Richard Stamelman
— October 1997 —

The Empire of Fashion

NEW FRENCH THOUGHT

Series Editors
THOMAS PAVEL AND MARK LILLA

The aim of this series is to bring to a cultivated public the best of recent French writing in the humanities in clear, accessible translations. The series focuses on the younger generation of philosophers, historians, and social commentators who represent the new liberal, humanistic bent of French intellectual life.

TITLES IN THE SERIES

Mark Lilla, ed., *New French Thought: Political Philosophy*

Gilles Lipovetsky, *The Empire of Fashion: Dressing Modern Democracy*

Pierre Manent, *An Intellectual History of Liberalism*

Gilles Lipovetsky

The Empire of Fashion

DRESSING MODERN DEMOCRACY

Translated by Catherine Porter

With a Foreword by Richard Sennett

 NEW FRENCH THOUGHT

PRINCETON UNIVERSITY PRESS · PRINCETON, NEW JERSEY

Translated from the French edition of Gilles Lipovetsky, *L'Empire de l'éphémère:*
La mode et son destin dans les sociétés modernes (Paris: © Editions Gallimard, 1987;
new Folio edition, 1991)

Library of Congress Cataloging-in-Publication Data

Lipovetsky, Gilles, 1944–
[Empire de l'éphémère. English]
The empire of fashion : dressing modern democracy /
Gilles Lipovetsky ; translated by Catherine Porter ;
with a foreword by Richard Sennett.
p.   cm. — (New French thought)
Includes bibliographical references and index.
ISBN 0-691-03373-0 (alk. paper)
1. Costume—History—20th century.   2. Fashion—
History—20th century.   I. Title.   II. Series.
GT596.L5713   1994
391'.009'04—dc20   94-4830   CIP

Published with the assistance of the French Ministry of Culture

This book has been composed in Adobe Bauer Bodoni

Princeton University Press books are printed on acid-free paper and meet the guidelines
for permanence and durability of the Committee on Production Guidelines for Book
Longevity of the Council on Library Resources

Printed in the United States of America

10 9 8 7 6 5 4 3 2 1

Contents

Foreword

IN THE PAST few years, several social thinkers in France and Italy have confronted the reign of mass culture as largely and searchingly as possible, while we in the English-speaking world have tended to narrow this subject to violence on television, the sexual ethics of rock stars, or the vices and virtues of an urban landscape increasingly resembling Disneyland. Perhaps the most provocative of these new European writers on mass society is the French philosopher Gilles Lipovetsky; in several books he has sought to explore the effect of mass culture on the practice of democracy. Does mass culture in fact create passive citizens incapable of political reasoning, as Tocqueville believed, today voting only for the candidate who simulates a movie star's version of The Statesman? Are the weak and unstable social bonds of people in a mass society necessarily a bad thing?

Lipovetsky, a young writer who follows in the footsteps of the critic Roland Barthes and the sociologist Edgar Morin, has yet to crystallize a firm and fixed answer to these questions, but on the one hand, he has moved far beyond the celebration of mass culture as popular expression that rules much of the contemporary discourse of "cultural studies" in the English-speaking world, and on the other hand, he is anything but a conservative holding his nose at how the present smells, hoping to inhale again the perfumes of the past. His books see-saw between a pessimistic reading of the democratic possibilities of mass culture, as in *The Empty Era*, and the peculiar hopes for the future rendered in this book, *The Empire of Fashion*.

Many English-speaking readers, I think, will find *The Empire of Fashion* as maddening as it is stimulating. This sociological tract celebrating the ephemeral and the playful aspects of modern society is written in a language of high seriousness, Immanuel Kant and St. Augustine rubbing shoulders with Pierre Cardin and the Red Hot Chili Peppers. Lipovetsky has based his arguments on the history of fashion, which the author believes is the leading edge of superficial experience, yet this is history such as few Anglo-Saxon historians would write it: the author often zig-zags over two thousand years in a single bound; his facts frequently cascade over each other; and he talks variously about clothing, bodily deportment, sex roles, sexual practices, political rhetoric, stage costume and set design, or acting techniques all as "fashion." The author calls upon his readers to put away outmoded tools of thinking like class analysis in favor of more modern toys of social understanding like advertising, yet the author has evidently never written an ad, sewn a hemline, or sold a shoe.

The divide between Anglo-Saxon empirical habits and a perhaps more French manner of seizing hold of social life ought not, however, blind us to the general import and real importance of *The Empire of Fashion*. For in this book, Lipovetsky tries to see the worth in those aspects of mass society particularly scorned by traditional critics such as Tocqueville and Ortega y Gasset: he tries to understand our consumer-driven, chameleon desires as real desiring, and he seeks to affirm, through the history of fashion, that this modern stream of ephemeral sensations serves something like the common democratic good. "The more progress the ephemeral makes," he declares, "the more stable, profoundly unified and reconciled with their pluralist principles the democracies become."

To be sure, this declaration is also an argument he makes to himself. In *The Empty Era*, Lipovetsky joins the company of writers like the philosopher Elaine Scarry, who believe this taste for ephemeral pleasure expresses in fact a fear of the pains entailed by deep engagement in the world and with oneself, the fear of experiencing disguised by a language of consumer pleasure.

Particularly shocking to the traditional liberal reader (I count myself as one) may be the assertion in *The Empire of Fashion* that democracy works better, the more superficial the social relations are between people in a democratic polity. Put another way, the author asks what will make it possible for people to live together in some harmony in a world no longer ruled by inherited caste or religious injunctions. Rather than concoct bureaucratic or procedural answers to this question, Lipovetsky deals directly with how people feel about one another: the less they feel, the better they will get along. To ask people to take a deep interest in each other's lives is to invite disaster—people are more likely to say, "I hate who you are" than to say, "let's work together." If this seems perverse, think only of what happens in erotic life, in its many lurches and disastrous turns, its frequent ruptures; a political regime simply cannot afford such jolts, and the only way to prevent them is to make people less mutually engaged, more tolerant because mutually indifferent. Whether he is wrong or right, this is the tough-minded core of Lipovetsky's enterprise; his book could equally well have been called *An Apology for Indifference*.

How are people to "achieve" such mutual indifference? This is fashion's role in Lipovetsky's scheme; in the course of Western civilization, fashion in the modern world has served the achievement of democracy by trivializing desire. People who see the world in terms of Gap ads feel very little about it, and about one another, but they see equally and easily; no barriers of caste, education, or indeed taste, stand in the way. Fashion is in this sense a uniform of desire. The author recognizes, of course, that

much advertising deals in social distinctions of class and age; his argument, however, is that advertising and other mass-media mechanisms
make everyone who looks at a Cartier ad feel, "I want that watch, and I
could enjoy it as much as anyone else—if only I had the money." The
author argues that this realm of consuming desires weakens anger against
those who actually have the money rather than sharpening resentment; in
perhaps the most interesting sections of the book, he explains how the
phenomena of "difference" in modern society have shifted to the realm of
fantasy rather than direct confrontation; in the erotic-tinged realm of consumer fantasy, all differences can be overcome—the man who dreams of
the Cartier watch has already possessed it, in a sense, because he has
dreamt it into his life.

As this brief summary may make clear, Gilles Lipovetsky has radically
challenged the assumptions we make in thinking about the social good. He
violates, for instance, the classic sociological opposition made by Ferdi-
nand Tonnies between *Gesellschaft* and *Gemeinschaft*—impersonal social
structure versus intimate social relations. In Lipovetsky's view, the impersonal is the realm of fantasy and desire, structured in such a way that
masses of people can get along with one another, whereas the personal is
a realm of social rupture, a lack of connection. Lipovetsky challenges
Tocqueville's assumptions about democracy: what Tocqueville called the
vices of democratic individualism—its weakening of a person's desire to
engage in the world—Lipovetsky sees as a genuine virtue; the only way to
make diversity work in society is to make people less interested, and so less
interfering, in the lives of people unlike themselves.

Lipovetsky also challenges the assumptions made by the Frankfurt
School about homogenized experience in a modern consumer society.
Fashion, he says, may homogenize particular veins of taste; for instance,
all jeans may look alike each year. But the economics of the fashion system
produces ever more different kinds of goods; in place of the trousers worn
by people in premodern societies, today there are jeans, corduroys, bell-
bottoms, slacks—every brand of each kind of men's pants much like other
brands, but the kinds of pants ever more diverse. Similarly, consumer
markets segment electronic machines and gadgets, foods, and home fur-
nishings. Thus, the things of the world become at once more homogeneous
of kind, and more various in kinds, and this leads—Lipovetsky claims—to
greater individuality through consumption even though each object consumed is a cliché. Through the pursuit of fashion, people become complex
selves, though this complexity differs radically from the interior, soulful
selfhood of the past.

Perhaps the most challenging part of Lipovetsky's argument lies here:
is a new form of individuality coming into being, one created by surface
complexity of desire rather than by deepening of the soul? His proposal

can be understood as taking to one extreme the idea of a secular self, a self no longer obliged to search for the secrets of faith, and the relation of faith to worldly desire; Lipovetsky's individual is liberated from all truth beyond the stimulating flicks of the desire to taste, own, consume.

To be sure, even in this book Lipovetsky pulls back from a pure celebration of this state of affairs. "The consummate reign of fashion smooths over social conflict, but it deepens subjective and intersubjective conflict; it allows more individual freedom, but it generates greater malaise in living." The reason for this is that the human capacity to desire far outstrips those icons of desire which can be so smoothed and shaped that they can be easily desired by all. "The euphoria of fashion has its counterparts," the author declares, "in dereliction, depression, and existential anguish."

The author leaves us there. What does this "existential anguish" mean about democracy? Does a politics of mutual toleration require privatized suffering? Could the political sphere possibly do something about that anguish? Lipovetsky's book unfolds like a fashion show, with Democracy, Subjectivity, Media, and Desire appearing down the runway as so many supermodels, each possessing the supermodel's gift of "the walk," that ability to show off to all sides of a crowded room. And yet when these high-priced bodies reach the end of the runway, they do something surprising, perhaps surprising most of all their designer: they break into speech. They are unhappy, they are human beings; more than to be desired, they want to be respected. If, when they burst into speech, we have to attend to them in another way, it is Gilles Lipovetsky's gift nonetheless to have dressed them so dramatically.

Richard Sennett

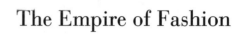

The Empire of Fashion

Introduction

T‌HE QUESTION of fashion is not a fashionable one among intellectuals. This observation needs to be emphasized: even as fashion goes on accelerating its ephemeral legislation, invading new realms and drawing all social spheres and age groups into its orbit, it is failing to reach the very people whose vocation is to shed light on the mainsprings and mechanisms of modern societies. Fashion is celebrated in museums, but among serious intellectual preoccupations it has marginal status. It turns up everywhere on the street, in industry, and in the media, but it has virtually no place in the theoretical inquiries of our thinkers. Seen as an ontologically and socially inferior domain, it is unproblematic and undeserving of investigation; seen as a superficial issue, it discourages conceptual approaches. The topic of fashion arouses critical reflexes even before it is examined objectively: critics invoke it chiefly in order to castigate it, to set it apart, to deplore human stupidity and the corrupt nature of business. Fashion is always other people. We are overinformed about fashion in terms of journalistic accounts, but our historical and social understanding of the phenomenon leaves much to be desired. The plethora of fashion magazines is matched by the silence of the intelligentsia, by its forgetfulness of fashion as both infatuation with artifice and the new architecture of democracy.

Many studies have been devoted to the subject, of course. We have masterful histories of costume, and an abundance of detailed monographs on the trades associated with fashion and its creators; we do not lack statistical information about its production and consumption, or historical and sociological studies of shifting tastes and styles. However, we must not allow these bibliographical and iconographical riches to obscure the most important thing about fashion: the profound, general, largely unconscious crisis that actually holds the key to an overall understanding of the phenomenon. The case of fashion may be unique in the universe of speculative thought. Here is an issue that has stirred up no real battles over its problematics; it has provoked no significant theoretical dissension. As a matter of fact, the question accomplishes the feat of bringing about a meeting of virtually all minds. For the last hundred years or so, the enigma of fashion has seemed by and large resolved. There has been no major dispute over its interpretation; the corporation of thinkers, with admirable collective momentum, has adopted a common credo on the subject. In this view, fashion's fickleness has its place and its ultimate truth in the existence of class rivalries, in the competitive struggles for prestige that occur among the various layers and factions of the social body. This underlying consensus leaves room—according to the theoreticians, of course—for interpretive nuances, for slight inflections, but with only a few exceptions the inconsistent logic of fashion and its assorted manifestations is invariably explained in terms of social stratification and social strategies for achieving honorific distinction. In no other realm is scholarly knowledge so firmly ensconced in the untroubled repetition of a single all-purpose recipe available for exploitation by lazy minds. Fashion has become a problem devoid of passion, lacking in theoretical stakes, a pseudo-problem whose answers and explanations are known in advance. The capricious realm of fantasy has managed only to impoverish the concept and reduce it to monotony.

The study of fashion needs new impetus, renewed questioning. Fashion is a trifling, fleeting, "contradictory" object par excellence; for that very reason it ought to provide a good stimulus for theoretical argument. The opacity of the phenomenon, its strangeness, its historical originality, are indeed considerable. How has an institution structured by evanescence and aesthetic fantasy managed to take root in human history? Why in the West and not elsewhere? How can an age dominated by technology, an age in which the world is subjugated by reason, also be the age of fashion in all its unreasonableness? How are we to conceptualize and account for the establishment of shallow instability as a permanent system? Once we resituate fashion within the vast life span of societies, we cannot see it as the simple manifestation of a passionate desire to be admired and to set oneself apart; it becomes an exceptional, highly problematic institution, a sociohistorical reality characteristic of the West and of modernity itself. From this standpoint, fashion is less a sign of class ambition than a way out of the world of tradition. It is one of the mirrors that allow us to see what constitutes our most remarkable historical destiny: the negation of the age-old power of the traditional past, the frenzied modern passion for novelty, the celebration of the social present.

The schema of social distinction that has come to be viewed as the sovereign key for understanding fashion, in the realm of objects and modern culture as well as dress, is fundamentally unable to account for fashion's most significant features: its logic of inconstancy, its great organizational and aesthetic mutations. This idea is the basis for the overall reinterpretation I propose here. By insisting on the idea of social distinction, theoretical reason has set up as the motive force of fashion what is actually its immediate, ordinary acceptation. Theoretical reason has remained in the thrall of the lived meaning of the actors on the social stage, positing as fashion's origin what is merely one of its social functions. This identification of origin with function lies behind the extraordinary simplification that characterizes genealogical explanations of the "invention" of fashion and its transformations in the West. A kind of epistemological unconscious underlying discourse on fashion, the problematics of social distinction has become an obstacle to a historical understanding of the phenomenon, an obstacle accompanied by an ostentatious play of conceptual whorls capable of concealing the deficiencies of scholarly discourse on the subject. A theoretical face-lift is in order. It is time to detach analyses of fashion from the heavy artillery of social class, from the dialectic of social distinction and class pretensions. Countering the imperialism of schemas of symbolic class struggle, I seek to show that, in the history of fashion, modern cultural meanings and values, in particular those that elevate newness and the expression of human individuality to positions of dignity, have played a preponderant role. These are the factors that allowed the fashion system to come into being and establish itself in the late Middle Ages; in an unexpected way, these same factors allow us to trace the major stages in fashion's historical evolution.

What I offer here, then, is an interpretive history of fashion: a conceptual and problematic history, governed not by a desire to set forth its inexhaustible contents but by a desire to present a general interpretation of the phenomenon and its metamorphoses over time. I shall not provide a chronological history of styles and social elegance; instead, I shall focus on the defining moments, the major structures, the organizational, aesthetic, and sociological modulations that have determined the centuries-long course of fashion. I have deliberately opted here for a clear and comprehensive overview at the expense of detailed analyses: what we lack most is not specific knowledge, but the global meaning, the underlying economy, of the dynamics of fashion. This book, then, has two goals. On the one hand, I seek to understand the emergence of fashion in the late Middle Ages and its principal lines of evolution over the centuries. In order to avoid psychosociological generalizations about fashion that manifest little historical understanding, and in order to resist resorting to broad parallelisms of a kind that are all too often artificial, I have chosen to confine my attention here to a relatively homogeneous object that best exemplifies the phenomenon in question: clothing and its accessories, the archetypal domain of fashion. On the other hand, I attempt to comprehend the rising power of fashion in contemporary societies, the central, unprecedented place it occupies in democracies that have set out along the path of consumerism and mass communications. For the dominant feature of our societies, one that has played a major part in my decision to undertake this book, is precisely the extraordinary generalization of fashion: the extension of the "fashion" form to spheres that once lay beyond its purview, the advent of a society restructured from top to bottom by the attractive and the ephemeral—by the very logic of fashion. Hence the unevenness in this book's organization, as measured by the yardstick of historical time. Part One, which deals with fashion in the narrow sense, covers more than six centuries of history. Part Two analyzes fashion in its multiple networks, from industrial objects to the culture of the mass media, from advertising to ideology, from communication technologies to the social sphere; it focuses on a much briefer historical period, the era of democratic societies oriented toward mass production, consumption, and communication. This difference in the way historical time is treated and explored is justified by the new, highly strategic place now occupied by the fashion process in the workings of free societies. Fashion is no longer an aesthetic embellishment, a decorative accessory to collective life; it is the key to the entire edifice. In structural terms, fashion has completed its historical trajectory; it has reached the peak of its power, for it has succeeded in reshaping society as a whole in its own image. Once a peripheral phenomenon, it is now hegemonic. In the pages that follow, I seek to shed some light on the historical rise of fashion, in an attempt to understand how its empire was established, how it evolved and reached its apogee.

In our societies, fashion is in the driver's seat. In less than half a century, attractiveness and evanescence have become the organizing principles of modern collective life. We live in societies where the trivial predominates, societies that constitute the last link in the centuries-old capitalist-democratic-individualist chain. Should we be dismayed by this? Does it announce the slow but inexorable decline of the West? Must we take it as the sign of the decadence of the democratic ideal? Nothing is more commonplace or widespread than the tendency to stigmatize—not without cause, moreover—the consumerist bent of democracies; they are represented as devoid of any great mobilizing collective projects, lulled into a stupor by the private orgies of consumerism, infantilized by "instant" culture, by advertising, by politics-as-theater. The ultimate reign of seduction annihilates culture, it is said, and leads to a general brutalization, to the collapse of a free and responsible citizenry: no intellectual tendency is more widely shared than the tendency to condemn fashion. The contradictory and paradoxical interpretation of the modern world I propose here, however, points in quite a different direction. Looking beyond fashion's "perversions," I attempt to reveal its globally positive power, with respect both to democratic institutions and to the autonomy of consciousness. Fashion holds more surprises in store: whatever deleterious influence it may have on the vitality of minds and democracies, it appears above all as the primary agent of the spiraling movement toward individualism and the consolidation of liberal societies.

To be sure, the frivolous new deal is apt to provide fodder for a certain number of anxieties. The society it outlines does not look much like the democratic ideal, and it does not offer the best conditions for getting out of the economic slump into which we have slid. On the one hand, our citizens take little interest in public affairs. Lack of motivation and indifference to politics prevail more or less everywhere; the voter's behavior is beginning to resemble the consumer's. On the other hand, isolated, self-absorbed individuals are not much inclined to consider the general good, to give up acquired privileges; preparing for the future tends to be sacrificed by individuals and groups to immediate satisfactions. Citizens' behavior is just as problematic where the vitality of the democratic spirit is concerned—that is, the capacity of our societies to take themselves in hand, to make timely conversions, to win the new market war.

All these weaknesses are well known, and they have been abundantly analyzed. The same cannot be said, however, for the future prospects of democracies. To put it succinctly, late-twentieth-century democracies, inconstant as they seem, do not lack weapons with which they can confront the future. The resources they now have at their disposal are priceless, although they are not measurable and not very spectacular: they consist of a human "raw material" that is more flexible than we used to think. This raw material has come to terms with the legitimacy of peaceful change; it has given up revolutionary and Manichean worldviews. Under fashion's reign, democracies enjoy a universal consensus about their political institutions; ideological extremes are on the wane and pragmatism is on the rise; the spirit of enterprise and efficiency has been substituted for prophetic incantation. Should these factors of social cohesion, of institutional solidity, of modernist "realism," be completely disregarded? Whatever social conflicts and corporatist reflexes may hinder modernization, the process is under way, and it is gathering steam. Fashion does not do away with the demands and defensive tactics of special-interest groups, it makes them more negotiable. Conflicts of interest and selfishness remain, but they are not obstacles; they never reach the point of threatening the continuity or the order of the republic. I do not share the gloomy outlook of some observers about the future of the European nations. These pages have been written with the idea that our history has not played itself out, that in the long run the consummate fashion system represents an opportunity for democracies. Now that they are free from the fervor of extremists, the democracies have been by and large won over to change, to perpetual reconversion, to the need to reckon with national and international economic realities. Here are the first paradoxes of our societies: the more seduction is used as a tool, the more people face up to reality; the more triumphant the element of playfulness becomes, the better the economic ethos is rehabilitated; the more progress the ephemeral makes, the more stable, profoundly unified, and reconciled with their pluralist principles the democracies become. Although these factors cannot be quantified, they constitute immense assets for the construction of the future. To be sure, on the level of short-term history, the data are not always encouraging; to be sure, not everything will be accomplished all at once, without collective effort, without social tensions, and without a political will to change. Still, in an age recycled by the fashion form, history is more open than ever. Modernism has won such a measure of social legitimacy that the recovery of Western European nations is more probable than irreversible political decay. Let us avoid reading the future solely in the light of quantified schemas of the present. An age that functions in terms of information, the seductive power of novelty, tolerance, and mobility of opinions, is preparing us, if only we can take advantage of its strong points, for the challenges of the future. We are going through a difficult passage, but we are not at an impasse. The promises of fashion society will not yield their fruits right away; we need to let time do its work. In the short run, we may see little beyond rising unemployment, a precarious labor market, weak growth rates, a flabby economy. If we fix our gaze on the horizon, however, reasons for hope are not entirely lacking. The mature phase of fashion is not the road to oblivion. Considered with a certain detachment, it leads to a dual view of our destiny: pessimism about the present, optimism about the future.

The denunciation of the consummate stage of fashion has taken on its most virulent tones in the domain of the life of the mind. In analyzing media culture as a reason-destroying machine, a totalitarian enterprise designed to do away with autonomous thought, the intelligentsia has made common cause, speaking with one voice to stigmatize the degrading dictatorship of the consumable, the infamy of the culture industries. As long ago as the 1940s, Theodor Adorno and Max Horkheimer were inveighing against the "monstrous" fusion of culture, advertising, and industrialized entertainment that led to the manipulation and standardization of consciousness. Later, Jürgen Habermas analyzed media-oriented consumer products as instruments designed to reduce people's capacity for critical thinking, while Guy Debord denounced the "false consciousness," the generalized alienation induced by the pseudo-culture of the spectacular. And today, although Marxist and revolutionary thought are no longer in season, the offensive against fashion and media-induced brain rot is again in full swing: new times bring new ways of saying the same old thing. In place of Marx-as-joker, out comes the Heidegger card. The dialectic panoply of merchandising, ideology, and alienation is no longer brandished; instead, we find musings on the dominion of technology, "the autonegation of life," or the dissolution of "life with the mind." We are invited to open our eyes, then, to the immense wretchedness of modernity. We are condemned to the degradation of a media-dominated existence. A soft totalitarianism, we are told, has infiltrated our democracies: it has successfully sown contempt for culture; it has generalized regression and mental confusion. We are fully ensconced in "barbarianism," according to the latest jingle of our antimodern philosophers. They fulminate against fashion, but they are quick to follow its lead, adopting similar hyperbolic techniques, the sine qua non of conceptual one-upmanship. There is no way around it: the hatchet of apocalyptic war has not been buried; fashion will always be fashion. Denunciation of fashion is no doubt consubstantial with its very being; such denunciation is part and parcel of the crusades of lofty intellectual souls.

The critical unanimity provoked by the empire of fashion is anything but accidental. It is deeply rooted in the thought process that underlies philosophical reflection itself. Ever since Plato's day we have known that the play of light and darkness in the cavern of existence blocks progress toward truth. Seduction and evanescence enchain the human spirit, and they are the very signs of its captivity. According to Platonic philosophy, rational thinking and progress toward truth can only come about through a fierce effort to root out appearances, flux, the charm of images. No intellectual salvation is to be found in the protean universe of surfaces; this is the paradigm that presides even today over attacks on the rule of fashion. Ready access to leisure, the ephemeral nature of images, the distracting seductiveness of the mass media—these phenomena can only enslave reason, beguile and disorder the mind. Consumption is superficial, thus it makes the masses childlike; rock music is violent and nonverbal, thus it does away with reason; the culture industries deal in stereotypes, thus television abuses individuals and creates couch potatoes, while "feeling" and "zapping" produce airheads. Superficiality is evil in any event.

Whether they see themselves as followers of Marx or Heidegger, our intellectual clerks have remained moralists trapped in the froth on the surfaces of phenomena; they are completely unable to fathom the way fashion actually works—what we might call the ruse of fashion's irrationality. Here is fashion's greatest and most interesting historical lesson: at the other extreme from Platonism, we need to understand that seduction now serves to limit irrationality; that the artificial facilitates access to the real; that superficiality permits increased use of reason; that playful displays are springboards to subjective judgment. Fashion does not bring about the definitive alienation of the masses; it is an ambiguous but effective vector of human autonomy, even though it functions via the heteronomy of mass culture. The paradoxes of what is sometimes called postmodernity reach their apogee here: subjective independence grows apace with the empire of bureaucratic dispossession. The more ephemeral seduction there is, the more enlightenment advances, even if it does so in an ambivalent way. At any given moment, to be sure, the process is hard to detect, so compelling are the negative effects of fashion. The process comes into its own only by comparison over the long term with the evils of

earlier eras: omnipotent tradition, triumphant racism, religious and ideological oppression. The frivolous era of consumption and communication
has been caricatured to the point of delirium by those on the right and the
left alike who hold it in contempt; it needs to be reinterpreted from start to
finish. Fashion cannot be equated with some gentle new realism. Quite to
the contrary, fashion has allowed public questioning to expand; it has
allowed subjective thoughts and existences to take on greater autonomy.
Fashion is the supreme agent of the individualist dynamic in its various
manifestations. In an earlier work I sought to identify the contemporary
transformations of individualism;[1] here I have tried to understand what
paths the process of individualization has taken, what social mechanisms
it has used in order to enter the second cycle of its historical trajectory.

Let me attempt to set forth briefly the idea of history implied by an
analysis that takes fashion as the ultimate phase of democracy. Clearly in
one sense I have returned to the philosophical problematics of the ruse of
reason: collective "reason" advances in fact through its contrary, distraction; individual autonomy develops through the heteronomy of seduction;
the "wisdom" of modern nations is constructed through the folly of superficial tastes. What is at issue is not the classic Hegelian model, the disorderly game of selfish passions in the achievement of a rational city, but a
formally equivalent model: the role of the frivolous in the development of
critical, realistic, tolerant consciousness. The erratic progress of the exercise of reason is brought about, as in Hegel's and Marx's philosophies of
history, by the action of its opposite. But my complicity with theories of the
ruse of reason ends here. I shall limit my purview to the dynamics of contemporary democracies alone; I shall not proceed to develop a global conception of universal history, nor do I intend to imply any metaphysics of
seduction.

To avoid misunderstandings, I need to add two further remarks. First,
the fashion form that I analyze is not antithetical to "rationality": seduction is already in itself, in part, a rational logic that integrates the calcula-
tions, technology, and information that characterize the modern world.
Consummate fashion celebrates the marriage of seduction and productive,
instrumental, operational reason. What is at stake is not at all a vision of
modernity that would affirm the progress of rational universality through
the dialectical play of individual tendencies, but the autonomy of a society
structured by fashion, where rationality functions by way of evanescence
and superficiality, where objectivity is instituted as a spectacle, where the
dominion of technology is reconciled with play and the realm of politics is
reconciled with seduction. Second, I do not subscribe unreservedly to the
idea of the progress of consciousness. In reality, as enlightenment advances it is inextricably mingled with its opposite; the historical optimism
implied by my analysis of fashion must be confined within narrow limits.

Human minds taken collectively are in fact better informed but also more disorderly, more adult but also more unstable, less subject to ideologies but also more dependent on fashions, more open but also more easily influenced, less extremist but also more dispersed, more realistic but also more fuzzy, more critical but also more superficial, more skeptical but also less meditative. An increase in independent thinking goes hand in hand with increased frivolity; tolerance is accompanied by an increase in casualness and indifference among thinkers. Neither theories of alienation nor theories of some optimal "invisible hand" offer an adequate model for fashion, and fashion institutes neither the reign of ultimate subjective dispossession nor the reign of clear, solid reason.

Even though it has links with theories of the ruse of reason, the model for the evolution of contemporary societies that I propose does not make the intentional initiative of human beings any less significant. Insofar as the ultimate order of fashion produces an essentially ambivalent historical moment of consciousness, the lucid, voluntary, responsible action of human beings is more possible than ever, and more necessary for progress toward a freer, better-informed world. Fashion produces the best and the worst, inseparably: news around the clock, and zero-degree thinking. It is up to us to stand our ground and challenge myths and presuppositions; it is up to us to limit the harmful effects of disinformation, to bring about the conditions for a more open, freer, more objective public debate. To say that the universe of seduction contributes to the dynamics of reason does not condemn us to nostalgia for the past; it does not mean that "everything is the same in the end"; it does not amount to a smug apology for generalized show business. Fashion is accompanied by ambiguous effects. Our job is to reduce its "obscurantist" dimension and enhance its "enlightened" dimension—not by seeking simply to eradicate the glitter of seduction, but by putting its liberating potential at the service of the greatest number. Consummate fashion calls neither for unconditional defense nor for unqualified rejection. If the terrain of fashion is propitious for the critical use of reason, it also makes manifest the exile and confusion of thought: there is much to correct, to regulate, to criticize, to explain ad infinitum. The ruse of fashion's irrationality does not rule out human intelligence and free initiative, or society's responsibility for its own future. In the new democratic era, collective progress toward freedom of thought will not occur apart from seduction; it will be undergirded by the fashion form, but it will be seconded by other agencies, reinforced by other criteria: by the educational establishment, by the openness to scrutiny and the ethical standards proper to the media, by theoretical and scientific works, and by the corrective system of laws and regulations. In the slow, contradictory, uneven forward movement of free subjectivities, fashion is clearly not alone on the slopes, and the future remains largely undetermined insofar as the specific features of individual autonomy are concerned. Lucidity is always hard-won; illusion and blindness, like the phoenix, are always reborn from their own ashes. Seduction will fully accomplish its democratic work only if it succeeds in allying itself with other parameters, if it avoids stifling the sovereign rules of truth, facts, and rational argument. Nevertheless, contrary to the stereotypes in which it is clothed, the age of fashion remains the major factor in the process that has drawn men and women collectively away from obscurantism and fanaticism, has instituted an open public space and shaped a more lawful, more mature, more skeptical humanity. Consummate fashion lives on paradox. Its unconscious is conducive to consciousness; its madness is conducive to the spirit of tolerance; its frivolity is conducive to respect for the rights of man. In the speeded-up film of modern history, we are beginning to realize that fashion is the worst scenario, with the exception of all the others.

PART ONE

The Enchantment of Appearances

Fashion does not belong to all ages or to all civilizations: it has an identifiable starting point in history. Instead of seeing fashion as a phenomenon consubstantial with human life and society, I view it as an exceptional process inseparable from the origin and development of the modern West. For tens of thousands of years, people lived together without a cult of fantasy and novelty, without the instability and ephemeral temporality of fashion. This does not mean that collective life lacked change, or curiosity, or a taste for exotic realities. But it was only at the end of the Middle Ages that the order of fashion itself became recognizable—fashion as a system, with its endless metamorphoses, its fits and starts, its extravagance. The renewal of forms became a social value; fantasy deployed its artifices and its excesses in high society. With the birth of fashion, inconstancy in matters of form and ornamentation was no longer the exception but the lasting rule.

In order to conceptualize fashion, we shall have to stop identifying it as a principle that is necessarily and universally inscribed in the evolutionary course of all civilizations,[1] and we must also stop viewing it as a historical constant with universal anthropological roots.[2] The mystery of fashion lies here, in the uniqueness of the phenomenon, in the way it sprang up and took hold in the modern West and nowhere else. Neither an elementary force of collective life nor a permanent principle of social transformation rooted in the human condition in general, fashion is essentially a sociohistorical formation limited to a single type of society. We can uncover its fascinating effects not by invoking its presumed universality, but rather by carefully determining the limits of its historical extension.

The history of clothing is unquestionably the privileged reference for such a problematics. The historical view of fashion imposes itself in particular when we look at the way styles have changed and at the rapid pace of change in dress. Fashion is exercised most ostentatiously, carried to extremes, in the sphere of personal appearance; for centuries, this sphere has represented the purest manifestation of the organization of the ephemeral. This privileged linking of clothing and fashion is not at all fortuitous; as we shall see, there are important reasons for the connection. Nevertheless, fashion has by no means remained confined to the domain of dress. In parallel developments, at different paces and to varying degrees, other sectors—furniture and decorative objects, language and manners, tastes and ideas, artists and cultural productions—have been won over by the fashion process, with its fads and its rapid shifts of direction. In this sense, from the moment of its inception in the West fashion has had no content of its own. Fashion is a specific form of social change, independent of any particular object; it is first and foremost a social mechanism characterized by a particularly brief time span and by more or less fanciful shifts that enable it to affect quite diverse spheres of collective life. But until the nineteenth and twentieth centuries the fashion process was most obviously embodied by clothing. Dress was the theater of the most accelerated, capricious, and spectacular formal innovations. For centuries on end, the role of personal appearance was preponderant in the history of fashion. Although personal appearance clearly does not communicate the full originality of the realm of ephemera and superficiality, it does offer the best way of getting at that realm, because it is the one that is best known, the most often described, the most fully represented and discussed. No theory or history of fashion fails to take personal appearance as its starting point and as its central object of investigation.

Although as a social phenomenon fashion is subject to considerable agitation, from a broad historical viewpoint its underlying mechanisms are not without stability and regularity. On the one hand, there are the ebbs and flows that feed the chronicles of elegance. On the other hand, we find an astonishing centuries-long continuity that calls for a very long range history of fashion, an analysis of its broad patterns and of the breaks that disturbed its order. If we are to conceptualize fashion, we have to veer away from positivist history and from the classical periodization by century and decade favored by historians of dress. That history has its legitimacy: it is the obligatory starting point, an indispensable source of information for any reflection on fashion. But it gives too much credit to the idea that fashion is merely an uninterrupted and homogeneous chain of variations, marked at more or less regular intervals by innovations of greater and lesser significance. That history has acquired considerable knowledge of the past, but little understanding of fashion's originality or of its real inscription in the great span of history in its collective dimensions. We have to go beyond painstaking transcriptions of fashion's novelties and try to reconstruct the great avenues of its history, try to understand how it works, try to uncover the various forms of logic that organize it and the ties that bind it to the collective whole. We need to piece together the history of the structures and logics of fashion, punctuated as that history is with twists and turns, with major discontinuities that initiate phases lasting a long—sometimes a very long—time. This is the problematics that governs the chapters that follow. It is important to specify, however, that the breaks in fashion's regime do not automatically imply thoroughgoing transformation or incomparable novelty. Over and above the great discontinuities, certain standards, attitudes, and processes have been repeated and maintained: from the late Middle Ages to our day, despite decisive shifts in the system, the values and invariants that constitute fashion have continued to reproduce themselves. The crucial turning points that are insistently underlined here must not be allowed to obscure the broad currents of continuity that have been perpetuated and that have guaranteed the identity of fashion.

In this trajectory spanning many centuries, an initial phase held sway for five hundred years. From the mid-fourteenth to the mid-nineteenth centuries, the inaugural phase of fashion, the precipitous rhythm of ephemera and the reign of fantasy were established in a systematic and lasting way. Fashion revealed its characteristic social and aesthetic features even then, but for very limited groups that monopolized the power of initiative and creation. This was the artisanal and aristocratic stage of fashion.

Fashion and the West: The Aristocratic Moment

The Instability of Personal Appearance

Fᴏʀ ᴍᴏsᴛ of human history, societies have gone about their business oblivious to the spirited play of frivolous change. For thousands of years, the so-called savage social formations, for instance, have remained unaware of, and implacably resistant to, the frenzy of change and the ever-increasing extravagance of individual fancy. The unchallenged legitimacy of ancestral legacies and the positive value placed on social continuity have served everywhere to impose a principle of immobility, the repetition of models inherited from the past, a seamless conservatism in modes of being and appearing. In such social systems, the process and the idea of fashion are completely meaningless. "Savages," even apart from ceremonial clothing, may have a pronounced taste for ornamentation, may well seek certain aesthetic effects; still, there is nothing that resembles the fashion system. Even though they may come in endless varieties, the types of decorations, accessories, hairstyles, body painting, and tattoos remain fixed by tradition, subject to norms that do not change from one generation to the next. Primitive society is hyperconservative: it excludes the emergence of fashion because fashion goes hand in hand with a relative devaluing of the past. Fashion always implies the attribution of prestige and superiority to new models and by the same token entails a certain downgrading of the old order. Completely centered on respect for the past and the meticulous reproduction of that past, primitive society cannot permit the consecration of novelty and individual fancy, the aesthetic autonomy of fashion. In a relation of strict dependence vis-à-vis its mythic past, primitive society is organized in such a way as to limit and reject the dynamics of change and history. How could such a society succumb to the whims of novelty when human beings are not recognized as the authors of their own social universe, when customs and principles for conducting one's life, social requirements and taboos, are held to result from a moment of origin that has to be perpetuated, changeless, and immobile; when antiquity and the continuation of the past are the foundations of legitimacy? What else can people do but continue as faithfully as possible to carry out practices dating back to the time of origin as reported by mythic narratives? So long as society's most basic and most meaningful activities are dictated by the deeds and gestures of founding fathers, and so long as individuals are unable to assert a relative independence with respect to the collective norms, the logic of fashion is excluded. Primitive societies erect prohibitive barriers against the constitution of fashion, inasmuch as fashion explicitly consecrates aesthetic initiative, fancy, and human originality; even more significantly, they do so because fashion implies an order of value that exalts the present and the new, in direct opposition to the model of timeless legitimacy based on submission to a collective past. If the reign of frivolous change is to have a chance of taking hold, not only must the power of human beings to modify the organization of their world be recognized, but also, at a later stage, the partial autonomy of social agents with regard to the aesthetics of appearance.

The emergence of the state and of class divisions has not altered the basic nature of the problem. Over the centuries, the same tastes, the same ways of doing, feeling, and dressing have been perpetuated unchanged. In ancient Egypt, the same type of tunic-dress, worn by both sexes, was maintained for nearly fifteen centuries with almost total consistency; in Greece, the peplos, a woman's outer garment, prevailed from the origins of Greek society to the middle of the sixth century B.C.; in Rome, the male garb of toga and tunic persisted with slight variations from the earliest period to the end of the empire. The same stability was characteristic of China, India, and other traditional Asian civilizations where modifications in dress were the exception. The Japanese kimono remained unchanged for centuries, while in China women's dress underwent no real transformation between the seventeenth and the nineteenth centuries. As nation-states emerge and conquests occur, the dynamic of historical change is undeniably at work: currents of importation and diffusion disrupt customs and dress from time to time, but this does not mean that they take on the character of fashion. Apart from some peripheral phenomena, a given change can be expected to crystallize in a new and lasting collective norm: the principle of immobility always wins out, notwithstanding openings to history. While change often results from external influences, from contact with foreign peoples from whom some particular type of clothing is copied, it may also be inspired by a sovereign to be imitated (the Greeks shaved their beards following Alexander's example and under his orders), or it may be decreed by conquerors who impose their form of dress on the conquered peoples (at least the upper classes): thus the Moghuls' dress became the rule in India after the Moghul conquest.[1] But in no case do the variations proceed from some autonomous aesthetic logic; they translate not the requirement of regular renewal characteristic of fashion, but rather circumstantial influences or relations of dominance. What is at issue is not the uninterrupted chain of small variations constitutive of fashion, but the exceptional adoption or imposition of foreign models that are instituted after the fact as stable norms. Although certain civilizations have been much less conservative than others, more open to innovations from without, more eager to display their wealth, they have never come close to what we call fashion in the strict sense—that is, the systematic reign of the ephemeral, of frequent evanescent fluctuations.

In this sense, the ages of fashion cannot be defined, as Gabriel de Tarde thought they could, simply in terms of the prestige of foreign or new models—which, for Tarde, amounted to one and the same process.[2] The prestige of foreign realities is not enough to upset the rigidity of tradition; the fashion system comes into play only when the taste for novelty becomes a consistent and regular principle, when it is no longer synonymous with simple curiosity about exogenous items, when it functions as an autonomous cultural requirement, relatively independent of chance relations with the outside world. Under these conditions, it is possible for a system of frivolous change to develop and maintain itself in perpetual motion as an endless interplay of innovations and reactions, a game based on the logic of one-upmanship.

Fashion in the strict sense scarcely existed before the mid-fourteenth century. This moment stands out, first and foremost because of the appearance of a radically new type of dress that was sharply differentiated according to gender: short and fitted for men, long and close to the body for women.[3] This revolution in apparel laid the groundwork for modern dress. The same long flowing robe that had been worn more or less indiscriminately by both sexes was replaced, on the one hand, by a costume for men composed of a doublet, a kind of short, narrow jacket connected to tight breeches that followed the contour of the legs; and, on the other hand, by a costume for women that perpetuated the traditional long dress but that was much more closely fitted and low necked. The major innovation was the replacement of men's long, flowing, smocklike surcoat with a short garment cinched in at the waist and fastened with buttons, leaving the legs uncovered except for tight-fitting stockings. The transformation instituted a quite pronounced difference between male and female clothing, one that persisted throughout the entire evolution of fashion up to the twentieth century. The new costume for women was also fitted, and it exalted the attributes of femininity: the garment lengthened the body with a train, while it emphasized the bust, the hips, and the small of the back. The chest was highlighted by the lowered neckline; the stomach itself was accentuated, in the fifteenth century, by the use of small protruding bags worn under the dress, as we see in Jan Van Eyck's famous painting "The

Marriage of Giovanni and Giovanna Cenami" (1434). While there is con-
troversy over where this major transformation in dress styles first occurred, we know that the innovations spread very rapidly throughout
Western Europe between 1340 and 1350. From this point on, one change
followed another: variations in appearance were more frequent, more extravagant, and more arbitrary; previously unknown rhythms and ostentatiously whimsical, gratuitous, decorative forms made their appearance,
defining the very process of fashion. Change was no longer an accidental,
rare, fortuitous phenomenon; it became a fixed law of the pleasures of high
society. Henceforth the transitory would come to function as one of the
constitutive structures of modern life.

Between the fourteenth and the nineteenth centuries, the fluctuations of
fashion did not always proceed at the same rapid pace. As the Middle Ages
waned, the rhythms of change were unquestionably less spectacular than
they became during the Enlightenment era, when vogues caught on
quickly and changed "every week, every day, almost every hour,"[4] re-
sponding to whatever was "in the air," registering the events of the day,
the latest triumphs. Nevertheless, starting in the late fourteenth century,
sudden shifts in tastes, fancies, and novelties proliferated rapidly and have
had free rein in worldly circles ever since. This is not the place to attempt
to list even in a cursory way the changes in cut and detail of the various
elements of dress; they have been too numerous, the rhythms of fashion
have been too complex and too variable in terms of place and period. The
documentation at our disposal is fragmentary and limited, but historians
of costume have managed to present quite a clear picture of the historical
introduction and establishment of fashion's brief cycles, starting in the
late Middle Ages.[5] The testimony of contemporaries reveals in a different
way the extraordinary emergence of this accelerated temporality. In the
late Middle Ages and the early modern period, a number of authors
sought—perhaps for the first time in history—to preserve the memory of
clothing worn during their lifetimes: there are the court chronicles of the
count of Zimmern, for instance, and the chronicle of Konrad Pellikan de
Ruffach, who recorded the emotions aroused by styles and extravagant
appearances, the sense of passing time conveyed by variations in modes of
dress. In the sixteenth century, Matthäus Schwarz, the financial director of
the House of Fugger, undertook to produce a book of watercolor illustrations in which he discussed the costumes he had worn from childhood on,
and those he had had made according to his own instructions. This unprecedented attention to ephemeral phenomena and to changes in forms
of dress, along with the desire to record them, has given Matthäus Schwarz
his reputation as the "first historian of clothing."[6] Curiosity about "old"
ways of dressing and a perception of the rapid variations in fashion appear

again as early as 1478, when King René of Anjou issued an order initiating research into the details of clothing worn by past counts of Anjou.[7] At the beginning of the sixteenth century, Vecellio designed a collection "of ancient and modern clothing." In sixteenth-century France, inconstancy in dress was noted by various authors, above all Montaigne, in his *Essays*: "We change so suddenly and promptly that the inventiveness of all the tailors in the world could never furnish us enough novelties."[8] In the early eighteenth century, the protean character of fashion and the great mobility of taste were widely discussed and criticized in literary works, satires, and opuscules: it became a commonplace to evoke the fickleness of fashion.[9] It is true that the superfluities of dress and feminine coquetry in particular had been the object of numerous complaints from ancient times on, but starting in the fifteenth and sixteenth centuries, denunciations were aimed at male and female clothing itself, at the inconstancy of tastes in general. Fashion's fickleness was self-evident in the eyes of its chroniclers: the instability and oddities of appearance became objects of questioning, astonishment, and fascination, as well as repeated targets for moral condemnation.

Fashion was in constant flux, but not everything in fashion was subject to change. Ornamentation and accessories, the subtle details of trimmings and fullness, were particularly influenced by fashion's rapid modifications, while the structure and general forms of dress were much more stable. Fashion change mainly affected the most superficial elements of clothing; it generally had less impact on the overall cut. The farthingale, a bell-shaped framework that made dresses stand away from the body, appeared in Spain around 1470, and continued to be worn through the middle of the seventeenth century. The rhinegrave (petticoat breeches) remained in use for nearly a quarter of a century, the jerkin for almost seventy years. The wig was fashionable for more than a century. The so-called gown *à la française* remained unchanged for decades, starting in the mid-eighteenth century. Frills and furbelows, colors, ribbons and laces, details of shaping, nuances of fullness and length: such elements underwent constant renewal. The success of the Fontanges hairstyle under Louis XIV lasted some thirty years, although with variant forms. It always entailed a complex raised construction of ribbons, laces, and bows, but its architecture offered considerable variation: there was the *culebutte* style, the *effrontée* style, the *palissade* style, and so on. The eighteenth-century panierruches, underskirts fitted over metal hoops, were popular for more than half a century, but with varying forms and dimensions: there was the round table style; the cupola style; the gondola style, which made women look like water carriers; the oval-shaped "elbow" style; the cadet style; the "shrieking" style (*criardes*), named after the noise made by the gummed linen used; and there were the lightweight short petticoats called *considérations.*

These were cascades of "little nothings," small differences that combined to make up fashion as a whole. Such differences immediately raised the standing of anyone who adopted them and lowered that of anyone who failed to adopt them, and they immediately rendered obsolete whatever had gone before. Fashion instituted the social power of infinitesimal signs, the astonishing mechanism of social distinction conferred on those whose dress is subtly novel. This escalation of superficial changes cannot be separated from the global stability of dress: fashion's mutability could only have come into being against a background of order. It is because the changes remained modest and preserved the overall architecture of dress that renewals could catch on and give rise to fads. Fashion did undergo authentic innovations, to be sure, but these were much less common than the succession of small modifications in detail. The logic of these minor changes is what truly characterizes fashion; in Sapir's terms, fashion is more than anything "a variation in an understood sequence."[10]

The temporal effervescence of fashion must not be interpreted as an acceleration of tendencies toward change, tendencies that are developed to a greater or lesser extent in different civilizations. Rather, this effervescence must be seen as inherent in the human social phenomenon.[11] What it translates is not the continuity of human nature (the taste for innovation and ornament, the desire to stand out, group rivalry, and so on) but a historical discontinuity, a major break—however circumscribed—with the form of socialization that had prevailed from time immemorial: the immutable logic of tradition. On the scale of the human adventure, the sudden appearance of fashion signaled a departure from the form of collective cohesiveness that had ensured the durability of custom; it signified the deployment of a new social bond and of a new social temporality.

Gabriel de Tarde has already proposed a penetrating analysis of this process. In his view, ages of custom are ruled by the prestige of antiquity and the imitation of ancestors, while ages of fashion are dominated by the cult of novelty and the imitation of local and foreign models: people want to look more like contemporary innovators and less like their forebears. Love of change and the determining influence of contemporaries are the two major principles governing eras of fashion; both entail a devaluing of the ancestral heritage and a tendency to dignify the norms of the social present. Fashion plays such a radical role in history because it institutes an essentially modern social system, freed from the grip of the past. The old is no longer deemed venerable; "the present alone seems to inspire us with respect."[12] The social space of the traditional order is rearranged in favor of a new type of interpersonal bond, one based on the changeable decrees

of the present. As an exemplary figure of modern socialization, fashion has
liberated an agency of collective life from the timeless authority of the
past: "In periods when custom is in the ascendant, men are more infatuated about their country than about their time; for it is the past which is
preeminently praised. In ages when fashion rules, men are prouder, on the
contrary, of their time than of their country."[13] High society was gripped
by the passion for innovation; it flared up with enthusiasm for the latest
finds. It imitated the reigning fashions in Italy, Spain, and France in turn;
anything that was different and foreign gave rise to a snobbish preference.
Fashion was the first manifestation of a passion characteristic of the West,
the passion for what is "modern." Novelty became a source of worldly
value, a mark of social excellence. People had to keep up with whatever
was new; they had to adopt the latest changes. The present took over as the
temporal axis governing a superficial but prestigious sector of the life of
the elites.

The modernity of fashion? The question warrants a closer look. On the
one hand, fashion indeed illustrates the ethos of aristocratic ostentation
and expense, an ethos diametrically opposed to the modern bourgeois
spirit devoted to savings, foresight, and calculation. Fashion runs counter
to the spirit of growth and the development of mastery over nature. On the
other hand, however, fashion belongs structurally to the evolving modern
world. Its instability signifies that appearances are no longer subject to
intangible ancestral laws, that they stem from human decisions and pure
human desire. Before being a sign of conceited unreasonableness, fashion
attests to the human capacity to change, the ability of men and women to
invent new modes of appearance. Fashion is one of the faces of modern
artifice, of the effort of human beings to make themselves masters of the
conditions of their own existence. Along with the agitation that is characteristic of fashion there arises an order of "autonomous" phenomena, re-
sponding only to the play of human desires, whims, and wishes. No longer
is some specific form of dress imposed from the outside, by virtue of ancestral practice. Everything connected with appearance is by rights at the
disposal of individuals who are henceforth free to modify the fleeting
signs, to make them more sophisticated; the only limitations are contemporary standards of appropriateness and taste. The age of efficiency and
the age of the ephemeral, rational mastery of nature and the ludic follies
of fashion: these are only in appearance antinomic. In fact, the two types
of logic are rigorously parallel: just as people have devoted themselves, in
the modern West, to intensive exploitation of the material world and to the
rationalization of productive tasks, through the fleeting nature of fashion
they have asserted their power of initiative over looks. In each case, human
sovereignty and autonomy are affirmed, exercising their dominion over
the natural world as they do over their own aesthetic decor. Proteus and

Prometheus are of the same stock; although their paths are radically different, together they have inaugurated the unique adventure of Western
modernity.

The Theater of Artifice

It is nevertheless true that at certain points in their history other civilizations have also witnessed the development of aestheticism and superficial
refinement. We know that in imperial Rome men curled and dyed their
hair, used perfume, and applied "beauty spots" to enhance their complexions and appear younger. Elegant women used makeup and perfume, and
wore false braids and wigs dyed blond or ebony black. During Flavius's
reign, elaborate raised hairdos appeared: hair was built up into elevated
diadems made of complicated bows. Under Oriental influence, precious
jewels and various ornaments, embroidery and braiding, came to compensate for the austerity of classical female garb. Should we conclude from
this that fashion manifested itself precociously in ancient Rome? It is important to be clear on this point: even if certain of these demonstrations of
elegance and luxury can be related to the logic of fashion, the most specific
feature of fashion is manifestly lacking: the rapid flux of variations. No
system of fashion exists without the conjunction of two logical systems: the
system of ephemera and the system of aesthetic fantasy. This combination, which formally defines the fashion mechanism, has been produced
only once in history, at the threshold of our modern societies. Elsewhere
we can find sketchy movements, premonitory signs of what we call fashion, but never a full-fledged system. The various decorative frills have
remained fixed within narrow limits; they cannot be compared to the excesses and repetitive follies of which the Western world has been the theater. If, as the Roman satires of the time attest, certain precious elements
did succeed in adding sophistication to masculine appearance, can these
elements really be compared to the uninterrupted deluge of frills and
ribbons, hats and wigs that modern fashion has brought forth in rapid
succession? To limit our consideration to Rome, fantasies did not modify
the austerity of traditional masculine dress; these were rare, and they
did not go beyond curled hair and the restrained use of makeup. We are
far removed from Western fashion and its permanent profligacy of
eccentricities.

It is more significant still that in eras governed by tradition fantasies are
structurally secondary with respect to the overall configuration of clothing. They may accompany and embellish it, but they always respect the
general arrangements defined by custom. Thus despite the taste for striking hair dyes, assorted jewelry, fabrics and trimmings, Roman women's

dress changed very little: the old outer tunic (*stola*) and the draped coat (*palla*) were worn without much modification. The search for aesthetic effects is extrinsic to the prevailing general style. It orchestrates neither new structures nor new forms of dress; it functions as a mere decorative complement, adding peripheral charm. With the fashion system, on the contrary, an unprecedented mechanism is in place. The artificial is not superimposed from without on a preconstituted whole; the artificial henceforth totally redefines forms of dress, both in their essential lines and in their details. By the same token, fashion shifts overall appearance into the order of theatricality, seduction, and enchanted spectacle, with its pro-fusion of frills and furbelows but also and especially with its outrageous, extravagant, "ridiculous" forms. The long pointed shoes and other foot-wear, the prominent trouser flies in the form of penises, the low-necked dresses, the two-color costumes of the fourteenth and fifteenth centuries, and later the immense ruffs, the rhinegraves, the hoop skirts, the monu-mental baroque hairstyles, all these more or less eccentric fads profoundly restructured male and female figures to varying degrees. Under fashion's regime, aesthetic artificialism is not subordinated to a stable order; it is at the very root of the arrangement of grooming, which appears as a strictly contemporary, modern, ludic party spectacle. The features it shares with the timeless past of decorative taste must not be allowed to obscure fash-ion's absolutely radical nature, or the logical reversal that it institutes his-torically. Until fashion came on the scene, "mannerism" was strictly sub-jected to a structure inherited from the collective past; with fashion, on the contrary, it has become primary in the creation of forms. Mannerism was once content to decorate; now it has full sway to invent everything related to appearance. Even when it was invested with fantasy, in traditional eras, personal appearance maintained a continuity with the past; it remained a sign of the primordial legitimacy of the ancestral tradition. The emergence of fashion has brought about a complete shift in the social meaning and temporal markers of dress. As a playful and gratuitous representation and a factitious sign, fashionable dress has broken all ties with the past; it draws the essence of its prestige from the ephemeral, scintillating, fasci-nating present.

From the fourteenth to the eighteenth centuries, this sovereignty of whim and artifice ruled both sexes in virtually identical terms. Fashion's defining feature during all that time was the impetus it gave to a plethora of theatrical excesses, for men as well as women. Just when fashion was introducing an exaggerated dissimilarity in the appearance of the two sexes, it was also consigning both sexes in equal measure to the cults of novelty and preciosity. In many respects, for all that, men's fashion en-joyed a relative preponderance in terms of novelty, ornamentation, and extravagance. With the appearance of the short suit, in the mid-fourteenth century, male fashion embodied the new logic of appearance—based on fantasy and rapid change—more directly and more obviously than the female version from the start. In the seventeenth century men's clothes were still more mannered, more beribboned, more playful (witness rhinc- graves) than those of women. Modifications of military equipment had an influence on men's fashions,[14] but this by no means kept the fanciful fash- ion process from regulating signs of virility and toying with them: fashion put the combatant's attributes (golden spurs, swords adorned with roses, boots embellished with lace, and so on) onstage and complicated them even as it simulated "naturalness." Not until the "great renunciation" of the nineteenth century was the masculine mode eclipsed by the feminine. From that point on, the new canons of male elegance, discretion and sobri- ety, the rejection of color and ornamentation, made fashion and its arti- fices a female prerogative.

Governed by the logic of theatricality, the fashion system was insepara- ble from excess, disproportion, outrageousness. It was destined to be car- ried away, inexorably, in an escalation of extremes, exaggerations of volume and amplifications of form that braved ridicule. Nothing managed to keep elegant men and women from "piling it on," from going one step further with respect to what was acceptable, from competing in extremes of formal and luxurious ostentation. The ruche that could scarcely be seen above the top of the shirt, under the doublet, thus grew slowly into the independent ruff, exaggerated in volume and fullness. Similarly, the far- thingale became wider and wider, in conformity with the hyperbolic pro- cess characteristic of fashion. However, the escalation of width was not unlimited. At one point or another the process was abruptly reversed, turned around: fashion rejected the previous trend, but it remained driven by the same logic of play, by the same capricious movement. In fashion, the least and the most, the sober and the flashy, fads and the reaction they provoke, are of the same essence, no matter what contrasting aesthetic effects they produce: what is at stake is always the realm of caprice, sub- tended by an unwavering passion for novelty and ostentation. The reign of fancy does not merely entail carrying things to extremes, but also shifting back, reversing direction: the vogue for simplicity and nature that came into being around 1780 was no less theatrical, artificial, and ludic than were the earlier excesses of precious refinement. If it is true that modifica- tions of the culture and spirit of an age are indeed at the root of variations in fashion, they can never suffice on their own to account for fashion's novelty, its irreducible aleatory character, its endless metamorphoses that are neither reasonable nor necessary. This is so because fashion cannot be detached from the logic of pure fantasy, from the spirit of gratuitousness

and play that inevitably accompanies the promotion of secular individualism and the end of the immutable preregulated universe of traditional
forms of appearance.

This is why fashion gave rise to endless criticism, why it clashed, often
head-on, with contemporary aesthetic, moral, and religious standards.
Critics were no longer content to denounce human vanity, the display of
wealth, and female coquetry; they came to look at forms of dress themselves as indecent, scandalous, and ridiculous. In the fourteenth and fifteenth centuries, bishops and preachers issued violent condemnations of
the *déshonnesteté*—the impropriety—of breeches worn with tails, "nudity
of the throat," and long, pointed shoes. The tight doublet, with a camber
that makes a man's chest "comparable to a woman's bust" and makes him
"resemble a greyhound," created as much scandal as did hairstyles in the
shape of horns. In the sixteenth century, farthingales were mocked, and
their diabolical artificiality was denounced; in the seventeenth century,
rhinegraves (which resembled skirts) and jerkins were objects of ridicule.
In the eighteenth century, people laughed at frock coats; the allegorical
and extravagant hairdos that put the wearers' eyes "in the middle of the
body," women's clothing inspired by men's, and the transparent tulle
dresses of the Directoire were targets for caricature artists. Without question, we can trace the tradition of denigrating frivolity, artifice, and
makeup back to ancient Greece and Rome;[15] decorative excesses are condemned in periods governed by this tradition, but the prevailing overall
standard of dress is exempt from sarcasm. With the emergence of fashion,
on the contrary, specific components of dress are themselves targets of
indignation. For the first time, personal appearance is no longer determined by social consensus; it affronts habits and prejudices; it is violently
condemned by church leaders; it is judged ridiculous, inappropriate, and
hideous by contemporary chroniclers. The latest vogue is viewed as sublime by the elegant set, as scandalous by the moralists, and as ridiculous
by the ordinary honest person; fashion and discordant opinion henceforth
go hand in hand.

The apotheosis of aesthetic gratuitousness has not failed to influence the
secular relations, tastes, and mental outlook of human beings; it has
helped forge certain characteristic features of modern individuality. By
creating an order made up simultaneously of excesses and minimal discrepancies, fashion has helped refine taste and sharpen aesthetic sensibility. It has civilized the human eye by teaching it to discriminate among
small differences, to take pleasure in small, subtle, delicate details, to welcome new forms. Norbert Elias has pointed out how the competitive universe of the court had given rise to the art of observing and interpreting
one's peers, the art of studying people's behavior and motives;[16] we may
add that fashion has worked in a similar way, via appearance and taste.

With fashion, human beings begin observing each other endlessly, appreciating each other's looks, evaluating nuances of cut, color, and pattern in dress. As an apparatus for generating aesthetic and social judgment, fashion has favored the critical gaze of the worldly-wise; it has stimulated more or less agreeable judgments of the elegance of others. Whatever the scope of the mimetic trends that subtend it, fashion has served as an agent for the autonomizing of taste.

Yet fashion has not been merely a stage for the appreciation of the spectacle provided by others; it has also unleashed an investment of self, an unprecedented aesthetic self-observation. Fashion goes hand in glove with the pleasure of seeing, but also with the pleasure of being seen, of exhibiting oneself to the gaze of others. While fashion quite obviously does not create narcissism out of whole cloth, it does reproduce narcissism in a particularly noteworthy way: it makes narcissism a constitutive and permanent structure of fashionable individuals, by encouraging them to pay more attention to the way they present and represent themselves, by inciting them to seek elegance, grace, and originality. The endless variations of fashion and the code of elegance invite individuals to study themselves, to adapt novelties for their own use, to concern themselves with their own dress. Fashion has not only made it possible to display one's membership in a given rank, class, or nation, it has also been a vector of narcissistic individualization, an instrument for enlarging the aesthetic cult of the self, even at the heart of an aristocratic age. The first major mechanism for the consistent social production of personality on display, fashion has aestheticized and individualized human vanity; it has succeeded in turning the superficial into an instrument of salvation, a goal of existence.

Fashion: Hierarchical Expression,

Individual Expression

Fashion is an original system for social regulation and social pressure. Its changes are constraining by nature: they carry with them the obligation that they be adopted and assimilated; they impose themselves with varying degrees of rigor on a specific social milieu. Such is the "despotism" of fashion, so frequently denounced over the centuries. It is a very special form of despotism, since it has no significant sanctions except perhaps for the laughter, scorn, or criticism of one's contemporaries. But however effective these means of ensuring social conformity may have been, especially in periods ruled by hierarchy and honor, they do not suffice to account for fashion epidemics. More fundamentally, it is by virtue of the human desire to resemble people deemed superior, people whose influence radiates via prestige and rank, that fashion's decrees succeed in spreading: the diffusion of fashion has mimesis at its core. In aristocratic periods and until recently, as Tarde observed, this mimesis was propagated essentially from the top down, from superior to inferior. Waves of imitation progressed accordingly: while the court kept its eyes on the king and the great lords, the city followed the example of the models prevailing at court and among the nobility. The diffusion of fashion has been less a form of social constraint than an instrument of social representation and affirmation, less a type of collective control than a sign of social pretension.

The social expansion of fashion did not win over the lower classes right away. For centuries, dress respected the hierarchy of conditions, by and large. Members of each estate wore clothing appropriate to that estate; the force of tradition prevented the confusion of status and the usurpation of privileges of dress. Sumptuary laws forbade commoners to dress like nobles; they could not display the same fabrics, accessories, or jewelry. Thus for a long time fashionable clothing remained a luxurious and prestigious acquisition confined largely to the nobility. Even so, as early as the thirteenth and fourteenth centuries, as commerce and banking developed, immense bourgeois fortunes were being constituted, setting the stage for the appearance of the grand upstart with a flashy retinue, dressed like a noble, draped in jewels and expensive fabrics, rivaling the born-and-bred nobility in elegance—even as sumptuary laws were proliferating in Italy, France, and Spain; they were designed to protect national industries and prevent the waste of rare metals and precious stones, but they were also intended to impose distinctions in dress that would remind all people of their estate and place in the hierarchical order. Confusion in dress, quite limited at the outset, did not increase until the transition from the sixteenth century to the seventeenth, when the imitation of noble dress spread into new social strata. Fashion penetrated into the middle and sometimes the lower bourgeoisie; many lawyers and owners of small businesses were already adopting the fabrics, headdresses, laces, and embroideries worn by nobles. The process continued into the eighteenth century, although it still excluded rural populations. The phenomenon was strictly limited to well-to-do city dwellers: artisans and merchants, for example, sported powder and wigs in the aristocratic manner.

Even if bourgeois dress was never a match for aristocratic flashiness, boldness, and panache, even if it only began to spread after the fact, when the custom was beginning to disappear from the court, a slow and limited tendency to democratize fashion, to mix up dress styles, appeared even despite the sumptuary laws that were still formally in place. For centuries, numerous highly detailed statutes forbade commoners to copy the fabrics, accessories, or even the patterns of noble dress. We know that despite the threats and fines these regulations entailed, they were never effective and were very often transgressed. The fate of the sumptuary laws is a perfect

illustration of the way the Old Regime worked, as Tocqueville summed it
up: strict rules, lax practices. The nobility never consented to stop spending money for prestige, and it never failed to find new ways to get around
the laws so as to display its wealth. As for the well-to-do bourgeoisie, alert
for visible signs of social respectability and advancement, over the centuries it repeatedly violated the rules by adopting one element of aristocratic
dress or another. Confusion in dress and the aims of the absolutist monarchy worked in such a way that in the 1620s, roughly speaking under Riche-
lieu's ministry, the sumptuary laws ceased to be explicitly segregative. Excessive spending on dress was still forbidden, but the prohibitions were
addressed from that point on to all subjects; they no longer mentioned
estate or condition.[17] Thus in this sense the Convention's 1793 decree de-
claring the democratic principle of freedom in dress only legalized and
burnished a reality that had already been in place for two centuries or
more in the upper and middle strata of society.

While the role of fashion in this partial process of equalizing appearances must not be overestimated, its contribution is nevertheless undeniable. By continuously introducing novelties, by legitimizing the practice of
taking contemporaries instead of predecessors as models, fashion permitted the immutable order of traditional dress and intangible distinctions
among groups to dissolve. It provided a climate favorable to acts of boldness and transgression not only for the nobility but also among the bourgeoisie. Fashion must be conceptualized as an instrument for the equality
of conditions. It disrupted the principle of inequality in dress; it undermined traditionalist behaviors and values in favor of the thirst for novelty
and the implicit right to "fine looks" and frivolities. But fashion could be
an agent of the democratic revolution only because it was accompanied,
more fundamentally, by a dual process with dramatic consequences for
the history of our societies: the economic ascension of the bourgeoisie on
the one hand, the growth of the modern state on the other. Together these
factors succeeded in giving reality and legitimacy to the desire for social
advancement on the part of the classes obliged to work. This is the crux of
fashion's originality and also its ambiguity: an instrument of social discrimination and a manifest mark of social superiority, fashion was nevertheless also a special agent of the democratic revolution. On the one hand,
it blurred the established distinctions and made it possible to confront and
confuse social strata. On the other hand, it reintroduced—although in a
new way—the timeless logic of signs of power, brilliant symbols of domination and social difference. Here is the paradox of fashion: its flashy displays of the emblems of hierarchy played a role in the movement toward
the equalization of appearances.

The spread of fashion coincided only partially with mechanical imitation. At a deeper level, it has to be identified with a selective and controlled
mimesis. Even if the middle classes did take the nobility as models, they

did not imitate everything; not all fleeting innovations were adopted, even at court. In sophisticated circles, not all the eccentricities of the nobility were accepted, and the more fanciful features of personal appearance provoked more disapproval than admiration among the bourgeoisie. In the early seventeenth century, a fashion system parallel to the system prevailing at court was already in place, the moderate fashion of the *honnête homme*, stripped of aristocratic excess and conforming to the bourgeois values of prudence, temperance, usefulness, cleanliness, and comfort. This "wiser" fashion,[18] rejecting the extravagances found at court, resulted from the filtering action of the bourgeois criteria; from court it retained only what did not run counter to its standards of good sense, moderation, and reason. Mimesis in fashion has the peculiarity of functioning at different levels: from the strictest conformity to a more or less faithful adaptation, from blind acceptance to thoughtful accommodation. Fashion is differentiated in terms of class and estate, but viewing it exclusively in these terms leaves out an essential dimension of the phenomenon: the play of freedom inherent in fashion, possibilities of nuance and gradation, opportunities to adapt or reject innovations. As an institution, fashion registers the rigid barriers of class stratification and class ideals within its own order; at the same time it is an institution in which individuals can exercise their freedom and their critical faculties. Notwithstanding the gulf between court and city, we cannot simply contrast an aristocratic fashion where individualism prevailed with a bourgeois fashion characterized by submission to custom and the community. Court fashion was obviously somewhat acquainted with conformity, and city fashion was quick to manifest significant features of the aesthetic emancipation of the individual. The most remarkable aspect of fashion lies in its relatively supple structure, one that leaves room for effects of gradation, for complex blends of refusal and acceptance. It is fashion as a system that is inseparable from individualism, from a relative latitude that allows people to reject, modulate, or accept the novelties of the day, from the principle that leaves people free to adhere to the canons of the moment or not. Notwithstanding the undeniable conformity of class behaviors and class differences, personal appearance disengaged itself from the traditional uniformity and became—very imperfectly and very unevenly, varying with the period, the milieu, and the individual—a matter of private taste, choice, and personal predilection.

If fashion saw waves of imitation unfold and spread from the higher to the lower orders, it nevertheless remained characterized by an entirely new, more strictly territorial mimesis: fashion in the aristocratic age was national fashion. Instead of the unity or even identity of dress that prevailed in Western Europe in the thirteenth century, each territorial state—beginning in the fourteenth century and continuing up to the nineteenth—

persisted in differentiating its forms of dress through special elements that
distinguished them from those of its neighbors. In its own sphere, fashion
registered the rise of the fact and feeling of nationhood in Europe, starting
in the late Middle Ages. In exchange, by producing national forms of dress,
fashion helped reinforce the awareness of belonging to a single political
and cultural community. Still, despite the national character of fashion
during that period of roughly five centuries, its multiple borrowings and
influences were largely a function of the prestige of nations themselves, not
as a function of a specialized institution, as was the case later on with the
development of haute couture. During this entire phase of the history of
fashion, artisans were simply and solely the executors of their clients'
wishes; lacking any power of initiative and any social status, they did not
succeed—apart from the eighteenth-century "fashion merchants"—in imposing themselves as creative artists. The tastes of elegant men and women
were liberated; the personality of the client—not that of the producer-
artisan—was affirmed. The principle of individuality, in the aristocratic
age, did not cross this boundary. Under such conditions, fashion's course
could not be determined by a body of tradespeople who lacked autonomy
and genuine legitimacy; its evolution was determined, at least in part, by
the political logic of the power of nations. After complex movements and
cycles of influence in which Italy, the Burgundian states, and Spain played
the major roles, from the mid-seventeenth century on it was French fashion that managed to establish lasting dominion and increasingly began to
look like a beacon of elegance.

This national individualism is echoed by what must be called *aesthetic
individualism*. As a collective constraint, fashion actually left individuals
with relative autonomy in matters of appearance; it instituted an unprecedented relation between individuals and the rule of society. Fashion's distinguishing feature was its imposition of an overall standard that nevertheless left room for the manifestation of personal taste. One must look
like other people, but not exactly; one must follow trends and also signal
one's own tastes.[19] This mechanism combining mimesis and individualism
occurs over and over at various levels, in all the spheres where fashion
operates; still, it is manifested nowhere more strikingly than in personal
appearance, because dress, hairstyles, and makeup are the most obvious
signs of self-affirmation. If fashion governs personal appearance to such
an extent, it is because fashion is a privileged way of expressing the
uniqueness of individuals. As much as it was a sign of condition, class, and
nation, fashion was also, from the outset, an instrument for inscribing
individual difference and freedom, if only at a superficial and generally
tenuous level. The logic of fashion implied wearing the shapes and styles
in favor at the moment, dressing in the garments currently viewed as essential, but at the same time it supported individual initiative and taste in

trimmings and little extras, in color and decorative motif. The structure of clothing was imposed, not the accessories and decorative elements; these left room for individual taste and personality. Personal choice was henceforth an inherent aspect of fashionable dressing, but it was strictly limited to colors and to certain formal details, such as the depth of the décolleté, bows and laces, decorative motifs, the width and height of ruffs, the fullness of petticoats. The strict uniformity of fashion trends and the process of individual differentiation were historically inseparable; fashion's great originality lay in the way it allied overall conformity with personal freedom in small choices and minor variations. Fashion can then be seen as the expression of the freedom of human subjects: this phenomenon has been quite well identified, even when it concerns dress styles prevailing outside court society, as numerous texts from the first half of the seventeenth century attest. "Four Frenchmen who meet on the Pont Neuf will each create his own fashion, and any Gascon who passes by will think of some way to create yet another. So this Fashion is not a fashion, for there are as many fashions as there are Gascons, and as many Gascons as there are Frenchmen."[20]

Paralleling this minimal yet widespread aesthetic freedom, individualism in fashion asserted itself more insistently and systematically in the sphere of power and at court. From the late Middle Ages on, fashion depended on the changing tastes of monarchs and great lords. Clothing no longer belonged to collective memory; it became the singular reflection of the predilections of sovereigns and other powerful people. Mimesis in fashion cannot be grasped apart from the historically unprecedented creative individualism of those at the top of the hierarchy: the power of highly placed people in this world to introduce an arbitrary break in the continuity of custom, to bring about changes in forms, dimensions, colors. The "device" used by King René in 1447–49 consisted in three colors, black, white, and grey; two years later, white and violet were used, and at the end of his reign his pages sported black and crimson, possibly echoing his political difficulties and the death of family members.[21] Dress changed according to the preferences of the powerful: clothes became signs and languages by the same token as all the embroidered devices, monograms, and emblems that were used in the fourteenth and fifteenth centuries as personal symbols adopted by knights. Later, Queen Jeanne of Portugal introduced the *verdugo* (a support structure anticipating the farthingale) to conceal her pregnancy; Louis XIII inaugurated the vogue of pointed beards; Louis XIV used male fashion to create a particular image of his power. Fashion, unlike tradition, requires free individual intervention, a singular and capricious power to disrupt the order of appearances.

In addition to sovereigns, over the centuries we find increasing numbers of individuals known as "arbiters and ministers of elegance," great lords capable of launching fashions to which their own names are sometimes attached: Pompignan-style shoes, spurs in the Guise manner, a Sévigné coiffure. Individualism in fashion is reflected in all its brilliance in the power of a few great nobles to promote innovations deliberately, to be leaders in taste and grace within high society. Individualism in fashion also became apparent, though not in the same way, in the ostentatious search for individual differences and originality on the part of courtiers, the lesser nobility, worldly types on display in attention-seeking outfits at court and later in the salons. *Muguets, petits-maîtres, muscadins, merveilleuses, beaux, fashionables* were incarnations of frivolous individualism who devoted themselves to the frenetic cult of personal and social distinction. Aesthetic excess and fanciful gratuitousness became components of fashion, possibilities open to the individual who was liberated from the traditional order of dress. Mimesis in fashion does not conflict with individualism. Rather, it embraces it, in two principal forms that are clearly opposed but that allow for subtle intermediate and composite degrees: on the one hand, the self-effacing individualism of the greatest number; on the other hand, the self-advertising individualism of worldly extravagance.

It would be inaccurate to claim that ancient societies were unfamiliar with individual efforts to achieve aesthetic effects, or with manifestations, in the realm of dress, of the desire to be seductive. In Greece, a large number of adjustments and drapings could be achieved from the single piece of rectangular cloth that was the basis for the classic draped costume for both sexes. Multiple arrangements were possible, and choices unquestionably arose out of personal taste and aesthetic talent; but this personal dimension can never be confused with the individualist logic that is constitutive of fashion. So long as the traditional costume prevailed, personal appearance turned out in law and fact to be subordinated to the ancestral common rule; nowhere were social agents able to transgress prevailing practices openly and invent new lines and styles one after another. Even when ways of arranging dress varied considerably, as they did in Greece, they were nevertheless ordered, predetermined by a closed set of possible combinations. An individual might vary and combine figures, but only within the bounds of an intangible repertory fixed by tradition: there were plays of combination and permutation, but there was no formal innovation. The emergence of fashion coincides, on the contrary, with the overthrow of this mechanism, with the advent of the principle of individual aesthetic autonomy in its two major manifestations: sovereign creation for some, adaptation of prevailing standards to individual tastes for the rest.

The collective standard no doubt continued to rule with an iron hand, as attested by mimetic trends and complaints about the despotism of fashion. But in the guise of the return of the same, a radical modification occurred: individuals won the right—not an unlimited right, to be sure, but a functional one—to display personal taste, to innovate, to outdo others in daring and originality. The individualization of appearance earned secular legitimacy; the aesthetic search for difference became a constitutive logic of the universe of appearances. Far from being wholly subordinated to an overall standard, the individual agent conquered a measure of creative, reformist, or adaptive initiative: the primacy of the immutable law of the group yielded to the valorization of change and individual originality. Historically, this is what counts: individualism in fashion is the possibility granted to an individual—even if that individual has to come from the highest ranks of society—to be a force for initiative and change, to transform the existing order, to take personal credit for innovations, or, more modestly, to introduce elements of detail that conform to the individual's own taste. Although individuals generally go on faithfully obeying the collective dress code, their subjection *in principle* is a thing of the past. Where it had once been necessary to submerge one's identity and bow to the law of the group, it is now possible to highlight some distinctive characteristic or personal idiosyncrasy. Where it was once necessary to return to the past, change and personal creative taste have now been legitimized. This transformation may not have had very profound effects on the behavior of the masses, but the break with the traditional system and the subjugation of the individual agent that it implies were nevertheless accomplished. A closed, anonymous, static system gave way to a system that in theory has no determinable limits, a system open to the personalization of appearance and intentional change of forms.

Individual initiative in ornamentation, creation of new signs in the realm of dress, triumph of the fashion arbiters: far from being antithetical to the affirmation of the individual personality, as some are overly fond of repeating, fashion is based historically on the value and claims of individuality, on the legitimacy of personal uniqueness. At the very heart of a world ruled by hierarchical values, the figure of the intraworldly individual that characterizes modern societies was erected in a position of dominance. An individualism of taste developed alongside economic and religious individualism, preceding the ideological individualism of the egalitarian age. Personal autonomy in the practice of elegance preceded the valorization of the individual that characterizes modern ideology; freedom in action, however limited, came ahead of the Declaration of the Rights of Man. Very early on in the era of fashion, we can mark the advent of secular individualism in every sense of that term, an individualism alert for signs of personal uniqueness as well as social superiority. Throughout this entire period, it must be acknowledged that individualism in fashion took the form of *aristocratic individualism*, a complex but exemplary case that allowed the "holistic" principle of social cohesiveness to coexist with

the modern principle of individual freedom. It is thus incorrect to claim
that fashion corresponded to the new "tyrannical" hold of the collective
that is denounced on all sides; it is much more accurate to say that fashion
reflected the emergence of human autonomy in the world of appearances.
It was an inaugural sign of the emancipation of aesthetic individuality, the
beginning of the right of personalization, although this right was obviously subject to the changing decrees of the collective whole. At its own
level, fashion marks a break in the timeless preponderance of holistic organization as well as a limit to the process of social and political domination in modern societies. The growth of states and administrations and the
perfecting of bodily programming together constitute a single facet of the
evolution of the modern world. Alongside disciplinary training and the
increased penetration of the political sphere in civil society, the private
sphere gradually broke free of collective prescriptions. Fashion was beginning to express, in luxury and ambiguity, an invention characteristic of the
West: the free, detached, creative individual and its corollary, the frivolous
ecstasy of the self.

Beyond Class Rivalries

Crude though it may be in its formulation, the question of fashion's origin
remains a stumbling block. Why did fashion appear and flourish in Western Europe and nowhere else? How can we account for the incessant ebb
and flow of forms and tastes that has marked Western societies for six
centuries? What is remarkable is how little elaboration and theoretical
interrogation this question has provoked. There is no getting around it: on
the origins and mainsprings of fashion, we are astonishingly ill informed.
The models that are generally invoked were developed in the nineteenth
century; since then, the basic theory of fashion has advanced very little. It
has been content, in the main, to rework and refine unchanging principles
established by sociological thought as quasi-dogmatic truths. The state of
the question has been treated to a good deal of overblown rhetoric but no
real renewal; the sociological paradigm of class distinction has come to
look more and more like the indispensable key to the phenomenon. The
pages that follow do not share that assurance. They begin with the idea
that the sociological models proposed are far from adequate to their explanatory ambition. The project has to be thoroughly reexamined; the
limits of the paradigm of distinction have to be demonstrated. We have to
complicate the analytical schemas by giving due credit to phenomena generally considered secondary. We have to undertake an overall reinterpretation of fashion, and in the process we shall have to reconsider the historical role of classes and their rivalries.

It is clearly impossible to understand the appearance of fashion without linking it to a set of general conditions characteristic of Western Europe after the year 1000. The economic and social conditions of the time must be taken into account, to be sure, but also, at a more subterranean level, the crucial phenomenon constituted by the end of the period of outside invasions. With the end of barbarian devastation and pillaging, the West came to know an immunity that was found virtually nowhere else in the world. The consequences of this phenomenon were considerable, not only for later economic development but also and especially for the flourishing of civilization as a whole, in a process that was not to be disrupted again by powers foreign to its cultural soil: intra-European wars were numerous and deadly, but they all took place within the family, in a closed receptacle, to use Marc Bloch's terms. This particular feature of the West, that it was to remain exempt from outside incursions, allowed its civilization to give itself over to the pleasures of sophisticated forms and ephemeral follies. The inordinate play of frivolity was made possible only by virtue of the profound cultural stability that guaranteed a permanent anchor point for collective identity: at the root of the principle of inconstancy is the constancy of Western cultural identity, an exceptional case in history.

The economic factors that characterized medieval Europe also played an important role. Starting in the eleventh century, we witness the beginning of continuous economic growth based on vast land clearings and an agricultural and technological revolution, as well as the development of commerce, a monetary renaissance, and the expansion of cities. The progress of material civilization, the establishment of the feudal system, and the decline of monarchic power resulted in an increase in the revenues of the nobility and an improvement in the aristocratic standard of living. With increased resources, rich and ostentatious princely courts came into being, courts that served as fertile ground for fashion and its displays of wealth. To this we must add the development of cities, the establishment of trade fairs and distant trading outposts, and the intensification of commercial exchanges that allowed new foyers of great financial fortunes to appear. In the thirteenth century, as expansion was more and more focused on cities, and the cities of Italy were at the center of the world economy, an upper bourgeoisie was beginning to copy the manners and tastes of the nobility. It was against this background of economic upsurge in the West, the enriching of the lordly and bourgeois classes, that fashion gained its foothold.

It would be inaccurate, however, to view the birth of fashion as a direct result of economic expansion. It was in fact at the very moment when the West was experiencing the return of famines and economic hardship, wars and armed marauders, decreased agricultural revenues, epidemics and the plague, that fashion came into its own. The upsurge of ephemeral passions coincided with the end of medieval growth, in a century when the great rural landowners were weakened economically by the peasantry's abandonment of the land and agricultural work. The flourishing of fashion went hand in hand with the financial difficulties, indeed the ruin, of a segment of the nobility. This ruin cannot be attributed to the decline in land use alone; fidelity to an ethos of sumptuary expense was also a contributing factor. It is true that the crisis of the fourteenth century did not affect all regions and all sectors of the economy in the same way. It did not prevent certain aristocratic landholders from maintaining their power or indeed from developing great rural exploitations in the fifteenth century. It did not keep bankers, businessmen, and merchants from pursuing trade in silver, spices, cloth, and wheat, or from buying fiefdoms complete with rights of banishment and royalties. Even if the mercantile activity of the late Middle Ages came up against hard times and declined in importance in comparison to the era of the Crusades, it allowed the cities of Italy and Hanseatic Germany to continue to develop, and it permitted the spectacular rise of prosperous new centers in Castille, southern Germany, Lombardy, and England. The misfortunes of the late Middle Ages did not have the same consequences for everyone everywhere: despite the general slump, some great fortunes were concentrated, and newly wealthy bourgeois families proliferated. Luxurious tastes and ruinous prestige-oriented expenses, especially in the realm of dress, did not decline; on the contrary, they spread within a bourgeoisie eager to display the signs of its new power, as well as within a lordly class concerned with maintaining its status. In this sense, the appearance of fashion reflects less a major economic change than the continuation, even the exacerbation, of an aristocratic habit of magnificence that the economic crisis did not by any means manage to dislodge.

The development of fashion was influenced not only by economic fluctuations but also—although quite differently—by other aspects of material civilization: the breadth of international exchanges, the urban renaissance, the new dynamism of the craft industries. In the Middle Ages, the textile industries and the far-flung commercial traffic fostered diversification in the materials used to make clothing: silk from the Far East, valuable furs from Russia and Scandinavia, cotton from Turkey, Syria, and Egypt, leather from Morocco, feathers from Africa, dyes (kermes, lacquer, indigo) from Asia Minor. Weavers and dyers were able to create luxury fabrics that circulated throughout Europe—the Europe of the powerful— by way of fairs and the sea trade: broadcloth from Flanders and England, linen from southern Germany, flaxen goods from the Saône and Bresse regions of France, velvet from Milan, Venice, and Genoa. The growth of medieval cities was especially influential in allowing the establishment of a high degree of intensive specialization and division of labor. By the middle of the thirteenth century, many trade corporations had developed a complex organization and collective regulations charged with controlling product quality as well as professional training. Etienne Boileau's *Livre des métiers* indicates that between 1260 and 1270 there were already some ten professions in Paris devoted to clothing and personal adornment: tailors, dressmakers, shoemakers, doubletmakers, bonnetmakers, and so on. The corporation of seamstresses was not constituted and authorized to make women's clothing—except for whalebone lining and trains—until 1675; before then, only tailors had the privilege of clothing both sexes. With their monopolies and rules fixed by tradition and codified by the corporations, the trades played a major role in the production of fashion through the mid-nineteenth century. On the one hand, the extreme specialization of trades and their corporate framework impeded their development, by stifling individual initiative and imagination. On the other hand, these same conditions allowed for numerous innovations in weaving, dyeing, and finishing, and the production they fostered was of very high quality. Fashion could come into its own, with its sophisticated production, its refined details, only on the basis of such a separation of tasks. To limit ourselves for a moment to the short masculine garb that ushered in the age of fashion, we may well wonder how it could have appeared without a body of trades that was already highly specialized. Unlike the medieval smock, which was a long, full garment pulled on over the head, the new masculine garment was very narrow at the waist and broader at the chest. Such a transformation in dress styles required a very careful cut, as well as innovative manufacturing techniques for buttons, laces, and so on. Even if tailors and other clothing professionals lacked social recognition and remained in the shadow of their prestigious clients, through their expertise and their countless anonymous innovations they contributed in a crucial way to the uninterrupted evolution of fashion. Thanks to the process of specialization, these professionals succeeded in giving concrete form to the aristocratic ideal of refinement and grace.

No theory of fashion can be based solely on economic and material factors. However important these factors may be, they shed insufficient light on the endless fanciful variations and transformations that define fashion per se. That is why we can only conclude that fashion is anchored more firmly in social logic than in an economic dynamic. The analysis is as classical as they come: fashion's instability is rooted in the social transformations that began to occur in the late Middle Ages and spread during the Old Regime. At the heart of the process, we find the growth in economic power on the part of the bourgeoisie, a growth that facilitated both the bourgeoisie's increased desire for social recognition and its increased tendency to imitate the nobility. The quest for symbols of distinction and class competition are the essential factors in the paradigm that has pre-

sided over accounts of fashion for more than a century. According to a
model that is customarily traced back to Herbert Spencer and that has
been used over and over ad infinitum since then, in their search for social
respectability the lower classes imitate the life-style and appearance of the
upper classes. The upper classes, in turn, in order to maintain social distance and set themselves apart, are forced to innovate, to modify their
appearance, once they have been overtaken by their rivals. As the bourgeois strata manage by virtue of their prosperity and daring to adopt certain marks of prestige that prevail among the nobility, change is required
in order to reinscribe the social gap. This dual movement of imitation and
distinction accounts for fashion's mutability.[22]

True, with the rise of the bourgeoisie, Europe unquestionably witnessed
an increase in the desire for social advancement and an acceleration of
imitative contagion; nowhere else were class barriers, estates, and conditions so widely crossed. Yet however accurate this account may be, the
social dynamic of class competition still cannot explain fashion, cannot
account for its extravagances and its accelerated rhythms. It is unlikely
that change in fashion comes about only because a phenomenon of diffusion and widespread imitation discredits elitist signs. The very rapidity
with which variations emerge contradicts this thesis: most often, novelties
are replaced much faster than they are popularized. They do not wait to be
"overtaken," as it were: they anticipate that process. It is not a matter of
an effect undergone but an effect desired, a largely autonomous power of
formal innovation. Change in fashion cannot be deduced from the widespread nature of its diffusion. It is not the inevitable effect of an external
social determinism; no mechanistic rationality of that sort is equipped to
grasp fashion's capriciousness. This certainly does not mean that there is
no social logic of fashion, but that in fashion the controlling, determining
factor is the headlong quest for novelty as such: not the cumbersome, de-
terministic mechanics of class conflict, but "modern" exaltation, the endless excitement of gratuitous aesthetic play. Fashion's turbulence depends
less on threats to social barriers than on the continuous, inexorable, but
unpredictable work carried out by the ideal of, and taste for, novelty that
characterize societies in the process of extricating themselves from the
prestige of the past. The weakness of the classical approach is that it sees
in fashion's fluctuations only a constraint imposed from without, an obligation resulting from the tensions that symbolize the prevailing social
stratification, whereas in fact these tensions correspond to the deployment
of new sociohistorical goals and aspirations.

A different version of the class-distinction model is currently in vogue
among theoreticians of fashion. This version no longer emphasizes the
headlong race between those at the bottom and those at the top of the
hierarchy, the phenomenon of "catching up," but struggles for prestige at

the heart of the dominant classes themselves. The development of the merchant and financier class set off a major process of social advancement. Newly wealthy members of the bourgeoisie acquired titles, bought fiefdoms and offices, and married their children into the nobility. From the fourteenth to the eighteenth centuries in Europe, royal power lent its support to a form of social osmosis within the dominant classes. The nobility was opened up to newly wealthy commoners; little by little a *noblesse de robe* took its place alongside the *noblesse d'épée*. It was precisely when the social stratification at the top of the hierarchy was no longer rigorously stable and when waves of commoners were climbing up the social ladder that fashion began to offer its volte-faces, subtended by strategies of distinction and class rivalries. As fortunes and ambitions became more mobile, as social barriers became less insurmountable, as privileges of birth found themselves rivaled by the power of wealth, accelerated processes of differentiation began to operate, inaugurating an age of endless competition for prestige and distinctive titles. Within the upper classes in particular, among factions within the dominant groups, between the nobility and the upper bourgeoisie, between the *noblesse de robe* and the *noblesse d'épée*, we can locate the competitive struggles that gave rise to the dynamic of fashion.[23]

Obviously, I do not mean to deny the internal struggles and the strategies of distinction that accompanied the upward movement and ennobling of the bourgeoisie. What I contest is rather the notion that these struggles and strategies were at the root of fashion and its vicissitudes. From the end of the Middle Ages on, we may ask, who were the tastemakers, the trendsetters and masters of fashion? Who gave impetus, and lent their own names, to novelties, if not the most highly placed individuals, the most prominent people at court, the royal favorites, the great lords and ladies, the king or queen in person? Competitive class struggles could not have played the role attributed to them, since the instigators of change were at the top levels of the hierarchy, people who, precisely by virtue of their prominent position, were immune to class anxieties and competition for social status. Once this is understood, the effort to locate the driving force behind fashion cannot fail to take into consideration the transformations that affected the attitudes and ambitions of the social elite. What has to be understood is how the uppermost layer of the hierarchy came to transform the realm of appearances as it did, how it managed to destroy the immutable order of tradition and give itself over to the interminable spiral of fantasy: it is a question of new reference points, new goals, not of social dialectics and struggle for status. If fashion also served as an instrument of class affiliation and class distinction, this function by itself does not explain the origin of the chain of innovations and the break with the timeless valorizations of the past. Strategies of social distinction undoubtedly enhanced fashion's diffusion and expansion; but the need for distinction alone does not account for the motive force behind novelties, the cult of the social present, or the legitimation of the unprecedented. It is impossible to accept the idea that competitive struggles for prestige among groups, struggles as old as the earliest human societies themselves, are at the root of an absolutely modern process that has no historical precedent. Furthermore, we must ask how such a schema would allow us to account for the unbridled quest for originality, or the nuanced quest for small individual variations in detail. What is the origin of the process of tenuous individualization of appearance that characterizes fashion? Theories of distinction elucidate neither the driving force behind perpetual innovation nor the freedom of choice concerning personal appearance.

Moreover, fashion is hardly foreign to phenomena of social competition. Veblen's celebrated analyses have taught us that upper-class consumption basically follows the principle of conspicuous waste, with the aim of attracting the admiration and envy of others. The motive underlying consumption is rivalry between individuals generated by self-love; in order to compare favorably with others, to earn and retain honor and prestige, members of the upper classes have to give and spend generously. They have to display their wealth and their luxuries; they have to demonstrate conspicuously, by their good manners, their decorum, and their surroundings, that they are not compelled to perform degrading, productive work. Fashion, with its rapid variations and its "useless" innovations, turns out to be particularly well suited for the intensification of ostentatious expense; for Veblen, it becomes a simple "corollary"[24] of the law of conspicuous consumption, an instrument for achieving social respectability. Veblen, who notes in passing that "no explanation at all satisfactory has hitherto been offered of the phenomenon of changing fashions,"[25] thought that such an explanation could be supplied only by the theory of visible waste. That theory alone makes it possible to explain the rejection of practical usefulness that characterizes fashion; that theory alone—still according to Veblen—underlies the vicissitudes and the obsolescence of forms. The requirement of magnificence leads to an escalation of fleeting innovations, a piling-on of superfluities without any functional goal, so that "the resulting conspicuous expensiveness of dress is therefore intrinsically ugly."[26] The law of unproductive expense has as its consequence both the speed of change and the ugliness of clothing that appeals to the tastes of the day. If fashions are this fleeting, it is because they are so grotesque and unaesthetic that we can tolerate them only briefly; hence the need to find relief from the preposterous effect of these forms in new costumes that are just as faithful to conspicuous consumption but that are also opposed to good taste: fashion and the artistic are opposites. Sociological reductionism is at its peak here: trends translate only our aspiration for social standing; we like contemporary styles only inasmuch as they allow us to categorize ourselves socially, to make ourselves stand out, to derive from them the benefit of distinction.

Veblen's theory unquestionably emphasizes an important aspect of fashion: ostentatious expense as a way to signify rank, arouse admiration, and display social status. But by what mechanism does the standard of conspicuous consumption manage to give rise to the cascades of novelties that constitute fashion? And why did it fail to trigger this folly of artifice for thousands of years? On this point, Veblen's analysis is brief: for the author of *The Theory of the Leisure Class*, what separates ages of fashion from ages of stability essentially depends on an exacerbation of the requirement to spend that is brought about by conditions proper to large cities where the upper classes are wealthier, more mobile, and less homogeneous than they were in traditional eras.[27] The law decreeing ostentatious waste and the race for social standing are thus imposed more imperiously, and they result in continually changing forms and styles. The fickle movements of fashion, in this sense, merely reflect an intensification of the rule of conspicuous consumption. But was this less true in other times? Did this rule prevail with less intensity at the time of Greek or Roman ostentatious spending, when leading citizens devoted astounding fortunes to feasts, buildings, distributions of coins, sacrifices, and spectacles of all sorts?[28] The standard of waste, in that context, was particularly imperious; yet fashion did not find space to flower in such a society.

In fact, the imperative to display one's wealth did not intensify in the modern West; rather, it manifested itself differently. More precisely, it allied itself structurally with the quest for individual difference and aesthetic innovation. Underlying the upsurge of fashion we find not an increase in waste for display purposes but new requirements, new values that are translated, to be sure, into the timeless code of ostentatious prodigality but that cannot be deduced mechanistically from that code. Here we have reached the limit of a sociology for which fashion functions solely as an instrument of social classification with no aesthetic aim. "When seen in the perspective of half-a-dozen years or more, the best of our fashions strike us as grotesque, if not unsightly," Veblen wrote.[29] This statement is clearly unacceptable: we may not agree at any price to wear styles that were in vogue a few years before, but there are innumerable earlier fashions that we continue to admire. Yesterday's fashion is boring; those of the day before yesterday and those of the distant past continue to hold charm: we admire their refinement, their abundant details, their outdated but delicate forms. Here is proof that fashion is inseparably linked to the *aesthetic* requirement, that it cannot be reduced to the order of aberrant superfluity for social quotation alone. Far from being "intrinsically ugly," fashion is defined, on the contrary, by the aspiration to refinement, ele-

gance, beauty, no matter what extravagances, excesses, and lapses in taste
have managed from time to time, over the centuries, to gain sway.

It is nevertheless true that fashion cannot be separated from conspicuous consumption—so long as its precise scope is spelled out, along with its
social and historical anchor points. In eras of inequality, conspicuous consumption has to be understood as a social norm consubstantial with the
aristocratic order, as a necessary imperative for the insistent representation of social distance and social hierarchy. As Max Weber had already
noted, " 'luxury' in the sense of rejecting purposive-rational control of consumption is for the dominant feudal strata nothing superfluous: it is a
means of social self-assertion."[30] The aristocratic ethos of largesse coupled
with disdain for work certainly was one of the conditions for the emergence of fashion: some sovereign ideal of that sort, embedded in the holistic order of societies, was a prerequisite for the gratuitousness and showy
play of adornment. The splendor of court life in the princely states and
later in the great absolutist monarchies was particularly dependent on that
standard of magnificence. As a place where nobles sought to shine and
stand out, a place of constant competition for status and prestige, a place
where an obligation to spend money on symbols of social distance was
imposed, the princely court was a decisive factor in the blossoming of fashion. As the great court societies evolved, moreover, fashion questions became matters of the highest importance for a nobility that had been dis-
armed, dispossessed of its ancient military and judicial prerogatives and
consigned to the realm of worldly pleasures. But fashion had been linked
to the change in status of the nobility even before the absolutist court came
into its own. Beginning in the late fourteenth century, at the very moment
when the extravagances of fashion were about to have free rein, the nobility found its prestige and political power diminishing. Knights were no
longer masters of war; their castles now succumbed to artillery fire; on the
battlefield it was infantrymen and archers on the ground who prevailed.
The decline of the cavalry was echoed not only in the rise of new chivalric
orders but also in an excess of spending on dress, an immoderate taste for
luxury and ostentation. Far from emblematizing the supremacy of the nobility, fashion attests much more to its continuous weakening since the late
Middle Ages, to its progressive metamorphosis into a "spectacular" class
that has self-advancement by sumptuary expense for display purposes as
one of its major obligations.

[However important these phenomena may be, we must make no mistake about it: they leave the heart of the problem unexplored. What caused
the rule of lavish expense to turn into an excess of precious elegance?
Always the same question: why the move beyond sumptuosity itself to the
escalation of change and extravagance? In opposition to the prevailing
theories, it is necessary to reassert that class rivalries are not the principle

underlying the incessant variations of fashion. No doubt class rivalries accompany these variations and determine certain of their aspects; they do not unlock their secret. The interrogation of fashion requires a paradigm change. This theoretical displacement can be outlined in broad strokes: fashion's constant shifts result above all from a new position and representation of the individual in relation to the collective whole. Fashion is not the corollary of conspicuous consumption and of strategies of class distinction, it is the corollary of a new relation between the self and others, of the desire to assert one's own personality, a desire that emerged among the upper classes during the late Middle Ages. It is because the role of the representation of the individual has not been given its due that the explanations of change in fashion remain so unconvincing. Far from being an epiphenomenon, the consciousness of being an individual with a particular destiny, the will to express a unique identity, the cultural celebration of personal identity were "productive forces," the very driving forces of the mutability of fashion. In order for the surge of frivolous changes to come about, a revolution was required in the *representation* of individual human beings and in their sense of self, upsetting traditional mentalities and values; we had to wait for the exaltation of human uniqueness and its complement, the social promotion of signs of personal difference.

At the end of the Middle Ages, indeed, we can observe an unprecedented increase in awareness of subjective identity, a new desire to express individual uniqueness, a new exaltation of individuality. In chronicles and memoirs, care is taken to mark the speaker's identity with a canonical formula, "the first-person pronoun followed by the author's name and surname, title and rank."[31] In poetic works, intimate confidences are intensified, expressing outpourings of the self, fleeting experiences, and personal memories. The appearance in the fourteenth and fifteenth centuries of "realistic" autobiographies, portraits, and self-portraits rich in accurate details also reveals the new dignity recognized in what is *singular* in human beings, although in contexts that were still chiefly coded and symbolic. What Philippe Ariès calls the "death of the self" is another illustration of that same tendency, one that breaks with the traditionally anonymous space of death: in the late Middle Ages, the iconography of the Last Judgment, the Book of Life, macabre themes, testaments, and personalized burial places were all signs of a desire for individualization, a concern with being oneself, a promotion of personal identity.[32] This new sense of personal identity and the legitimation of individual expression, even if they prevailed only within the confines of the small world of the social elite, and even if they were more a matter of formulas and life experience than of doctrine, allowed the protean logic of fashion to come into play. The requirement that one be oneself, the passionate attachment to marks of personality, and the social celebration of individuality had a number of effects: they facilitated the break with respect for tradition, they allowed sites of initiative and innovation to proliferate, they stimulated private imagination in a quest for novelty, difference, and originality. The affirmation of the *uomo singolare* set off a process of constant innovation in forms and styles, a process of rupture with respect to the fixed traditional standard. By the end of the Middle Ages, the individualization of appearance had been legitimized: to be unlike others, to be unique, to attract attention by displaying signs of difference— these became legitimate aspirations and passions in the world of the courts. Under such conditions, the precipitous movement of fashion is comprehensible. Self-awareness and the desire to stand out foster rivalry, competition among individuals, a race toward difference; they authorize and encourage the expression of individual tastes. Under such conditions, the acceleration of new ideas and the speeded-up and lasting search for new signs are virtually inevitable.

Innovation unquestionably remained a class privilege, an attribute of those at the top of the social hierarchy. But its importance lies elsewhere: the people at the summit had begun to glory in their ability to modify their environment, to invent new artifices, to personalize their own appearance. Such a transformation in the behavior of the social elite attests to the infiltration of a new social representation of individuality in the aristocratic universe. This was not a class phenomenon as such, but rather the penetration into the upper classes of a new way of looking at individual personality. The new ideas helped unsettle the immobility of tradition; they allowed individual difference to become a sign of social excellence. The perpetual variations of fashion cannot be separated from the more or less ostentatious personalization of appearance; the two phenomena are rigorously complementary faces of the new social valorization of the singular. Theories of fashion have been mistaken in viewing these two issues as unrelated; in reality, a single phenomenon is involved. Fashion was able to become the permanent theater of ephemeral metamorphoses because the individualization of appearance had won a new status of social legitimacy. Conversely, all the changes and trends would allow private individuals at least a minimal margin of freedom, choice, and autonomy in matters of taste.

At the same time, the meaning of change in cultural affairs was turned inside out. What had previously inspired fear and mistrust became a social value, an object of unbridled passions in the highest social circles. "Everything that changes loses value," a twelfth-century poem maintained, remaining within the rigid confines of the traditional mentality. The inconstancy of fashion reveals, on the contrary, that that traditional system was being left behind, at least in part. An unprecedented social value was beginning to radiate, that of *novelty*.[33] Fashion could not have existed without this reversal of the relation to historical evolution and to ephemera. In order for fashion to come into being, the "modern" had to be accepted and desired; the present had to be deemed more prestigious than the past; in an unprecedented move, what was novel had to be invested with dignity. The sources of this fundamental reversal in the temporal orientation of social life are quite complex, but the shift has to be linked in particular to the recognition of the right of private individuals to set themselves apart, to singularize their own appearance, and thus to change. With the new position of the social body in relation to the collective standard, a new social relationship to movement was established: the legitimacy of innovation and of the social present was tightly linked with the advent of the individualist-aesthetic logic as a logic of difference and autonomy. ⌉

The Aesthetics of Seduction

However fundamental the consecration of individuality and novelty may have been for the establishment of fashion, it does not suffice to make the phenomenon fully intelligible. A logic as complex as that of fashion, embracing so many aspects of social, individual, cultural, and aesthetic life, could emerge only owing to the synergistic interaction of a multitude of factors, each of which, while not always absolutely independent of the others, had its own impact. In addition to the social phenomena already mentioned (court society, the status of the aristocracy, the development of cities), other phenomena also played crucial roles. The encouragement of secular individuality, the overinvestment in personal appearance, the refinement and aestheticization of the forms that characterize fashion are all rooted in a cluster of cultural factors distinctive to the West. This point must be emphasized: in the genealogy of fashion, the factors that were determining in the last analysis were the values, meaning systems, tastes, and standards, the "superstructures" that accounted for the emergence—unique in human experience—of the passion for novelty.

By substituting reference to the present for reference to the past, fashion instituted a radical break in the order of legitimate time. However, this historical discontinuity does not preclude viewing fashion as a system that maintained the tastes, life-styles, and secular ideas that preceded the sense of modernity. The consecration of ephemera lies indeed in a straight line of descent from the standards of chivalric, courtly culture, with its aspiration to terrestrial joy and happiness: the joys of fighting in wars and tournaments, the joys of hunting, the pleasures of elegant feasts and festivals, the pleasures of games and of gallant verse, the love of display and spectacle.[34] The ethos of aristocratic pleasure was unquestionably a crucial factor in the appearance of the *homo frivolus*: fashion is a practice of pleasures, synonymous with the pleasure of pleasing, surprising, or astonishing. Furthermore, it is a pleasure produced by the stimulus of change, the metamorphosis of forms, of self and others. Fashion is not merely a mark of social distinction, it is also an enhancement, a pleasure for the eye, the pleasure of difference. The reign of fashion that was instituted at the end of the Middle Ages must not be conceived as an escape, as a way of inuring oneself to the misfortunes and anxieties of the times. It had much more direct continuity with the standards and mind-sets characteristic of lordly circles, of aristocrats avid for worldly satisfactions. That quest for enjoyment grew apace with the development of the great courts and courtly civility, and it also paralleled a new feeling for the duration of human life. From the humanists' writings we know that starting with the trecento the sense of the fleeting nature of earthly time was intensified: expressions of regret about aging, nostalgia for youth, a sense of the imminence of the end took on new accents.[35] This new collective sensibility, henceforth inseparable from modernity, unquestionably fostered the accelerated quest for pleasure. Fashion reflects a passionate love of life and happiness, an exacerbation of the desire to make the most of the earthly joys made possible by the values of chivalric life and court society, as well as by a modern sensibility already marked by a melancholy sense of time and anguish at the prospect of departing earthly life.

Increased intensity and precipitation in the quest for worldly pleasures were coupled with a process of stylization of tastes and standards of living. The emergence of fashion cannot be dissociated from the cultural revolution that was launched in the lordly class, at the turn of the eleventh century, by the development of courtly values. The ideal of chivalrous life was updated: the traditional requirements of strength, prowess, and generosity were supplemented by new standards advocating the idealization of women, delicacy of speech, good manners, literary talent, and gallant preciosity. The knight was transformed into a literary figure, a poet; the love of fine language and later of fine objects gained sway in worldly circles. Fashion was forged by this slow civilizing of manners and pleasures, by the new refined, aestheticized ideal. In a sense, the way had been paved for fashion more than two centuries before it emerged, with the advent of the courtly spirit that outdid itself with poetry and delicate preciosity. An art of nuances and surface refinements, fashion coupled a passion for beautiful objects and works of art with the aspiration to a more beautiful and stylized life that arose at the dawn of the twelfth century.

Fashion appeared in the century in which art presented a clear tendency toward decorative excess: the proliferation of ornament, the profusion of caprices in flamboyant architecture, the exacerbations of *Ars Nova*, the elegant modulations of Gothic miniatures. This is also the age of eccentric dress, culminating at the court of Charles VI and the dukes of Burgundy with clothing that was half-red, half-purple, or blue and yellow, with women's hairdos in sugarloaf style, the hennin, heads shaved at the temples and above the forehead, capes in the form of cockscombs, sleeves wide enough to touch the ground. There is no denying it: all these novelties, with their exaggerations and their excesses, constituted just one manifestation among many others of the need for aestheticism, the cult of ornament and spectacle that characterized the late Middle Ages but lasted well beyond that time. The fourteenth and fifteenth centuries saw the emergence of a baroque spirit, a taste for theatrical and fanciful decors, an attraction to exoticism and rarity, gratuitous fancies corresponding to the triumph of courtly culture with its ideal of play and worldly preciosity. The undulating circuit of forms and the profuse wealth of ornamentation in art were now echoed by the strange, extravagant, sophisticated costumes of the court and nocturnal festivals. The influence of the spirit of play dominating the courtly imagination gave rise to an optics of theatricality, an imperious need for effect, a propensity for emphasis, excess, and the picturesque that are particularly characteristic of fashion; this courtly art remained dominated by the baroque spirit at least until the purist and modernist ruptures of the twentieth century. For from the mid-fourteenth century on, at the deepest level, fashion has remained under the sway of fascination with effect and artifice, with luxuriance and refinement in decorative detail. In art, baroque and classical forms alternate and sometimes merge; in fashion, the baroque spirit has never ceased to reign. The emergence of fashion attests to an evolution of taste infatuated with the mannered embellishment of forms; it is much more a sign of the progress of aesthetic enjoyment than a sign of the rise of wealth or even of the new system of social relations characteristic of court societies.

As an art of small differences and subtleties in personal appearance, fashion expresses a refinement of visual pleasure. The time has come to offer a slight correction to Lucien Febvre's now classic thesis concerning the "underdevelopment of sight" and the absence of visual poetry in the Renaissance.[36] Even if writers and poets of the period did make greater use of acoustic and olfactory images and did not evoke physical shapes, figures, or colors to any significant extent, that observation hardly suffices to justify a diagnosis according to which sight plays a subordinate role with respect to a dominant sensitivity to odors, perfumes, sounds, and voices. The development of fashion compels us to reconsider that judgment in part, if it is true that we cannot conceive of fashion without scrupulous attention to individual details, without a search for nuances, without a poeticization of the morphological differences between the sexes. How can we see Renaissance men only as creatures lacking a cultivated visual sense, not very sensitive to the grace of forms, attracted only by bright and contrasting colors, when we see fashion coming into its own in all its ornamental sophistication, when we see sixteenth-century braiding, lace, and

embroidery motifs being diversified, when we see dress following and em-
phasizing the lines of the body? Fashion and visual refinement are inseparable: fashion consecrates the progress of the aesthetic gaze in worldly
spheres.

We must take another look at courtly culture and its most original invention, love, and briefly recall what courtly love instituted that was new:
sublimation of the sex drive, a "detached" cult of love, along with the
overvaluation and lyric celebration of the beloved, submission and obedience on the part of the lover toward the lady; all these features characteristic of Provençal love gradually succeeded, in courtly circles, in transforming the relations between the sexes, and more specifically the relations of
seduction. From time immemorial warriors have won women's love by
accomplishing feats and exploits in their honor; love is earned by masculine virtues, daring, and heroic devotion. This chivalric notion of love had
been pursued for centuries; however, beginning around 1100 it became
subject to the civilizing influence of courtly love. Thus warlike heroism
gave way to a lyric and sentimental heroism; according to the new code of
love, the lord plays the *game* of living on his knees before the woman he
adores. He languishes; he showers her with attention; he shows that he is
a slave to her whims; and he is obliged to celebrate her beauty and her
virtues in verses of praise. This is the beginning of what René Nelli calls
"the poeticization of courtship";[37] vulgar language, traditional jokes, rib-
aldry, and obscenities are ruled out in favor of discretion and respectful
humility, noble language and gallant exaltation on the lover's part. From
this point on, seduction required attentiveness and delicacy toward
women; it required stylized play, a poetics of language and behavior.
Fashion, with its variations and its subtle play of nuance, must be viewed
as a continuation of this new poetics of seduction. Just as men had to
please women through good manners and lyricism, so they had to present
an increasingly sophisticated appearance; they had to offer a studied look
just as they offered studied speech. Preciosity of dress was an extension
and a counterpart of the stylization of love. Fashion and the artifice it
requires cannot be detached from the new image of femininity, from the
strategy of seduction by aesthetic signs. At the same time, within the
higher reaches of lay society the overvaluation of women and the way
feminine beauty was extolled helped expand and legitimize women's taste
for ornamentation and makeup, although the taste itself had been present
from earliest antiquity. Courtly love is doubly implicated in the genesis of
fashion. On the one hand, by decreeing that true love should be sought
outside marriage, that pure love was extraconjugal, courtly love discredited the institution of marriage; it legitimized a lady's free choice of lover
and thus supported autonomy of feeling. In this sense, courtly love contributed to the process of human individualization; it helped encourage

the development of the worldly individual with relatively independent tastes, detached from the traditional standard. We have already noted the intimate link that connects fashion with the modern consecration of individuality. On the other hand, more directly, courtly love produced a new relationship between the sexes; it inaugurated a new mechanism of gallant seduction that played a major role in the process of aestheticizing appearance that we know as fashion.

The modifications in the structure of men's and women's clothing that held sway from 1350 on are directly symptomatic of this aesthetic of seduction. From then on, dress marked a radical difference between the masculine sphere and the feminine; it sexualized appearance as never before. As we saw earlier, masculine clothing outlined the waist with the short doublet, and it emphasized the legs by encasing them in long breeches; simultaneously, the new feminine line molded the body and emphasized the hips, while low necklines revealed the shoulders and bust. Clothing thus made a point of exhibiting the charms of the body by accentuating the differences between the sexes. The padded doublet added contour to the male chest; trouser openings sometimes had a phallic shape. Beginning somewhat later and continuing for four centuries, the framework of the whalebone corset made it possible to compress the female waist and raise the bustline. Fashionable clothes became seductive costumes outlining the attractions of the body, revealing and concealing the allure of sex, stirring up erotic charms: no longer merely a hierarchic symbol, a sign of social status, dress had become an instrument of seduction with mysterious secret power, a means of pleasing and attracting attention that connoted luxury, fantasy, and stylized grace. Seduction broke loose from the timeless order of ritual and tradition; it started on its lengthy modern career by individualizing, at least partially, the signs associated with clothing, by idealizing and exacerbating the sensuality of appearance. As a dynamic of excess and amplification, an accumulation of artifice and ostentatious preciosity, fashionable dress attests that we have already moved into the modern age of seduction, the age of the aesthetics of personality and sensuality.

But a change in sexual strategies of seduction is not the only thing at stake. We cannot fail to connect the emergence of fashion with another form of seduction that is represented, beginning in the thirteenth century, by perceptible manifestations of the world in Western art. Life on earth had become an object of delectation; it was judged beautiful and worthy of attention, and it gave rise, among artists, to an increasingly pronounced attention to aesthetic considerations. Medieval art developed a new way of looking at the terrestrial world, at the material environment: expressions of unknowable mystery and the impersonal superhuman dimension lost ground to the discovery and description of real life on earth in all its diversity. Gothic sculptors replaced fantastic monsters with the living animals, woodlands, gardens, and leaves of their immediate surroundings. They represented handmade works, and brought God closer to human beings by propagating a more feminine and maternal image of the Virgin and a Christ marked by gentleness and humanity. This artistic realism of medieval origin took on a new dimension in the Renaissance, with the quest for depth and relief in the arts of portraiture, landscape, and still life. The sense of the concrete, the interest in visual experience and appearances in art, is extremely important: it reflects a glorification of the created world, a valorization of the beauties of human life on earth. The new investment in the secular realm turns up again in fashion and contributes to its development. Indeed, fashion represents the frivolous dimension of this new love of appearances, this new spectacle of human beings that was taking shape in the West. The cult of fantasy that is manifested in fashion and the "realism" that in one sense has never ceased to preside over the evolution of art are part of the same whole; in both cases, the same exaltation of the visible is at work, the same passion for perceptible detail, the same curiosity about individual features, the same immediate delight in surfaces, the same goal of aesthetic pleasure.

The revolution in clothing that is at the basis of modern dress was supported by the artistic rehabilitation of the world. The love of the real in all its singularity, first manifested in Gothic art, favored the advent of a dress style expressing the charms and the individuality of human bodies. It is appropriate to stress that the fourteenth-century male garb with its short jacket was inseparable from "realism," that it was not a result but rather a forerunner of the fifteenth-century revolution in representation, that it played a role in the discovery of the human body by allowing artists to have "an almost anatomical vision of the trunk and the limbs."[38] Such views are legitimate, provided one does not go too far in the portrayal of fashion as autonomous with respect to medieval art. It is not true that the new form of dress owed nothing to previous stylistic research; the short male costume is not the "earliest realism."[39] Even if it did in fact antedate the Renaissance style, it actually extends over a longer time span the observation of and curiosity about reality that were already manifest in Gothic art. At the end of the Middle Ages, fashion extended to personal apparel a process of promoting appearance whose forerunner we have seen in Gothic art.

Thus it is no accident that fashion and nude figures in painting belong to the same era: both phenomena manifest the same consecration of our earthly sojourn. No doubt nude figures stem from a return to the classics, from a renewed admiration for ancient models; but beyond the resurrection of antiquity we must not lose sight, as Emile Mâle reminded us, of the continuity in which Western art is inscribed, inasmuch as it allowed for the rehabilitation of visible things, the love of divine creatures, as early as the Gothic era. In the same way, if the emergence of fashion coincided with the advancement of secular values at the heart of the upper classes, that advancement was inseparable from a religious framework, in this case that of Christianity. The Christian faith, which had offered the most categorical opposition to worldly vanities, contributed, although indirectly, to the establishment of fashion's reign. Through the dogma of the God-man and the correlative revalorization and legitimation of the terrestrial sphere, of perceptible and visual data,[40] the religion of the Incarnation facilitated the appearance of fashion. Just as Christianity, at least as a symbolic framework, made possible the modern possession and exploitation of nature,[41] so the Christian religion provided the matrix of meaning that allowed fashion to develop as an autonomous aesthetic order that could become the exclusive province of human caprice. Christianity was able to accomplish this paradoxical task, one so obviously in contradiction to its imperative of salvation, chiefly through the mediation of art. Christian art reconciled itself to our earthly sojourn; its stylistic glorification of the reign of creatures had eventual repercussions in the sphere of adornment in dress. Fashion was not born of the social dynamic alone, nor even of the emergence of secular values; at the deepest level, it required a unique religious schema, that of the Incarnation, which led to an investment in the here and now, lending dignity to the terrestrial sphere, to individual forms and appearances. Within the framework of a religion based on the full humanity of the Savior, the created world can be lauded for its beauty; the originality and charms of appearance can gain legitimacy; costume can outline and amplify the beauties of the body. Fashion succeeded in taking root only in the West, precisely where the Christian religion developed. This is no accident: an intimate although paradoxical bond unites the *homo frivolus* and the *homo religiosus* in the specific case of Christianity.

CHAPTER II

A Century of Fashion

Fashion as we understand it today emerged during the latter half of the nineteenth century. Not everything about it was brand-new, of course; far from it. Still, it is clear that an unprecedented system of production and diffusion appeared during that period and was maintained with great consistency for a century. This historical phenomenon is what I want to emphasize here: technological progress and its own endless stylistic reversals or revolutions notwithstanding, fashion has not escaped what might be called a long-term structure. From the mid-nineteenth century to the point in the 1960s when the system began to crack and to transform itself to some extent, the organization was so stable that it is legitimate to speak of a fashion that lasted a hundred years. This was the first phase of the history of modern fashion, its sublime, heroic moment. A century of fashion: doubtless this is one way of saying that a cycle has ended, while stressing everything that continues to connect us most deeply to the phase that instituted a durable organization of the ephemeral. Of this hundred years' fashion, one might say without exaggeration what Tocqueville said of America:[1] more than a fashion, it is a metaphor for the advent of modern bureaucratic societies. More than a page in the history of luxury, class distinctions, and rivalries, it is one facet of the ongoing "democratic revolution."

Fashion and Its Double

Modern fashion is articulated around two new industries that might seem to have little in common. Their goals and methods, the articles they produce, and the prestige they earn are undeniably incommensurate; nevertheless, these two industries together form a single configuration, a homogeneous system in the history of the production of ephemera. *Haute couture*—initially known as *couture*—on the one hand, industrial clothing manufacture (*confection*) on the other: these were the two keystones of the century of fashion. The system was bipolar: at one extreme there were luxury items and made-to-order creations, while at the other there were inexpensive, mass-produced, ready-to-wear articles that imitated more or less closely the prestigious "labeled" models of haute couture. The creation of original models coupled with the industrial reproduction of copies: the emerging fashion system was characterized by a marked differentiation in techniques, prices, reputations, and objectives, as befitted a society itself divided into classes with quite distinct life-styles and goals.

The system as thus described is only a partial transcription of a more complex historical reality. There have always been intermediate organizations, low-level and middle-level couture, between the two poles. In France in particular, during the period in question, large numbers of women (60 percent in the 1950s) continued to use dressmakers or made their own clothes from patterns sold in stores or through fashion magazines. At the same time, especially in the highly industrialized countries (the United States, for example) where haute couture models could be reproduced legally and rapidly, manufacturing was not limited to low-priced production; manufacturers diversified their offerings and produced articles across a wide quality range, from modest to near luxury. Still, the overall schema can fairly be characterized as one in which haute couture had a monopoly on innovation and set the annual trends; clothing manufacturers and related industries followed along, producing goods inspired more or less directly and more or less immediately by haute couture but in any event offered at very different prices. If modern fashion was undergirded, then, by two principal axes, it nevertheless became for the first time clearly monocephalic.

To the extent that haute couture can be described as an unrivaled laboratory for novelty, the hundred years' fashion was essentially synonymous with feminine fashion. This does not mean that a parallel masculine fashion did not exist; however, the latter was not rooted in any institution comparable to that of haute couture, with its illustrious houses, its seasonal renewals, its parades of fashion models, its bold strokes, and its "revolutions." Compared to couture fashion, masculine fashion could be characterized as slow, moderate, steady, "egalitarian," even if it was also articulated according to the opposition between made-to-order and ready-to-wear. Haute couture is without question the most significant institution in modern fashion. No other fashion institution has had to keep on mobilizing a legal arsenal to protect itself against plagiarists and imitators; no other has given rise to passionate debates or enjoyed worldwide fame; no other has benefited from the steady, intense publicity of a specialized press. Extending a phenomenon that was already visible in the eighteenth century, modern fashion is feminine in essence.

The two-tiered order of fashion was not structured around an explicit objective; it did not even arise within an entirely synchronous time frame. Industrial manufacturing came before haute couture. Starting in the 1820s in France, following England's example, an industry for producing new, inexpensive, ready-to-wear clothing was established; it was flourishing by 1840, even before the age of mechanization inaugurated around 1860 with the advent of the sewing machine. As department stores gained a foothold, as technology progressed and production costs were lowered, manufacturers diversified the quality of the goods they offered the lower and middle bourgeoisie. After the First World War, manufacturing was profoundly transformed under the influence of an increased division of labor, improved machinery, breakthroughs in the chemical industry allowing richer colors, and—as of 1939—new textiles based on synthetic fibers. But despite this progress, the organization of fashion remained unchanged; until the 1960s, all fashion industries were subject to the dictates of haute couture.

In the winter of 1857–58, Charles-Frédéric Worth set up his own fashion house in Paris in the rue de la Paix. This was the first in the line of houses that would soon be known as haute couture. Worth advertised "ready-made dresses and coats, silk goods, top-notch novelties"; however, his real originality—to which contemporary fashion is still heir—lay in the fact that for the first time brand-new models, prepared in advance and changed frequently, were presented to clients in luxurious salons, then made to measure according to the client's choice. This revolution in the process of creating fashion was accompanied, moreover, by a major innovation in sales technique that was also initiated by Worth: the models were worn and presented by young women, prototypes of today's mannequins or fashion models, known then as *sosies*, "doubles." Fashion became an enterprise involving not only creativity but also advertising spectacles. In France, dozens of fashion houses sprang up following Worth's example and organized along similar lines. The 1900 World's Fair included twenty houses of haute couture, including Worth, Rouff (established in 1884), Paquin (1891), and Callot Soeurs (1896). Doucet, which later hired Poiret, opened its doors in 1880; Lanvin was founded in 1909, Chanel and Patou in 1919. The 1925 decorative arts show welcomed seventy-two fashion houses; in 1959, some fifty were registered with the Chambre syndicale de la Couture parisienne. These houses, many enjoying illustrious reputations, employed from one hundred to two thousand people, depending on their size and on the year, but their impact on the national economy was clearly out of all proportion to the number of their employees. The luxury industry represented by haute couture came to play a major role in the French economy, above all in clothing exports; owing to the prestige of the great Paris houses, this sector occupied second place in France's external trade in the mid-1920s.[2] During that period, an exceptionally prosperous one to be sure, prior to the Great Depression and its severe impact on high fashion, haute couture accounted single-handedly for one-third of

France's export sales in clothing.[3] Haute couture sales represented at that point roughly 15 percent of all French exports.[4] Nevertheless, by the mid-1950s the situation had already changed significantly: the House of Dior, which accounted all by itself for more than half the total sum of visible and invisible haute couture exports, represented no more than .5 percent of all France's visible exports.

Although it came into being in the mid-nineteenth century, not until the beginning of the twentieth century did haute couture adopt the rhythm of creation and presentation that is familiar today. At the outset there were no collections to be presented at fixed dates, for models were created throughout the year, varying only according to the season. Nor were there organized fashion shows: these began in 1908 and 1910 and became authentic spectacles, presented at a fixed hour of the afternoon in the great fashion house salons. After the First World War, as foreign professional buyers acquired more and more models, the seasonal shows began to be organized at more or less fixed dates. From then on, twice a year, in late January and early August, every great fashion house in Paris presented its summer and winter collections; later, in response to pressure by foreign buyers, fall and spring (half-season) collections were presented in April and November. Collections were first shown to foreign agents, especially American and European buyers; private clients were admitted two or three weeks later. The foreign professionals bought models of their own choosing, generally with the right to reproduce them in major lines in their own country. Supplied with models and reference slips that provided the information needed to reproduce the garment, manufacturers—except for those in France, who, for obvious reasons of exclusivity, did not have immediate access to the season's novelties—could reproduce simplified versions of the Parisian creations very rapidly; in just a few weeks, their foreign clients could thus be dressed in the latest haute couture craze at reasonable cost, sometimes even at very little cost, depending on the manufacturing techniques used. As a result, and contrary to widespread belief, the effect of haute couture was not so much to accelerate fashion change as to regularize it. In fact, the tendency to rapid change in fashion did not arrive simultaneously with haute couture but preceded it by more than a century: by the end of the Old Regime in France, fashion had already acquired its frenetic rhythm. But prior to the haute couture period, the rapidity of change in fashion had remained a random phenomenon, driven somewhat chaotically by one variable arbiter of elegance or another. With the age of haute couture, however, renewal in fashion was for the first time institutionalized and orchestrated. Fashion became for the most part a biennial affair: the half-season collections did little more than offer hints of the fashion to come. In place of a fortuitous logic of innovation, we find a normalization of change in fashion, an obligatory renewal brought about at fixed dates by specialized groups. Haute couture brought discipline to fashion at a time when fashion was giving rise to an unprecedented process of innovation and creative fancy.

Fashion's decrees originated in Paris. With the hegemony of haute couture, a hypercentralized fashion appeared, entirely indigenous to Paris and yet at the same time international: Parisian fashion was followed by all the "up-to-date" women in the world. In this respect, moreover, fashion bears some resemblance to modern art, for its pioneers were concentrated in Paris and they developed a style from which national characteristics were expunged. The phenomenon is certainly not an entirely new one: from the seventeenth century on, France was increasingly recognized as the beacon of fashion in Europe. Dealings in "fashion dolls," those earliest ambassadors of fashion, became commonplace in the eighteenth century, betraying both the tendency toward uniformity of dress in Europe and the tendency for Paris to serve as the pole of attraction. Nevertheless, throughout this entire period the way people dressed continued to present certain recognizable traits characteristic of their respective countries: like painting, fashion retained a certain national character. Aided by manufacturing, haute couture on the contrary allowed fashion to break loose from the national grip by leaving intact only the model and its many copies, which were identical in all countries. Thus even though it remained subject to the luxurious authority of haute couture, modern fashion stands out as the earliest manifestation of mass consumption: homogeneous, standardized, indifferent to frontiers. Under the Parisian aegis of haute couture, fashion approached worldwide uniformity, a homogenization in space with a parallel diversification in time linked to the regular cycles of the seasonal collections.

As fashion was centralized and internationalized, it was also *democratized*. The rise of industrial dressmaking on the one hand and of mass communications on the other, the dynamics of modern life-styles and values, led not only to the disappearance of diverse regional folk costumes but also to the attenuation of heterogeneous class differences in dress: dressing in the fashion of the day become possible for an increasingly broad social spectrum. The most remarkable thing about this whole process is the contribution made by haute couture—a luxury industry par excellence—to the democratization of fashion. From the 1920s on, with the simplification of women's clothing that was symbolized, in a way, by Chanel, fashion indeed became less inaccessible because it was easier to imitate: the gap between dress styles inevitably narrowed. As soon as the display of wealth became a sign of poor taste, as soon as true elegance required discretion and the absence of show, women's fashion entered the era of democratic appearances. In 1931, the journalist Janet Flanner noted that Chanel inaugurated the "poor" style, introduced the apache sweater to the Ritz, lent elegance to the housemaid's shirt collar and sleeves, exploited the workman's scarf, and dressed queens in mechanics' overalls. Clear separations continued to set apart the dress styles of the various social strata, but what matters is that it was no longer obligatory for the upper classes to dress with ostentatious luxury. Such dress was legitimate only if it was discreet or even imperceptible; a certain "impersonal" and apparently standardizable simplicity took over the scene of feminine elegance. "Here is Chanel's Ford": the American edition of *Vogue* came to that conclusion in 1926 about a simple long-sleeved black dress. At the opposite extreme from aristocratic emphasis, the modern democratic style was incarnated in simplified, supple lines, in ostensibly unostentatious "uniforms." While the first revolution instituting the look of the modern woman can be traced to Poiret's suppression of the corset in 1909–10, the second and unquestionably more radical one arrived in the 1920s under the impetus of Chanel and Patou. Paul Poiret abandoned the corset and gave feminine allure a new suppleness, but he remained faithful to the taste for elaborate ornamentation, to a traditional sumptuousness in dress. Chanel and Patou on the contrary repudiated the strident look of luxury; they stripped away frills and affectations from women's clothing. Women would henceforth wear simple sheaths, cloche hats, pants, and sweaters. Chanel managed to dress society women in tailored jersey suits and grey, black, or beige pullovers. Patou created sweaters with geometric motifs and straight pleated skirts. From that point on it was chic not to appear rich. What Brummell's aesthetic claimed for men in the nineteenth century had won over the feminine universe in an entirely different way: flamboyant display was eclipsed in favor of the democratic aesthetic of purity, restraint, and comfort.

The heterogeneity of dress styles characteristic of the aristocratic order, in which ostentatious display was a social imperative intended to mark human and social differences in no uncertain terms, was replaced at the beginning of the twentieth century by a fashion that was "homogeneous" in tendency, based precisely on a rejection of the principle of lofty, majestic exhibition of hierarchy. "Before," according to Poiret, "women were architectural elements, like ships' prows, and they were beautiful. Now they resemble underfed little telegraph operators."[5] Social difference, no longer oversignified by dress, was now obscured by the decline in marks of visible sumptuousness. This dissolution of symbols of social distance clearly cannot be detached from the imagined democratic ideal of equality of conditions: in the long run, creatures recognized as being of the same essence cannot help offering self-images from which extreme disparities, blatant marks of a hierarchical gulf, are absent. At the deepest level of this revolution in women's clothing, following on the heels of an earlier revolu-

tion in men's dress, we find the advent of a society governed by the ideal
of democratic equality.

The process was not lacking in a certain ambiguity, however. Indeed,
luxury did not disappear, but it had to be treated euphemistically, as an
irreplaceable value of taste and class refinement at the heart of haute couture. The democratization of fashion did not mean that appearances had
to be uniform or equalized; new signs, more subtle and more nuanced,
particularly in the realm of labels, shapes, and fabrics, ensured that dress
would continue to mark social distinctions and social excellence. Democratization signified a lessening of the marks of social distance, a muting of
the aristocratic principle of conspicuous consumption, along with the new
criteria of slenderness, youth, sex appeal, convenience, and discretion.
The fashion system that lasted for a century did not eliminate signs of
social rank, but it attenuated them by promoting values that stressed more
personal attributes.

Nor did the restrained democratic style carry the day with perfect uniformity. Alongside simple, lightweight daytime outfits, haute couture went
on creating sumptuous, elaborate, hyperfeminine evening attire. The hundred years' fashion deepened the gulf between the types of women's clothing. On the one hand, there were daytime fashions for city and sports,
governed by discretion, comfort, and functionality. On the other hand,
there were enchanting evening fashions designed to bring out the seductiveness of femininity. The democratization of fashion was accompanied
by a *disunification* of feminine appearance: women's dress became much
more varied in form, much less homogeneous. It could play on a greater
number of registers, from the voluptuous woman to the relaxed woman,
from the "schoolgirlish" woman to the professional woman, from the
sportswoman to the sexy woman. The rejection of showy signs brought the
feminine into the cyclic play of complete metamorphosis, the coexistence
of disparate and sometimes antagonistic images.

More directly than the idea of equality, cultural and aesthetic factors—
sports, in particular—played a primordial role in the democratic revolution of feminine appearance. Even though they were not widely practiced,
activities such as golf, tennis, cycling, swimming, mountain climbing, hik-
ing, hunting, winter sports, and automobile driving helped modify the
shape of women's clothing, slowly at first, then much more quickly after
the First World War.[6] The cardigan sweater came in with golf; around
1890, the bicycle allowed for bouffant pants drawn in below the knee and,
in 1934, summer shorts; at the turn of the century, swimming gave impetus
to the innovation of sleeveless bathing suits with a rounded décolleté, followed in the 1920s by one-piece suits with bare legs and arms. In the 1930s,
two-piece bathing suits left backs completely exposed. Skirt lengths grew

shorter for hockey, skating, and tennis starting in the 1920s; in 1921, Suzanne Lenglen caused a sensation by playing tennis for the first time in a sleeveless white cardigan and a pleated skirt that came just below the knee. From the end of the nineteenth century on, sports clothes proliferated: in 1904, Burberry devoted a 254-page catalog almost entirely to ready-made sportswear. In the early 1920s, haute couture plunged into the sportswear sector: in 1922, Patou offered a first showing of sportswear and outdoor outfits; he opened his shop, "Le Coin des Sports," in 1925. Sportswear made its first "classy" appearance in that era: it was considered chic even for walking about town and eating in restaurants. Going out in shorts, exposing one's legs, arms, back, or midriff, gradually became acceptable: the bikini appeared in the late 1940s. The new supple, functional, sexy styles cannot be detached either from the growing popularity of sports or from the democratic-individualist universe affirming the primordial autonomy of individuals; these two things together set off a process that bared the female body and reduced the rigid constraints of clothing that had hampered the free expression of individuality. Sports lent dignity to the natural body; they allowed it to be displayed more directly, relieved of the excessive armature and trappings of dress.

Sports not only prompted an evolution in specialized dress, they made a crucial contribution to the changing lines of women's clothing in general by creating a new aesthetic ideal of femininity. Through the cult of sports, the prototype of the slim, svelte, modern woman who plays tennis and golf took over from the sedentary woman hobbled by her flounces and lace. The simplification of clothing in the 1920s, the elimination of gathers and frills in favor of restrained, clean lines, was a response to this new idea of lightness and energy drawn from sports. Between 1924 and 1929, Patou created all his designs on the same principles as his outdoor clothing and sportswear: "My clothes are made to practise *le sport.* . . . I have aimed at making them pleasant to the eye and allowing absolute liberty of movement."[7] Forty years later, Courrèges's futurist lines of the 1960s, the "Courrèges effect," did nothing more than radicalize this process in the name of the identical values of physical comfort and well-being: "I have sought a dynamic fashion, with constant concern for freedom of movement. . . . Today's woman is liberated. She must also be liberated physically. She cannot be dressed as a static, sedentary figure" (Courrèges).

In addition, it is impossible to ignore the considerable influence of trends in modern art on the democratic transformation of fashion following the First World War. The straight, flat-chested figure of the 1920s woman harmonizes perfectly with the cubist pictorial space comprising planes and angles, vertical and horizontal lines, geometrical contours and flattenings; it echoes Léger's tubular universe, the stylistic austerity introduced by Picasso, Braque, and Matisse in the wake of Manet and Cézanne.

Feminine voluminousness and roundness yielded to a purified, simplified appearance analogous to the work of the artistic avant-gardes. Fashion learned a lesson from the modernist project that began with Manet, a project characterized, according to Georges Bataille, by the "negation of eloquence," by the rejection of "grandiloquent verbiage," and by the majesty of images. By abandoning the poetics of ornamentation and glittering display, couture fashion worked to desublimate and deidealize the female figure, in part; it democratized clothing styles in the climate of the new modernist aesthetic values that tended toward the purification of forms and the rejection of the decorative.

The democratization of appearance was matched by the extension and eventual generalization of a *desire for fashion*, a desire previously confined to the privileged strata of society. The hundred years' fashion not only brought divergent ways of dressing closer together, it also turned frivolous ephemera into objects of desire for the masses as it gave tangible form to the democratic right to fashion. Although increasingly broad strata of society had been gaining access to fashion over the centuries, it was only after the two world wars that the "right" to fashion gained a real foothold and won mass-market legitimacy. Earlier, when members of the lower classes imitated aristocratic dress they had been subject to sarcasm; that time had long since passed. What was deemed ridiculous in the democratic age was not so much imitation in fashion (apart from manifestations of snobbery) as being out-of-date; that was the new mass "taboo." The hundred years' fashion simultaneously freed personal appearance from traditional norms and imposed on all and sundry the ethos of change, the cult of modernity. Fashion was more than a right; it had become a social imperative. Through the magic of haute couture, fashion magazines, and fashion-plate celebrities, the masses were trained in the code of fashion, in the rapid variations of the seasonal collections, while at the same time the code of originality and personality was becoming sacred. One defining characteristic of the hundred years' fashion lies in the way an increasing demand for originality was accompanied by a synchronized, uniform, compulsory obedience to the codes of haute couture. Just as novelties were regularly prescribed for every season, immediately making everything that was done earlier out-of-date, fashion was followed step-by-step, as closely as possible; gaps, challenges, and antifashions began to be significant only in the 1960s. On the one hand, homogeneous trends were imposed and an "official" fashion was proclaimed every season; on the other hand, the public at large conformed and submitted to uniform standards of dress. Despite its organizational specificity, the moment just described was related to the rigid and standardized age of the fashion trades.[8] The fashion system that had been constituted in the name of the principle of individuality managed to spread only by imposing uniform, standardized norms, swallowing up the free play of personal difference. Along with disciplinary organizations and democratic institutions, the hundred years' fashion helped detach our societies from the holistic, traditional order; it contributed to the establishment of universal centralized standards, and to the institution of the first phase of modern, authoritarian, individualist societies.

Fashion as One of the Fine Arts

Haute couture is responsible for the organization of fashion as we know it today, at least in its broad outlines: seasonal renewal, presentations of collections on live models, and, most important of all, a new vocation coupled with a new social status for the dressmaker. Here is the heart of the matter. Ever since Worth's day, the couturier has been recognized as a creator with a mission: to develop brand-new models, to launch new lines of clothing on a regular basis, lines that ideally reveal a special, distinctive, incomparable talent. Worth's move marked the end of fashion's traditional era and the beginning of its modern artistic phase, for Worth was the first to introduce constant change in forms, fabrics, and accessories. It was he who disrupted the uniformity of style to a degree that shocked public taste; it was he who dethroned crinolines and could thus be credited with starting a fashion "revolution." After centuries of relegation to subordinate status, the couturier had become a modern artist, one whose commanding law was innovation. In this context, fashion was increasingly identified with the creative abundance of haute couture. Before 1930, the great houses presented collections that included 150 to 300 new designs each season; in the 1950s, when the average number still varied between 150 and 200, some 10,000 prototypes were created in Paris each year.

The break with the past was clean and decisive. No longer a traditional artisan, a creature of routine, the couturier had become a designer, a modern artistic "genius." Up to that point, the tailor or dressmaker had little room for initiative: the patterns in use were obligatory. The general architecture of clothing and its basic elements were more or less immutable during a given period; only certain limited aspects of dress authorized a fanciful cut and style. The dressmaker had no creative role to play; not until the second half of the eighteenth century did "style merchants" appear. By then the fashion trades had won a certain creative autonomy, although that autonomy was confined under the circumstances to the ornaments and trimmings of dress. The artistic talent attributed to fashion merchants at that point thus consisted in a talent for decoration, the capacity to enhance and ennoble dress by means of fashionable accessories and conceits (hats, bonnets, gewgaws, braiding, ribbons, feathers, gloves,

fans, scarves, and so on), not in the invention of original lines. Conservatism and uniformity in the construction of the whole, more or less pronounced fancy and originality in the details: this sums up the logic that
had governed fashion ever since it came into being in the West, starting in
the middle of the fourteenth century. And this is the mechanism that haute
couture managed to overturn, by attributing to the designer a supreme
vocation, the incessant creation of original prototypes. The shape of the
garment itself took center stage; the garment's originality was no longer
limited to furbelows and accessories, but now involved the pattern itself.
As Chanel put it later on: "Start with the dress, not the trimmings."[9]

In theory, the designer was now a "free" creator, operating without any
constraints. In reality, at the head of an industrial and commercial enterprise, the great couturiers found their creative autonomy restricted by the
mores of the times, by the styles in vogue, and by the particular nature of
the product to be created, namely, clothing, which had to appeal to the
customer's aesthetic values and not just satisfy the designer's pure creative
inspiration. That is why the parallelism between the emergence of the couturier-creator and that of modern artists in the narrow sense can be carried only so far. The new indeed had become the rule, but painters, writers, and musicians had a freedom to experiment, a power to push back the
frontiers of art, that had no parallel in fashion. Even if it was new, an
article of clothing still had to appeal to the person who wore it, and it had
to be becoming to that person; even if it was new, it must not appear
prematurely or be overly contemptuous of conventions and tastes. The
advent of haute couture did not change everything, then: as before, what
was new in fashion remained a set of necessarily slow variations in the
style of an epoch, a "comfortable adventure" (Sapir) and a "riskless" one
compared to the harsh ruptures, the dissonances and provocations of
modern art. Haute couture was indeed accompanied by organizational
discontinuity, but against a background of continuity proper to fashion
and its imperative of immediate seduction.

Despite this conservatism that was consubstantial with fashion, haute
couture systematized the logic of innovation to such an extent that we may
legitimately see it as a special case, a less radical but nevertheless significant instance, of an unprecedented mechanism that was making its appearance in Europe: the avant-garde. It is more than a coincidence that
certain great turn-of-the-century couturiers admired and befriended certain modern artists: Poiret's friends included Picabia, Vlaminck, Derain,
and Dufy; Chanel had connections with Pierre Reverdy, Max Jacob, and
Juan Gris; she made the costumes for Cocteau's *Antigone*, while Picasso
did the sets and Honegger the music; Schiaparelli's collections were inspired by surrealism. Although it came about slowly, a proliferation of
bold innovations in clothing challenged the aristocratic tradition (Poiret

made fun of Chanel's famous "luxurious poverty"), the aesthetic tastes
and the archetypal image of woman (the boyish look, eccentric evening
dresses, shocking pink), and the prevailing mores and standards of de-
cency: let us recall the knee-length dresses of the 1920s, the deep décolleté
in back and the general skimpiness of summer outfits and beach wear in
the 1930s, the miniskirt of the 1960s. In the 1920s, some American states
passed laws designed to stem the tide of immodesty linked with shorter
dresses;[10] earlier, in the 1900s, the archbishop of Paris had allied himself
with a protest holding couturiers responsible for indecent and provocative
fashions. By the 1920s, Chanel and Patou had already replaced the time-
honored logic of complex ornamentation with that of style and austere
lines; the revolution in women's dress that ensued in some sense "wiped
the slate clean" with respect to the past, abandoning the ceremonial imperatives and luxurious trimmings characteristic of earlier fashion. A relative desublimation of fashion (the shirtdress) and the use of inexpensive
materials (jersey, then burlap and sacking, or in Schiaparelli's case synthetic materials) paralleled trends in modernist art: the simplification or
purification of fashion had its counterpart in certain efforts undertaken by
cubists, abstract artists, and constructivists. Like art itself, haute couture
plunged into a process of ruptures, escalations, and profound changes that
related it—with all its nonlinearity, its zigzags, its apparent about-faces
(Dior's New Look)—to the avant-garde. Even if the headlong forward
movement was not reflected in extremist and destructive signs of disloca-
tion, fashion was conquered, on its own scale, in a spirit of play, by a
modern revolutionary logic; it had its discontinuities, its infatuation with
newness, but also its excommunications, its rivalries, the factional struggles that are endemic to the world of creators.

The new vocation of the couturier was coupled with an extraordinary
rise in social status. Under the Old Regime, tailors and dressmakers were
anonymous individuals relegated to the inferior sphere of the "mechanical
arts"; their names, in the opuscules and texts that evoked fashion directly
or indirectly, were almost never recorded. The novelties in current vogue
bore the name of the important personage, the noble man or woman who
had launched a given fashion. This changed in the nineteenth century:
from Worth's day on, couturiers enjoyed unprecedented prestige. They
were recognized as poets; their names were celebrated in fashion magazines; they appeared in novels in the guise of the aesthete, the unchallenged arbiter of elegance. Like a painter's, their works were signed, and
they were protected by law. Through their ostentatious disdain for money
and commerce, through their discourse on the necessity of "inspiration,"
the great couturiers became recognized as "artists of luxury" (Poiret) who
collected artworks and lived in sumptuous, refined decors surrounded by
poets and painters; they themselves created costumes for the theater, bal-

let, and cinema, and they subsidized artistic creation. Artistic allusions were all the rage in characterizations of designers: Dior was the Watteau of couturiers, Balenciaga the Picasso of fashion.[11] Fashion creations themselves quoted works of art: there were the Mondrian or pop-art dresses, and Yves Saint-Laurent's Picasso skirts. High society, followed by the trade press, allowed the great couturiers not only to shore up their self-image as artists but also to acquire enormous international reputations: in 1949, the Gallup Institute named Christian Dior as one of the five best-known personalities in the world.

However spectacular it may have been, this sort of rise in social status was not entirely unprecedented. Beginning in the mid-eighteenth century, in the fashion trades, hairdressers, shoemakers, and "fashion merchants" considered themselves—and were increasingly viewed by others as—sublime artists. The first treatises on the art of the coiffure, most notably those by Le Gros and Tissot, appeared around the same period. In his *Traité des principes et de l'art de la coiffure*, Diderot's coiffeur Lefèvre wrote: "Of all the arts, that of hairdressing ought to be one of the most highly valued; painting and sculpture, which allow men to live on for centuries after their death, cannot challenge its right to the status of fellow art; they cannot deny that they need it to complete their own works." The era of the great hairdressing artists was beginning: they worked in dress clothes, swords at their sides; they chose their own clientele and called themselves "creators." Le Gros put his art above painting, and he opened the first professional school for his trade, calling it the "Académie de Coiffure." Not long afterward, the name of Léonard was on everyone's lips: possibly the most famous coiffeur of them all, he was the object of Mme de Genlis's remark in 1769: "Finally Léonard came; he has arrived, and he is king."[12] The same period witnessed the ascension of "sublime bootmakers," "artists" of footwear,[13] and the success of certain milliners was even more striking, as L. S. Mercier points out in *Tableau de Paris*: "The dressmakers who cut and sew the individual parts of the female garment are the masons of the building. The milliner, on the other hand, who produces the trappings, giving grace and the correct swing to the drapery, is the actual architect and decorator."[14] Milliners, who had recently supplanted haberdashers, made fortunes and enjoyed immense renown: Beaulard was hailed in song as a poet; Rose Bertin, Marie Antoinette's "Minister of Fashion," was celebrated in verse by the poet Jacques Delille, and her name turns up in letters, memoirs, and gazettes of the period. At this point, refinement, preciosity, and impudence were the order of the day among fashion artists, whose bills were exorbitant. Rose Bertin responded cynically to a client who was haggling over prices: "Is [Horace] Vernet paid simply for his canvas and paints?"[15] Taking any event—the success of a play, a death, a political incident, a battle—as a pretext, the fashion merchants exercised their art on countless frills and furbelows: their artistic creations are what made prices go up. "In the selling price of a dress, as it appears in the fashion merchants' account books, the fabric (99 ells, or 107 meters of black velvet) is priced at 380 pounds, the cost of sewing is 18 pounds, and the trimmings come to 800 pounds."[16] During the Empire period, Leroy, as fatuous as he was famous, elevated tailors themselves to the rank of artists. As a fashion journal of the period remarked: "Messires the tailors disdain sewing today, and only concern themselves with what they call the design of the suit." At the same time, Mme Raimbaud, a famous dressmaker, was nicknamed "the Michelangelo of fashion" by the gazettes. Under the July Monarchy, Maurice Beauvais was consecrated "the Lamartine of fashion," while new dressmakers, both women (Vignon, Palmyre, Victorine) and men (Staub, Blain, Chevreuil), came into prominence. By the time Worth took over as an "autocrat of taste," the principals of the fashion business had long since become artists. Worth's fame, followed by that of the great fashion houses, his condescension toward his clients, his wealth and his refinement, his artist's manners and his astounding bills, did not designate a historical turning point; they prolonged an ethos and a process of social ascension that had already been under way for more than a century.

The consecration of the fashion trades cannot be separated from the new social representation of fashion that was emerging at roughly the same time. Fashions had come and gone for centuries without being objects of description for their own sake; there were no specialized journals, no professional chroniclers. When texts and opuscules referred to a fashion, it was assumed that readers were already familiar with it; any specific indications provided by moralists, religious writers, or preachers were merely pretexts for mocking or denouncing contemporary mores and human weaknesses: the pretensions of bourgeois social climbers, the passion for "appearances" of courtesans, the extravagance, inconstancy, jealousy, and covetousness of women. Whenever fashion was evoked, the satirical genre predominated. In their memoirs, great lords did not deign to mention fashionable trivia, nor did the highbrow literature where such lords were represented. Works that acquaint us in detail with the forms and features of clothing are rare; generally speaking, that sort of information was less important than the stylistic niceties of versification, or the jesting to which the trivia of fashion gave rise. With the appearance of the first illustrated fashion magazines at the end of the Old Regime, the treatment of fashion changed. From that point on, it was regularly described for its own sake and put on display: *Le Magasin des modes françaises et anglaises*, which appeared from 1786 to 1789, is subtitled "Ouvrage qui donne une connaissance exacte et prompte des habillements et parures nouvelles" (Work that gives timely and accurate information about the new clothing styles and accessories). Discourse on fashion proliferated not only in the specialized magazines, of which there were increasing numbers in the nineteenth and twentieth centuries, but also among literary figures, especially in the nineteenth century, when they turned fashion into a subject worthy of attention and respect. Balzac wrote *Traité de la vie élégante* (1830), and Barbey d'Aurevilly published *Du dandysme et de George Brummell* (1845) along with various articles on fashion. Baudelaire wrote "In Praise of Cosmetics": he saw fashion as a constitutive element of beauty, a "symptom of the taste for the ideal," and he set out to "vindicate the art of the dressing-table from the fatuous slanders with which certain very dubious lovers of Nature have attacked it."[17] Mallarmé himself wrote *La Dernière Mode*; at century's end, Goncourt, Maupassant, and Paul Bourget produced detailed and accurate portrayals of elegant living, depicting the surroundings of the "high life" and its delicate, refined, luxurious settings. Somewhat later, Proust described worldly rivalries and explored the psychological wellsprings of fashion and snobbery in the salons of the faubourg Saint-Germain. By the latter half of the eighteenth century, fashion was acknowledged as an entity to be glorified, described, exhibited, and dealt with philosophically; like sex, if not more so, it became a prolific machine for the production of texts and images. The new age of fashion was characterized by an overinvestment in issues of appearance and an unprecedented interest in novelty—those democratic passions that allowed people in the fashion trades, and especially the great couturiers, to rise to glory.

Just as fashion was asserting itself as a sublime object, the epoch witnessed an outpouring of invented words designating fashionable individuals and the "latest thing" in the realm of elegance. In France, starting in the nineteenth century, the terms *beaux*, *fashionables*, *dandys*, *lions* and *lionnes*, *cocodès*, *gommeux* and *gommeuses* came into use; by century's end, *smart* had replaced *urf*, *chic*, *copurchic*, *v'lan*, *rupin*, *sélect*, *ha*, and *pschutt*. The early decades of the twentieth century saw the appearance of *dernier bateau*, *dans le train*, and *up-to-date*. The multiplication of discourses on fashion was accompanied by an accelerated proliferation of "in the know" (*dans le vent*) vocabulary paralleling the modern cult of the ephemeral.

The elevation of fashion to social and aesthetic dignity went hand in hand with the promotion of numerous minor topics that came to be treated with the greatest seriousness, as we can judge from the tastes of dandies as well as from such works as Berchoux's *La Gastronomie* (1800), Grimod de la Reynière's *Almanach des gourmands* (1803), Brillat-Savarin's *La Physiologie du goût* (1825), Émile Marc Hilaire's *Art de mettre sa cravate* (1827) and his *Art de fumer et de priser sans déplaire aux belles* (1827), Eugène Ronteix's *Manuel du fashionable* (1828), and Balzac's *Théorie de la démarche.* In a movement of which dandyism offers an idiosyncratic but exemplary illustration, useless entities (decorations, gathering places, outfits, horses, cigars, meals) became primordial concerns, on equal footing with the traditionally noble preoccupations.

The social ascension of people in the fashion trades is hardly an unprecedented phenomenon; in a sense, it can be linked with a much older set of claims, one inaugurated in the fifteenth and sixteenth centuries by painters, sculptors, and architects who persisted in seeking for their professions the status of liberal arts, a status radically distinct from that of the mechanical or artisanal trades. But if the struggle of corporations to accede to the condition of artists and to enjoy social recognition was by no means new, the fact remains that the process was enhanced in the eighteenth and nineteenth centuries by the values characteristic of the modern age. What is remarkable, in fact, is the way in which the demand for a new status was manifested: all the evidence suggests that fashion artists exhibited an implausible degree of impudence and arrogance toward their clientele, even when dealing with the highest society. It is not easy to assess the insolence of a Charpentier, a Dagé,[18] or a Rose Bertin, of whom Mme d'Oberkirch could say that she seemed to be "a strange person, very full of her own importance, and who treated princesses as her equals."[19] The sublime milliners not only advanced the view that their art was as noble as that of poets and painters, they behaved as if they themselves were equal to nobles. From this standpoint, the claims of the fashion trades cannot be separated from the modern egalitarian ideal. The phenomenon is unprecedented, and it reveals the impetus of social ambition that was a corollary of the dawning age of democracy. Tocqueville had already made a similar observation: "When this same equality was first established in France, it gave birth at once to almost unlimited ambitions. . . . Every revolution increases men's ambitions, and that is particularly true of a revolution which overthrows an aristocracy."[20] Moreover, such haughtiness and impudence were by no means confined to the fashion trades; they appeared just as often in the behavior of young people who prided themselves on being fashionable, refined, and elegant (*petits-maîtres, muscadins, incroyables, fashionables, dandys*), as well as in literature, where a new attitude toward the reader was beginning to appear. Authors such as Stendhal, Mérimée, Alfred de Musset, and Théophile Gautier manifested their contempt for the tastes of the general public and their fear of being thought common by using a style that consists in impudent badinage, scornful allusions, and cavalier remarks addressed to the reader.[21] Artistic pretensions and the insolence of people in the fashion trades cannot be separated from the tendency of ambition, conceit, and vanity to appear outside the upper classes, a tendency that characterizes the passage of societies into the era of equality.

It is quite obvious that the consecration of fashion creators can be explained only in part through corporatist ambition, even if such ambition is exacerbated by claims to equality. If fashion people won recognition as artists of genius, it is because a new sensitivity to ephemera and new aspirations had come into play, offering new ways of valorizing phenomena that had previously been unworthy of notice. Since the Renaissance, fashion had unquestionably enjoyed a certain degree of respect as a symbol of social excellence and of court life. Not to such an extent, however, that it deserved to be exalted and depicted in its down-to-earth details. In aristocratic eras, fashion is too material an expression of hierarchy to warrant attention. The elevated style in literature featured heroic exploits, the glorious, magnanimous attitudes of exceptional beings, the ideal, pure love of great souls, rather than the obvious little things, the concrete realities—however luxurious—that common folk can attain and possess. The only legitimate models were found in figures of devotion, glory, and sublime love, not in images of fashion. Frivolities could be promoted only because new standards were imposed, standards that disqualified not only the essentially feudal heroic cult, but also the traditional Christian morality that considered frivolities as signs of the sin of pride, offenses against God and one's neighbor. Linked to the progressive disaffection from heroic values and religious morality, fashion's ascent was inseparable from the new credit it enjoyed at court and in town, especially from the eighteenth century on, by pleasure and happiness, novelty and material comfort, freedom conceived as the satisfaction of desires and the relaxation of strict conventions and moral prohibitions. From that point on, personal enjoyment tended to take precedence over glory, agreeableness and refinement over grandeur, seduction over sublime exaltation, voluptuousness over ostentatious majesty, the decorative over the emblematic. The modern cult of fashion grew out of this lowering of the idea of grandeur and its corollary, the raising of human and worldly concerns to a higher dignity. The defense of happiness, the quest for what was agreeable, and the aspiration to a freer, happier, easier life brought about a gradual humanization of the sublime, a less majestic, less lofty conception of the beautiful along with an ennobling of useful things, "little pleasures," decorative fancies, secular beauties and refinements: trimmings, trinkets, "little apartments," interior decoration, miniatures, small theater boxes, and so on. The hegemony of the majestic was replaced by an aesthetic of graceful forms, praise for seductive lightness, for variety as the source of pleasure and excitement. At the heart of fashion's modern status, we find the new individualist morality that lent dignity to freedom, pleasure, and happiness: *Le Magasin des modes*, whose epigraph indicates that "uniformity gave birth one day to lassitude," was quite in tune with the hedonistic spirit of the century (however compatible it may also have been with reason, moderation, and

virtue); it was infatuated with unexpected sensations, surprises, and renewals. At the heart of fashion's ascent, there is the repudiation of sin, the
rehabilitation of self-love, of human passions and desire in general. The
same magazine defined its goals as follows: "Give all individuals the opportunity to satisfy the passion with which they are born for the objects
that will allow them to appear to the best advantage and get the most
attention." The individualist ideology and the sublime age of fashion were
thus inseparable. They both entailed a cult of self-development and well-
being, material enjoyment, the desire for freedom, the will to diminish
authority and moral constraints: "holistic" and religious standards, incompatible with the dignity of fashion, were undermined not only by the
ideology of freedom and equality but also by the ideology of pleasure,
which is just as characteristic of the individualist era.

As we have already seen, the triumph of pleasure and ephemera was
facilitated by a number of factors: the increase in wealth, the development
of "court society" and salons, the strengthening of the absolutist monarchy, and the new position in which the nobility found itself. Dispossessed
of any real power, the nobility was reduced to finding its symbols of excellence in artifices and superfluities at a time when the wealthy bourgeoisie
was seeking to imitate noble manners as never before. The Revolution and
the abolition of privilege further accentuated the process by fostering the
desire to raise one's station in life, to excel, to cross barriers, to stand out
above the common people, the vulgar herd. At the same time, the Revolution maintained the aristocracy as the beacon of worldly existence, and
fostered a heightened aestheticization of appearances. Nevertheless, it
would be far too simplistic to equate the phenomenon of fashion with an
elitist device for class recognition and differentiation in a society in which
inequality of birth was no longer legitimized, in which stable criteria of
social dignity were dissolving, and in which prestige was no longer so
much awarded as conquered. Viewed in a long-term perspective, fashion
in its new status has to be interpreted rather as a phase and an instrument
of the democratic revolution. Indeed, the artistic consecration of fashion
means nothing if not a lowering of the sense of the sublime, a humanization of ideals, a new primacy of "small pleasures" accessible to all and a
corresponding obsession with small differences and subtle nuances. The
democratic ideal of seduction, rapid success, and immediate pleasure won
out over the heroic exaltation of greatness and the excesses of aristocratic
morality. Moreover, by attributing greater dignity to inferior phenomena
and functions, by blurring the boundary between noble art and modest
art, the empire of fashion helped promote equality. The dissolution of the
hierarchy of genres and trades, which instituted theoretical equality
among formerly heterogeneous realms, allows the celebration of fashion to
appear as a manifestation of democracy, even though fashion arose in the
name of distinctive differences within a world of privilege.

Significantly, as fashion and the people engaged in it were winning their own letters of nobility, people engaged in intellectual pursuits—philosophers, writers, poets—were also acquiring immense prestige. They were sometimes viewed as the "equal of kings" (this was Voltaire's case, for example), and they took on the preeminent roles of guides, educators, and prophets to the human race.[22] Just as the fashion artist took over as arbiter of elegance, intellectuals, poets and, later, scientists claimed the right to legislate values, to educate the populace, and to govern public opinion in the interest of progress and public welfare. However, alongside this triumph of intellectuals and artists with a mission, another phenomenon emerged in the Romantic period, around the middle of the nineteenth century in particular, when artists began to offer ambivalent, mocking representations of themselves.[23] The artist's glory and downfall, the supreme splendor of art and its illusory nature, went hand in hand. Later, avant-garde creators even undermined their own work as artists, sought out "anti-artistic" moves, and declared art inferior to life. This tragic aspect of artistic representation contrasts with a triumphant, wholly positive image of fashion and the great couturier; the latter is an artist who understands frivolous mockery as a necessary game: "The spirit of contradiction in Fashion is so frequent and so regular that one can see in it almost a law. Do not women wear fox furs on light dresses, velvet hats in August, and straw ones in February? . . . There is in the decisions of fashion and of women a kind of provocation to common sense that is charming."[24] While the great couturier basked in worldwide fame, avant-garde artists, painters in particular, experienced an unmistakable lowering of status and social rejection: in the 1860s their works created a scandal, giving rise to a storm of public mockery, contempt, and hostility. A rift opened up between academic art and the new art: innovative painters were doomed to be misunderstood by the vast majority of the public and thus condemned to lead a precarious bohemian life of rebellion; the fate of the "accursed artists" stood in sharp contrast to that of the great couturiers with their fortunes, their flashy displays, their acceptance of the prevailing values. The glory of the couturiers corresponded to a decline in the prestige of innovative artists: the former were celebrated, the latter degraded. Here too, democratic logic pursued its task of equalizing conditions, dissolving extreme differences and hierarchies, raising the status of one group while lowering that of another, however ambiguously—for modern art never ceased to draw from its very degradation a confirmation of its own supremacy.

The epoch that glorified fashion also put it off-limits to men. Fantasy was banished; men's tailors never shared in the aura of the great couturiers, and no specialized press was devoted to men's clothing. Modern societies divided up the empire of fashion in a radical way: the apotheosis of feminine fashion was paralleled by the repression or denegation of masculine fashion, a repression symbolized by the use of black dress clothes and, later, the suit and tie. To be sure, dandyism undertook to "spiritualize" fashion, and the issues of male elegance, posture, and correctness came up again and again. For the most part, however, fashion and its prestige were now restricted to the universe of women; fashion had become an art in the feminine gender. If the modern era broke down the division between noble art and fashion, it paradoxically accentuated the division between men's and women's appearance as never before; it gave birth to an obvious inequality in the way the sexes presented themselves and in their relation to seduction.

Little remains to be said about the "great male renunciation" of fashion and its connection with the rise of democracy and the bourgeoisie. The neutral, austere, sober masculine costume reflected the consecration of egalitarian ideology as the conquering bourgeois ethic of thrift, merit, and work. Costly aristocratic dress, a sign of celebration and pomp, was replaced by clothing that expressed the new social values of equality, economy, and effort. Men were excluded from the glitter of artifice in favor of women, who for their part were destined to reintroduce symbols of luxury, seduction, and frivolity. Still, must we see this new distribution of appearances as merely a form of what Veblen called "vicarious consumption," a way of continuing, through women, to display financial clout and male social status? To do so would be to underestimate the weight of the cultural and aesthetic representations that have been attached for millennia to the position of the feminine. Whatever role may be played here by ostentatious class spending, women's monopolization of artifice can only be understood in relation to the collective representation of the "fair sex" as destined to please and seduce by its physical attributes and by the play of the factitious. Fashion's new gender disjunction and the preeminence of the feminine that it instituted extended the social definition of the "second sex," its timeless taste for artifice as an aid to seducing and appearing beautiful. By putting women's fashion on a pedestal, by reaffirming the primordial requirement of feminine beauty, the hundred years' fashion represented a continuation of the representations, values, and predilections of the feminine that had ruled for centuries.

Seduction in Power

The creative vocation of the couturier that defined haute couture itself was inseparable from a new logic that governed the mechanism of fashion: an organizational mutation marked fashion's entry into the age of modern production. Until Worth's day, tailors, dressmakers, and fashion merchants had gone on working in direct contact with clients, collaborating in

putting together complete outfits. The elegant woman made her own tastes
and preferences known, and in that way gave direction to the fashion
trades; thus Rose Bertin could refer to her hours of "work" with the queen.
Fashion professionals had not yet achieved a sovereign right to creative
freedom; they were subordinate, at least in principle, to the wishes of their
individual customers. In the mid-eighteenth century, the fashion trades
were clearly valorized in a new way, but there was no corresponding transformation in the way the work itself was conceived and organized. Professionals of fashion had won glory and social status, to be sure, but not
creative autonomy. In relation to this artisanal structure, the move Worth
made was crucial: it amounted to abolishing the millennial logic of subordination and collaboration between dressmaker and client in favor of a
logic that honored the designer's independence. By repeatedly dreaming
up original designs among which the client had only to choose, by having
his own wife serve as a model at the races or in the Bois de Boulogne,
Worth implemented the dual principle that constitutes fashion in the current sense of the term: the designer-couturier gained autonomy in theory
and in fact, while the client lost the initiative in the matter of dress. This
shift marks the unmistakable historical novelty of haute couture: the era
in which clients cooperated with dressmakers on a design that was in the
final analysis unchangeable gave way to an era in which articles of clothing were invented, created from start to finish, by professionals according
to their own "inspiration" and taste. The woman became a mere consumer, albeit at the level of luxury, while the couturier was transformed
from artisan into sovereign artist. Worth's arrogance, the authority with
which he addressed women of the highest society, must be understood in
this context: more than a character trait, it must be seen as a rupture, as
the assertion of a newly acquired right on the dressmaker's part to legislate
freely in matters of elegance.

The revolution in the way fashion was organized did not emerge with
the radical consistency of a logical schema at the start. Until the beginning
of the twentieth century, designs were sometimes exclusive, adapted to the
tastes of each client. Poiret tried to downplay the couturier's newly acquired importance by insisting on the still-crucial role of a certain clientele: "A Parisienne, especially, never adopts a model without making in it
changes of capital importance, and particularising it to suit herself. An
American woman chooses the model presented to her, and buys it just as
it is, while a Parisienne wants it to be blue if it is green, or garnet if it is
blue, and adds a fur collar, and changes the sleeves, and suppresses the
bottom button."[25] Still, whatever psychological truth these considerations
may hold, they must not be allowed to obscure the main point: the advent
of demiurgic power on the couturier's part, and the concomitant exclusion
of the wearer. The couturier had the upper hand in the conception of the

garment; at best, the elegant woman had the privilege of introducing modifications in certain details. The overall design belonged to the couturier;
minor details were left to the client, with advice from the saleswoman, who
took care to see that the couturier's spirit and trademark were not disfig-
ured. Moreover, as private customers grew fewer in number over time, and
as haute couture produced more and more prototypes destined for export,
the more or less "discretionary" power of the modern couturier continued
to increase.

Haute couture thus entailed more than anything else the constitution of
a specialized power that exercised its own separate authority, in the name
of elegance, creative imagination, and change. Viewed in these terms,
haute couture has to be resituated within a much broader historical movement, precisely that of the rationalization of power in modern societies.
Since the seventeenth and eighteenth centuries, our societies have in fact
witnessed the emergence of new forms of management and control that
can be called bureaucratic, and that typically aim to penetrate and
reshape society, to organize and reconstitute forms of socialization and
behaviors in their smallest details from a "rational" viewpoint. Bureaucratic control takes over the elaboration of the social order from start to
finish, through a distinct power structure based on a systematic separation
of functions: direction is disconnected from execution, the creative process
detached from manufacturing. As it happens, this is precisely the structure
we find in haute couture. With the de facto exclusion of the user and the
monopolization of power in the hands of those who specialized in elegance, an identical bureaucratic logic came to organize fashion, factories,
schools, hospitals, and barracks. There was just one difference: couturiers
set forth their laws in the name of taste and novelty rather than in the
name of positive rational knowledge. This bureaucratic logic ended up
structuring the entire organization of the great fashion houses; they were
henceforth arranged in a pyramid with the studio where designs were developed at the top, and specialized workshops (sleevemakers, bustmakers,
skirtmakers, "mechanics," and later hemstitchers and the workers who
produce formal dresses, suits, and so on) at the bottom; the workers'
places were marked hierarchically as well ("first" and "second" in the
workshop, first and second hand, *petite main*, apprentice). Haute couture's status as a luxury industry with women of the highest society as its
clients did not alter the historically crucial fact that it was responsible for
fashion's shift from the artisanal order to the modern bureaucratic order.

Furthermore, one cannot help recognizing the bonds of kinship that
united haute couture with the very purpose of modern bureaucratic organization, that is, its will to dissolve the stability of traditional social forms
in favor of an operative, well-informed, and goal-oriented rationality. It is
finally a question of disengaging fashion from a still fundamentally tradi-

tional order in which novelty was a random and irregular occurrence, and in which the right to initiate change remained an aristocratic privilege rooted in the structure of a caste society. With haute couture, innovations may have remained unpredictable, but they became obligatory and part of a regular process; no longer a birthright, they became a function of a relatively autonomous specialized apparatus defined by talent and worth. Fashion, like the other dimensions of the human world, was opened up to accelerated experimentation, to the modern voluntarist era of ruptures and revolutions.

It is important to note at once that the bureaucratic organization in question was of a rather special type, for the great fashion houses were headed not by some anonymous power independent of the person who exercised it, as is the case in many modern democratic institutions, but by artists who were at least in theory irreplaceable and unique, by virtue of their style, their tastes, their "genius." In the case of haute couture, unlike strictly bureaucratic organizations, the individual was inseparable from the function. Couturiers were defined by their unique talent, their label— which in the case of the greatest couturiers might be "immortalized," perpetuated even after their death (the Chanel style offers one example). In a unique way, haute couture brought together the bureaucratic process and a process of personalization manifested by the couturier's aesthetic, irreplaceable "omnipotence." In this sense, haute couture belonged to those new institutions that were inseparable from a sacralization of persons, whereas modern society is defined in just the opposite way by an anonymous disembodying of political and administrative power.[26] The diluted, impersonal logic of domination characteristic of the bureaucratic democratic states is complemented by the magical power of superindividuals on whom the masses bestow their adulation: great actresses and great couturiers, sports figures and popular singers, movie stars and show-business idols. As political agencies stop displaying signs of superpower, symbols of their otherness with respect to society, quasi-divine figures arise in the "cultural" field; such sacred monsters enjoy unparalleled honor and thus restore a certain hierarchical difference at the very heart of the egalitarian modern world.

Haute couture is an emblem of the modern bureaucratic age. Still, it would be inaccurate to link it with the historically dated form of bureaucratic control constituted by the disciplinary apparatus as described by Michel Foucault. Indeed, instead of the production of useful bodies, with haute couture there is a glorification of luxury and frivolous refinement; instead of stylistic uniformity there is a plurality of models; instead of prescriptive programming and the minutiae of rules, there is an appeal to personal initiative; instead of regular, constant, impersonal coercion, there is the seduction of the metamorphoses of appearance; instead of a micropower exercised over every little detail, there is a power that relinquishes control over accessory elements to individuals and concentrates on the essentials. Quite clearly, even though it was bureaucratic, haute couture as an organization put into play not the technologies of disciplinary constraint but previously unknown processes of *seduction* that inaugurated a new logic of power.

Seduction appeared at the outset, in techniques for commercialization of the new styles. In the nineteenth century, by organizing fashion shows and using live models, haute couture—like department stores, indoor galleries (the Parisian "passages"), and World's Fairs—was already establishing an advanced tactic of modern commerce, based on the theatricalization of merchandise, fanciful advertising, and appeals to desire. The idealized models of haute couture were the luxurious live counterparts of attractive shopwindows. Thus haute couture contributed to the great commercial revolution that is still under way. The aim is to encourage people to spend and consume without guilt, through strategies that use advertising displays and product overexposure. Still, the seduction process at work goes well beyond these devices of magical display, even if they are reinforced by the canonical and unreal beauty of models or the photogenic quality of cover girls. At a deeper level, the seduction process works through intoxication with change, the multiplication of prototypes, and the possibility of individual choice. We must not be too quick to rule out the dimension of freedom of choice, although some theorists hasten to call it illusory on the grounds that fashion is tyrannical, that it dictates the chic line of the year to all women. Actually, an enormous gulf separates pre–haute couture fashion with its uniform patterns from plurivocal modern fashion with its highly diversified collections, no matter how much overall homogeneity there may be. The rigid imposition of a particular cut yielded to the seductiveness of choice and change, which had as its subjective counterpart a myth of individuality, originality, and personal metamorphosis, dreams of an ephemeral harmony between one's inner self and one's outward appearance. Haute couture did not discipline fashion or make it uniform so much as it individualized fashion: "There ought to be as many models as there are women."[27] The distinguishing feature of haute couture is not so much that it imposed homogeneous standards as that it diversified styles in order to emphasize individual personalities, to consecrate the value of originality in dress, even to the point of extravagance (as with Schiaparelli). "What have you got to do with fashion? So, don't bother yourself with it, and simply wear what becomes you."[28] Haute couture, an organization with an individualist orientation, took a stand against standardization, against uniformity of appearance, against mass mimicry; it upheld and glorified the expression of personal differences.

Moreover, haute couture unleashed an original process within the fashion order: it psychologized fashion by creating designs that gave concrete form to emotions, personality, and character traits. Henceforth, depending on her clothes, a woman could appear melancholy, casual, sophisticated, severe, insolent, ingenuous, whimsical, romantic, gay, young, amusing, or athletic; furthermore, the fashion magazines chose to stress these psychological essences and their original combinations.[29] The individualization of modern fashion is inseparable from the personalizing and psychologizing of elegance; by the same token, what formerly appeared as signs of class and social hierarchy had a tendency to become increasingly, although not exclusively, psychological signs, expressions of a soul or personality. "Visit the great dressmakers, and you will not feel that you are in a shop, but in the studio of an artist, who intends to make of your dresses a portrait and a likeness of yourself."[30] The psychologizing of appearance is accompanied by the narcissistic pleasure of transforming oneself in one's own eyes and those of others, of "changing one's skin," feeling like— and becoming—someone else, by changing the way one dresses. Haute Couture offered new ways for women to realize their desires for metamorphosis; it broadened the scope of seduction through appearance. Women could look athletic in shorts or trousers, highfalutin in a cocktail dress, businesslike in a suit, haughty or vampish in an evening sheath; the modern seductiveness of haute couture stems from the way it has managed to bring into coexistence luxury and individuality, "class" and originality, personal identity and the ephemeral alteration of the self. "At each season, what [women] are seeking is perhaps, even more than a dress, a renewal of their psychological makeup. Fashion has a role to play vis-à-vis women: it helps them to exist. It can even take the place of drugs!"[31]

The break with the disciplinary order is revealed just as clearly by the logic of indetermination, which was henceforth consubstantial with fashion. No doubt the prototypes were quite carefully conceived and prepared separately, in the laboratories of haute couture; nevertheless, couturiers were by no means the sole artisans of fashion. Fashion took shape after the collections were presented; much depended on the particular patterns chosen by clients and by certain fashion magazines. The fashion of the year appeared only when the selections of a certain clientele and the press had converged on particular patterns. This is a crucial point: the couturiers did not know in advance which of their designs would be successful. Thus haute couture created fashion without knowing precisely what its destiny would be, without knowing which fashion would prevail. Fashion remained subject to public choice; it was indeterminate, even though its prototypes were arranged from beginning to end by the great couturiers. "Couturiers propose, women dispose," someone has said: it is easy to see what distinguishes this mechanism, which integrates the unpredictability of demand into its own workings, from the disciplinary power that consists essentially in leaving nothing to individual initiative, in imposing standard traditional rules from on high, in controlling and planning the chain of behavior from beginning to end. This indeterminacy is not residual; it is constitutive of the system itself. This is obvious when one knows that only one-tenth of the designs in a collection, in the early decades of this century, won the backing of clients. "The total balance sheet of a season is thus about thirty successful patterns out of the three hundred presented."[32] Public tastes, the choices made by magazines and movie stars— factors such as these came to play a central role, to such an extent that they were able to counter the tendencies of haute couture. Thus the fashion of the 1920s was imposed more by women customers than by haute couture: "In 1921 Haute Couture declared war on short hair—without success. In 1922 it fought against short dresses, and in fact skirts suddenly became long again, but with the waist very much lowered. The winter collections were very colourful in an attempt to banish the black preferred by women. It was a failure; in the spring collections, everything was black once again."[33] The lean and delicate shape of the Adonis-woman in a shirtdress gained ground, countering the dominant trends of haute couture, which continued for a time—before finally giving up—to offer women collections that were rich in trimmings, "looseness," rounded and draped forms.

Programming fashion while remaining unable to impose it, conceiving of it as a whole while simultaneously offering an array of choices, haute couture inaugurated a new type of supple power that functioned without issuing rigid injunctions and that incorporated into its processes the unpredictable and varied tastes of the public. This mechanism had a bright future: it was to become the preponderant form of social control in democratic societies as they embarked on the era of consumption and mass communication. In consumer societies, products are governed in fact by the same principle that underlies the designs of the couturiers' collections. They are never offered in just one unique form; increasingly, the consumer is invited to choose between one variant and another, between one set of accessories, or gamuts, or programs, and another, and to combine the elements of each more or less freely. Like haute couture, mass consumption implies the multiplication of models, the diversification of series, the production of optional differences, the stimulation of a personalized demand. More generally speaking, in open societies, the bureaucratic apparatuses that currently organize production, distribution, the media, education, and leisure activities reserve a growing, systematic place for individual desires. We are in the second generation of the bureaucratic age: after the era of compulsory discipline, we have entered the era of personalization, choice, and combinatory freedom. This immense upheaval in modalities and goals of power is winning over increasingly broad sectors of social life today, and haute couture was the first link in the chain. With haute couture an experiment was undertaken, prior to psychoanalysis but analogous to it, involving a new logic of power that renounced mastery and flawless foresight; it no longer worked through imperative, impersonal, global constraints, but it left individuals and society room for initiative. The comparison with psychoanalysis should not come as a surprise, for the same reversal of disciplinary power is at work there in an exemplary manner. On the one hand, psychoanalysis is based on the patient's free associations, on the analyst's silence, and on transference, as if medical power had taken note of the ineradicable component of subjective singularities and the impossibility of totally dominating or controlling individuals.[34] On the other hand, modern fashion diversifies models, solicits differences, and opens up the indeterminate space of choice, preference, or random taste. This constitutes not an abdication of power but the emergence of an open, flexible power, a power of seduction that prefigures the very power that is to become dominant in the society of excessive choice.

What we know as fashion "trends," that is, the similarities existing among the designs of different collections in a given year (waistline placement, skirt length, shoulder width) often lead to the mistaken belief that fashion is decreed through deliberate concert among the couturiers. Instead, these "trends" only confirm the "open" logic of haute couture's powers. On the one hand, trends are inseparable from haute couture viewed as a closed, bureaucratic phenomenon in Paris: the couturiers, though they go to great pains to assert their uniqueness, cannot develop their own collections without taking into account the original contributions of their competitors, since fashion's vocation is to astonish and to invent endless novelty. A couturier's unprecedented idea, often tentative and not fully exploited at first, is under these circumstances very quickly recognized as such; it is seized upon, transposed, and developed by others in subsequent collections. This is how fashion changes, first by groping and sending out trial balloons, then through sedimentations and mimetic "amplifications" that are nevertheless in all cases individual. All these processes are brought about by the professional logic of constitutive renewal, and they explain why abrupt shifts in fashion (the New Look, for example) are much rarer than slow changes, contrary to common belief. And yet trends escape bureaucratic logic in that they also result from the choices made by the clientele and, since the Second World War, by the press, which at any given moment favors particular sorts of designs. Trends tell us as much about the power of public or journalistic infatuations as about the power of the couturiers, for the latter are constrained by the threat of commercial failure to follow the public's movement, to adapt to the tastes of the times. Similarities among collections are by no means signs of a secret agreement among the couturiers (quite to the contrary, the latter hide their prototypes jealously), nor does it signify omnipotence on the part of designers; instead, it is the effect of the encounter between an aesthetic bureaucracy and the logic of demand.[35]

A Brief Genealogy of Haute Couture

If we go by the standard studies of modern fashion, there is nothing complicated or mysterious about the genesis of haute couture. Its relations with the capitalist order, with the profit system, and with class rivalries are presented as determining. Without question, indeed, haute couture is an industrial and commercial luxury enterprise; its goal is profit making and its endless creations produce an obsolescence that promotes ever more rapid consumption. Without question, too, the idea (borrowed from working-class and then petit bourgeois industrial manufacturing) of grouping previously separate operations—direct purchasing at the factory, fabric sales, the manufacture of ready-made garments—is inseparable from the capitalist motivation of realizing a "triple benefit," as Worth's son was quick to recognize.[36] Without doubt, finally, the idea of displaying designs on live models is a well-conceived advertising scheme inspired by the same profit motive. Still, however important a role economic motivation may have played, it obscures the original fact that haute couture always appears as a formation with two faces, the economic and the aesthetic, the bureaucratic and the artistic. The logic of profit making fostered the creation of novelties; by itself, however, and even in concert with the principle of competition among fashion houses, it cannot explain either the escalation in the number of creations in the collections or the stylistic research, sometimes avant-garde in nature, that characterizes modern fashion. Haute couture set in motion a permanent process of aesthetic innovation that cannot be deduced mechanically from the logic of economics.

For this reason, the classical theory of social distinction and class competition has been widely invoked. At the most basic level, the emergence of haute couture has to be related to the principle according to which the dominant classes are in search of honorific recognition. Within this theory, haute couture appears to be a class institution expressing in its own particular register the ascendancy of the bourgeoisie, and the bourgeois desire to earn social recognition through the intermediary of sumptuous feminine emblems at the very moment when masculine clothing had ceased to be flashy, and when the democratization of appearance was being consolidated owing to the rise of industrial manufacturing of clothing. In this view, haute couture represented a reaction against the modern "leveling" of personal appearance; it was a product of "internal struggles within the dominant class." In short, haute couture won out, as it were, through a kind of sociological imperative, given the competitive struggles and strategies for distinction attributed to the upper classes. Under these conditions, haute couture was nothing but an "apparatus for the production of class emblems" corresponding to "symbolic struggles"; these emblems were intended to supply the dominant class with "profits of distinction" proportionate to its economic position.[37] The mechanistic economic interpretation is coupled with the sociological dialectic of distinction.

If the role of the quest for social distinction in fashion is undeniable, the fact remains—and needs to be emphasized—that that quest cannot shed any light on the emergence of that feature of haute couture that constitutes its incomparable historical originality, namely, its bureaucratic organizational logic. The argument that haute couture grew up *in reaction* to the manufacturing of clothing, and in the service of class distinctions,[38] does not stand up to an examination of the historical facts. Under the Second Empire, the manufacture of women's clothing, although it was already reaching a bourgeois clientele, remained limited, since the technologies did not yet permit precise fitted manufacturing for a whole sector of feminine apparel: the first dresses made according to standard measures did not appear until after 1870. Manufacturing techniques mainly produced the loose-fitting elements of dress (lingerie, shawls, mantillas, coats, and mantelettas); for the rest, women continued to turn to their dressmakers, and went on doing so for a long time. Mass production was therefore a long way from invading the marketplace when Worth set up his fashion house. In fact, manufacturing was not a "threat" to the upper classes, since the quality of the fabrics, the luxuriousness of the trimmings, and the fame of the dressmakers continued to permit the display of prestigious differences. Factional rivalries within the dominant class, competition between those who had "arrived" and those who claimed they had, between the wealthier and the less wealthy, the old and the new, certainly existed. Still, how can such phenomena, which are by no means unprecedented, account for the institutional break represented by haute couture? In terms of the dynamics of symbolic struggles alone, haute couture and its modern bureaucratic mechanism did not win out entirely, for the old production system managed perfectly well to keep on furnishing emblems of "class." Yet an organizational mutation did in fact occur: it consisted in the separation of professionals from customers and the regular creation of new designs. The new bureaucratic-artistic organization cannot be interpreted as an echo of social distinction.

At a more basic level, haute couture is inconceivable without the revolutionary overturning of the social and juridical order of the Old Regime that occurred in France at the end of the eighteenth century. Thus the histori-

cal possibility of an unfettered production of clothing can be traced back
to the abolition of the corporations by the Constituent Assembly in 1791.
Up to that point, the custom- and rule-based policies of the Old Regime
had prevented tailors and dressmakers from stocking and selling fabric;
thus they could not produce clothing they had created in advance. The
idea of producing ready-made garments, of combining the purchase of
fabric, its sale, and its "fashioning," was first introduced in the industrial
production of items destined for the lower and middle classes; it was later
brought into play at the level of luxury items, first by Mme Roger,[39] and
then, more significantly, by Worth and haute couture. This practice stems
from the democratic dissolution of the corporate regime, the abolition of
maîtrises and *jurandes*. Nevertheless, even though this change was crucial, it was by no means a historically sufficient condition to account by
itself for the emergence of a bureaucratic and artistic organization. Without the legitimizing of new historical values, sociological and juridical factors alone could never have given rise to the separate institution of haute
couture. The conclusion is inescapable: the ideas and social representations of the modern world were not secondary superstructures; they were
at the heart of the bureaucratization of fashion.

If class competition, the profit motive, and the abolition of corporations
succeeded in giving haute couture its well-known aspect, they did so
chiefly by reinforcing the legitimacy of the social value of novelty, a reinforcement triggered by the advent of democratic individualist societies.[40]
Since the end of the Middle Ages, the value of newness had certainly
gained a foothold, but from the eighteenth century on, its social valorization increased significantly. This is directly attested by the artistic celebration of fashion, and indirectly by the proliferation of social utopias, the
cult of the Enlightenment, the idea of revolution, and demands for equality and freedom. The ecstasy of newness is consubstantial with democratic
eras. This crescendo in desires for change contributed importantly to the
birth of haute couture as a bureaucratic formation based on the separation
of the professional and private spheres and devoted to continuous creation. The modern religion of novelty, an emphatic devaluation of the old
in favor of modernity, was a prerequisite if women were to give up their
traditional control over their own dress, if society was to abandon the
timeless principle according to which those who provide work for artists
have "a choice and a voice" in the products they order. Through the intermediary of the new, the artisanal organization, with its sluggish motion
and its random innovations, could yield precisely to "an industry whose
very raison d'être is to create novelty."[41] Indeed, when newness asserts
itself as the supreme requirement, a second requirement necessarily accompanies it in the short or the long run: the couturier's independence

becomes legitimate and obligatory. Hence the existence of a separate
agency entirely devoted to creative innovation, detached from the ineluctable conservatism and inertia of social demand.

The bureaucratic autonomy of fashion could not have come about without the simultaneous recognition of the ultimate value of individual freedom. Like modern art, haute couture is inseparable from the individualist
ideology. According to this new ideology, autonomous independent individuals are freed of the age-old obligation to conform to the rites, customs,
and traditions that prevail in society as a whole. The advent of the representation of the self-sufficient individual means that preexisting norms no
longer have an absolute foundation with respect to human will; there are
no more sacred rules; lines and styles are to be invented from a position of
sovereignty, in conformity with the modern right to freedom. This new
situation gives rise to the possibility of pushing back the frontiers of appearance further and further, of creating new aesthetic codes; the emergence of the independent couturier is one manifestation of the individualist conquest of unfettered creativity. It is far too simplistic to explain the
multiplication of designs, the stylistic breaks, and the couturiers' excesses
by invoking the sociological constraints of distinction and economic motivation: the headlong advance of modern fashion, however useful it may
have been to business, was possible only thanks to the modern ideal of
newness and its corollary, creative freedom. The revolution accomplished
by Poiret at the beginning of the twentieth century sheds retrospective
light on the ideological genesis of haute couture; thus when Poiret writes
that "it was equally in the name of Liberty that I proclaimed the fall of the
corset and the adoption of the brassière,"[42] what is at issue is less women's
freedom, we might say ("Yes, I freed the bust but I shackled the legs"),[43]
than the freedom of couturiers themselves, for whom the corset represented an ancient code blocking the imagination of new designs, a framework resistant to sovereign creativity.

It is important to emphasize yet again how much haute couture owes
the modern cult of individuality. In essence, haute couture substituted a
multiplicity of styles for a uniform cut; it diversified and psychologized
dress. It was pervaded by a utopian vision according to which each woman
of taste had to be attired in a distinctive fashion adapted to her own particular "type" and personality. "The high art of dressmaking consists precisely developing the individuality of each woman."[44] The diversification
of models requires something quite different from the quest for profits. It
requires the ideological celebration of the principle of individualism; it
requires that full and complete legitimacy be conferred on personalized
self-presentation; it requires that originality take precedence over uniformity. True, the creations of haute couture were adopted as class

emblems; yet haute couture owes its very existence to the modern individualist ideology that subtended it. That ideology, because it recognized the
individual as a virtually absolute value, had a number of repercussions:
increased taste for originality, nonconformism, fantasy, uniqueness of the
individual personality, eccentricity, comfort, and bodily display. Only
within the framework of this new individualistic configuration could the
earlier logic of fashion be destroyed, the logic that had limited originality
to the accessories of attire. Haute couture was not the product of a natural
evolution; it was not a simple extension of the productive order of ephemera. From the fourteenth century to the mid-eighteenth century, fantasy in
fashion was strictly limited in theory and in fact. Subordinated to a general structure of dress that was identical for all women, fanciful innovations were not at all likely to spread. And even when trimmings did come
into their own, the architecture of clothing remained uniform. Haute
couture, on the contrary, brought about a complete change of direction:
overall originality became a requirement, an a priori and ultimate goal;
commercial factors alone intervened to put the brakes on the creative
imagination. Such a reversal could have come about only in the wake of a
revolution in legitimate social representations—the very revolution that
recognized the individual as supreme value. Despite its character as a luxury industry aimed at making the social hierarchy visible, then, haute
couture was a democratic individualistic organization that adapted the
production of fashion to the ideals of the sovereign individual—even
though, as was the case for women, that individual remained in a "minor"
position within the political order. Haute couture was a compromise formation between two ages. On the one hand, it reintroduced the time-
honored aristocratic logic of fashion with its luxurious emblems; on the
other hand, it orchestrated a modern, diversified production in conformity
with the ideological referents of democratic individualism.

The values of the individualist age contributed decisively to the orchestration of modern fashion, playing the same role with respect to fashion
that they played with respect to the modern state. In conformity with the
principle of equality, in each instance the majestic emblems of hierarchical
otherness, both human and political, were repudiated; in each instance,
power was increased and bureaucratized, with a growing and penetrating
dominion of specialized agencies over society, even while emancipatory
values—the principle of the new or the principle of collective sovereignty—were being invoked. What is more, like the democratic state that
derived its own legitimacy from its homogeneity with the society it represented and of which it was nothing more than the strict executor, modern
couturiers never lost sight of their democratic function as instruments of
collective desire. "The truth is that I respond by anticipation to your secret

intentions. . . . I am only a medium sensitive to the reactions of your taste and meticulous in registering the trends of your caprices."[45] Unlike artists and the avant-garde that proclaimed their sovereign independence long and loud, haute couture, true to its bureaucratic essence, largely concealed its new power to legislate fashion at a time when it was gaining unprecedented access to powers of initiative, leadership, and stylistic hegemony.

Open Fashion

Today's fashion is no longer modeled on the system embodied in the hundred years' fashion. Since the 1950s and 1960s, organizational, social, and cultural transformations have thoroughly disrupted the earlier structure; we can reasonably conclude that a new stage in the history of fashion has come into view. One thing needs to be made clear at the outset: the emergence of a new system does not by any means signify a historical rift, a total break in continuity with the past. At the deepest level, the second phase of modern fashion continues and extends the most modern contributions of the hundred years' fashion, namely, a bureaucratic production orchestrated by professional creators, an industrial logic of mass production, seasonal collections, fashion shows with live models used for advertising purposes. However, this large-scale organizational continuity is matched by an equally large-scale reconfiguration of the system. New centers of creation have emerged, and new criteria have been imposed. The earlier hierarchical and unitary configuration has exploded. The individual and social meanings of fashion have changed along with the tastes and behaviors of women and men. These are all aspects of a crucial restructuring that nevertheless continues to reinscribe the secular preeminence of the feminine and to perfect the triple logic of modern fashion, with its bureaucratic and aesthetic face, its industrial face, and its democratic individualist face.

Ready-to-Wear: The Democratic Revolution

The golden age of modern fashion had Parisian haute couture as its epicenter: a laboratory for the creation of novelty, a global pole of attraction, and the focus of imitation for both manufacturing and small-scale dressmaking. This aristocratic and centralized phase is over. The haute couture houses continue to present their sumptuous twice-yearly creations in Paris, of course, before the international press. They still enjoy an illustrious reputation, and can boast of continually growing worldwide profits throughout economic slumps.[1] Nevertheless, beneath the surface continu-

ity, haute couture has lost its earlier avant-garde status. It has ceased to be
the focal point and center of live fashion, even though its vocation and
activities have undergone a significant updating. In the 1960s, certain
fashion houses could still survive, for the most part, on made-to-order
work. In 1975, the made-to-order component accounted for no more than
18 percent of direct profits (excluding perfumes) of the haute couture
houses; in 1985, the figure was down to 12 percent. Employment figures
also reflect this irreversible evolution. In the 1920s, Patou employed thirteen hundred people in its workshops; before the war, twenty-five hundred
people worked for Chanel; in the mid-1950s, Dior had twelve hundred
employees. In 1985, the twenty-one houses classified as "Couture-Crea-
tion" employed only two thousand workers altogether in their made-to-
order workshops, and they provided made-to-order clothing for no more
than three thousand women throughout the world.

In fact, the haute couture houses remain prosperous now solely through
their ready-to-wear lines, licensing contracts, and perfumes. Since the
turn of the century, these houses have always been associated with perfumes and cosmetics. Paul Poiret was the first to launch a line of perfumes
("Rosine"), in 1911. Chanel followed suit, with the celebrated "No. 5," in
1921. Mme Lanvin created "Arpège" in 1923; Patou came out with "Joy,"
"the world's most expensive perfume," in 1930. The idea bore fruit: in
1978, Nina Ricci's perfumes made a profit of 1.2 billion francs, accounting
for more than 90 percent of the brand's overall profits; Chanel's perfumes
accounted for 94 percent of overall profits. In 1981, haute couture's overall
profits, excluding perfume, came to 6 billion francs; with perfumes, the
total was 11 billion. In the mid-1980s, Lanvin's perfumes accounted for 50
percent of the firm's overall profits, and Chanel's "No. 5," the most widely
sold French perfume in the world, is thought to bring in more than $50
million a year all by itself. Since the 1960s, all the couture houses have
embarked on a lucrative race for licensing agreements that involve not
only perfumes and cosmetics but also a great variety of other articles:
glasses, leather goods, tableware, cigarette lighters, pens, underwear, sailboards, men's and women's ready-to-wear. As of the mid-1980s, Saint-
Laurent was deriving nearly 68 percent of its profits from royalties, Lanvin 60 percent, Dior 30 percent. Cardin was relying on more than 600
French and foreign licenses; Lanvin had 120, Nina Ricci 180. Even though
some houses have a much more restricted licensing policy (licensing accounts for just 3 percent of Chanel's profits), the haute couture sector as a
whole can survive only because of the substantial profits realized by the
sale of its prestigious brand names: perfumes and cosmetics aside, royalty
profits are seven times higher than profits from direct production.

Not only has couture's made-to-order role—the sublime expression of
the hundred years' fashion—atrophied due to a drastic reduction in its

clientele, but haute couture no longer dresses women in "the latest thing."
It aims much more at perpetuating the great tradition of luxury and professional virtuosity. Its goals are essentially promotional: brand-name advertising for high-fashion ready-to-wear and the other items sold under its
labels worldwide. Neither classical nor avant-garde, haute couture no
longer produces the latest fashion; instead, it reproduces its own "eternal"
trademark by creating masterpieces of execution, prowess, and aesthetic
gratuitousness: unprecedented, unique, sumptuous attire transcending
the ephemeral reality of fashion itself. Once the spearhead of fashion,
haute couture today is becoming a fashion museum, in a pure aesthetics
that has shed its earlier commercial obligations. The new haute couture is
paradoxical: it couples fashion with absolutes, frivolity with perfection; it
no longer creates for *anyone*. It enacts a detached aesthetic folly all the
better in that this approach best corresponds to market interests. In this
new phase, in which haute couture has been transformed into a display
window for advertising pure prestige, there is more than the peculiar fate
of a dynamic institution that has made a successful conversion to ready-
to-wear and licensing; there is also a change of fundamental importance
for the centuries-long history of Western fashion. Supreme luxury and
fashion have gone their separate ways: luxury is no longer the privileged
embodiment of fashion, and fashion is no longer identified with ostentatious expense, even euphemistically.

However, the real revolution that destroyed the architecture of the hundred years' fashion is the one that overturned the logic of industrial production. This revolution corresponds to the emergence and development
of what Americans were the first to call *ready-to-wear*. J. C. Weill introduced the corresponding term *prêt-à-porter* in France, in an effort to dis-
engage manufactured clothing from its poor public image. Unlike traditional manufacturing, ready-to-wear committed itself to a new path: an
industrial production of clothing accessible to all that would nevertheless
be "fashion," inspired by the latest trends of the day. Whereas manufactured apparel was often characterized by defective cuts, careless finishing,
poor quality, and a lack of imagination, ready-to-wear sought to blend
industry and fashion; it sought to put novelty, style, and aesthetics on the
streets. Starting in the early 1950s, Parisian department stores such as
Galeries Lafayette, Printemps, and Prisunic introduced fashion advisors
and coordinators into their purchasing departments in order to win over
the manufacturers and offer their own clientele more up-to-date products.[2] In the United States and later in France, the ready-to-wear industry
gradually became aware of the need to hire designers, to offer apparel that
had added aesthetic value, that was fashionable. The first women's ready-
to-wear salon in France was held in 1957, and toward the end of the decade
the first independent Office of Fashion Advisors (Conseils et Styles) ap-

peared. In 1958, C. de Coux founded "Relations Textiles"; in 1961, Maïmé Arnodin created a fashion bureau that was a forerunner of Promostyl, set up in 1966.[3] To a certain extent, mass production of clothing followed the same path industrial design had followed in the 1930s. It was a matter of producing cloth and woolen fabrics that integrated novelty, fantasy, and aesthetic creation, following the model of fashion with its seasonal collections. With the advent of designers, mass industrial apparel changed status: it became a full-fledged fashion product. The earliest ready-to-wear labels appeared in advertisements shortly thereafter.

Still, before the late 1950s, ready-to-wear was not very creative in aesthetic terms. Governed by an earlier logic, it was a watered-down imitation of the new forms introduced by haute couture. Ready-to-wear finally came into its own, as it were, in the 1960s, by creating clothes in a spirit oriented more toward daring, youthfulness, and novelty than toward "class" perfection. A new breed of creators rose to the top, people who—for the first time—were not part of haute couture. In 1959, Daniel Hechter launched the Babette style and the cassock-style coat; in 1960, Cacharel reinvented women's blouses, using madras in a simple style that closely resembled men's shirts. In 1963, in London, Mary Quant created the Ginger Group, which came up with the miniskirt. In 1963, too, Christine Bailly began to innovate with her wide capelike coats. Michèle Rosier revolutionized winter sports clothes by offering a close-to-the-body silhouette with a cosmic flair. Emmanuelle Kahn and Elie Jacobson (Dorothée Bis) were also part of that first generation of designers who presided over the birth of sportswear, unconfining apparel that was youthful in spirit.[4] In the 1970s and 1980s, a second and third wave of designers gave impetus to the most important innovations in professional fashion. Kenzo galvanized fashion in the early 1970s with his flat-chested cuts derived from kimonos, his taste for colors and flowers, his blend of East and West. Mugler offered a feminine archetype from cinema and science fiction. Montana created voluminous, broad-shouldered garments. Chantal Thomas revealed an elegant and mischievous silhouette that was at once decent and insolent. J.-P. Gaultier played at being the bad boy of fashion by using humor and mockery and by blending genres and periods. The Japanese creators Issey Miyake and Rei Kawakubo upset the traditional structure of clothing. Since 1975, some of these designers and a few others (P. Moréni, Sonia Rykiel, A. Alaïa, and so on) have had ties to the major couturiers and their establishment: they have been designated creators of fashion.

During these transitional years, nevertheless, haute couture did not stand still. The 1960s were the last decade in which haute couture continued to fulfill its revolutionary vocation in matters of style—above all via the "Courrèges effect." Indeed, Courrèges's 1965 collection, in which he introduced a short, structured style, constituted a fashion event to such a degree that the publicity impact of the press photos published around the world was evaluated at four to five billion francs in 1965 terms. Courrèges's modernism was resolutely future oriented: the fashion he developed emancipated women from high heels, constraining bustlines, tight clothing, and closely fitted hips in favor of structured attire that allowed freedom of movement. The miniskirt had already appeared in England in 1963, but Courrèges managed to put his own stamp on it. With its low-heeled boots, its use of pure white, its references to schoolgirls wearing socks, its geometric dynamism, the Courrèges style registered the irresistible rise of specifically juvenile or teenage values in fashion. After the young woman of the 1920s, it was unequivocally the young girl who now found herself on a pedestal as the prototype of fashion. In addition, haute couture sanctioned women's trousers: in 1960, Balenciaga began to create evening outfits based on white pants, and Yves Saint-Laurent included pants in his collections in 1966; he had his models wear evening trousers and women's tuxedos. In 1968, Saint-Laurent launched the bush jacket: his safari style was highly influential in the 1970s. In an interview at about the same time, he proclaimed: "Down with the Ritz; long live the street!"[5] Coming from a major couturier, such a provocative statement verges on dandyism; nevertheless, it does express the new position of haute couture in the creation of fashion. Haute couture had in fact stopped setting the tone in fashion matters; ready-to-wear, off-the-rack clothing had been constituted as an "autonomous" fashion center. By the time haute couture introduced women's pants into its collections, women had already adopted them on a massive scale: in 1965, more women's pants were produced industrially than skirts. And in 1966, when Saint-Laurent included jeans in his collections, they had long since been adopted by the young as the apparel of choice. "You have to go into the streets."[6] After playing a pioneering role, haute couture in the narrow sense had become primarily a prestige-generating institution that did more to consecrate innovations produced elsewhere than to drive the cutting edge of fashion.

Haute couture, initially reticent if not actively hostile toward ready-to-wear, finally grasped how valuable the new methods could be when they were coupled with its own capital of prestige. In 1959, Pierre Cardin presented the first ready-to-wear couture collection at the department store Printemps; he later remarked, speaking of this event: "I established the T.N.P. [National Popular Theater] of couture."[7] He opened the first ready-to-wear department in 1963, and he was also the first of the couturiers to sign agreements with the major ready-to-wear manufacturers, exploiting the prestige of his label. In 1966, Yves Saint-Laurent created the first ready-to-wear collection conceived in terms of industrial requirements and not as an adaptation of haute couture. At the same time, he opened the first Saint-Laurent Rive-Gauche shop, and in 1983–84, the

Saint-Laurent Variation line, at prices 40 percent lower than Rive-Gauche. In 1985, women's ready-to-wear amounted to 33 percent of haute couture's direct profits, excluding perfume.

The refocusing of haute couture turned it not only toward mass production but also, starting in 1961 under Cardin's initiative, toward men's ready-to-wear. The institution that had symbolized the influence of the feminine for a century now created and presented seasonal collections for men. Far from being a passing fad, the new niche continued to expand. In 1975, men's ready-to-wear represented 8 percent of haute couture's direct profits; by 1985, the figure had gone up to 19.5 percent.

The end of made-to-measure and thus of two-tiered fashion under the aegis of haute couture on the one hand, a generalization of ready-to-wear and a dissemination of creative centers on the other hand: this schema summarizes the transformation of the fashion system. Technological improvements in the garment industry coupled with the emergence of designers and ready-to-wear virtually abolished the opposition that had structured the hundred years' fashion, the opposition between made-to-order and ready-to-wear. The age of made-to-order was past,[8] and even where it subsisted it had lost its premium on taste; on the contrary, ready-to-wear creations came to embody the spirit of fashion in its most vital expression. Whatever differences in value and quality might characterize ready-to-wear articles, the new age marked a supplementary stage in the democratic organization of fashion, since an essentially homogeneous industrial production had been substituted for a heterogeneous system of made-to-order and mass production. The hundred years' fashion, with its dual made-to-order/mass-produced organization, was a hybrid formation, half aristocratic and half democratic. By getting rid of the ostentatiously elitist sector and by universalizing the system of mass production, ready-to-wear gave a boost to the democratic dynamics that had been partially put into play in the earlier phase.

Thus the opposition between original luxury creation and industrial mass production ceased to govern the operation of the new system. True, avant-garde collections still appeared every season, presented by the great creators of ready-to-wear; still, mass industrial fashions for their part could no longer be written off as vulgar and degraded copies of the most admired prototypes. The distribution of ready-to-wear took on relative autonomy with respect to the quest for innovation: fashion's new deal took the form of spiraling audacity and extravagance on the creators' part, decreased mimetic subordination on the part of the major industrial producers. As the ready-to-wear manufacturers began to appeal to designers, as fantasy, sports, and humor came into their own as dominant values, as fashion stopped obligatorily excluding the previous year's trends from one year to the next, apparel in the major mass-production lines gained in

quality, aesthetic value, and originality, even if there was no comparison
with the "follies" of the couturiers' and creators' collections. The disjunction between luxury models and industrial or artisanal imitations was preponderant when the legislation of haute couture still had its full authority;
it faded away as fashion became multifarious and allowed the most disparate styles to coexist. How can we still speak of imitation when the industrial ready-to-wear collections are prepared two years in advance, when
fashion bureaus take it upon themselves to invent and define their own
fashion themes? This does not mean that avant-garde creations are no
longer taken into account, but it does mean that they no longer have the
power to impose themselves as exclusive models for reference. High fashion is now no more than one source of free inspiration; many others (life-
styles, sports, films, the prevailing mood, exoticism, and so on) are equally
important. While centers of inspiration are proliferating, and subordination to models viewed as *le dernier cri* is weakening, industrial apparel has
entered the era of aesthetic creation and personalization. The mass-market product is no longer an inferior reflection of a prestigious prototype, it
is an original re-creation, a specific synthesis of industrial requirements
and the designer system. It takes concrete form in clothing that offers diversified, consumer-oriented combinations of classicism and originality,
seriousness and frivolousness, reasonableness and novelty.

The ready-to-wear system tends to lessen the anonymity characteristic
of earlier industrial production, and to produce articles with a creative
"bonus," added aesthetic value, and a personalized cachet. The de-
mocraticization of fashion continues apace: the epoch in which mass industrial fashion arose, a period of mediocre quality lacking in style and
inspiration, has given way to a period in which the ready-to-wear industry
offers explicitly fashion-oriented products of aesthetic quality at reasonable prices. The democratization of the system depends not only on the de
facto dismissal of haute couture, but especially on the concomitant promotion of fashion quality in mass apparel. The qualitative progress made by
industrial fashion is difficult to deny. Whereas couturier- and designer-
based ready-to-wear accounts for roughly 40 percent of the national market in France, many highly reputed creators work or have worked as free-
lance designers for mass-market ready-to-wear firms. The *Trois Suisses*
catalog has even proposed clothing signed P. Moréni, Alaïa, J.-P. Gaultier,
and I. Miyake, at mass-market prices. The logic of mass production has
been overtaken by a process of personalization that gives priority to creative dynamism wherever it is found, that multiplies styles and variations
and substitutes aesthetic innovation for mimetic reproduction.[9] Mass fashion has changed character in the democratic age of overabundant choice,
in the era of modest items and inexpensive "coordinates," under the se-

ductive influence of what is "nice and inexpensive" and of the relation between aesthetic value and price.

The ready-to-wear industry has managed to turn fashion into a radically democratic system only because it has succeeded in meeting the democratic aspiration to fashion. The ready-to-wear revolution is inseparable from the significant progress achieved in the technology of clothing manufacture, progress that has made it possible to produce articles of very good quality in huge quantities at low cost. But the revolution cannot be detached, either, from a new state of demand. After the Second World War, the desire for fashion spread widely; it became a generalized phenomenon involving all levels of society. At the heart of ready-to-wear we find this ultimate democratization of tastes in fashion, conveyed by movies and women's magazines, but also by the appetite for living in the present that has been stimulated by the new hedonistic mass culture. The rise in standards of living, the cult of well-being, leisure, and instant happiness have led to the ultimate stage in the legitimizing and democratizing of enthusiasm for fashion. Fashion's aesthetic and ephemeral signs no longer strike the lower classes as an inaccessible phenomenon reserved for others; they have become a mass demand, a life-style decor taken for granted in a society that holds change, pleasure, and novelty sacred. The era of ready-to-wear coincides with the emergence of a society oriented more and more toward the present, a society rendered euphoric by novelty and consumption.

Along with hedonistic culture, the emergence of "youth culture" has been an essential element in the stylistic evolution of ready-to-wear. This youth culture is undoubtedly linked to the baby boom of the 1950s and to the rising buying power of the young, but at a deeper level it also appears as a broadened manifestation of individualist, democratic dynamics. This new culture was at the root of the rise of design in the 1960s, a phenomenon not so much concerned with perfection as it was alert for creative spontaneity, originality, and immediate impact. In concert with the democratic exaltation of youth, ready-to-wear itself embarked on a democratic rejuvenation of fashion prototypes.

Labels Transformed

Along with the aestheticization of industrial fashion, ready-to-wear succeeded in democratizing a symbol of high distinction that was once very selective, available to few consumers: the label. Prior to the 1950s, in France, only a few haute couture houses had the privilege of being universally known; other couturiers had limited local reputations. The haute couture label and its immense notoriety were in striking contrast to the impersonality of industrial production. With the advent of ready-to-wear and its earliest advertising efforts came a mutation that was not only aesthetic but also symbolic. Industrial mass production emerged from anonymity; it became personalized as it won brand-name recognition, with names henceforth widely displayed on advertising billboards, in fashion magazines, in shopwindows, and on articles of clothing themselves. This democratic advancement and inflation of brand names constituted a major change of direction. Since the eighteenth and nineteenth centuries, the best-known names and the most prestigious ones had been identical; now, consumers commit to memory certain mass-market brand names at least as readily as high-status labels; examples in the French context might include Levi's, Rodier, New Man, Mic Mac, Marithé and François Girbaud, Lee Cooper, Manoukian, Benetton, Naf-Naf, and Jousse. This shift reflects the power of advertising, and above all the power of the industrial designer system, which succeeded in getting the public to recognize and covet clothing produced in huge quantities at accessible prices.

But the real revolution in the symbolic system of labeling came about with ready-to-wear creators. As early as the 1960s, with the designer phenomenon, new names came quickly to the fore, familiarizing the fashion world with labels as recognizable as those of haute couture. The fashion most prominent in the public eye was no longer the exclusive property of haute couture; the new-wave creators and designers who followed and continued to proliferate represented the dynamic spearhead of fashion from that point on. Their prototypes regularly made the front pages of the trade publications; their collections were the objects of reports and evaluations on the same basis as those of haute couture. The ready-to-wear system gave rise to a new breed of innovators, and at the same time to a new category of labels that were well known in various circles. Of course, they were not so prestigious as the great names from the heroic period of couture. Indeed, no single name today, including those from the realm of haute couture, can achieve the extraordinary international acclaim that went along with the hundred years' fashion; no single name can compete any longer with the Chanel or Dior effect. On the one hand we find a proliferation of labels, and on the other a tendency toward a lowering of prestige from which everyone can profit. But above all, we encounter a diversification of the underpinnings of the system of legitimacies: fame is no longer tied to the art of embodying the ne plus ultra of upper-class chic. The factors that allow creators and designers today to distinguish themselves from their competitors and to make their names known on the scene of elegance through the trade press are, increasingly, startling novelty, spectacular effects, departures from the norm, and emotional impact. In this period of eclectic legitimacies, creators whose collections depend on radically heterogeneous criteria can achieve equal notoriety. After the monopolistic and aristocratic system of haute couture, fashion has arrived at a democratic pluralism of labels.

If creators and certain brands of ready-to-wear are praised to the skies, haute couture labels for their part are less subject to idolatry and worship than before. Haute couture is gradually—slowly and unevenly from house to house—losing its position of lofty preeminence even as it comes to depend more and more on a politics of licensing contracts covering a wide range of articles. The decline in prestige is quite relative, moreover, as we can tell from the very comfortable—and rising—profit figures of the great houses that have been able to perpetuate and exploit the notoriety of the Parisian label worldwide. Nevertheless, the licensing mechanism and especially the appearance of new centers of creation have led to the destabilization of the label system, a shift in the social representation of brand names. Thus the women interviewed for a survey published in the September 1982 issue of *Elle* magazine did not make a meaningful distinction between the labels of couturiers, avant garde creators, and mass-market ready-to-wear. Kenzo stands next to Ted Lapidus and Cardin, Yves Saint-Laurent is cited alongside Cacharel, New Man, Karting, and Sonia Rykiel. The earlier pyramidal system is becoming blurred: for most people, telling brand names apart has become an uncertain exercise, and haute couture no longer occupies a position of unchallenged leadership. Clearly this does not mean that all brand names are equivalent: few consumers are unaware of the considerable variations in price that accompany the various labels. But despite the price discrepancies, a homogeneous hierarchy no longer presides over the fashion system; no longer does a single agency monopolize taste and the aesthetics of forms.

This erosion of status and value must not be mistaken for ideological mystification, as if society were deluding itself about the way the field of fashion is actually divided up. Quite to the contrary, the phenomenon is in a way an accurate social perception of the transformations of the fashion system disengaged from the strict regime of haute couture and devoted to the creativity of the designer system and a multiplicity of criteria for appearance. On the one hand, ready-to-wear brand names are taking on heightened dignity; on the other, haute couture is undergoing a relative decline in notoriety. In the world of fashion, the blurring of lines continues the secular work of the equalization of conditions. This democratization of labels does not entail a homogeneous leveling by any means; coteries and hierarchies remain, but except for small minorities the frontiers are less clear-cut and less stable. The democratic process in fashion does not wipe out symbolic differences among brands, but it does reduce extreme inequalities; it destabilizes the division between old-timers and newcomers, between the top level and the middle level, and it even allows certain mass-market articles to attain celebrity status.

From a Class Aesthetics to a Youth Aesthetics

The end of haute couture's symbolic preeminence has as its corollary the loss of its clientele. Some houses get a few dozen orders; the most highly rated may get a few hundred.[10] This is the harsh reality, in figures, of the present commercial situation of made-to-order couture. To be sure, the shrinking of its clientele cannot be separated either from haute couture's prohibitively high prices or from the fact that ready-to-wear now offers fashionable clothing of good quality, design, and originality at far lower cost (the average price of a designer's ready-to-wear dress is ten times lower than the price of a made-to-order haute couture dress). But no matter how significant the price factor may be, it does not suffice to explain why French haute couture has no more than three thousand clients worldwide. This apparently straightforward phenomenon warrants closer study. The example of the sociology of distinction might lead us to relate the decline of interest in haute couture to the restructuring of the dominant classes, to the emergence of a bourgeoisie typified by modernist and dynamic managers, a bourgeoisie that is defined less by economic capital than by "cultural capital" and that seeks more sober and more manifestly elitist signs in order to distinguish itself from the traditional bourgeoisie, in conformity with the primacy of the cultural capital that defines it and the "self-legitimacy" it procures.[11] But that would amount to offering only a partial explanation. The access of women to higher education and to professions at the managerial level cannot provide a fundamental explanation for the decline in prestige of ostentatious luxury in dress, a decline that originated largely in an earlier period. The cultural capital of the dominant classes is not the most crucial factor; at the heart of the reorientation of haute couture lies something more than the emergence of a class "sure enough of its own legitimacy not to need to wear emblems of its authority."[12] Assuming that the new bourgeoisie is indeed asserting itself more forcefully now than it did before, the mechanism that would allow its social legitimacy to neglect symbols of power is not clear. Quite to the contrary: even when it went unchallenged, the social hierarchy exhibited blatant signs of power and domination for thousands of years. And how could cultural capital on its own lead to the decline of marks of hierarchical superiority? As we have seen, the goal of understatement has its deepest roots less in symbolic—and episodic—class struggles than in the action, over time, of values that are consubstantial with modern society.

Through its very problematics, the sociology of distinction is deaf to long-term movements; it cannot account for the threads linking the new with the old. The current situation of haute couture is a case in point: on the one hand, unquestionably, today's haute couture has broken with the hundred years' fashion; on the other hand, today's haute couture appears as the culminating moment of an age-old tendency constitutive of democratic societies. There is historical discontinuity, indeed; but there is also, and to just as great an extent, an extraordinary consistency in the destiny of individual appearance, from the advent of the black dress suit for men to the contemporary desertion of made-to-order couture. The modern world could hardly have been propelled in that same direction, toward the reduction of insistent signs of appearance, if, over and above the interplay of symbolic class rivalries, consistent values providing direction to the desire for distinction had not come into play. If the logic of distinction were to govern the course of fashion in such a thorough way, we would see in fashion only chaos, momentary crazes, and sudden reversals. Yet that is hardly the case: over the long haul, modern fashion has obeyed an ordering principle, an influential tendency that is intelligible only when it is related to social and aesthetic goals that transcend class rivalry.

Inconspicuous consumption originates in the convergent action of a cluster of values including the egalitarian ideal, modern art, sports, and—closer to home—the new individualist ideal of the youthful look. Strategies for distinction have been not so much "creative" forces as instruments of this fundamental democratic movement, this synergistic constellation of new legitimacies that discredit strident markers of hierarchical superiority. The vogue for men's dark suits marked the break with the aristocratic imperative of lavish spending on clothes; thus men—who were in fact the first to enjoy modern democratic rights to the fullest—were the first to manifest the democratization of elegance. In the course of the twentieth century, women's fashion has come to align itself increasingly with the same democratic logic. With the demise of the made-to-order end of the couture spectrum, conspicuous consumption was definitively repudiated after the transitional moment represented, starting in the 1920s, by haute couture's euphemized but still luxurious fashion. After that, not only were flashy displays rejected, but the very principle of luxury apparel lost its prestige and its age-old legitimacy, its capacity to arouse women's admiration and acquisitive desire.

Women's fashion has been able to break free from the dominion of haute couture only with the help of the new values manifested by free societies in the stage of mass production and consumption. The universe of objects, media, and leisure has encouraged a hedonistic, juvenile mass culture to emerge; this culture is at the root of the ultimate decline of sumptuary fashion. The rise of a youth culture in the 1950s and 1960s

accelerated the diffusion of hedonistic values and helped give a new aspect
to individualist claims. This new culture proclaimed its nonconformity
and promoted new values: individual expression, relaxation, humor, and
spontaneity. The Courrèges effect, the success of "style," and the first
wave of ready-to-wear creators in the 1960s all reflect, within the fashion
system, the rise in the new contemporary values featuring rock stars and
youthful idols: within a few years, "juniors" had become the prototypes of
fashion. Aggressive forms, stylistic collages and juxtapositions, the careless look—such trends carried the day only because they were embodied in
a culture ruled by irony, play, emotional shock effects, and liberated
mores. Fashion began to connote youthfulness; it had to express an emancipated life-style, free of constraint, relaxed with respect to the official
canon. This mass-culture galaxy is what undermined haute couture's predominance; the idealized meaning of "youthfulness" led to a detachment
from luxury clothing, which was identified with the "old" world. Chic
good taste and the distinction and "class" of haute couture were discredited by a new value system that advocated the destruction of conventions,
that promoted boldness and complicity, that privileged ideas over accom-
plishments, emotional impact over virtuosity, youthfulness over social respectability. This new system brought about a major reversal in models of
behavior: "Before, a girl wanted to look like her mother. Today, it's the
other way around."[13] Looking younger than one's years became much
more important than exhibiting one's social rank: haute couture, with its
great tradition of refinement, its styles intended for adult women who have
"made it," was disqualified by the new requirement of modern individualism: a youthful appearance. The fate of haute couture did not depend on
the dialectic of social pretension and class distinction; it depended on the
age-old principle of the display of social excellence and its corollary, a
promotion of an age-based code imposed on everyone in the name of the
increasingly compelling code of individualism. Thus if individualist values
made a critical contribution to the birth of haute couture at the outset,
in a second phase they also lay behind the disaffection of its traditional
clientele.

Just as the requirement of dressing expensively was waning, all forms,
styles, and materials were becoming legitimate in fashion. Clothes could
be casual, crude, torn, worn, unstitched, sloppy, ripped, or frayed: all
these features, which had been strictly taboo, began to be incorporated
into the field of fashion. By recycling signs of "inferiority," fashion pursued its democratic dynamics, just as modern art and the avant-gardes
have done since the mid-nineteenth century. The modernist integration of
all subjects and materials into the noble field of art has as its counterpart
the democratic respectability of faded jeans, sloppy sweaters, threadbare
sneakers, "vintage" apparel, comic-strip graphics on T-shirts, ragged

clothing, the "down-and-out" look, and high-tech diversions. The process of desublimation that had begun in the 1920s came into its own. Elegance was reduced to a minimum; artificiality toyed with primitivism or the apocalypse; the "dressed-up" look was scrupulously avoided; the well-dressed look gave way to tattered pauperism; "class" appeal was replaced by irony and eccentricity. The end of conspicuous consumption in clothing and the introduction of humor and irreverence go hand in hand: together they mark the supreme stage in the democratization of fashion, the moment when fashion makes fun of itself, when elegance indulges in self-mockery. Only fashion photographs and the major fashion shows retained their magical dimensions and partly escaped the prevailing trend. The hushed ceremonial of haute couture pageants gave way to sound shows, unreal performances involving groups of models, hyperspectacular and fantastic podium effects—sublime advertising instruments for the artistic hallowing of labels. Still, this ultimate liturgy addressed to a select public did not exclude the process of democratic deidealization and proximity: not only did certain creators begin to open their shows to an undifferentiated public through paid admissions, but also, here and there, irony, humorous gags, and mockery were used to reduce tension and decrease the sophistication of the sacred ritual of showing a collection. Some of the models even appeared less canonical, less unreal, closer to ordinary standards. Fashion was emerging, however timidly, from the grandiose era of self-infatuation.

As long as haute couture kept the prestige of luxury clothing intact, as long as the assertion of hierarchical rank enjoyed de facto primacy over individual self-assertion, fashion remained at least partially dependent on a holistic social code. As soon as that primacy was discredited, not only aesthetically but socially, fashion completed its entry into a new phase governed wholly by the logic of individualism. Clothing was less and less a sign of social respectability. A new relation to the other appeared in which seduction prevailed over social representation. "People don't want to be elegant anymore; they want to be seductive."[14] The important thing was not to follow the latest fashion dictates as closely as possible; what counted was to valorize oneself, to please, astonish, disturb, and look youthful.

In youthful styles, a new principle of social imitation has gained currency. It has become less a matter of striving to present an image of one's social position or aspirations than to appear "in the know." Few people now seek to display their "success" through their clothes; but there are fewer still who do not make some effort to present a youthful and liberated self-image, not necessarily by adopting the latest thing in junior fashions, but by capturing the allure of youthfulness, the youthful gestalt. Even adults and the elderly have taken up sportswear, jeans, amusing T-shirts, sneakers, and the braless look. With the advance of youthful styles, mimesis has become democratic; it has shed its fascination with the aristocratic model that had prevailed through the ages. The exaltation of the youthful look is a new focal point for social imitation, inseparable from the modern democratic individualist age whose logic it carries to its narcissistic conclusion. All individuals are in fact urged to work on their own personal images, to adapt, to keep fit, to recycle themselves. The cult of youth and the cult of the body go hand in hand; they require the same constant self-scrutiny, the same narcissistic self-surveillance, the same need for information, and the same adaptation to novelty: "At forty, you become more serene, more yourself, and also more demanding. Your skin changes too. It needs special attention now; it needs appropriate care. . . . The time has come for you to adopt Lancaster's Hyperactive Treatments, specially designed to give your skin a more youthful look." An incontestable agent of social normalization and incitation to fashion, the imperative to appear youthful is also very much a vector of individualization: people owe it to themselves to pay closer attention to themselves.

The code of youthfulness contributes even more strikingly, in its way, to the pursuit of equality between the sexes. Under this code, men take better care of themselves, are more open to the novelties of fashion, care more about the way they look; in the process, they enter the narcissistic cycle that was once perceived as feminine. "Yves Saint-Laurent for Men. An elegant, masculine man, a man who cares how he feels, how he looks. He takes special care of his face, with a cleansing face cream and a moisturizing face cream, followed by the whole gamut of perfumed lotions." Men now spend nearly as much time as women caring for their bodies and looking after their appearance: a survey shows that while women are still ahead, the gap amounts to only about ten minutes a day, over an average of nine hours a week. And the most significant gap occurs not between women and men but between older men (twelve minutes thirty-five seconds a day) and male students (six minutes twenty seconds). In an astonishing reversal, in France older men now devote more time to personal care than older women.[15] Men and women have ceased to behave as opposites in the realm of personal care and appearance; the phase of maximal disjunction between the sexes has given way to a narcissistic democratization, in particular owing to the imperative of youthfulness.

Fashion in the Plural

The end of the hundred years' fashion coincided not only with the collapse of haute couture's hegemony, but also with the appearance of new centers of creativity and with the simultaneous proliferation and lack of coordination of fashion criteria. The earlier system had been characterized by a strong homogeneity of taste; the existence of relatively uniform annual trends could be attributed to the role and the preeminence of haute couture. The legendary hatreds and rivalries among the great couturiers, who all had their own recognizable styles, must not be allowed to obscure the profound consensus that governed fashion's operation throughout the entire period. Haute couture imposed a common aesthetic of grace; following its dictates, women were to dress becomingly, with delicacy and care, engaged in a common quest for "high class" and feminine charm. All aspired to be supreme embodiments of luxurious elegance and refined chic, valorizing a precious and ideal femininity. During the 1960s and 1970s, this aesthetic consensus was shattered by the rise of sportswear, marginal youthful fashions, and ready-to-wear creations: the homogeneity of the hundred years' fashion gave way to a patchwork of disparate styles. The process is most obvious at the level of seasonal creation: no doubt some similarities in shoulder width or hemline could still be found, here and there, in the seasonal collections, but what were once imperatives had become inessential options, treated freely according to the item and the whim of the designer. The phenomenon of seasonal trends, so noteworthy in the earlier phase, was undergoing a gentle meltdown. The hundred years' fashion had freed couturiers to be creative; nevertheless, their creativity was hemmed in by trade criteria and "perfectionism," aesthetic principles of distinction; they all had to follow the same lines. A further step was taken when fashion professionals achieved creative autonomy. We have now reached the age of proliferation and fragmentation of the canons of appearance, the juxtaposition of the most disparate styles. Modernism (Courrèges) and sexiness (Alaïa) are both legitimate, as are layered styles and close-fitting styles, short styles and long styles, the classically elegant look (Chanel) and the Hollywood vamp look (Mugler), ascetic monasticism (Rei Kawakubo) and the "monumental" woman (Montana), the "down-and-out" look (Comme des Garçons, World's End) and the refined look (Saint-Laurent, Lagerfeld), ironic mixtures of styles (Gaultier) and the "Japanese look" (Miyake, Yamamoto), vivid exotic colors (Kenzo) and dusty earth tones. Nothing is taboo any longer; all styles are accepted and exploited unsystematically. There is no longer a fashion, there are fashions.

This is the ultimate stage in the process of personalization of fashion that was started early on by haute couture but restrained by the dominant values of luxury and class refinement. A new era in the individualization of fashion has arrived, characterized by the new values of humanity, youthfulness, cosmopolitanism, casualness, and the appearance of poverty. Fashion erupts in unique and incomparable collections; designers all pursue their own paths by advancing their own particular criteria. In this way, fashion has come closer to sharing the logic of modern art, with its multidirectional experimentation, its absence of common aesthetic rules. The rule in fashion now, as in art, is one of free, untrammeled creation. Just as, in the contemporary theater, directors feel free to appropriate the official repertory and transgress it, abolishing the authority of the text and of any principles extrinsic to creation for the stage, designers have done away with the implicit reference to universal taste and have reinvested ironically and anarchically in styles from the past. The theater of texts has given way to a theater of images, intensities, and poetic shocks; fashion, for its part, has turned its back on discreet parades in haute couture salons in favor of the "podium effect," sound-and-light shows, the spectacle of astonishment. As Rei Kawakubo writes, "fashion has no reality except in stimulation."[16]

Even the private collections are no longer governed by the unity of style, positioning, and length that was so clearly apparent in the New Look, in Dior's A or Y lines, and in Saint-Laurent's trapeze line. Thus Kenzo characterizes his own style as consisting of four recurrent looks: first, the wide blouses that double as minidresses; next, the feminine, sweet, high-necked "Victorian" fashion; then there is the "doll" look, amusing, pretty, and gay; and finally, the "boyish" look, sporting and masculine. According to Kenzo, each of his collections is based on these four looks. Eclecticism is the supreme stage of creative freedom. Short skirts no longer exclude long ones; designers can play at will with shapes, lengths, and widths. "External" unity is no more required in a collection than it is in a contemporary stage setting, with its multiple, nested "readings," its references to all periods and contexts, its heterogeneous "collages." The principle established by Dior according to which collections have themes no doubt remains intact, but the themes now serve only as motifs for free or metaphorical inspiration; they no longer function as exclusive formal rules. Nothing counts but the spirit of the collections, the poetic value of the label, the wide-open field available to artistic creativity.

The fragmentation of the fashion system still holds despite the emergence of the historically unprecedented phenomenon of youthful, marginal styles based on criteria unknown to professional fashion. After the Second World War, the first minority youth fashions appeared ("zazous," Saint-Germain-des-Prés, beatniks); these early "antifashions" took on new scope and meaning in the 1960s. With later trends—hippie, "baba," punk, new wave, Rasta, ska, skinhead—the codes proliferated by way of the anticonformist youth culture, which had multiple manifestations in dress and appearance and also in values, tastes, and behavior. The exacerbated nonconformity of this youth culture had its roots not only in strategies of differentiation with respect to the world of adults and other youth, but also, more profoundly, in the development of mass hedonistic values and in young people's desire for emancipation in connection with the progress of the democratic individualist ideal. Historically speaking, what matters most is that the impetus for these trends came from outside the bureaucratic system that characterizes modern fashion. Certain segments of civil society thus seized the initiative in the realm of appearance; they attained a degree of autonomy that revealed an astonishing social creativity in the area of fashion, a creativity that was a major source of inspiration for professional designers as they renewed the spirit of their collections.

The youthful fashions stamped personal appearance with a strongly individualist character, triggering a wave of something like a neodandyism that consecrated the extreme importance of appearance. Neodandies set themselves radically apart from the ordinary; they play on provocation, excess, and eccentricity in order to displease, surprise, or shock. As with classical dandyism, what is at stake here is increasing distance, separating oneself from the herd, provoking astonishment, cultivating personal originality. There is just one difference: with neodandyism it is no longer a matter of displeasing in order to please, of seeking social recognition by way of scandal or the unexpected; rather, neodandies seek to make the most drastic break possible with dominant codes of taste and appropriateness. The reserved, sober costume of a Brummell, the high-life quest for refinement and nuance in the choice of tie or gloves—such manifestations are over and done with. Neodandyism functions by means of outrageous marginality, exoticism and folklore (hippies), the blurring of distinctions between the sexes (long hair for men). Neodandies let themselves go, exaggerating ugliness and repulsiveness (punk) or ethnic self-assertion (Rasta, Afro). Personal appearance is no longer an aesthetic sign of supreme distinction, a mark of individual excellence; it has become a comprehensive symbol designating an age group, existential values, a life-style independent of social class, a culture at a breaking point, a form of social challenge. Through their excesses, these fashions undoubtedly entail a break with ordinary appearance; nevertheless, in one sense they merely announce and accompany—however spectacularly—a general tendency to want to be less dependent on the official dictates of fashion. These youthful fashions have to be viewed less as absolute deviations than as mirrors of a wave of generalized individualization of fashion behavior characteristic of a new age of personal appearance.

The expression "antifashion" has been used in this connection, but the term is not entirely satisfactory. To be sure, norms openly hostile to those of the official canon have found social expression; however, far from destroying the principle of fashion, they have simply made its overall architecture more complex and more diverse. The new era of fashion entails the combining of absolutely incompatible criteria, the coexistence of professional parameters and "wild" criteria, the disappearance of a legitimate standard imposed on the entire social edifice. We have reached the end of the consensual age of appearances. Thus fashion can no longer be defined as a system ruled by an accumulation of small nuances, since radically dissident codes that can lay claim even to ugliness are juxtaposed with the system of countless small differentiating details of elegance. On the one hand, there are fewer and fewer clear-cut divergences in clothing styles from class to class and between the sexes; on the other hand, extreme dissimilarities are returning, in particular in the minority fashions of young people and in those of the "adventurous" stylists. Unlike avant-garde art, contemporary fashion is not running out of steam; its horizons are not bounded by either homogeneity or repetitiveness.

Obligatory trends are behind us, while canons of elegance have proliferated and youthful styles have emerged; the fashion system has unquestionably moved beyond the normative, uniform cycle that, in spite of the process of aesthetic diversification unleashed by haute couture, continued to link the hundred years' fashion with the age of the fashion trades. With its polymorphous fragmentation, the new fashion system turns out to be fully compatible with the "open society" that is more or less universally instituting the reign of à la carte formulas, flexible rules, overabundant choice, and generalized self-service. The controlling imperative of seasonal trends has yielded to the juxtaposition of styles; the injunctive and uniform mechanism of the hundred years' fashion has given way to an optional and playful logic in which one chooses not only among different clothing designs, but among the most incompatible principles of appearance. This is *open fashion*, the second phase of modern fashion, with its heteromorphic codes, its nondirectivity, its supreme ideal known in France as *le look*. Running counter to all aligned fashions, including the antiseptic preppie code and the code of casualness, the "in" look of the 1980s encourages the sophistication of appearances, the free invention and alteration of one's self-image; it reintroduces artifice, play, and singularity.[17] All the same, there is no reason to speak of a Copernican revolution in looks.[18] In reality, the age of *le look* is nothing but the end point of the individualist dynamic that has been consubstantial with fashion from its earliest moments; it only carries to the extreme the taste for singularity, theatricality, and difference that the earlier eras also manifested, even though clearly in quite different ways and within much narrower limits. From Henri III's *mignons* to the nineteenth-century dandies, from the *lionnes* to the tastemakers of contemporary fashion, anticonformism, fantasy, and the desire to be noticed have not lacked practitioners at the higher levels of society. *Le look* constitutes less a break with this age-old individualist "tradition" than an exacerbation of it. Everyone is invited, now, to decompartmentalize styles, to blend them, to do away with stereo-

types and copies, to abandon rules and fossilized conventions. In this respect the hedonistic and hyperindividualist ethic generated by the latest
developments in consumer society is registered in the world of fashion. *Le
look*, intoxicated with artifice and the spectacular, with individual creation, is a response to a society in which the primordial cultural values are
pleasure and individual freedom. What is valued is the deviation, the creative personality, the astonishing image, rather than, as before, the perfection of a design. Linked to the rise of pop psychology, to the desire for
increased independence and self-expression, *le look* represents the theatrical face of the neonarcissism that is allergic to standardized imperatives
and homogeneous rules. On the one hand, the contemporary Narcissus is
in search of interiority, authenticity, psychic intimacy; on the other hand,
he tends to rehabilitate the spectacle of self, playful and out-of-phase exhi-
bitionism, the celebration of appearances. With *le look*, fashion is becoming young again; it has only to play with the ephemeral, to erupt without
complexes in the ecstasy of its own freely invented and freely renewed
image. It enjoys the pleasures of metamorphosis in the spiral of fanciful
personalization, in the baroque play of individualist overdifferentiation,
in the artificialist spectacle of the self offered to the gaze of the other.

Masculine/Feminine

The hundred years' fashion relied on a pronounced opposition between
the sexes in terms of personal appearance, backed up by a production
system in which fashion creation for women obeyed different imperatives
from creation for men. In this system, the feminine pole embodied the
changeable essence of fashion in all its glory. Since the 1960s, various
transformations of unequal importance have altered this age-old distribution of masculine and feminine roles. On the organizational level, for example, in the early 1960s, the feminine sanctuary of haute couture invaded
the masculine sector. Certain creators and designers for their part now
produce avant-garde men's ready-to-wear lines. Although some collections feature male and female models indiscriminately, the most prestigious haute couture labels have launched advertising campaigns for toilet
water and beauty products for men. After a long period of exclusion,
marked by the conservative dark suit, men are "back in style."

But the real novelty lies chiefly in the extraordinary development of
sportswear. With mass leisure apparel, men's clothing has made its authentic entrance into the cycle of fashion, marked by frequent changes,
compulsory originality, and playfulness. Moving away from austere stiff-
ness and dark or neutral colors, men's clothing has taken a step in the
direction of women's fashion by integrating fantasy as one of its basic

parameters. Bright, cheerful colors are no longer inappropriate; underwear, shirts, jackets, and tennis attire all now allow a free play of color in
multiple combinations. T-shirts and sweatshirts display amusing texts
and drawings; features that are comic, childlike, or unserious are no
longer off-limits to men. "Life is too short to dress drably": while signs of
death are vanishing from the public arena, the clothing of both sexes is
attuned to the mass happiness characteristic of consumer society. The disjunction between the sexes that characterized the hundred years' fashion
has been replaced by a gradual reduction of the gap in dress styles. This
process can be observed on the one hand in the at least partial inclusion of
men's clothing in the euphoric logic of fashion, and on the other hand in
women's increasingly widespread adoption, since the 1960s, of men's
clothing styles (pants, jeans, jackets, tuxedos, ties, boots). The emphatic
and obligatory dichotomy in personal appearance between the sexes is
being blurred; we see equality of conditions progressing as it ends the
female monopoly of fashion and partially "masculinizes" the feminine
wardrobe.

This development certainly does not mean that fashion no longer has its
privileged locus in the feminine sphere. Even if haute couture and the
designers do present collections for men, the women's collections are the
ones that continue to make certain houses and designers famous, and they
are the ones that are discussed and advertised, for the most part, in fashion
magazines. Creators like Jean-Paul Gaultier have made efforts to speed up
the promotion of the "male object" by creating an avant-garde male fashion with no holds barred; however, this fashion remains highly circumscribed, or at all events less varied, less spectacular, than women's fashion.
In men's attire, two antithetical logics coexist: the fashion of sportswear
and the "nonfashion" of the classic costume, fanciful dress for leisure time
and the sober, conservative suit and tie for work. Such a dissociation does
not occur as such in women's wear, where fanciful fashion enjoys much
wider social legitimacy. The opposition that, in France at least, governs
feminine fashion operates less between leisure dress and work clothes than
between daytime wear, which is more or less "practical," and evening attire, which is more dressed-up or elaborate. If men's attire can be seen as
precisely embodying the opposition between hedonistic values and technocratic values that characterizes capitalist societies, for French women
the privilege of fashion sets aside that disjunction in favor of a permanent
right to frivolity, even though in the workplace that right is undeniably
somewhat muted.

Men's clothing has become less austere, while women's clothing shows
increasing signs of masculine origin; still, these phenomena do not justify
a diagnosis of uniformity in fashion, or the eventual disappearance of gen-
der-linked fashions. Men may have long hair; many women wear clothing

that originates in masculine styles; there are unisex garments and unisex stores; but all this is far from sufficient to support the idea of a final unification of fashion. What are we seeing, then? Unquestionably, a gradual reduction of the emphatic difference between masculine and feminine forms, a movement that is essentially democratic in nature. But the process of "equalization" in clothing quickly betrays its limits. It is not pursued to the very end, to the complete abolition of all difference; its culmination is not—as one might logically expect, extrapolating from the egalitarian dynamic—a radical unisex identity. While women are turning in vast numbers to masculine clothing styles and men are reappropriating their right to a certain level of fantasy in dress, new distinctions are arising that reconstitute the cultural cleavage in the realm of appearance. Homogenization of men's and women's fashion exists only at the level of the superficial survey; in reality, fashion has not stopped incorporating differentiating signs—which may be minor without being inessential—into a system in which it is precisely the "little nothing that makes all the difference." Just as an item of clothing may be out of fashion, may please or displease depending on some minimal nuance, so a single detail can suffice to discriminate between the sexes. Examples abound: men and women alike wear pants, but the cuts and often the colors are different; shoes have nothing in common; a woman's shirt is easy to tell from a man's; the shapes of bathing suits differ, and so do those of underwear, belts, pocketbooks, watches, and umbrellas. More or less everywhere, fashion articles reinscribe difference in appearance by way of "little nothings." That is why short hairstyles, pants, suit coats, and boots have never succeeded in desexualizing women; these features are always adapted to the specificity of the feminine, reinterpreted for women in view of their difference. If clear-cut class distinctions in appearance are being lost, the division between the sexes remains, except perhaps for certain categories of adolescents and young people who wear more frankly androgynous clothing. But as these cohorts age, the masculine/feminine distribution tends to reassert itself. The representation of gender difference is proving much sturdier than the representation of social class. The marking of social identity by way of clothing has been blurred, but not that of sexual identity, although it is true that sexual dimorphism no longer has the pronounced character it manifested in the hundred years' fashion. The originality of the process that is under way lies precisely here: the progressive, undeniable tendency toward the reduction of extremes does not culminate in the unification of appearances, but in a *subtle differentiation*, something like the minimal distinctive opposition between the sexes. Differences of appearance between the sexes are becoming less blatant, but with the reduction of distance, discreet oppositions are coming to light. It would be a serious mistake to view the horizon of the democratic movement as one of sexual indistinction or nondifferentiation. The democratization of fashion functions by way of the interminable reproduction of small disjunctive oppositions, of coded differentiations that may be minor or optional but are nevertheless intended to designate gender identity and to eroticize the body.

The process of minimal differentiation between the sexes is paralleled by a process of *obvious differentiation* via exclusively *feminine* markers such as dresses, skirts, women's suits, stockings, pumps, makeup, depilatories, and so on. The variable geometry of fashion now permits a system of major oppositions to coexist with a system of minor ones; that dual logic is what characterizes open fashion, rather than the alleged generalization of unisex trends whose sphere, strictly speaking, remains circumscribed and whose elements are often associated in one way or another with sex-linked signs. There is no cause for alarm: the end point of the democratic age is not androgyny. With its juxtaposed codes of major and minor differentiation, the separation of the sexes in the realm of dress persists; it has fallen into step with the optional à la carte systems.

In the new gender-based constellation of appearance, the positions occupied by women and men are not equivalent; a structural dissymmetry continues to organize the world of fashion. While women can allow themselves to wear virtually anything, can include items of masculine origin in their wardrobe, men for their part are subject to a restrictive code based on the exclusion of feminine emblems. Here is the most important point: under no circumstances may men wear dresses or skirts, or use makeup. Behind the liberalization of mores and the destandardization of roles, an intangible prohibition still continues to organize the system of appearances at the deepest levels with a power of subjective internalization and social imposition that has few equivalents elsewhere. Dress and makeup are, at least for now, the property of the feminine; they are strictly forbidden to men. Here is proof that fashion is not a system of generalized commutation in which everything is exchanged in the indeterminacy of codes, in which all signs are "free to commutate and permutate without limits."[19] Fashion does not eliminate all referential content; it does not send reference points floating off toward equivalence and total commutability. The antinomy between masculine and feminine remains in force as a rigorous structural opposition in which the terms are anything but exchangeable. The taboo that presides over masculine fashion is so integral, it enjoys such a degree of collective legitimacy, that no one would dream of challenging it; it does not give rise to protest movements or serious attempts at rebellion. Only Jean-Paul Gaultier has gone so far as to present skirt-pants for men, but more as a provocative publicity stunt than as a quest for a new male fashion; the endeavor has had no effect on the way men actually dress. It could not have been otherwise: a skirt worn by a man appears immediately as a "perverse" emblem; the effect is inevitably burlesque and parodic. The masculine appears condemned to play indefinitely at being masculine.

Is this a vestigial condition destined to disappear, as the movement toward equality gathers momentum and the values of individual autonomy prevail? Nothing is less certain. It is true that the appearance of both men and women has been considerably altered since the 1960s. In addition to women's widespread adoption of pants, men can now wear long hair, bright colors, and earrings. But the movement toward convergence has done nothing to dislodge the underlying taboo that prevails in men's fashion. The inegalitarian logic of fashion remains the rule: the boyish look for women has gained social recognition, but unless men are willing to risk laughter and scorn, they cannot adopt the emblems of femininity. In the West, dresses have been identified with women for six hundred years; this age-old factor is not without effect. If dresses are off-limits to men, this is because dresses are culturally associated with femininity and thus, for us, with fashion, whereas since the nineteenth century masculinity has been defined, as least in part, in contradistinction to fashion, to the ephemeral and the superficial. For men to adopt feminine symbols in dress would be to transgress, in the realm of appearance, the very essence of modern masculine identity. We have not reached that point, and no sign of the times leads us to anticipate any shift in that direction. Despite the multiple forms of its democratization, fashion remains essentially inegalitarian, at least where gender is concerned. The masculine pole still occupies the inferior, stable position, as opposed to the free, protean mobility of the feminine pole. The new fashion system, however open it may be, has by no means abandoned all continuity with the previous arrangements; it reintroduces the feminine preeminence of the hundred years' fashion in new ways. Today, as before, the play of charm and dramatic metamorphosis is off-limits to men. The masculine remains inseparable from a process of individual and social identification that minimizes the principle of artifice and play, in a direct line from the "great renunciation" of the nineteenth century.

This continuity on the masculine side corresponds to an even deeper continuity on the feminine side. Since the 1960s, to be sure, the female silhouette has undergone a decisive "revolution," with the widespread wearing of pants. Still, however significant this phenomenon may be, it has by no means discredited the traditional female emblems of dress. In 1985, 19.5 million pairs of women's pants were sold; but so were 37 million dresses and skirts. Over a ten-year period, the average rhythm of pants purchases increased (in 1975, women purchased 13 million pairs), but the same is true of skirts and dresses (in 1975, 25 million were sold). Since 1981, dress sales have weakened, but skirt sales have risen. Dresses and skirts accounted for 13.4 percent of clothing purchases in 1953 and 16 percent in

1984: if large numbers of women have taken to wearing pants, they have by no means abandoned the properly feminine component of their wardrobe. Pants did not gradually replace the archetypical women's attire; they appeared alongside traditional clothing as a supplementary option. The persistence of a specifically feminine wardrobe must not be construed as a vestige destined to disappear, but as the condition of greater and more varied freedom in dress. This is why dresses keep on evolving, despite the gains made by pants. The maintenance of dresses does not signify a return to staking out a minority position for women, but just the opposite: it signifies the aspiration to increased choice and autonomy in clothing. This aspiration devolves directly, of course, from the classical feminine passion for modifying personal appearance, but it also derives from the optional contemporary individualism. At the same time, dresses allow the female body to be valorized in specific ways: it can be rendered ethereal, virtuous, or sexy; legs can be displayed; the attractions of the figure can be emphasized; dresses can facilitate flirtatiousness as well as discretion. If dresses have not been subject to collective disaffection, it is because they belong to an open tradition, one that is endlessly renewed by fashion in answer to women's most fundamental objectives in the realm of appearances: seduction and metamorphosis.

The continuity in which women's fashion is inscribed is even more manifest if we consider makeup and other beauty products. Since the end of the First World War, modern societies have experienced a constant increase in the consumption of cosmetics, an extraordinary democratization of beauty products, and an unprecedented vogue for makeup. Lipstick, perfume, cream, blush, eyeshadow, and nail polish are all mass-produced industrially and inexpensively; after thousands of years during which they were luxury items reserved to a tiny elite, they have become popular consumer items used more and more frequently in all classes of society.[20] There have been changes, of course, in the market for beauty products. The market currently registers an increased preference for skin-care products as opposed to makeup. But there is still a strong popular demand for makeup bases and products for nails, lips, and eyes. Men's colognes and aftershave lotions are increasingly successful, although in 1982 men's products still represented only one billion of the eleven billion francs of French profits from perfume and cosmetics. No matter how much women's preferences may be shifting and the men's segment growing, makeup still remains an exclusively female practice that appeals even to quite young girls; the amount of eye and lip makeup used by this sector has increased over the last several years. Among the host of hedonistic and narcissistic values, makeup has acquired broad social legitimacy; it no longer marks young people as part of a "bad lot," but at the most connotes "poor taste"; young girls who use makeup are subject to no more con-

demnation than mature women are. On the other hand, the use of eye
makeup by men remains marginal, limited to a small number of young
people. Naturalness, casualness, and practicality are more and more the
rule in fashion, yet makeup is still in continuing demand: here is proof not
of the power of the advertising artillery, but of the effectiveness of the
timeless valorization of feminine beauty. Women's social emancipation
has by no means led the "second sex" to stop using cosmetics; at most, we
can see a growing tendency toward discretion in makeup, along with a
desire for embellishment on the part of the majority.

Beauty products and makeup, like female coquetry itself, have en-
dured. In France, the hyperfeminist moment that denounced women's en-
trapment by fashion has had only superficial effects; it has not succeeded
in overturning the age-old strategies of feminine seductiveness. By the
mid-1980s, denunciation of "woman-as-object" was no longer in style; it
no longer had authentic social reverberations. But did it ever? Have we
come full circle? In reality, feminine frivolousness does not so much perpetuate a traditional image as it contributes to bringing about a new figure
of the feminine in which claiming the right to charm does not preclude
claiming the right to work and responsibility. Women have conquered the
right to vote, the right to sex, the right to free procreation, the right to a full
range of professional activity; at the same time, they have retained the
ancestral privilege of coquetry and seductiveness. It is this patchwork that
defines the French "adult woman," who is constituted by the juxtaposition
of once-contradictory principles. That a woman likes fashion no longer
implies that she is submitting to destiny; self-adornment and beautifica
tion no longer have anything to do with alienation. It does not make sense
to keep on speaking of manipulation or reification when a large majority
of women declare that, far from "oppressing" them, the proliferation of
cosmetics gives them more independence, more freedom to please whom-
ever they wish to please, whenever they like and however they like.[21] Making themselves beautiful has become a way for women to play with the
archetype of femininity, a form of second-degree frivolousness in which
the desire to please and detached self-awareness are juxtaposed. Glamour
has been pried loose from ceremonial rituals; it is celebrated in conscious
fantasies that make multiple references and allusions. Through dress
and makeup, women play at being vamps, stars, tuned-in trendsetters,
"women's women." They reappropriate styles, airs, myths, and epochs at
will; seduction has a good time and enjoys its own spectacle without taking
itself too seriously. Like messages in consumer society, fashion and seduc
tion have given up their earlier earnestness; from now on they function
largely by way of humor, pleasure, and playful spectacles.

The persistent disjunction between the sexes has echoes even in the new
dominant figure of contemporary individuality that men and women now

share, psychological and corporeal narcissism. The new narcissism does entail a blurring of previous gender roles and identities in favor of a vast "unisex" wave of personal autonomy and attention to self, along with hyperattention to the body, health, and personal relationships. But we can see that this destabilization of the gender divide does not entail a straightforward homogeneous narcissism once we take into account the way people relate specifically to aesthetics. Male neonarcissism views the body primarily as an undifferentiated reality, an overall image to be maintained in good health and good shape. Men take little interest in details; few specific areas of the body mobilize aesthetic concern, except for certain inevitably critical areas: facial wrinkles, the "gut," thinning hair. What counts above all for men is conserving the gestalt of a slender, dynamic young body through sports or dieting; male narcissism is more synthetic than analytic.

In contrast, for women the cult of the self is structurally fragmented. A woman's image of her body is rarely global; the analytic gaze predominates over the synthetic. Young women as well as mature women see themselves in "parts." There is ample evidence of this in letters published in women's magazines: "I am sixteen years old. My skin is awful—I have blackheads and pimples all over." "I've just turned forty. I really don't look my age, except for my upper eyelids—they're slightly wrinkled, and they make me look sad." "I'm 5′2″ and I weigh 108 pounds, but my hips and stomach are too big." All zones of the female body count; analytic narcissism breaks down the face and body into distinct elements, each endowed with a more or less positive value: nose, eyes, lips, skin, shoulders, breasts, hips, buttocks, and legs are all objects of self-evaluation, a self-surveillance that entails specific personal practices designed to enhance or correct a given body part. This analytic narcissism is essentially rooted in the preponderant force of the code of feminine beauty. The value placed on women's beauty sets off an inevitable process of comparison among women, a careful scrutiny of one's own physique in relation to the recognized canons, an evaluation of all body parts with nothing left out. If fashion in dress is now polymorphous, if its norms have a much less restrictive character, the celebration of female physical beauty, in contrast, has lost none of its power. It has even been reinforced, generalized, and universalized, along with the desire for a youthful appearance, the parallel development of casual clothes, beach attire, and sportswear, and the proliferation of stars and pinups on display in the media. "'Fat is beautiful!" "Ugly is beautiful!" Such are the new watchwords of minority demands, the ultimate democratic avatars of the quest for personality. So be it; but who actually makes such claims? Who believes them? The chances that such voices will move beyond the stage of dissident symptom look virtually nil when we see the depth of the phobia against gaining weight, the growing success of cosmetic products, of weight-loss techniques and diets: the passionate desire to be beautiful remains widespread. Men are unquestionably more preoccupied now than they once were with their waistlines, their skin, their appearance; this transformation, among others, serves to confirm the hypothesis of male neonarcissism. But the ideal of beauty does not have the same impact on men as it does on women. It has different implications for the relation to the body, different functions in individual self-identification, and different social and personal valorizations. The exaltation of feminine beauty reinstitutes a major division between the sexes at the very heart of mobile and "transsexual" narcissism, a division that is not merely aesthetic but also cultural and psychological.

There is a dissymmetry between masculine and feminine appearance. We need to take another look at the dichotomy, which may be optional and imprecise but which remains enigmatic in relation to the historical thrust of modern democracies. The social meaning of equality has undermined the idea that human beings are fundamentally heterogeneous. The principle of equality is at the root of the representation of the sovereignty of the people and of universal suffrage; it has contributed to the emancipation of women, to the destabilization of roles, statuses, and identities. However, it has not succeeded in uprooting the "will" of both sexes to manifest their differences by superficial signs. Even as the most obvious symbols of the division between the sexes are weakening (with the emergence of a feminine fashion that has room for straight lines, short hair, and trousers), others are arising, countering the democratic tendency to bring extremes closer together: examples include the demand for lipstick after the First World War, for nail polish after 1930, for eye makeup starting in the 1950s. It is as if the principle of equality had come up against a threshold, as if the democratic ideal had come into conflict with the imperative of gender differentiation. Here we encounter one of the historical limits of the idea of equality of conditions and its progressive reduction of substantive forms of human difference.[22] We all recognize ourselves as having a common nature, and we all claim the same rights; yet we do not want to look like members of the opposite sex. Tocqueville wrote that "in democratic ages even those who are not alike are bent on becoming so and copy each other."[23] Where gender-related fashion is concerned, that statement is clearly unacceptable: when women wear pants, they are not seeking to resemble men, they are attempting to offer a different image of women, freer in their movements, sexier or more casual—not mimicry of the other, but reaffirmation of a more subtle difference accentuated by the particular cut of clothes or the signs conveyed by makeup. Yet the persistence of a gender-based disjunction in appearance marks something like a failure of the egalitarian dynamic, which cannot succeed in taking the final steps toward eliminating difference.

This stubborn resistance to the trend toward equality betrays the power of an ancient antinomic social principle, the sacralization of feminine beauty. Ever since the days of the ancient Egyptians and Greeks, among whom the aesthetic use of makeup is attested, women have presumably always used beauty products as part of their toilette, although proportions have varied. Makeup becomes a ritual women use to make themselves more beautiful, to be desirable and charming, even though beauty products have been regularly subject to denigration and disapproval. What is astonishing is that despite the endless religious and moral denunciations that the use of cosmetics has elicited for thousands of years, their use has continued to be valorized and practiced by women, not only by courtesans and older women but by the female population at large. Neither the misogyny of mores nor the Christian dogma of sin has kept women from being coquettish, from seeking to appear beautiful and pleasing. By what miracle could equality succeed in putting an end to such a durable phenomenon that nothing else has managed to interrupt? Why would women give up the timeless rituals of seduction, when from the Middle Ages and the Renaissance on feminine beauty has found itself increasingly rehabilitated and exalted? With the cult of feminine beauty and the repudiation of the image of woman as Satan, women's desire to embellish themselves, to please, takes on profound social legitimacy. By this token, modern societies rest not only on the principle of equality among human beings, but also on the inegalitarian principle of the "fair sex": beauty remains an attribute, a specific feminine value; it is admired, encouraged, and displayed in ample proportions by women, and not very much by men. The democratic movement of societies seems powerless to block this calling to please, this inegalitarian celebration of feminine beauty as well as the ancestral means for enhancing it. In modern societies, we have even witnessed a reinforcement of the prestige and the requirement of feminine beauty, with the cult of stars and pinups, the importance of sex appeal, the mass production of cosmetics, the proliferation of beauty institutes and magazines offering aesthetic advice, the national and international beauty contests that sprang up after the First World War. The persistent inequality in the means of seduction and in the appearance of the sexes stems essentially from this unequal valorization of the feminine aesthetic. A culture of the "fair sex" could hardly avoid seeking to put beauty in the foreground, along with specific fashions intended to valorize the female body and face. Is this a stage on the way to the definitive triumph of equality in appearance? If we note the prosperity of the cosmetics industry along with recent developments in fashion and advertising images, we find nothing to justify an affirmative response. On the contrary, there is every reason to imagine the perpetuation of a system characterized by two antithetical systems of logic, egalitarian and inegalitarian, allowing for greater personalization of feminine appearance in keeping with the hyperindividualist values of our time. To be sure, the principle of equality is working to wipe out differences, but the ideal of individuality is working to reinscribe them: the code of the "fair sex," which specifically helps produce difference and valorize aesthetic individuality, still has some good days ahead. While the ideal of equality will undoubtedly continue to move the two sexes closer together in appearance, the sacralization of feminine beauty, for its part, will have the effect of reproducing new differentiations in fashion and seduction rituals.

The limit encountered by the egalitarian dynamic extends beyond the sphere of fashion, for it involves the subjective representation of the ego. In the modern era, the essential similarity of women and men is recognized, certainly, by both sexes—so long as we add, paradoxically, that this essential likeness does not preclude a feeling of anthropological otherness. It is not true that owing to the principle of equality sexual identities have been marginalized, relegated to the background in relation to a fundamental substantive identity. Ideologically, we might say, we are alike; but intimately and psychologically we all immediately identify with our own sex: we see ourselves first of all in our difference as men or women. This is not a superficial phenomenon, even in the context of the immense disruption provoked by the democratic social order: what is at stake here is the very image of the self, of one's own identity, one's most intimate reference points in relation to others, to one's own body and one's own desires. The undoing of social alterity by democratic equality is stymied in this instance, to such an extent that one can doubt the real power of the egalitarian ideal to penetrate the depths of subjective existence. May we not see contemporary feminism and its specific demands, the explosion of feminine writing, the countless speeches and statements made by women, as social symptoms of this limit to equality? The distinctive feature of equality is not that it puts a profound ideological identity tidily in place, it is that it engenders an essential similarity between the sexes that is nevertheless accompanied by a personal feeling of difference. We are alike and not alike, indissociably, and we cannot tell where the anthropological difference lies; we cannot fix the dividing line cleanly. Such is the astonishing outcome of the equality that destines us not to likeness but to indeterminacy, to the intimate juxtaposition of contraries, and to an endless questioning of sexual identity.

A Fashion for Living

While the reference points for legitimate appearance are being fragmented, new individual and collective tastes are emerging that represent a break with what came before. Neonarcissism is the chief characteristic of contemporary personalities. Even though the hundred years' fashion fostered an expansion of the taste for originality and vastly increased the number of available styles of dress, that fashion system developed in a unified, orderly way: it maintained the traditional primacy of overall aesthetic conformity, the classic "despotism" of fashion. Under the rule of haute couture and fashion magazines, annual and seasonal trends were imposed as so many diktats. In order to be fashionable, one had to adopt the latest trends as quickly as possible; one had to change one's wardrobe according to the whims of the great couturiers and up-to-date women. Open fashion marks the end of this uniform, disciplinary "central planning," the end of the unprecedented gap that had come to exist between innovation and diffusion, between the creative avant-garde and consumers. Now the "street" is no longer mesmerized by fashion leaders; it incorporates novelties only selectively and at its own pace. Where appearance is concerned, the public has acquired a heightened power to select and reject, a power that reflects the individualist escalation of the quest for personal autonomy.

The miniskirt fad in the mid-1960s was doubtless the first link in this process of becoming autonomous. Here was a fashion that no longer took as a model the classic thirty-year-old woman, but rather a fifteen- to twenty-year-old girl. A rift between "the latest thing" and mass diffusion was becoming inevitable; past a certain age, women rejected miniskirts as clearly not intended for them, as decidedly too unflattering. Manifestations of independence with respect to the latest canons continued to proliferate: the "maxiskirt" introduced at the end of the 1960s did not really catch on, and the most noteworthy innovations of the 1970s barely crossed the borders of a very narrow province. Where did one see the very square shoulders introduced in the late 1970s by Mugler and Montana? Who wore the multiple layers of the Japanese designers? Today, no new style succeeds in taking over instantly in the street. Extreme diversity from one creator to another and an increased desire for autonomy among consumers have led to more detached and more relative behavior with respect to flagship fashions. One is more or less aware of the latest look at the beach, but one does not copy it slavishly; one adapts it for oneself, and one may even ignore it altogether in favor of an entirely different style. The situation is paradoxical: whereas avant-garde creations are increasingly spectacular, mass diffusion is increasingly placid, affected only gradually by innovations at the top (broad shoulders began to appear widely some ten years after they were introduced). These are the defining characteristics of open fashion: the public has gained a new level of autonomy with respect to fashion trends, while prestigious styles have lost much of their dictatorial power.

Thus the propagation of fashion has been curiously slowed down, after a long phase of acceleration and synchronic adoption. The phenomenon is sufficiently unusual in the sphere of fashion to warrant emphasis. Fashion now progresses globally without feverish haste, without any pressure for instant assimilation. Not that fashion is suffering from burnout or any deficit in creativity; the change it has undergone is not so radical. Rather, a double logic has been established, a dual system in the world of appearances. On one side, the supply issues forth as precipitously and changeably as ever. On the other side, there is a demand that is no longer dependable; it is "liberated," it no longer falls into line. A cycle has ended: fashion in dress, which for centuries had been the very symbol of rapid changes in adoption and diffusion, has slowed down to cruising speed. Increasing individual autonomy, far from producing increasingly rapid change in tastes and styles, inclines rather to a certain frivolous "wisdom," generates a certain moderating force among consumers.

In the new era of slowed-down fashion, the earlier clear-cut opposition between what was outdated and what was in fashion has been undermined, its borders blurred. No doubt there is still such a thing as "the latest thing," but its social perception is less clear, for the latest thing is lost in a plethoric confusion of creators and diversified looks. Most people no longer know just what is in the forefront among novelties. Fashion increasingly resembles a vague set that can be known only imprecisely and from a distance. At the same time, unfashionableness is moving to a less extreme position: even if the notion is not disappearing, it has become less clear; it is less hastily attributed, and conveys less ridicule. When all lengths and widths are possible, when multitudes of styles go side by side, when vintage clothing is in style, when looking old-fashioned might be the height of fashion, it becomes difficult indeed to be categorically unfashionable. In fashion's new configuration, the new no longer abruptly discredits the old; the drastic injunctions of fashion are fading away as the values of popular psychology, communication, and humor take over. Despite its widespread democratization, the hundred years' fashion still functioned as a massive exclusionary system. That time is past; fashion's "dictatorship" is over, along with the social rejection of unfashionableness. Fashion's new configuration is open, uncompartmentalized, and nondirective. By doing away with the guilt and scorn that had been attached to unfashionableness, the democratization of fashion has entered its culminating phase. Individuals have gained increased freedom in dress; the social pressure to conform has lost much of its force, its homogeneity, and its durability. Just as people have by and large stopped making fun of the defects of others, so they no longer laugh at outdated clothing. This pacification of fashion reflects and embodies a growing tolerance, an increased gentleness in mores. Flexibility in fashion, a deep aversion to violence and cruelty, a new sensitivity toward animals, an awareness of the importance of listening to others, a comprehensive education, efforts to find peaceful solutions to social conflicts—these are all aspects of the same general process of modern democratic civilization. Hence we have a new system of fashion "with a human face," in which pretty much anything goes, in which others are judged less and less often in terms of some official standard. Euphoria over *le look* now occurs against a background of widespread tolerance in matters of dress, a context in which people have become less uptight and less passionate about fashion.

To say that the public has become increasingly autonomous in relation to fashion obviously need not imply the disappearance of social codes and mimetic phenomena. Social constraints clearly continue to apply to individuals. However, they are less uniform; they allow greater initiative and freedom of choice. Repetitive declarations that personal autonomy is an illusion of naive, presociological consciousness do little to advance our understanding of what is changing in the modern world. It is time to give up the sterile debate between determinism and metaphysical freedom. If it is clear that individual independence, in the absolute, is a myth, it does not follow that individuals living in society do not enjoy varying degrees of autonomy. Even if social obligations quite clearly persist, even if numerous codes and models structure the presentation of the self, private individuals have much broader latitude now than before. There is no longer just one single standard for acceptable appearance; people can choose among multiple aesthetic models. Women continue to be attentive to fashion, but in a different way; they follow it less faithfully, less scrupulously, more freely. The controlled mimicry characteristic of the hundred years' fashion has given way to an optional, flexible mimicry. One imitates the model of one's choice, in whatever style one prefers. Fashion is no longer injunctive; instead, it incites, suggests, hints. In the era of accomplished individualism, *le look* functions à la carte, in terms of mobility and nondirective mimeticism.

At the same time, fashion no longer arouses the interest or passion it used to elicit. How could it, when such a broad tolerance rules in matter of dress, when the most heterogeneous styles coexist, when fashion is no longer uniform? In an era when increasing numbers of women have professional ambitions and activities, when their intellectual, cultural, and recreational interests are similar or identical to those of men, interest in fashion is no doubt more widespread but also less intense, less vital, than in aristocratic periods when the play of appearances had crucial significance for human lives. Narcissistic individualism leads to a relaxation of concern with fashion. The moments of enchanted ecstasy (the New Look) and scandalized indignation (the Boyish Look) that punctuated the hundred years' fashion are behind us. No novelty quite manages to provoke that sort of collective emotion now; nothing shocks people any longer, or sets off massive controversies. Since the Courrèges revolution—probably the last fashion event that entailed a certain degree of effervescence—fashion has been running its course in a climate in which indifference is combined with admiration in equal proportions, notwithstanding the abundant media coverage offered by the specialized press. Nevertheless, fashion is successfully pursuing its own creative dynamics. Collections by such creators as Montana, Mugler, Gaultier, or Rei Kawakubo have seriously disrupted the image of elegance and the feminine archetype, although not enough to reinvigorate the social reception of fashion. Even truly spectacular novelties no longer succeed in seriously jarring the public at large; they scarcely reach beyond the circle of initiates. It is as if in the course of only a couple of decades fashion has lost its power to inspire and irritate the masses. Fashion still arouses interest, it is still attractive, but from a distance; it no longer has unbridled magnetism. "Cool" logic has taken over the space of fashion as it has taken over the ideological space and the political scene. Fashion has entered the relatively dispassionate era of consumption, of casual and amused curiosity.

The way people relate to issues of dress has undergone noteworthy changes as well. For more than thirty years, in the developed Western countries, the proportion of family budgets devoted to clothing has been constantly declining. In France, it fell from 16 percent in 1949 to 12 percent in 1959 and 8.7 percent in 1974. In 1972, 9.7 percent of the average household budget went for articles of clothing; in 1984, the figure was only 7.3 percent. The decline has not been uniform, of course, and it has more significance for low-income groups than for the well-to-do; the reduction in the percentage of income spent on dress during this period is highest in the case of blue-collar workers and people not in the work force. At present, while it is not clear whether the figures indicate a major trend or a temporary phenomenon, the proportional disparity in spending on dress among the various socioprofessional groups is increasing. In 1956, workers' households devoted 12.3 percent of their budgets to clothing, as compared to 11.4 percent for those of independent or liberal professionals. In 1984, clothing expenses were down to 6.8 percent of workers' budgets, while independent and liberal professionals spent 9.3 percent. Except for people who are not in the work force, workers now spend less on clothing than anyone else. But even if the decline is unevenly distributed, the overall place allocated for clothing in budgets has gone down by one-third over the past thirty years; all socioprofessional categories have participated in the same downward trend. Clothing accounted for 12.5 percent of the budget for someone in an upper-management position in 1956; in 1984, it represented only 8.7 percent. Salaried employees devoted 13.1 percent of their budgets to dress in 1956, as opposed to 8.4 percent in 1984. Although the social disparities are real, they must not be allowed to obscure the broader underlying phenomenon: the decline in the proportion of budgets devoted to clothing, the diminished consumer attachment to dress.

The disappearance of made-to-order clothing, the possibility of buying fashion items at accessible prices in various price ranges, the decline in the relative price of clothing—all these factors contributed to the steady decline in the budget share allotted to clothing, but they do not explain everything. Along with the decline in the clothing category in household expenses came a new distribution of purchasing, a new wardrobe configuration for men and women alike. This new distribution of purchases and the new tastes also helped cut down on consumer investment in clothing. Over a thirty-year period, people have completely reorganized the way they outfit themselves. The most significant trends are, on the one hand, a declining interest in the so-called major items (overcoats, raincoats, men's and women's suits), and on the other hand, an increased interest in minor items, sportswear, and casual clothing. In 1953, men bought suits once every six years. Major articles of outerwear represented 38 percent of men's expenses in 1953, as opposed to 13 percent in 1984. Sportswear and leisure apparel represented 4 percent of men's purchases in 1953 and 31 percent in 1984. The feminine wardrobe has undergone a similar evolution: wool or fur coats, raincoats, and suits represented 33 percent of women's expenses in 1953, 17 percent in 1984. On the other hand, the purchase of "middle-range" clothing (sweaters, jackets, sportswear, jeans, pants) went from 9 percent of women's clothing budgets to 30 percent.[24]

It may be useful to break down the impact of this trend by socioprofessional category. Surveys of clothing expenditures reveal that working-class households prefer quantity to quality; their purchases fall chiefly in the inexpensive range, unlike those of more affluent wage earners, who are drawn to more expensive, high-quality clothing. Blue-collar workers do not often wear suits and ties, while managers, company heads, and professionals buy suits, blazers, and dress shirts much more frequently. Wives of company heads and professionals are more apt to buy classic items such as suits, between-season dresses, and high-heeled shoes at full price, while wives of managers and engineers spend more money on the latest trends.[25] Still, these differences must not be allowed to obscure the overall movement, the market's tendency toward casualness and practicality as exemplified by sportswear. Even if the way the wardrobe is stocked varies from one social class to another, even if purchases vary in price and quality, in overall terms the taste for casual dress, fanciful clothing, and leisure attire is spreading in every milieu. "Major" items do not sell well, while "minor" articles (jackets, pants and leisure clothes, sweatshirts, T-shirts, and so on) are doing better and better. In every age group and in all classes of society, people are more and more inclined to wear casual clothing: sports and leisure outfits, light jackets, and tennis shoes have all become city attire. In 1985, only 1.7 million pairs of women's dress pants were sold, and 12 million pairs of leisure and sports pants. In 1974, women bought 4.5

million pairs of jeans and leisure pants; ten years later, the number had risen to 18 million. Sportswear is gaining ground everywhere. Even so, this trend is clearly not about to abolish either dressier or more classic clothes for the office and for evening wear, or characteristically feminine outfits.

The preference for casual clothing is symptomatic of the new age of individualism. The recent flare-up of demands for autonomy in personal and sexual relationships, in sports and at work, has as its counterpart the desire for supple, loose, free clothing that does not impede people's movement and comfort. The vogue for sportswear reflects, in the sphere of dress, the demand for greater personal freedom; this freedom is reflected in fashion, in turn, by casualness, the relaxed look, flexibility, and humorous decorations and inscriptions. Sportswear and the decline of "major items" mark the rise of neonarcissism in fashion, the emergence of a personality more insistent on individual autonomy, less dependent on standards of prestigious display, less concerned with competition and obvious social differentiation in appearance. The notion of "Sunday best" has disappeared, along with fascination with the opulent dress of the upper classes; increasingly, fashionable clothing is losing its role as a mark of excellence and social respectability. It expresses less a position in the social hierarchy than a desire for personality, a cultural orientation, a life-style, an aesthetic outlook. Fashionable clothing has always been a sign of class and an instrument of seduction. Contemporary individualism is the primary force responsible for reducing the dimension of the status symbol in clothing and promoting pleasure, comfort, and freedom. People today seek less to elicit social admiration than to seduce and to be at ease; they are less interested in expressing their social standing than in displaying their aesthetic taste; they are less anxious to signify their class position than to look young and relaxed.

In this context, the blue-jeans phenomenon deserves special attention. The rage for jeans among all social classes and all age groups, the success of jeans over the last thirty years, is so considerable that it is not an exaggeration to see blue jeans as one of the most characteristic symbols of taste in fashion in the latter half of the twentieth century. It is true that jeans sales have been dropping steadily since the early 1980s: the drop from 8.8 million pairs sold (for women) in 1982 to 5.8 million in 1985 represents a significant decline in favor of corduroy and linen in particular. But denim is already making a comeback: the jeans odyssey is far from over. What is at issue is no longer even a fad, but a style that echoes the most cherished values of contemporary individualism: "Be part of the legend," as a Levi's ad puts it. The impression of uniformity and conformity produced by this sort of clothing has often been stressed. Everybody looks like everybody else: the not-so-young resemble the truly young; girls resemble boys; onlookers cannot always tell people apart. In this view, jeans seem to consecrate the mass standardization of appearances, the negation of individualism in dress. However, this is an illusion that misses what is most specific about the phenomenon. Jeans, like any other fashion, are selected, not imposed by some tradition; in this respect, they must be linked to the free appreciation of individuals able to adopt them, reject them, or combine them at will with other elements. We can read the massive social propagation of jeans as evidence that fashion always conjugates individualism with conformity; individualism is deployed only through mimeticism. But private individuals are always free to accept or reject the latest fad, to adapt it for themselves, to exercise a personal preference for one brand over another, for different shapes and cuts. We could argue that this amounts to giving individualism short shrift; but to do so would be to dismiss all that jeans have signified, and still signify, in the realm of individual freedom properly speaking. Jeans do not show dirt easily; they can be worn in a wide variety of contexts; they do not require ironing or meticulous cleaning; and they are still useful when they are worn, faded, or even torn. Intrinsically invested with anticonformist connotations, jeans were first adopted by young people who were resisting the conventional norms still in place and who were also opposed to the new hedonistic values of liberal consumer-oriented societies. The rejection of strict conformist codes was immediately exemplified by rock music and casual clothing; all things considered, it is fair to say that the inclination for jeans foreshadowed the counterculture explosion and the general protest movements of the late 1960s. As an expression of the desire for a freer, less confining, more flexible private life, jeans were the manifestation of a hyperindividualistic culture based on the cult of the body and the quest for a less theatrical sensuality. Far from serving as a uniform, jeans underline body shapes; they emphasize the hips, buttocks, and legs. Recent Lee Cooper advertisements have exploited this "sexy" register freely; jeans outline the unique aspects of physical individuality. In place of clothing that dissimulates and exercises its charm with discretion, we find clothing with a more "tactile," more immediately sexual resonance. We have moved beyond represented sensuality toward a more direct, more natural, livelier sensuality. Feminine seductiveness in jeans has hardly been abandoned; it has relinquished its earlier affectation in favor of more emphatic, more provocative, more youthful signs. Jeans illustrate, in seduction and fashion, the eclipse of distance that is at work in modern art, in avant-garde literature, and in rock music. Seduction is separated from the sublimation of artifice; it requires fewer mediations, more immediacy, the democratic signs of stimulation, naturalness, proximity, and equality. With jeans, democratic individualist appearance has taken another step forward: it has become the expression of individuality disengaged from social status. Distinguished and distanced refinement has given way to the ostentation of simplicity, to an extreme equalization of the signs conveyed by dress, to a relaxation of attitudes and postures. A certain unisex ideal has won over the modern world, yet it has not destroyed the sexualization and seductiveness of appearances.

By doing away with complicated signs of strategies for charm, sportswear has profoundly altered the register of seduction. Seduction has certainly not disappeared, but there is a new configuration in which pleasure in personal appearance is less alienated by the gaze of others, less dependent on an imperative need to subjugate. The new approach allows the individual to please while remaining at ease: seduction has achieved increased autonomy by privileging comfort, practicality, ease, and rapidity of use. We have entered the era of instant seduction: it is still a matter of exerting charm, but without devoting excessive time to the process, without detracting from other activities. In its relaxed mode, fashion entails an almost imperceptible one-minute seduction. Contemporary fashion does not strive to eliminate seductive strategies; it strives rather, in the daytime, to make them more and more discreet, if not invisible. This temporally minimal seduction coexists quite well, moreover, with the more elaborate rituals used for evening, when women want to dress up in order to please. Seduction remains a feminine code, but it becomes more and more a matter of choice and pleasure. In a recent survey, 70 percent of the women respondents felt that maintaining and embellishing one's body was first and foremost a pleasure. Seduction has been recycled: it has been partially reconstituted from the standpoint of neonarcissistic individualism, with the emergence of the à la carte aesthetic and subjective autonomy.

The new distribution of wardrobes attests equally well to the upsurge in hedonistic and psychologizing values characteristic of our societies. A growing number of people prefer to make more frequent purchases rather than to buy expensive items less often; they prefer to buy small articles rather than "major" items: this is a typical expression of the new age of individualism in the realm of dress. With the purchase of small items, not only do we have the opportunity to make more frequent choices, but we give ourselves more frequent pleasure. We may prefer to change often for the sheer pleasure of changing, for the fun of disguising and transforming ourselves, rather than out of a desire for social display. Buying clothes is not a strictly egocentric enterprise, to be sure; it is always linked to the relation to the Other, to the desire for seduction —but seduction brought into line with hedonistic democratic culture. The goal of social standing is giving way to the goal of playful renewal and the pleasure of change. Wardrobe renewals are governed increasingly not only by personal taste, but also by the desire to "create a new you." Many women make no bones about it: they do not buy a given article of clothing because it is in fashion, or because they need it, but because they need a lift, because they are depressed and want to change their mood. By going to the hairdresser or buying something to wear they feel they are "doing something," becoming different, growing younger, getting off to a fresh start. "Make me over": as fashion ceases to be a directive and uniform phenomenon, the purchase of fashion items is not governed by social and aesthetic considerations alone; it has become a therapeutic phenomenon as well.

With open fashion and the process by which the social recognition accorded clothing has been reduced, a new regime of imitation in fashion has been inaugurated. For centuries, the diffusion of fashion was by and large achieved with the court and the aristocracy as starting points; the lower classes invariably copied the manners and dress of their betters. Gabriel de Tarde could thus treat the imitation of superiors by inferiors as a law governing the process of social emulation. The hundred years' fashion did not infringe on this law; the models for imitation were those set forth by haute couture and women of high society. But the situation is different today, when casual styles and sportswear are in fashion, when even stars dress "like everyone else." The change that has occurred has radically undermined the age-old law of imitative contagion: one no longer imitates one's betters, one imitates what one sees in the vicinity—simple and amusing outfits, inexpensive models seen with increasing frequency in magazines. The vertical law of imitation has been replaced by a horizontal law, in keeping with a society of individuals recognized as equals. As Tocqueville had already noted on the subject of opinions and beliefs, progress toward democracy leads to majority rule, to the influence of the greatest number. Fashion does not escape this rule. The influence of the "average" person is now preponderant; this is attested by the increasing success of "minor" items, leisure clothes, and sportswear.

The statistical data on clothes-buying trends over time provide further indications that the diffusion of fashion is less and less subject to the classical schema according to which the lower classes try to catch up with the upper classes. The pyramidal model in which new articles are progressively diffused from the upper classes down is no longer generally applicable. The pullover, for example, over a twenty-year period beginning in the early 1950s, was purchased primarily by upper-echelon managers and independent professionals. But its spread did not follow the hierarchical order of social categories. After 1972, white-collar employees surpassed the level of consumption of the higher categories; however, not only did farmers and blue-collar workers fail to follow the white-collar pattern, they gave up pullovers even before the higher categories tired of them. Similarly, the spread of jeans did not follow the rule of hierarchical descent: the wearing of jeans did not start with the upper classes, but was first adopted by the young. In the early 1970s, the wives of upper-echelon managers were the leading purchasers of jeans. But in the years that followed, it was not middle managers or independent professionals who spent the most money on jeans, it was the wives of white-collar workers and farmers.[26] Imitation in fashion obeys a complex logic from this point on; it is no longer mechanically ordered according to the principle of social catch-up. More often, an article is adopted not because it is in use at the top of the social pyramid, but because it is new. One dresses fashionably not so much to distinguish oneself from lower orders of society or to display one's own rank as to change, to be modern, to please, to express one's own individuality. To be sure, from the very outset fashion has never been motivated entirely and exclusively by social distinction; the taste for novelty and the desire to manifest aesthetic individuality have always been at work as well. But one can scarcely doubt that the desire for social differentiation was a preponderant and particularly intense motive over the centuries. What we are seeing now is the recomposition of the space of motivations in fashion. The distinctive dimension of class is not disappearing, but it is losing its importance and its impact in favor of the desire for novelty, seduction, and individuality. In our day, the new is loved for itself; it is no longer a class alibi but a value in its own right, one that makes it possible, moreover, to display a modern, changing aesthetic individuality. Fashionable clothing is less and less a means for social distancing, more and more an instrument for individual and aesthetic distinction, an instrument of seduction, youthfulness, and emblematic modernity.

Ever since it began, fashion has blended conformity with individualism. For all its openness, contemporary fashion still has not escaped that basic structure. But there is a difference: individualism has become by and large less competitive, less concerned with what others think, less exhibitionist. No doubt eccentric young minorities exist, but they only serve to make the majority's tendencies stand out, the majority being less concerned with originality than with understated elegance, comfort, and casualness. If small numbers of people pile on one extravagance after another, the vast majority manifest increasing discretion. Everything goes, and yet the streets look drab, devoid of originality for the most part; designers' follies are countered by the monotony of everyday appearance. Such are the paradoxes of open fashion, at the very moment when *le look* and unbridled fantasy are exalted. The privatization of existence, the rise of individualist values, the diversification of ready-to-wear, far from leading, as might have been expected, to a burst of individualist originality, have led to a progressive neutralization of the desire for distinction in dress. In this sense, it is true that there is less individualism than in earlier eras when the frenetic search for social and personal differentiation was a source of rivalry and jealousy, eras when it was imperative to set oneself apart through details, accessories, and nuances, when it was intolerable for two women to be dressed alike.

But beyond all this, it is perhaps even more accurate to say that individualism in dress has significantly increased. In our day we dress more for ourselves, more as a function of our own tastes, than in terms of an obligatory, uniform standard. For centuries, individuals could assert autonomy only in the choice of styles and variants; the overall aesthetic standard was not accessible to the exercise of individual freedom. Today, personal autonomy is manifested even in the choice of criteria of appearance. Individualism is less visible because the concern for originality is less flagrant; in reality, individualism is more fundamental than ever, because it can permeate the very reference points of personal appearance. Individualism in fashion today is less glorious but more free, less decorative but more optional, less ostentatious but more combinatorial, less spectacular but more varied, than ever before.

PART TWO

Consummate Fashion

Where does fashion begin and where does it end, in the era of exploding needs and proliferating media, mass advertising and mass leisure, stars and "hits"? What is left that fashion does not rule, at least in part, when the ephemeral governs the world of objects, culture, and meaningful discourse, and when the principle of seduction has profoundly reorganized the everyday environment, news and information, and the political scene? The fashion explosion no longer has an epicenter; it has ceased to be the privilege of a social elite. All classes are caught up in the intoxication of change and fads; the infrastructure and the superstructure alike are subject, although to different degrees, to fashion's rule. We have reached the era of *consummate fashion*, the extension of the fashion process to broader and broader spheres of collective life. Fashion is not so much a particular peripheral sector, now, as a general form at work in society as a whole. Everyone is more or less immersed in fashion, more or less everywhere, and the triple operation that specifically defines fashion is increasingly implemented: the operation of *ephemerality*, *seduction*, and *marginal differentiation*. Fashion has to be delocalized. It can no longer be identified with the luxury of appearances and superfluity; it has to be identified with the trivalent process that is thoroughly overhauling the profile of our societies.

With the extraordinary expansion of this tripolar structure, modern societies have undergone a major shift that radically separates them from the type of society that developed in the seventeenth and eighteenth centuries. A new generation of bureaucratic and democratic societies has come into being; their dominant tone is lightness and frivolity. The coercive imposition of disciplines has been replaced by socialization through choice and image; revolution has given way to infatuation with meaning. Communication via advertising has replaced ideological solemnity, while the seductiveness of consumption and pop psychology has displaced rigorism. In a few short decades, we have shed the primacy of rigid ideologies and the disciplinary schema characteristic of the heroic stage of democracies; contemporary societies have recycled themselves in kit form and as express service. This does not mean, of course, that we have broken all ties with our roots. Frivolous society does not leave the competitive bureaucratic universe behind; rather, it carries that universe forward into the flexible, communicative stage. Nor does it leave the democratic order behind: it achieves that order in the frenzied passion for the spectacular, in the inconstancy of opinions and social mobilizations.

The supremacy of the fashion form must not be mistaken for a form of decadence that would characterize Western societies given over to private pleasures and stripped of all faith in higher ideals. The fashion form has nothing to do with posthistorical "snobbery," the Hegelian-Marxist end of history as Kojève analyzed it in the late 1940s.[1] Consummate fashion does not imply the disappearance of social and political content in favor of a pure, snobbish, formalist gratuitousness lacking in historical negativity. Rather, it implies a new relation to ideals, a new investment of democratic values, and at the same time an acceleration of historical change, a greater collective opening to the challenge of the future, even if this opening comes by way of present pleasures. The end point of fashion entails the fading away of the great prophetic references, the end of the traditional forms of socialization, the permanent circulation of things and meanings. It brings about a decline in social resistance to change, and it mobilizes more consciously historical human beings who are more scrupulous in dealing with the requirements of democracy.

There is no cause for alarm: I am by no means purporting to define all Western societies in terms of a homogeneous and unique supersystem. It is perfectly clear that essential aspects of collective life have very little to do with the fashion form. Economic spirals, the escalation in war technology, terrorist attacks, nuclear catastrophes, unemployment, the distribution of labor, xenophobia—widely disparate phenomena such as these lie at the opposite pole from a frivolous image of our time. The euphoria of fashion is certainly not omnipresent: the age of seduction coexists with the arms race, with lack of personal security in daily life, with the economic crisis and the subjective crisis. The point warrants reiteration: postindustrial societies are not unified entities that can be understood solely in the light of the fashion process. Science, technology, art, conflicts of interest, nations, politics, social and humanitarian ideals are based on their own specific criteria and have their own autonomy. The fashion form only encounters them in passing; it can sometimes rearticulate them, but it does not absorb them entirely in its own logic. My aim in this book is not to homogenize disparate entities, but to grasp a dominant historical tendency that is restructuring entire areas of our collective universe.

The idea that contemporary societies are being organized under the laws of imperative renewal, planned obsolescence, images, spectacular solicitation, and marginal differentiation has been advanced for a long time, at various levels and with considerable skill, by such writers as David Riesman, Vance Packard, Daniel Boorstin, Herbert Marcuse, and later in France by Jean Baudrillard and the situationalists. Starting in the 1960s, the perception of a "new society," governed, as it were, by the fashion process, was presented by the theoreticians most attentive to modernity; however, their analysis remained confined to the conceptual framework inherited from an earlier, revolutionary mentality. The hegemony of fashion was denounced with a sort of critical overkill, while the denouncers failed to notice that the radical-subversive perspective was itself becoming a fad in use among intellectuals. No theoretical leitmotif can be seen more plainly: the trajectory of fashion in our societies has been identified with the institutionalization of waste, with the large-scale creation of artificial needs, with the standardization and hyperregulation of private life. Consumer society entails the programming of everyday life; it manipulates and regulates individual and social life rationally in all its aspects; everything becomes artifice and illusion in the service of capitalist profit and the dominant classes. In the "swinging sixties," critics went all out to stigmatize the empire of seduction and obsolescence, alleging the rationality of irrationality (Marcuse), the totalitarian organization of appearance and a generalized alienation (Debord), global conditioning (Galbraith), terrorist society (Henri Lefebvre), a fetishist and perverse system leading back to class domination (Baudrillard). The supremacy of fashion has been read in the light of the schema of class struggle and bureaucratic capitalist domination. Behind the ideology of the satisfaction of needs, the conditioning of existence, or "augmented survival," has been denounced (Debord), along with the rationalization and extension of domination. Shored up by the conceptual tools of Marxism, the classic reflex of condemning appearances and seduction has played its hand fully; it has found its ultimate expression at the level of the social body as a whole.

The dossier needs to be thoroughly reexamined. In their feverish haste to denounce, these theoreticians have fundamentally misunderstood the historical work of the reign of fashion. Its real long-term effects lie light-years away from those that critical thinkers and, in many respects, common sense itself have castigated and continue to attack. With total fashion, the ruse of reason is convoked as never before to the podium of history. Behind the scenes of seduction, the Enlightenment is at work; underneath the escalation of the ephemeral, the centuries-old struggle to conquer individual autonomy is under way.

CHAPTER IV

The Seduction of Things

W̶E CAN CHARACTERIZE "consumer society" empirically by listing some of its features: a higher standard of living, an abundance of goods and services, a cult of objects and leisure, a hedonistic and materialistic morality. However, the generalization of the fashion process is what defines consumer society in properly structural terms. A society that hinges on the expansion of needs is above all a society that reorganizes mass production and consumption according to the law of *obsolescence, seduction,* and *diversification*; this is the law that tilts the economy into the orbit of the fashion form. "Every industry tries to emulate the women's fashion industry. This is the key to modern marketing."[1] What Louis Cheskin wrote in the 1950s has not been contradicted by the subsequent evolution of Western societies; the fashion process has not ceased to extend its sovereignty. The organizational logic established in the sphere of appearances in the mid-nineteenth century has in fact spread to the entire array of consumer goods. Everywhere, specialized bureaucratic agencies define objects and needs; everywhere, the logic of precipitous renewal and the diversification and stylization of models prevail. Manufacturers take independent initiatives in developing merchandise; forms of merchandise vary regularly and rapidly; models and series proliferate. These three major principles, which were introduced by haute couture, no longer belong exclusively to luxury clothing; they constitute the very core of the consumer industries. The bureaucratic-aesthetic order governs the consumer economy that has now been reorganized by seduction and accelerated obsolescence. Light industry is structured like fashion.

Objects the Way You Like Them

The fashion form is manifested most radically in the accelerated pace of product change, the instability and precariousness of industrial objects. Economic logic has simply swept away any idea of permanence; the rule of the ephemeral governs the production and consumption of objects. The reduced temporality of fashion has engulfed the universe of merchandise:

that universe has been transformed, since the Second World War, by a process of renewal and "planned" obsolescence suited to an ongoing re-stimulation of consumption. I am thinking less about all the products that are designed not to last—tissues, disposable diapers, paper napkins, bot-tles, lighters, razors, cheap clothing—than of the overall process that forces companies to innovate, to keep on introducing new articles that are sometimes truly new in conception, but that sometimes (most often) sim-ply incorporate minor refinements of detail in order to give the products an edge in global competition. In fashion's consummate stage, its abbrevi-ated time span and its systematic obsolescence have become characteris-tics inherent in mass production and consumption, following an inexora-ble law: a firm that does not regularly create new models loses its market penetration and weakens its image of quality in a society where consumers spontaneously hold that the new is by nature superior to the old. Scientific progress, the logic of competition, and the dominant taste for novelty all contribute to the establishment of an economic order organized like fash-ion. Supply and demand revolve around novelty; our economic system has been propelled into a spiral in which innovation is sovereign whether on a large scale or a small one, and in which obsolescence is accelerating: spe-cialists in marketing and innovation can assure us that within ten years 80 percent to 90 percent of our current products will be outmoded; they will appear in new forms, with new packaging. "It's new, it's a SONY." All the ads emphasize novelty: "New Pampers," "New Ford Escort," "New Egg Pudding, Franco-Russian Style." Newness appears to be the categorical imperative of production and marketing; our fashion economy advances in a forced march, as it were, with the indispensable seduction of change, speed, and difference.

Gadgets symbolize the frivolous economy. Electric oyster knives, elec-tric window washers, electronic razors with three cutting positions: we are swimming in overkill and a profusion of automatisms, in an environment of instrumental fairyland. During the 1960s and 1970s, this neokitsch economy devoted to waste, futility, and the "pathology of the functional" was widely denounced.[2] Gadgets—utensils that are neither truly useful nor truly useless—could appear as the essence and truth of the consumer object. Every area is potentially open to gadgetry; from the nine-position electric toaster to the sophisticated stereo system, all our objects are hand-maidens of fashion, of more or less ostentatious technological gratuitous-ness. With the hegemony of gadgetry, the material environment comes to resemble fashion; the relations we entertain with objects are no longer utilitarian but playful in nature.[3] What we find seductive above all are the games for which gadgets provide the opportunity; we like the play of mechanisms, manipulations, performances. Without in any way calling into question the place of play in our relation to the technological environment, we may wonder whether this sort of analysis is still in touch with the contemporary universe of consumerism. Is it legitimate to consider gadgets as the paradigm of the consumer object? Behind the denunciations does there not lurk one of the typical forms of the antimodern attitude, which holds that programmed innovations are futile, inauthentic, and artificial compared to the age of artisanship? Not everyone is willing to see that beyond some of the ridiculous new manifestations of preciosity we find an ongoing process of objective progress, increased comfort, and efficiency. "Functional uselessness" is not emblematic of our technological universe. That universe is propelled more and more in the direction of high tech, high fidelity, and computerization; gadgets are giving way to "intelligent terminals," flexible videocommunications, autonomous and on-demand programming. The intellectual triumph of gadgetry will doubtless turn out to have been no more than a reflection of the inaugural moment of mass consumption intoxicated with the sparkle of technology. At the moment, attacks on gadgetry are muted. Gadgets are less objects of scandal than amusing trinkets; we are going through a period of reconciliation with our material environment. Consumers are less dazzled by the pretensions of utensils; they are better informed about product quality; they compare advantages and disadvantages; they look for optimal use value. Consumption does not rule out a heightened desire for functionality and individual independence. The cult of gratuitous manipulations has yielded to the cult of comfort and livableness; one wants dependable objects, "cars for your life-style." Fashion in objects has found its cruising speed; it is accepted as a not-so-tragic destiny, a source of well-being and of welcome small excitements in the humdrum routines of everyday life.

The industrial imperative of newness is currently embodied in a coherent politics of products, the diversification of production. The fashion process destandardizes products. It multiplies choices and options; it manifests itself in policies that consist in offering a wide gamut of models and versions constructed on the basis of standard elements and distinguished at the end of the assembly line only by small combinatorial differences. While mass production, at least in the automotive sector in the United States, began to put into practice the principle of full product lines and annual renewal of models as early as the 1920s,[4] the process did not reach its full magnitude until shortly after the Second World War. With the proliferation of lines, versions, options, colors, and limited series, the sphere of merchandising entered the realm of personalization. The principle of "marginal differentiation,"[5] long a specialty of clothing manufacture, was generalized. The fashion form became sovereign. In every realm, alongside the growing individualization of tastes, we find diversity substituted for uniformity; nuances and small variations replace likeness. All sectors have been conquered by the fashion processes of variety and secondary distinction. The Renault Supercinq came in twenty-two different versions in a single year. If we include color choices and optional accessories and take all models and options into account, we can say that Renault produced about two hundred thousand different cars that year. Nike and Adidas each offer several dozen models of running shoes in various colors. In 1986, SONY proposed nine new compact-disc players, and dozens of speakers, amplifiers, and cassette players. Soft drinks have gotten on the bandwagon: Coca-Cola has created a whole range of sodas—Classic Coke, New Coke, Diet Coke, Caffeine-Free Coke, Caffeine-Free Diet Coke, Cherry Coke—sold in different packaging and bottles. Consummate fashion entails the generalization of the system of small differences multiplied to excess. Along with the process of technological miniaturization, the fashion form generates a universe of products organized in terms of microdifferences.

With the extension of the policy of product lines, the opposition between model and series, which was still quite obvious during the early phases of mass consumption, no longer determines the status of modern objects,[6] although there is still a disjunction between luxury items and mass-produced articles. Assembly-line objects have been contrasted with luxury models in terms of two major features: on the one hand, the "technological deficit" that consigns the assembly-line object to functional mediocrity and to more rapid abandonment; on the other hand, the "stylistic deficit" that condemns the mass-produced object to bad taste, to a lack of formal integrity, style, and originality.[7] But how can we fail to see the changes that have taken place in both the technological and the aesthetic qualities of mass-produced objects? The widespread idea according to which mass production works systematically to reduce the life span of a product by deliberately introducing manufacturing defects and lowering the product's quality needs serious reexamination.[8] While the observation may be accurate for certain appliances, it does not apply to others that have a stable or even an increasing life span (e.g., television sets and automobile engines).[9] A 1983 survey showed that 29 percent of all refrigerators owned by the respondents were more than ten years old; one-fourth of the coffee mills, hairdryers and vacuum cleaners were also more than ten years old. Mass-produced objects are not condemned to see their reliability and their durability keep on declining; technological degradation is not an inexorable destiny. There is rather a tendency to add an "edge," in the form of finishing touches or "zero-defect" products. The same reservation applies to the aesthetic qualities of objects: the increased number of designers and the policy of creating a whole gamut of products has led to increasing numbers of mass-produced items of undeniable formal quality. The age of the Citroën Deux-Chevaux, a robust vehicle entirely lacking in sculptural pretensions, is over; one automobile may cost 50 percent less than another that has precisely the same outward form. As much care is taken with the external appearance of mass-produced articles as with top-of-the-line versions; small cars are models with elegant aerodynamic silhouettes, not very different in their formal conception from big cars. Our society is not carried away by the kitsch logic of mediocrity and banality. The difference that matters is less and less one of formal elegance and more and more a matter of technical performance, quality of materials, comfort, and sophistication. Stylistic originality is no longer reserved for luxury items; the aim of seductive appearance presides over the rethinking of all products; the opposition between model and series has been blurred, has lost its hierarchical and ostentatious character. Industrial production pursues the democratic project of equalizing conditions in the sphere of objects: in place of a system made up of heterogeneous elements, a graduated system made up of small distinctions and nuances is emerging. The extremes have not disappeared, but they no longer proudly exhibit their incomparable difference.

Charm by Another Name Is Design

With the systematic incorporation of the aesthetic dimension in the development of industrial products, the expansion of the fashion form is finally complete. Industrial aesthetics and the world of objects are henceforth subject to the design system and the rule according to which appearances must have charm. The decisive step in this advance goes back to the 1920s and 1930s, when industrialists discovered, after the Great Depression in the United States, that the outward aspect of consumer goods could play a crucial role in promoting sales: "Good design makes for good business." Increasingly, a new principle took hold: manufacturers grasped the value of doing aesthetic studies of the shape and presentation of mass-produced articles; they learned to embellish and harmonize their forms so as to seduce the eye, in keeping with R. Loewy's famous dictum: "Ugliness doesn't sell." A revolution in industrial production ensued: design became an integral part of the conception of new products; the industry at large adopted the perspective of elegance and seduction. With the predominance of industrial design, the fashion form no longer refers simply to the whims of consumers; it is a constitutive structure of industrial mass production.

The frequent alterations imposed on the aesthetics of consumer products correlate with the new position attributed to seduction. By periodically introducing changes in model shapes, the consumer industries aligned themselves openly as early as the 1950s with the methods used in women's fashion: they shared the same formal inconstancy that allowed a product to become outmoded through a simple change in style and presentation. The consumer age coincides with this process of permanent formal renewal, a process whose goal is the artificial triggering of a dynamic of aging and market revitalization. The frivolous economy that ensues is oriented toward the ephemeral and the latest fads. Vance Packard's description of it is ferocious, but highly characteristic: cars, domestic appliances, dishware, bedding, furniture—the whole world of objects waltzes to the rhythm of "styling," with annual changes in color and shape.[10]

It would not be at all difficult to show how much still links us to that universe of the "fashion plot." The initial appearance of a product and its stylistic renewal always occupy a crucial place in industrial production; the way objects are "dressed" is always a crucial element of their success in the marketplace. In France at least, advertisements are strangely similar in their insistent references to the fashion look. Some three decades ago, we might have read about "the best-dressed car of the year" (De Soto), or "the latest thing in fashion" (Ford). Now we see "a haute couture style, a ready-to-wear price" (Peugeot), "the hit of the year, the Fiesta Rock, the look of a star" (Ford). Whereas the major automobile manufacturers regularly propose models with new lines, the most varied products enter into the endless cycle of fashion operation and design. Even food products are beginning to be subject to the industrial aesthetic: the Italian designer Giugiaro has developed a new form of pasta. More and more small items—clocks, eyeglasses, cigarette lighters, pencils, pens, ashtrays, notebooks—are losing their traditionally austere character and are becoming cheerful, playful, malleable accessories. The watch industry has succeeded particularly well in its fashion aggiornamento: Swatch brings out some twenty fanciful models a year in colorful plastic presentations; we have entered the era of the clip watch, which "is worn anywhere except on the wrist," or the gimmick watch, whose hands move backward.

Whatever the contemporary taste for quality and reliability may be, the success of a product depends largely on its design, presentation, and packaging. If in the 1940s R. Loewy succeeded in restimulating Lucky Strike sales by renovating their presentation, Louis Cheskin gave Marlboro a new lease on life more recently when he invented its famous red-and-white hard package. It is said that packaging can improve the distribution of a product by 25 percent; often a new wrapper is all it takes to bring back a product that has been losing ground. Now, as before, clients make up their minds in part on the basis of outward appearances: in makeup and fashion, design still has a bright future.

This does not mean that nothing has changed since the heroic era of consumerism. The age of the "art of waste," of the automobile as reigning queen of fashion, the era in which all General Motors automobile bodies were altered every year, the era in which variations followed the rhythms and the eccentricities of fashion and in which technological quality seemed inexorably doomed to deteriorate, did not come into being without some significant transformations. The present moment places more value on comfort, naturalness, maneuverability, security, economy, and performance. "The new Escort has arrived! A new look, new technology, new performance. More efficient, with new suspensions on four independent MacPherson wheels; extraordinary handling and comfort. More appealing, with a completely redesigned interior: a highly readable dashboard, ergonomic seats for the ultimate in comfort, very practical shelves and compartments, a huge adjustable trunk, not to mention record-breaking livability." Values less dependent on the intoxication of appearances have been imposed on a massive scale. In Europe at least, it is no longer possible to maintain that household appliances can become outmoded by the introduction of simple, small innovations in form or color. In many sectors, such as mass-market electronics, household appliances, or furniture, a formal classicism prevails. The form of electric razors, television sets, or refrigerators changes very little; no stylistic innovation manages to make them obsolete. The more technological complexity increases, the more the external aspect of objects becomes sober and streamlined. The ostentatious forms of automobile fenders and the gleam of chrome have given way to compactness and integrated lines; stereo systems, VCRs, and laptop computers appear with serious, streamlined forms. The frivolous complication of forms has been superseded by a high-tech superfunctionalism. Fashion is embodied less in decorative gaudiness than in the luxury of precision, of striking perceptible touches. Incorporating less formal play and more technical aspects, fashion tends toward a kind of upscale chic.

At the heart of the fashion-oriented redeployment of production, there is industrial design. There is a paradoxical element here, if we think of the initial intentions of the movement that was articulated and implemented early in this century in the Bauhaus and later in the positions of "orthodox design." From the Bauhaus on, in fact, design has been directly opposed to the fashion spirit, to the gratuitous play of the decorative, of kitsch and aesthetic superfetation. Hostile in principle to superfluous elements and superficial ornamentation, design in the strict sense is basically looking for the functional improvement of products; it is a matter of conceiving of formal economic configurations defined above all by their semantic or semiologic richness. Ideally, design does not assign itself the task of coming up with objects that will please the eye, but rather with finding rational and functional solutions. Design in this respect is not a decorative art but "informational design,"[11] aimed at creating forms adapted to needs, functions, and the conditions of modern industrial production.

In practice, the opposition to fashion was not nearly so radical. For one thing, in the United States, where industrial design developed most rapidly, its chief aims were the embellishment of objects and the seduction of consumers: styling, prettifying, dressing up, or making over through design. Then too, once they had moved beyond the intransigent, puritanical approach of the Bauhaus, designers took on less revolutionary tasks. Purist efforts to perfect the design of industrial products were supplanted by the more modest project of "resemanticizing" the sphere of everyday objects, that is, of incorporating into that sphere the rhetoric of seduction.[12] The functionalist program was humanized and relativized; it opened itself up to people's multiple needs—aesthetic, psychological, emotional. Design abandoned the purely rational viewpoint in which form was to be rigorously deduced from the material and practical requirements of the object alone: "Aesthetic value is an inherent *part* of function."[13] If the supreme ambition of design is to create useful objects adapted to essential needs, its other ambition is to "humanize" industrial projects; the quest for visual appeal and formal attractiveness must have its place. In this sense, design is not opposed to fashion; rather, it institutes a specific fashion, a new elegance, an abstract beauty consisting of rigor and architectonic coherence. This is fashion of a special sort, in that it is unidimensional and functional (at least with the exception of recent "new design" fancies). Unlike "fashion," characterized by perpetual stylistic reversals, design is homogeneous; it restructures the environment in a consistent spirit of simplification, geometry, and logic. The design process does not keep objects from being presented in styles common to a given epoch or from eventually becoming unfashionable.

In its reaction against the irrational sentimentality of objects, in its use of raw materials, in its consecration of orthogonal streamlining and aerodynamics, design does not leave the order of seduction behind; instead, it invents a new morality for this order. Staging and artificiality have not disappeared; they have become accessible via the unprecedented pathway of minimalization, letting the "truth" of objects speak for itself,[14] with the discreet charm of simplification, economy of means, and transparency. After the seduction of caprice and ornamental theatricality, we have a cold, univocal, modernist seduction. With design, the world of objects is purged of reference to the past; everything belonging to collective memory is abolished in favor of a hypercontemporary presence. In creating contemporary forms that exclude relationships with other times (copies of ancient models) and places (floral motifs inspired by nature), design becomes a paean to rigorous modernity; like fashion, design connotes and valorizes the social present. The design object appears to lack roots; it does not arouse the imagination through allegorical or mythological references; it offers a sort of absolute presence without the slightest allusion to anything other than itself, without any temporality other than the present. The design object functions in the here and now; its attraction stems from the constitutive charge of pure modernity that it legitimizes. Hostile to futility, design is nevertheless subtended by the same temporal logic as fashion: the logic of the contemporary. Thus design appears as one of the figures of the sovereignty of the present.

Nevertheless, design is by no means wedded in its essence to the geometric and rationalist aesthetic. For one thing, an artisanal design style of warmer, more intimate forms has prevailed for some time (Scandinavian design, Habitat, and so on); furthermore, in the late 1970s, new design trends began to rehabilitate emotion, irony, unpredictability, and fantasy, along with the misappropriation of objects and heterogeneous collages. Reacting against the rational and austere modernism inherited from the Bauhaus, the Nuovo Design (Memphis, Alchimia) presented improbable, provocative, almost unusable "postmodern" objects; articles of furniture became toys, gadgets, playful and expressive sculptures. With the trend toward poeticization and postfunctionalism, design displays its fashion essence all the more openly even as it enacts a spectacular change of direction. Fantasy, playfulness, and humor, which are constitutive principles of fashion, have won a place in the modernist environment; they have managed to become inseparable from design itself. Hence the juxtaposition of stylistic contraries, the coexistence of ludic and functional forms. On the one hand, we encounter increasing fantasy and irony; on the other, increasing minimalist functionality. And the process is only beginning; in the world of objects, uniformity is not on the horizon.

The rift introduced by design and the Bauhaus may be compared to the rift opened up by haute couture: design and modern fashion both participate, paradoxically, in the same historical dynamic. By refusing gratuitous ornamentation, by redefining objects in terms of combinatorial and functional arrangements, the Bauhaus sanctioned the autonomy of creators of objects, in a context of rigorism and formal asceticism; it established in the realm of objects what the couturiers had achieved, in a different way, for clothing: the demiurgic freedom of the creator, now independent—at least in theory—of the client's spontaneous tastes. Even if, unlike the Bauhaus (which was completely committed to a functionalist and utilitarian rationalism), haute couture perpetuated the tradition of elitism and ornamentation, in structural terms design is to objects what haute couture was to clothing. At the core, we find the same modern project of wiping the slate clean, the same wholesale reconstruction of an environment freed from tradition and national idiosyncrasies, the same institution of a universe of signs attuned to the new needs. Haute couture remained faithful to the tradition of luxury, gratuitousness, and artisanal work, while the Bauhaus accepted the challenge of being "useful" and took industrial constraints into account. But together they helped revolutionize and denationalize styles; they helped promote the cosmopolitanism of forms.

The radical nature of design prevents it from being reduced to a class ideology. It cannot be viewed purely and simply as an effect of the new conditions of capitalism oriented toward mass consumption and the marketing effort. A whole literature of Marxist inspiration has delighted in demystifying the creative and humanistic ideology of design by stressing its subjection to the imperatives of mercantile production and the profit motive. This criticism is partly warranted; however, it leaves unexplored the historically complex factors involved in the emergence of design. While the impact of the new technologies, the new conditions under which articles are produced and marketed (industrial mass production of standardized articles), must not be underestimated, they cannot account on their own for the appearance of the functionalist aesthetic. Design is inseparable from the work of modern plastic artists and, less obviously, from democratic values. The debt the design aesthetic owes to the work of avant-garde painters and sculptors—cubism, futurism, constructivism, de Stijl—can hardly be missed.[15] Just as modern art achieved formal autonomy by freeing itself from faithfulness to models, so the Bauhaus movement was committed to producing forms defined through their internal coherence, without reference to any standard but the way the object was to function. Modern painting has created works valued in and for themselves: the Bauhaus for its part has extended that gesture by imagining strictly combinatorial objects. The functional style exalts the process of paring down, stripping away; it glorifies right angles and formal simplicity. This style is in fact the end result of the modern artistic spirit in rebellion against the aesthetics of display, emphasis, and ornamentation. The functional environment only brings to completion the essentially democratic modern artistic revolution that was inaugurated around 1860, jettisoning majestic solemnity and strong idealization. Seen as a negation of convention and a rehabilitation of the prosaic, all of modern art is inseparable from a culture of equality that dissolves the hierarchies of genre, subject, and material. Thus the functionalist aesthetic is subtended by revolutionary and democratic modernist values: it wrenches objects away from ornamental uses, abolishes the poetic models of the past, uses "vulgar" materials (projectors and table lamps in chrome or aluminum, Breuer's 1925 chairs and stools made of metallic tubes). The movement toward equality has eliminated signs of ostentatious difference; it has legitimized the new non-noble industrial materials; it has facilitated the promotion of "authenticity" and "truth" as values attributed to the object. The celebration of functional beauty owes little to the diverse social strategies of distinction; it is rooted in the industrial techniques of mass production, the effervescence of the avant-garde, and the revolution in aesthetic values characteristic of the democratic age.

The Consuming Passion, or Ambiguous Rationality

Among the theoretical works that have analyzed the extension of the fashion form in contemporary societies, those of Jean Baudrillard occupy a special place. Baudrillard deserves credit for being one of the first to see the fashion form not as an epiphenomenon but as the backbone of consumer society. By analyzing fashion and the process of consumption as part of the open logic of society and not as a manipulation of consciousnesses, he unquestionably helped overturn Marxist dogmas and succeeded in restoring vitality and theoretical nobility to the issue. Baudrillard coupled his radical hypothesis with close attention to concrete details; his texts remain an important contribution to the theory of fashion in Western societies.

The challenge to Marxist dogma and the desire to understand novelty have included the keystone of all problematics in fashion since the nineteenth century: social classes and their competition for status. Baudrillard's analyses are based on an effort to demystify the ideology of consumption as a utilitarian behavior on the part of an individual subject whose goal is pleasure and the satisfaction of desires. In Baudrillard's eyes, this ideology is deceptive: far from being rooted in a logic of individual desire, consumption is based on a logic of performance and social distinction. Veblen's theory of conspicuous consumption as a social institution charged with signifying social status becomes a major reference; in its wake, consumption is seen as a social structure of segregation and stratification. In this view, one never consumes an object for its own sake or because of its use value, but only by virtue of its signifying value in a system of exchange, that is, by virtue of the prestige, status, and social rank that it confers. Beyond its role in the satisfaction of needs, consumption has to be recognized as an instrument of the social hierarchy, and objects have to be seen as loci for the social production of difference and of status values.[16] By the same token, consumer society, with its orchestrated obsolescence, its marks of greater or lesser value, its product lines, is nothing but an immense production process for "sign values" that serve to connote rank and reinscribe social difference in an egalitarian age that has destroyed hierarchies based on birth. The hedonistic ideology that subtends consumption is only an alibi for a more fundamental determination: the logic of social overdifferentiation. The race to consume and the passion for novelty are not rooted in the pleasure principle; they are driven by competition for status.

According to such a theory, the use value of merchandise is not the principal motivation for consumers, whose primary concerns are social standing and rank. Objects are merely "class exponents," social signifiers and discriminants; they function as signs of social mobility and social aspirations. This logic in which objects are signs is what drives the accelerated renewal of objects and their restructuring under the aegis of fashion: systematic ephemerality and innovation exist only in order to reproduce social differentiation. Thus, the most orthodox theory of fashion has come galloping back: the ephemeral is based on symbolic class competition; the bold, bizarre novelties of fashion serve to recreate distance, to exclude the greatest number—for the masses are incapable of assimilating them right away—and on the contrary to set apart, for a time, the privileged classes that can appropriate these novelties: "Formal innovation in the realm of objects is not aimed at an ideal world of objects; it is aimed rather at a social ideal, that of the privileged classes, which involves a perpetual renewal of their cultural advantage."[17] Novelty in fashion is above all a distinctive sign, a "luxury of the well-to-do." Far from undermining social disparities in terms of objects, fashion "speaks to everyone, the better to put everyone in his or her place. It is one of the institutions that most successfully restitutes cultural inequality and social discrimination—it establishes them under the pretext of abolishing them."[18] What is more, fashion contributes to social inertia in that the renewal of objects can compensate for an absence of real social mobility and a disappointed desire for social and cultural progress.[19] As an instrument of class distinction, fashion reproduces social and cultural segregation; it participates in the modern mythology that masks the inaccessibility of equality.

These classic analyses raise endless questions. However interesting they may be, as I see it they have missed the most important aspect of the explosion of consummate fashion: they have been blind to the new type of social regulation based on inconsistency, seduction, and a surfeit of choice. I would not dream of denying that objects may on occasion be social signifiers and signs of ambition. Rather, I am contesting the idea that mass consumption is governed chiefly by a process of status distinction and differentiation, that it is fully identified with the production of honorific values and social emblems. What is strikingly original, in historical terms, about the rise of needs is precisely that it inaugurated a trend in which *consumption has been desocialized*, in which the age-old primacy of the status value of objects has given way to the dominant value of pleasure (for individuals) and use (for objects). This reversal of direction is the distinguishing feature of the work of consummate fashion. We acquire objects less and less in order to acquire social prestige, in order to set ourselves apart from groups of lower status and to affiliate ourselves with groups of higher status. In acquiring objects, we are aiming not so much at social legitimacy and social difference as at a *personal* satisfaction that is less and less concerned with the judgments of others. Consumption, by and large, is no longer an activity governed by the quest for social recognition; it is undertaken in an effort to achieve well being, functionality, pleasure for its own sake. Consumption has very largely ceased to be a logic of status display; it has shifted into the order of utilitarianism and the individualist quest for privacy.

It is true that in the early stage of the rise of mass consumption, certain objects—the earliest automobiles, the first television sets—could be elements of prestige, more heavily invested with distinctive social value than with use value. But it is perfectly obvious that those days are past. Today, we feel we have a natural right to new objects; we know nothing but the ethic of consumption. Even the new goods that appear in the marketplace (videocassette players, microcomputers, laser-disc players, microwave ovens, the Minitel in France) have not won recognition as articles charged with connotations of social standing; they are more and more rapidly absorbed by a collective avidity not for social differentiation but for autonomy, novelty, stimulation, information. To interpret the rapid infatuation of the middle and lower classes with videocassette players or sailboards in terms of the social logic of difference and distinction is the worst of misreadings: social pretension is not at stake. What is involved, rather, is the thirst for image and spectacle, the taste for autonomy, the cult of the body, the intoxication of sensation and novelty. The purpose of consuming is less and less to impress others and to earn social consideration; we consume more and more for ourselves. We consume for the objective services that things afford us: this is the path of narcissistic individualism, which corresponds not only to the development of the craze for psychological and bodily well-being, but also to a new relation to others and to objects. It is no more accurate, now, to represent consumption as a space ruled by the constraint of social differentiation than as an unbridled "mimetic rivalry" and the envious war of all against all.[20] The unleashing of waves of imitation and the equalization of conditions do not lead to more interpersonal rivalry and competition; quite to the contrary, what others think matters less and less in our acquisition of things. We are witnessing a pacification, a neutralization, of the universe of consumption. Neonarcissism has reduced our dependence on social norms and our fascination with them; it has individualized our relation to social status. What counts is less the opinion of others than the made-to-order management of our own time, our own material environment, our own pleasure.

This obviously does not mean that objects have no more symbolic value, or that consumption has nothing to do with competition for status. In a good many cases, the purchase of a car, a second home, or top-of-the-line designer articles signals an explicit desire to set oneself apart socially, to display one's rank. As we know, luxury products have not suffered from the economic crisis. They continue to be sought after and valorized; among other things, they reflect the persistence of the code that relates differences in social status to the consumption of specific products. But prestigious consumption must not be viewed as a model for mass consumption; the latter depends much more on the personal values of comfort, pleasure, and practical use. We are living in an era in which use value is getting its revenge over status value; private enjoyment is winning out over honorific value. As evidence, we can cite not only the emergence of contemporary consumerism, but also advertising itself, which puts greater emphasis on an object's qualities, on dreams and feelings, than on the values of social status: "Own the road, rule it, triumph over it, thanks to the engine's terrific power, and even more to its fantastic intelligence. . . . Touch the steering wheel, caress it and feel the reaction of a fine, impetuous and docile beast. . . . Glide into space with the superb serenity of total pleasure. All that and more in the Golf GTI." Baudrillard's critique of Marx's critique of the political economy has been misguided: far from initiating the "relegation of use value," consummate fashion brings that process to an end. The fetishism of the sign-object belongs more to the past than to the present; we are on equal footing in the age of use value, reliability, use warranties, tests, reports on the relation of quality to price. Above all, we want appliances that work, that ensure good quality in terms of comfort, durability, and ease of use. This does not keep consumption from being associated with any number of psychological dimensions and images. But images of the product are at issue rather than signs of class, which constitute only one feature of the product image among many. When we purchase an object with a brand name we are consuming dynamism, elegance, power, defamiliarization, masculinity, femininity, age, refinement, security, naturalness—all these images may influence our choices, and it would be simplistic to write them off as indicative of social class alone, at a time when tastes are becoming increasingly individualized. With the reign of heterogeneous, polymorphous, proliferating images, we leave the primacy of class logic behind and enter the age of intimate and existential motives, psychological gratification, personal pleasure, and product quality and usefulness. Not even the success of products with designer labels can be explained simply in terms of the constraint of social standing; that success also attests to the neonarcissistic tendency to please oneself, to a growing appetite for quality and aesthetic value in broader social groupings.

The materialism of contemporary societies is widely deplored. But why do the critics not stress that consummate fashion also helps detach human beings from objects? Under the regime of use value, we no longer become attached to things; we readily trade in our houses, our cars, or our furniture. The age that imparts social sanctity to merchandise is an age in which people part from their objects without pain. We no longer love things for themselves or for the social status they confer, but for the services they render, for the pleasures they provide, for a perfectly exchangeable use value. In this sense, fashion makes things less real; it takes away their substance them through the homogeneous cult of utility and novelty. What we own we will replace; the more objects become our prostheses, the less we care about them. Our relation to things stems now from an abstract, paradoxically disembodied love. How can we continue to talk about alienation at a time when, far from being dispossessed by objects, individuals are dispossessing themselves of objects? The more consumerism advances, the more objects become disenchanted means, mere instruments: so it goes, as the democratization of the material world proceeds.

These phenomena contribute to the adoption of an entirely new perspective on the historical role of consummate fashion. Far from being a vector for the reproduction of social differentiations and segregations, the expanded fashion system more than anything else has facilitated the pursuit of the age-old quest for individual autonomy. The fashion system is an instrument for the individualization of persons, not for the reintroduction of social distance. By institutionalizing the ephemeral, by diversifying the range of objects, the consummate stage of fashion has multiplied opportunities for personal choice. It has forced individuals to inform themselves, to embrace novelty, to assert subjective preferences: each individual has become a permanent decision-making center, an open and mobile subject viewed through the kaleidoscope of merchandise. Whereas even the everyday environment is increasingly conceptualized and configured from the outside by specialized bureaucratic agencies, under the reign of fashion we as individuals function increasingly as subjects of our own private existence; we are free operators of our lives, owing to the surfeit of choices in which we are immersed. The empire of fashion indeed signifies a universalization of modern standards, but in a process that promotes an unprecedented emancipation and destandardization of the subjective sphere. Absorbed by the project of demystifying the ideology of consumption, the critical tradition has been blind to the power of individual autonomy that has been ineluctably encouraged by mass hedonism, that cultural epicenter of consummate fashion. To see hedonism merely as an instrument of social control and manipulation is a serious error; in fact it is above all a vector of the affirmation of private individuality. Marcuse could write, without hedging, that "the scope of society's domination over the individual is immeasurably greater than ever before. . . . The productive apparatus . . . obliterates the opposition between the private and public existence, between individual and social needs,"[21] just when a hyperindividualist explosion was about to occur that would affect all areas of private life. His analysis was particularly blind to the movement of social modernity, if we can judge by the extraordinary process of personal emancipation of individuals today in the sphere of sexual relations, family life, women's behavior, procreation, dress, sports, and interpersonal relations. The goal of realizing one's potential, of deriving immediate pleasure from life, cannot simply be equated with the training of the *homo consumans*: far from lulling people into a stupor with programmed entertainment, hedonistic culture stimulates us all to take greater charge of our own lives, to assume more self-mastery, to achieve self-determination in relationships with oth-

ers, to live more for ourselves. The euphoric assimilation of programmed
models is only one manifestation of fashion; on the other side, there is a
growing indeterminacy of existence, the morality of "fun" working toward
the individualist assertion of personal autonomy.

The frivolous economy has definitively uprooted traditional standards
and behaviors. It has generalized the spirit of curiosity, democratized
tastes and the passion for novelty at all levels of existence and in all social
ranks. The result is a fundamentally labile type of individuality. To the
extent that the ephemeral has invaded the everyday, novelties come on the
scene more and more rapidly and are more and more readily accepted.
The fashion economy has engendered a social agent in its own image: the
fashion person who has no deep attachments, a mobile individual with a
fluctuating personality and tastes. Such openness to change on the part of
social agents requires a rethinking of the classic charges brought against
frivolous society, accusing it of organized waste and bureaucratic-capital-
ist irrationality. The arguments are familiar, and examples are legion.
Why have ten different brands of identical detergent? Why spend money
on advertising? Why so many models and versions of cars? Lofty souls
may lament the fact: an immense irrationality lies at the heart of the technocratic universe. But the critics are tarred with their own brush: critical
intelligence is the paradoxical victim here of what is most superficial. The
critics fail to see the forest for the trees. How, indeed, can one evaluate all
the implications of the development of a flexible ethos for modern society?
Or the implications of a new type of kinetic, open personality? Is this not
what societies in perpetual motion need most? How could our societies fall
into step with constant change and bring about the requisite social adaptations if individuals were wedded to intangible principles, if novelty had
not won broad social legitimacy? Innovative societies engaged in international competition have an urgent need for flexible attitudes, for nonrigid
outlooks. The reign of fashion leads precisely in this direction, as much by
way of the economy of objects as by way of information. We have to move
beyond moralistic vituperation against fashion. Its irrationality and its
apparent wastefulness aside, fashion contributes to a more rational edification of society because it socializes human beings to change and pre-
pares them for perpetual recycling. Capable of softening rigidities and
resistances, the fashion form is an instrument of social rationality, an *invisible* rationality; while it cannot be measured, it is irreplaceable for a
rapid adaptation to modernity, for the acceleration of transformations in
progress, for the constitution of a society equipped to face the endlessly
variable requirements of the future. The system of consummate fashion
puts civil society in a state of openness with respect to historical movement; it creates receptive mentalities characterized by fluidity that are inherently prepared for the voluntary adventure of the new.

It is true that consummate fashion is also at the heart of certain difficulties in social adaptation, certain more or less chronically dysfunctional aspects of the democracies. Individuals brought up in the hedonist ethic are not much inclined to give up the advantages they have acquired (salaries, retirement benefits, working hours), to accept sacrifices, or to see their standard of living decline; they tend to make demands or to seek benefits in terms of their own social category alone. By exacerbating individualist passions, consummate fashion has followed the path of indifference to the public good. It feeds the propensity of individuals to look out for themselves; it gives the present priority over the future; it promotes special interests and corporate interests; it undermines the sense of duty or debt toward the surrounding community. The promotion of corporate interests corresponds unmistakably to the context of economic crisis, but also to the new era of individualism reshaped by the fashion form. The most challenging social struggles that are emerging in France in our day are no longer those concerning global objectives of general interest, but those concerning the conquest or defense of highly localized advantages; they reflect the fraying of class consciousness and class ideologies, the preponderance of group self-interest over the search for overall social progress. The neoindividualist aspiration threatens group identities and class solidarities; it turns its back on macroeconomic constraints and leads to the defense of factional interests at all costs, to status-linked protectionism and the denial of mobility. In France, in some sectors of the economy, entire facets of national life can be paralyzed; consumers and society can be taken hostage in the name of narrow demands. Neocorporatism on the part of wage earners coupled with corporatism on the part of professions protected by long-standing legislation: we must not underestimate the capacity of such manifestations to block the dynamics of change, to perpetuate sameness, to slow down the unavoidable transformations required by the modernization of democracies and international competition. We must take note of the contradictory nature of the historical work of consummate fashion: in one respect it generates a positive attitude toward innovation, while in another respect it freezes the ductility of the social body. Fashion society at once accelerates and rigidifies the tendency toward social mobility; paradoxically, it gives impetus to modernism and conservatism alike.

The contradiction is perhaps not absolutely insurmountable, if we look at it in terms of different levels of historical temporality: the cultural and social effects of consummate fashion appear in different lights according to the temporal reference points selected. No doubt in the short run fashion does contribute to immobility, defensive attitudes, and the reinforcement of archaism. The same does not hold true for the middle run and the long run. On the deepest level, the frivolous age of free societies loosens up behavior; it legitimizes modernization, adaptation, and mutability on a

massive scale. The general acceptance of different levels of severity in efforts to scale down the work force in industrial sectors in decline reveals,
grosso modo, the "wisdom" of contemporary nations, the relative lucidity
of the social actors involved in the economic crisis, even though this consciousness may be somewhat belated. While various blockages and resistances continue to appear, consummate fashion permits democracies to
accelerate the dynamics of modernization.

At the national level, the problem is that, given the mobility required for
international competition, nations do not all start with the same weap-
onry; they are not all equal in their capacity to take the offensive in the
new form of warfare that is a war of time, the speeding-up of time. Corporate interests, the aspiration to personal well-being, the demand for security and state protection do not carry the same weight everywhere; they do
not impede change in the same way everywhere. In theory, the fashion
form points contemporary societies in the right historical direction; in
practice, it allows some nations to get bogged down in the immobility of
special interests and acquired advantages; it institutes a delaying action
that is fraught with consequences for the construction of the future. Political agencies have the responsibility of managing the effects of consummate fashion, in an effort to optimize its modern potential, to reduce its
conservative aspect. In nations without a strong liberal tradition, the state
has the historical responsibility of bringing off this vital enterprise in as
short a time as possible: the trick is to control the deficit of modernity by
using the powerful sense of the legitimacy of change that coexists with the
collective fear of change. Western European governments need to move as
quickly as possible from the stage in which modernization is both desired
and feared to the stage in which modernization is actually carried out
without major social disruption; indeed, that is their most important task,
if we do not want to come out last in the war of time, if we want to stay in
the running in the competitions of the future. In strongly individualist
societies focused on the cult of the present, such a modernization clearly
cannot be carried out in a forced march, or decreed by fiat from above.
Public power must prepare for the future while taking present aspirations
into account (these are necessary, moreover, in the long run, for the
growth of our societies); it must find a social equilibrium between the ne-
cessities of the future and the demands of the present. Destined inexorably
to accelerate the flexibility and the competitiveness of our societies, the
state, in the European context, has a chance to succeed in this task only if
it can handle the various resistances of the collective body with flexibility
but also with firmness, while imagining new ways of resolving the conflict
between the need to position oneself advantageously in the war of time and
the requirements of life in the present for individual citizens. On the one
hand, the task is to forge a united Europe, to strengthen the competitive-

ness of our industries, to encourage investment; on the other hand, it is necessary to negotiate social peace, to invent reasonable compromises for the partners in the social enterprise. A difficult and uncertain task, but not an impossible one, for it is collectively subtended by the revolution in subjectivities embodied in consummate fashion.

The Power of Novelty

On the "supply" side, the reasons for the boom in the fashion economy are not hard to fathom. The acceleration in scientific progress, combined with the system of economic competition, clearly underlies the world of generalized ephemera. Driven by the profit motive, industrialists create new products, innovating continually in order to increase their market penetration, gain new clients, and revitalize consumption. Consummate fashion is indeed the daughter of capitalism. On the "demand" side, the problem is more complex. As soon as people stop settling for a mechanical determinism that functions via production and advertising of the "revised sequence" type (Galbraith), the evolution of fashion desires calls for closer attention. Why do the countless little novelties "hook" consumers? What brings them acceptance in the marketplace? What permits the economy to function on the basis of rapid obsolescence and tiny combinatorial differences? The prevailing sociological response at least has the merit of clarity: class competition and strategies of social distinction sustain and accompany the dynamics of supply. This type of analysis underlies Baudrillard's earliest work as well as that of Bourdieu. For the latter, it is hardly astonishing that novelties always find a clientele. Neither a matter of conditioning nor of adapting production to public taste, the "almost miraculous correspondence" between the products supplied and the field of consumption results from the "objective orchestration of two logical structures that are relatively independent" but functionally homologous: on the one hand, the logic of competition inherent in the field of production, and on the other hand, the logic of symbolic struggle and strategies of class distinction that determine consumer tastes.[22] Both supply and demand are structured by competitive struggles that are relatively autonomous but strictly homologous; together they ensure that consumption is adequate to production at all times. If new products, as they are developed, are immediately adapted to needs, this does not result from a top-down imposition, but from "the encounter between two systems of differences," the encounter between the logic of conflicts internal to the field of production on the one hand and to the field of consumption on the other. Fashion grows out of this correspondence between the differential production of goods and the differential production of tastes, a correspondence that finds its place in symbolic class struggles.[23]

Even in conjunction with capitalist production processes, the strategies of class distinction do not suffice to explain the workings of an economy restructured by the fashion form. Can we account for the thousands of versions of automobiles, the endless varieties of soft drinks, stereo sets, cigarettes, skis, or eyeglass frames through the mechanics of class distinction? Can we explain the proliferation of pop idols and pop music through the dynamics of social distinction and pretension? The explanatory effort can hardly fail to involve some acrobatic contortions. To which dominant or subordinate faction will a given color correspond, or a given engine, or product line, or category of cigarette, or high-top shoe? The logic of distinction provides a crude map of the fashion economy; it is incapable of accounting for the endless escalating diversification and industrial surfeit of choice. The permanent installation of consummate fashion in our societies will never be understood until we restore cultural values to their rightful place, a place continually obscured by Marxism and sociology alike. No economy of the ephemeral can exist without the synergistic action of major cultural objectives such as comfort, aesthetic quality, individual choice, and novelty. The innumerable improvements in large and small home appliances could hardly have proliferated so rapidly if those improvements had not also responded to individual desires for well-being, to the modern taste for material comfort, to the satisfaction of saving time and doing less work.[24] We cannot understand the success of color television, hi-fi, or compact-disc players without relating this success to a widely shared desire for quality images and music. We cannot comprehend the politics of product lines without taking into consideration the democratic value attributed to personal choice, the individualization of tastes, the desire to have made to-order articles adapted to the consumer's own idiosyncratic preferences. Even if all these mechanisms and meanings were initially embodied at the higher levels of society, they have acquired their own autonomy, a diffuse legitimacy in all social strata. The fashion process that governs our economy is less dependent, in the last analysis, on class oppositions than on orientations shared by the social body as a whole, and these orientations taken together open up the social possibility of an endless dynamic of renewal and diversification. The impact of symbolic class rivalries is secondary with respect to the power of these imaginary significations that have penetrated all classes and have taken on a life of their own.

In the empire of fashion, what amounts to the cultural power of novelty requires special emphasis. Class rivalry is insignificant compared to the effects of the social signification that single-handedly generates the taste for difference, that precipitates boredom with anything repetitive, that makes people love and want anything that changes, almost before the fact. The "planned" obsolescence of industrial products is not simply a result of the capitalist technostructure. It has been grafted onto a society that has been converted in very large measure to the incomparable thrill of newness. At the root of the demand for fashion, the imperative of setting oneself apart socially is less and less operative, while the thirst for novelty comes increasingly into play. Consummate fashion, like the first historical manifestations of fashion at the end of the Middle Ages, is essentially dependent on the emergence of a certain number of social meanings; in the foreground of these meanings we find the exaltation and legitimization of novelties. While the ethos of novelty may have been the exclusive property of the aristocratic and bourgeois social elites for centuries, it is henceforth applicable at all levels of society. And while there is no doubt about the contribution of mass production to developing the desire for novelty, other factors have made major contributions as well. The code of the new in contemporary societies is inseparable, in particular, from progress in the equalization of conditions and from individualist claims. The more individuals keep to themselves and remain absorbed in themselves, the more different tastes there are, and the more room for novelties. The value of the new proceeds apace with the appeal to the private personality and personal autonomy. At the end of the Middle Ages, fashion was already intertwined with the aspiration to individual personality, with the assertion of individual uniqueness in an aristocratic social and ideological world. The process was simply exacerbated with the reign of equality and democratic individualism. Tocqueville stressed this point: democratic individualism is the burial ground for the reign of the past; all people recognized as free aspire to shed the constraining and compulsory bonds that attach them to the past. Submission to the tacit rules of tradition is incompatible with individual mastery of the self. "Those who have gone before are soon forgotten": whereas the ancestral legacy is discredited in the era of *homo aequalis*, the present and the changing standards that are offered as optional behaviors are correspondingly elevated in status; they prevail not by authority but by persuasion. In submitting to the new decrees, "the modern man flatters himself that he is making a *free choice* of the propositions that are made to him."[25] While obedience to the ancient prescriptions is antithetical to the assertion of individual autonomy, the cult of novelty promotes a feeling of independent individuality: one is free to choose; one no longer makes decisions on the basis of a preexisting collective legitimacy but on the basis of the impulses of one's own heart and mind. With modern individualism, the new receives its full consecration: on the occasion of each shift in fashion, there is a feeling, however tenuous, of subjective freedom, of liberation from past habits. With each novelty, some inertia is shaken off, a passing breath of fresh air becomes a source of discovery, of subjective positioning and availability. In a society of individuals committed to personal autonomy, it is clear why what is new offers such a lively attraction: it is experienced as an instrument of personal "liberation," as an experiment to be undertaken, an experience to be lived, a little adventure of the self. The consecration of the new and modern individualism go hand in hand; novelty is in phase with the aspiration to individual autonomy. If consummate fashion is shored up by the logic of capitalism, it is equally sustained by cultural values that find their apotheosis in the democratic state.

CHAPTER V

Advertising on the Offensive

ADVERTISING has grounds for optimism. The overall amount of money spent on it keeps rising, and advertising itself keeps invading new spaces: state-owned television channels, colloquia, artistic events, sports events, and movies, as well as consumer goods of all sorts, from T-shirts to windsurfer sails. Brand names appear on virtually everything in our everyday environment; today's advertising knows no bounds. We have seen campaigns for "generic" items, products without brand names; we turn to advertising to "have fun" on Minitel or over telephone lines; places for prayer are set aside in supermarkets; spot ads fill the gaps between numbers in recorded music; campaigns are organized to sell stock in de-nationalized enterprises on the open market. Publicity is in its heyday. This expansive logic is enjoying something like a state of grace: children love it, older people condemn it less forcefully than they used to, and people in general in growing numbers look on it more or less favorably. A socially legitimate form of communication, advertising has been conse-crated as an art form as well. Museums make room for it; retrospective poster exhibits are organized; prizes for excellence are awarded; advertise-ments are featured on postcards. The age of mere advertising is dead; long live creative communication! Advertising conspires with art and cinema, and dreams of embracing history.

Political parties, major government agencies, and even whole nations are adopting it freely: as early as 1980, in France, the state could be viewed as the number one advertiser. Brand-name advertising is increasing, matched by public-service and general-interest advertising. Major cam-paigns have been launched on behalf of traffic safety, employment, women's issues, energy-saving measures, and the elderly. Railway and telephone systems, the Paris subway, and the postal service all enjoy the plugged-in delights of communication. Advertising as a strategy is coming into its own. Advertising, not propaganda: these two forms of mass com-munication have too often been amalgamated, when they are actually poles apart. With advertising, communication takes on an entirely original profile; it is caught in the net of the fashion form. At the opposite extreme from totalitarian logic, it is immersed in superficiality and frivolous seduction, in fantasy and gimmickry; at the opposite extreme from the total control that is rather too readily attributed to the unreasonable forms of commercial and political reasoning, advertising embodies a new deal whose fundamentally democratic position and effects we are only beginning to comprehend.

Advertising: Chic Value and Shock Value

One of advertising's key weapons is surprise. At the heart of advertising, we discover the very principles we have seen at work in fashion: originality at any price, perpetual change, ephemera. Anything is better than lulling the audience to sleep; nothing is worse than becoming invisible through familiarity. In France, a poster campaign lasts, on the average, seven to fourteen days. It is essential to keep on creating new texts, new visuals, new spots. Even when slogans or jingles are repeated, the scenarios and images change. Brand-name competition and industrial standardization lead to an endless race for unprecedented effects, for difference; it is a race to capture consumers' attention and memory. The requirement of novelty nevertheless respects the inviolable rule according to which messages must be immediately readable and the conventions of the moment must be followed. This in no way prevents advertising from cheerfully upsetting a certain number of conventions, from pushing back limits, from getting carried away, intoxicated by hyperbole. "In the long run, all fashion is excessive," as Paul Poiret used to say. For its part, advertising does not shy away from excess; indeed, it manifests a wild imagination (witness Grace Jones swallowing a Renault CX) and an inclination to overstatement (witness the Cinzano slogan, "Time is on our side," or "the Pepsi generation"). Advertising is a form of communication based on controlled excess in which the superlative is always counterbalanced by playfulness and humor. "Tomorrow, I'll take the bottom off"; and there are the Wrangler skeletons, or the Visa cards that take off from an aircraft carrier. Advertising uses the discourse of fashion, and like fashion it is fed by shock effects, minitransgressions, spectacular stagings. It depends entirely on "getting noticed" without ever tilting too far toward aggressive provocation.

Advertising's tendency toward excess does not rule out less outrageous campaigns designed explicitly to persuade consumers through the credibility of the message. For a long time, advertising has tended to make apparently plausible statements that assert the unparalleled quality of a product ("Omo washes whiter"), sometimes calling upon the testimony of well-known stars or ordinary individuals in "slice-of-life" sequences. This sort of ad has led Daniel Boorstin to maintain that advertising is situated beyond truth and falsehood, that its register is one of "credibility"[1] rather than truth: in advertising, it is less a matter of delivering verifiable facts than of making declarations that seem plausible, that are more or less credible. We see this with claims backed up by plausible arguments:[2] "When you're Number Two, you try harder" (Avis); "We've been in the business for thirty-two years" (Bis). Still, the evidence suggests that this trend is declining; at the moment, advertising is less interested in convincing than in amusing, astonishing, getting a laugh. Boorstin's cherished "self-fulfilling prophecies," declarations that are neither true nor false, have been replaced by associative plays on words and short circuits of meaning, in increasingly nonrealistic, delirious, preposterous, and extravagant communications. This is the era of creative, spectacular advertising: products have to become stars, they must be transformed into "living beings"; humanized brands have to be created, with their own style and character.[3] It is no longer a question of checking off anonymous performances and flatly objective qualities, but of communicating a "brand-name personality." Seduction through advertising has shifted to a new register; seduction is henceforth invested in the personalized look. Brand names have to be humanized, given a soul and a psychology: the calm Marlboro man; Dim's liberated, sensual, humorous woman; Eram's mischievous, carefree shoes; the with-it Parisian subway system; the Perrier craze. Just as fashion individualizes the appearance of each human being, advertising aims to personalize each brand name. If it is true, as Jacques Séguéla says, that "real" advertising has adopted the methods of the star system, it is even more accurate to say that advertising is communication structured like fashion, more and more under the sway of the spectacular, personalized appearance, pure seduction.

The apotheosis of seduction. Previously, advertising's appeal had remained subject to marketing constraints. Advertisers had to make concessions to rational argument; they had to be able to justify their basic promises. Under the regime of "copy strategy," seduction had to be reconciled with reality, in terms of the merchandise; the product's advantages, its excellence, had to be demonstrated. With advertising's redundant and explanatory slogans, the empire of seduction was limited by the preeminence of plausibility, quantitative measures, and other "objective" virtues of things. Today, creative advertising takes the high road. It gives priority to the realm of a virtually unadulterated imagination. Seductiveness can now be freely exploited for its own sake; it shows off as hyperspectacle, displaying the magic of artifice in stagings indifferent to the reality principle and to the logic of plausibility. Solicitude, warm attentiveness, and gratification function less and less as tools of seduction; instead, we find a playful Hollywood-style theatricality, a superlative gratuitousness (Citroën's AX model billed as "Revolutionary!"). For too long, the essence of advertising was thought to lie in its power to distill communicative warmth; it supposedly won us over by becoming a maternal agency full of little attentions for us.[4] To be sure, even today the affective card may be played ("You love Channel One, Channel One loves you"), the note of solicitude may be sounded ("We put everything we have into the details, so you won't have to. For us, a business trip has to be a success all along the line"—Air Canada). However, we are also starting to see ads that adopt a cynical tone: thus, in the "U.T.A. for U.S.A." campaign, in case you have not caught on, you get this: "Consult your regular doctor." There is also the Epson computer commercial: "Inhuman, our PC A.X.? One hundred percent!" What seduces is not the effort to seduce or cajole or valorize the consumer (compare Kipling toilet water, "for the men who move the world"), but rather the original, spectacular, fantastic aspect of the ad. Seduction proceeds by suspending the laws of the real and the rational, by lightening the seriousness of life, by celebrating artifice.

Even if we have entered the era of "concepts" and creative communication, even if making beautiful and attractive posters is no longer enough, aesthetic considerations remain primordial in the work of advertising. The sculptural valorization of a product, retouched photos, luxury interiors, refined decors, beautiful bodies and faces—by such means, advertising poeticizes products and brand names and idealizes the ordinariness of the merchandise. However important humor, eroticism, or extravagance may be, the most classic weapon of seduction—namely, beauty—continues to be widely exploited. Cosmetic products and perfumes in particular depend systematically on refined, sophisticated ads that feature sublime creatures, the profiles and makeup of one's dreams. But many other ads— for women's underwear, fashion clothing, alcohol, cigarettes, coffee—strive just as hard for the chic effect. High-precision technology is joining the bandwagon: Sharp and Minolta have launched poster campaigns with streamlined designer images. Just as fashion is inseparable from the aestheticization of the individual, so advertising fulfills a cosmetic function for communication. Like fashion, advertising appeals first and foremost to the eye: more than information, it promises beauty, the seductiveness of appearances, an idealized ambiance. Advertising takes its place alongside industrial design, neighborhood renovation, antenna disguises, shopwindow dressing, and landscape renewal, in the generalized process by which we aestheticize and embellish everyday life. Everywhere we turn we encounter reality cosmeticized, value added in the fashion mode.

In addition to aesthetic charm, seduction exploits the fanciful paths of untrammeled creativity. Word plays ("Fran-Choix Ier"—Darty), alliterations and childlike repetitions of syllables ("Qu'est-ce que tu bois, doudou, dis donc"—Oasis), shifts and displacements of meaning ("Do you want to sleep with me?"—Dunlopillo), appeals to emotion (a weeping statue—BASF audiotapes), fantastic or surrealist imagery (a little girl walking on water—Schneider): advertising does not seduce *homo psycho-analyticus*, but *homo ludens*. Its effectiveness has to do with its playful superficiality, with the cocktail of images, sounds, and meanings it offers without any concern for the constraints of reality or the seriousness of truth. "There is Urgo in the air, there is air in Urgo": nothing needs to be deciphered, everything is right there in the simplicity of the wordplay, in the lightness of the complicitous wink. Profundity is dissolved and surfaces are celebrated; advertising is the luxuriousness of game playing, the futility of meaning, creative intelligence at the service of superficiality. If it is true that advertising can help launch fashions, it is truer still that advertising is fashion itself in the realm of communication. More than anything else, it is frivolous communication, a communication in which the "concept" is the gimmick: "Paris-Baghdad: 120F" (Eram). And if fashion is the fairyland of appearances, advertising is without question the fairyland of communication.

People in today's advertising world delight in stressing the radical novelty of their methods. No more claims, no more copy strategy: communication and the creative idea are everything. While we should not underestimate the changes that are under way, it may nevertheless be useful to point out how much still links the new with the old. It is true that today's advertising wants to be seen as "conceptual." This does not keep it from being an extension of an earlier logic, one that is constitutive of modern advertising: the logic of fantasy and play. Before, there were slogans like "Dubo, Dubon, Dubonnet," or "Le chausseur sachant chausser"; now, we see "Mini Mir, mini prix, mais il fait le maximum." Above and beyond the difference of register, advertising still remains a matter of insights, clever ploys, playful combinations, games with meaning. Lacking any other mainsprings but lightheartedness and superficiality of meaning, advertising remains in the realm of superficial and euphoric communication. No wholesale mutation in advertising has occurred, but rather an inflection of its trajectory, in a process that works continually to make communication more flexible, to eliminate the solemnity and ponderousness of discourse, to promote the frivolous world of signs.

The current aggiornamento of advertising has to be understood in the context of the profound transformations our era is experiencing in its mores and its dominant personality. The phenomenon echoes the metamorphoses of the contemporary individual, who is less concerned with displaying external signs of wealth than with fulfilling his or her ego. By turning away from spelling out the anonymous qualities of products, creative advertising registers its own neonarcissistic sensibility, a sensibility detached from the ethic of social status, absorbed by personal subjectivity, by "hunger for life" and the quality of the environment. Advertising films

and slogans seek less to prove the objective excellence of the products involved than to provoke laughter and emotion, to trigger aesthetic, existential, and affective resonances. This spiral in the realm of the imaginary
corresponds to the profile of the postmodern individual. To come into
play, it requires the combined action of the code of novelty and the hedonistic and psychological values that have fostered extremism in the search
for the absolutely unprecedented. The age of pleasure and self-expression
requires a decrease in tedious repetition and stereotyping, an increase in
fantasy and originality. Advertising discovered very early on how to adapt
these cultural transformations to its own ends. It has succeeded in con-
structing a system of communication in harmony with contemporary
tastes—for autonomy, personality, quality of life—while eliminating the
ponderous, monotonous, infantilizing forms of mass communication.
Wrangler features skeletons; the Avenir-Publicité agency promises that
"tomorrow, I'll take the bottom off." Creative advertising has an emancipated appeal; it is addressed to adults who are not particularly conformist,
who are largely indifferent to the major taboos, who are capable of enjoying a commercial on more than one level. All this still does not allow us to
imagine (as Séguéla does) that advertising is taking the place of a faltering
cinema as a mechanism for mythmaking. By its very rhythms and the
perceptions it invites, advertising constitutes an obstacle to dreaming and
prolonged evasion. It has no subjective resonance; it elicits no emotional
involvement. Like fashion, it is made to be forgotten at once; it enters into
the growing gamut of products without residue in our biodegradable culture. Still, it is undeniable that, reoxygenated in this way, advertising succeeds better in its mission, which entails establishing a positive brand
image for products while retaining the public's attention, limiting the
practice of channel hopping. Is that not the real dream of everyone in
advertising?

Advertising's new directions cannot be separated, however, from the
self-promoting desires of advertising people themselves. In a society that
sanctifies novelty, imaginative boldness works better than anything else as
a way to assert oneself in the field of culture and communication. For
someone in advertising, there is no better image than a hyperspectacular
superproduction—no matter how effective it really is in commercial terms,
for its effectiveness is not always in proportion to its creative qualities. The
future of advertising is in large part the work of the logic of advertising
itself, of the fashion imperative that imposes the search for an artistic
image. Alongside ready-to-wear designers and business leaders who have
become "creators," hairdressers who call themselves "facial designers,"
artisans who see themselves as artists, advertising people have plunged
into the immense wave of social valorization characteristic of democratic

societies: they are recognized as "creative types." So it goes, in the age of equality: business gains a supplement of soul. Lucrative activities never come into their own more fully than when they succeed in hoisting themselves up to the level of expression and artistry.

A Tranquil Force

Advertising is communication in the fashion mode; that does not make it any less representative of the modern process of bureaucratic control. As a message of persuasion developed by specialized concept engineers, for some theorists advertising is linked with the logic of bureaucratic power that characterizes modern societies: even though it uses gentle methods, it is always in the process—as are all disciplinary institutions—of guiding behavior from the outside, of penetrating society in its innermost recesses. An exemplar of the benevolent management of human beings, advertising broadens the rationalizing work of power. It reflects the extension of the modern bureaucratic organization that is defined by the way it produces, reorders, and programs the collective whole from an external and scientific viewpoint. This analysis is now a classic one: with the development of the revised sequence,[5] needs are directed and manipulated; the consumer's autonomy is eclipsed in favor of a prepackaged demand orchestrated by the technostructural apparatus. The impetus of bureaucratic power toward rationalizing and planning makes a leap forward here: after production, demand itself turns out to be a target for global planning. Advertising produces needs that are precisely adapted to the supply; it allows producers to program the marketplace, to subvert the freedom of consumers. Society as a whole tends to become a circular system, without exteriority, without difference, without randomness. By scientifically designing tastes and aspirations, by conditioning private lives, advertising only hastens the advent of a fundamentally totalitarian society.[6] In its determination to subject society through and through to the standards of bureaucratic power, to reorchestrate a daily life that has been stripped of all depth and all autonomy, advertising reveals its complicity with totalitarianism, a totalitarianism that is compatible, moreover, with free elections and the party system.

These arguments have had their day. They continue in considerable measure to provide background for our understanding of the advertising phenomenon,[7] even though society's rejection of advertising is on the decline. As I see it, the entire field of problems needs an overhaul. It is exemplary of the speculative slippage that hypocritical thinking can produce. For my part, I shall register a serious objection to the wholesale identification of the advertising order with the totalitarian order. The disjunction is

in fact considerable. Advertising has nothing in common with the efforts
of political power to absorb civil society and the unlimited project of
changing men and women. Nor has it anything in common with the process of tenuous control of the "disciplines" (military service, for example)
that are equally totalitarian in essence, in their goal of standardizing and
programming bodies. According to Foucault's analysis, the disciplines depend structurally on totalitarian logic:[8] the agencies of power work toward
a thorough reconstitution of the movements of bodies; they think in the
place of subjects; they direct them "rationally," orchestrating the most
minute details of behavior from without. Advertising does nothing of the
sort. In place of hit-or-miss coercion there is communication; in place of
regimented rigidity there is seduction; in place of mechanistic training
there is playful entertainment. Where the disciplines categorize bodies according to fixed grids and block the initiative of subjects by minute regulations, advertising opens up a space of broad indeterminacy. It always
leaves open the possibility that one can evade its persuasive action: one
can change the channel, turn the page. The fashion form has no relation
to panoptic totalitarian logic. Advertising integrates individual freedom
and the randomness of subjective movements into its own order. With
advertising, a new level of control is in place: it is no longer a question of
illuminating every dark corner, of controlling every aspect of life, but
rather of influencing a collective whole while leaving the individuals who
constitute that whole free to opt out of its action. Advertising acts on
masses, not individuals; its power is not mechanical but statistical. The
discipline of the infinitesimal has given way to a mode of action that ig-
nores the universe of the minuscule. Neither a form of "political anatomy"
nor a technology of subjection, advertising is an agent of stochastic stimulation.

The totalitarian enterprise, as we know, acquires its singular historical
identity only in relation to its goal of complete absorption of civil society
by the agency of the state. As collective life becomes an object for the state
to control and organize down to the smallest details, all elements that appear foreign to the standards of the party-state are subject to limitless
domination and repression. Everything that exists independently of the
power structure, anything that weaves links of sociability arising from
earlier states of humanity, has to be excluded and destroyed. As Hannah
Arendt put it, totalitarianism is rooted in the phantasmagoric belief that
everything is possible; its aim is "the transformation of human nature."[9]
Human beings and human societies are experimental fields, blank slates,
pure amorphous matter inherently subject to shaping by the unlimited
power of the state. A new spirit, a new human being, must be formed and
educated. This truly demiurgic project has nothing in common with the
much more limited enterprise of advertising and the "revised sequence."

Only through an insidious analogy has it been possible to see the "programming" of daily life and the creation of needs as a totalitarian manifestation of power. Advertising does not aim to reform people and mores; in reality, it takes people as they are, attempting only to stimulate a preexisting desire to consume. By continually establishing new needs, advertising settles for exploiting the common goals of well-being and novelty. It is not a utopia; it is not a project for transforming minds: advertising considers human beings in the present, with no vision of the future. It is less a matter of reconstituting humanity than of making pragmatic use of existing tastes for material enjoyment, well-being, and novelty. Whatever the critics of generalized conditioning may argue, the management of demand and the creation of desire still remain within a libertarian horizon in which power is in fact limited. The individual is subject to many pressures, to be sure—but always within the framework of autonomous choice and the possibility of refusal or indifference, always within the context of enduring human aspirations and ways of life. This is a critical point. Advertising is a renunciation of total power. It does not attempt a wholesale re-creation of thoughts and attitudes; it acknowledges a human spontaneity that eludes dominating schemes of overarching power. The bureaucratic administration of everyday life stands out paradoxically against an irreducible human background with which advertising quite knowingly coexists.

Advertising can of course serve purposes other than consumption. It is called on more and more often in an effort to make citizens more aware of the great problems of the day, and in an effort to modify various behaviors and inclinations: alcoholism, drug use, reckless driving, selfishness, irresponsible procreation, and so on. Advertising does sometimes seek to change certain attitudes, even moral or existential ones; still, nothing justifies our seeing it as a manifestation of totalitarianism. Advertising campaigns are intended to "sensitize" rather than to indoctrinate. Using humor and catchy phrases, they have nothing to do with central planning or the platitudes of the tribunal of history. Advertising does not promulgate truth and justice from on high. It offers gentle advice; it addresses adults who are capable of grasping the seriousness of the problems that underlie its games and spectacles. Advertising does not resort to invoking traitors, plots, or the sweep of history; it does not call for denunciation, social violence, or self-sacrifice. Its register is not dramatization but goodwill, relaxation, and seduction, in keeping with a peaceful society that valorizes supple dialogue, personal autonomy, and private interests. Advertising influences, but it does not threaten; it suggests, but it does not seek doctrinal domination; it functions without invoking Manicheanism or inducing guilt, in the belief that individuals can correct their own behavior almost on their own, once they are aroused to responsible awareness by the media. As with brand-name advertising, public-interest advertising—

contrary to appearances—does not seek to invent a new human being ex nihilo on the basis of ideological and political requirements running against the tide of spontaneous mass desires. Rather, it seeks to diffuse standards and ideals that are actually accepted by everyone but are not always put into practice. Who does not agree that alcohol has harmful effects? Who does not care about babies? Who is not outraged by world hunger? Advertising does not take on the task of completely redefining the human race; it exploits embryonic tendencies that are already present by making them more attractive to more people. Far from signifying an exponential race toward total domination, the spread of advertising reflects the reinforcement of a modality of power with minimal ideology and with strictly limited goals.

A good deal has been said and written about the diabolical power of advertising. And yet, if we consider the issue more closely, if we ask what is affected by advertising, it is hard to think of a power whose impact is as modest. At most it succeeds—not automatically and not systematically, moreover—in getting people to buy one brand as opposed to another: Coca-Cola instead of Pepsi, the Renault 205 instead of the Supercinq. That does not add up to very much. Vital for the growth of businesses, advertising plays an insignificant role in individuals' lives and their most important choices. The power of advertising is paradoxical: crucial for businesses but without major consequences for individuals, it acts effectively only in the sphere of the inessential and the irrelevant. Conforming to the superficiality of its own messages, advertising itself is only a surface power, a sort of zero-degree power as measured by the standard of individual existence. It undoubtedly carries some weight in individual decisions, but only in the state of relative indifference that tends to be generated by the expanding universe of industrial hyperchoice. Things have to be put back into perspective. The influence of advertising does not abolish the reign of human freedom. Rather, its action is exercised at the lowest level of that freedom, the level where a state of indifference reigns, where there is an excess of choice among scarcely differentiated options.

In the cultural sphere, the situation is in the last analysis quite similar. Of course the highly concentrated offering of the latest hits on radio stations means that records are sold. Of course movie posters and top billings draw the public en masse toward dark rooms. But these things always happen with a large measure of unpredictability and they meet with decidedly uneven success. Of course media-based promotional techniques manage to beef up book sales, and they have some influence on the choices made by buyers. Still, does that justify the charge of brainwashing? What is it that the media actually have the power to do? To get people to read some hastily pieced-together autobiography rather than a novel etched in gold? In what respect is this a scandal for democracy? Is it because the media lend their authority to some trivial essay or some telegenic author rather than to a major work? But we need to be perfectly clear about one thing: the power of advertising, whether it is used directly or, as in the case in point, indirectly, is only short-term power; its resonance is basically superficial. The public at large absorbs the latest success like anything else: out of curiosity, in order to be in the know, in order to have seen. Nothing more. Its reading is empty, devoid of effect and certainly devoid of major or lasting intellectual impact when the work itself is only a dazzling facade. Advertising is anything but a force for the totalitarian formation and direction of consciousness; it is a power without consequences. It may lead to big sales, but not to intellectual repercussions: media coverage may be in stereo, but its effects are inaudible, for they are drowned out at once in the baffles of the next new best-seller. If the nonspecialist public is susceptible to the loud voice of advertising, this does not mean that there is no space for public reflection, for the propagation and collective discussion of new ideas. More or less quickly, more or less indirectly, counter-fires are lit, and new titles and new evaluations appear, raising doubts in readers' minds or directing their curiosity elsewhere. Nothing impedes this process: the real questions, the great works, inevitably bounce back onto the media stage; they can never stay very long in the shadows, by virtue of the very bulimia of advertising and the fashion spirit. It is permissible to deplore that our era puts trash on its pedestals, but it is not legitimate to denounce the destruction of the democratic public space where in fact intellectual reference points are merely becoming more complex and less firmly anchored. Media effects are only skin-deep. Advertising does not have the power with which it is widely credited. Promotional techniques do not destroy the space of critical discussion. Instead, they put intellectual authorities into circulation; they multiply references, names, and celebrities; they blur reference points by treating a piece of hackwork and a masterpiece as if they were equivalent, by failing to differentiate between the superficial and the serious. As they continue to heap praise on second-class works, they undermine the old aristocratic intellectual hierarchy; they place academic values and media values on the same plane. They offer a thousand thinkers, ten thousand contemporary works to be reckoned with: we may smile condescendingly, but a systematic process of *desacralization* and an accelerated *rotation* of works and authors is inaugurated in this way. It is not true that the great names are obscured by cultural impostors; it is only that media harassment and the proliferation of names causes the great ones to lose their aura, their unchallenged authority, their sovereign, untouchable position. In this sense, the marketing of "thought" carries out a democratic task; even if it regularly pays homage to insignificant starlets, at the same time it dissolves absolute figures of knowledge and attitudes of immutable reverence in favor of a space of interrogation that is undoubtedly more confused but also broader, more mobile, and less orthodox.

"Advertising makes everyone want the same thing": few ideas are more widely accepted than this one. Advertising is accused of making tastes uniform, of laminating individual personalities; it is seen as brainwashing, the rape of the masses; it is held responsible for the atrophy of individual judgment and personal decision making. It would indeed be hard to deny that advertising succeeds in increasing sales volume and in directing public taste toward certain products on a massive scale. But if we fail to look beyond this process of standardization, we miss the other facet of advertising's work, a much less obvious but much more crucial one with respect to the future of the democracies. As a strategic vector of the redefinition of life-styles centered on consumption and leisure, advertising has helped discredit the ethics of saving in favor of the ethics of spending and immediate gratification. Thus we must render it its due: paradoxically, from the standpoint of the hedonistic culture that it inseminates, advertising must be seen as an agent of human individualization, a force accelerating the quest for personality and individual autonomy. Beyond the real manifestations of social homogenization, advertising not only promotes objects and information, it also works to emphasize the principle of individuality. In the here and now, it generates mass phenomena; in the longer run, and less visibly, it produces destandardization and subjective autonomy. Advertising has a role to play in the progress of the democratic social state.

Can we do better if we apply the psychoanalytic grid to the effects of advertising? In what respect, for example, is its originality illuminated if we acknowledge that it manifests a logic of perversity? One can always maintain, of course, that advertising alludes to desire while proceeding at once to cover up the constitutive absence of desire; one can always say that advertising allows lack of desire to be masked by proposing an escalation of fetish objects.[10] But if we were to do that, we would lose sight of one of advertising's much more significant effects, namely, the way it systematically destabilizes and galvanizes movements of desire even in the sphere of everyday needs. Advertising helps stir up desire in all its states, helps institute it on a hypermobile base. It detaches desire from the closed and repetitive circuits inherent in traditional social systems. Along with mass production, advertising is a technology of disconnection and acceleration of the displacements of desire. We have moved away from an order in which one whole sector of desire was largely stationary into an open, mobile, ephemeral register. Advertising has given rise to a broad-based fashion desire, to desire structured like fashion. In the process, the social significance of consumption has been transformed on a vast scale: by glorifying novelty, by removing the element of guilt from the act of purchasing, advertising has taken the tension out of consumption, has rid it of a certain seriousness that went along with the ethics of saving. Consumption as a whole now operates under the sign of fashion. It has become a casual practice that has internalized the legitimacy of the ephemeral and of permanent renewal.

Politics Takes the Top Off

Politics, in turn, has jumped on the bandwagon. All things considered, it has made a fairly rapid accommodation to advertising and image making. In the United States, since the 1950s, political communication has come increasingly to resemble modern advertising; it uses the same principles, the same techniques, the same experts. Electoral campaigns are orchestrated by publicity agents and media advisors; one-minute spots modeled on commercials are produced; methods derived from motivational research are applied to speech writing and image building on behalf of political figures. After commercial marketing comes political marketing: it is no longer a matter of ideological conversion of the citizenry, but of selling a product in the best possible package. The austere heavy-handedness of propaganda has given way to the seduction of contact, simplicity, and sincerity; prophetic incantations have given way to the enticements of personalized shows and the transformation of political leaders into stars. Politics has shifted to a new register; it has been annexed in large measure by seduction. Everything possible is done to give our leaders an image of warm and sympathetic competence. Private lives are exposed in intimate little interviews or two-way tussles; no holds are barred in the effort to reinforce or correct an image, to arouse a response of emotional attraction that transcends rational motives. Seduction works through intimacy and proximity: political figures participate in variety shows; they appear in jogging clothes; they no longer hesitate to get up on stage. Valéry Giscard d'Estaing has played the accordion in public; Lionel Jospin has sung "Les Feuilles mortes"; François Mitterand has tried to look trendy. The political scene is veering away from pompous detachment in favor of glitter and variety: screen and stage stars are trotted out for electoral campaigns; funny T-shirts, stickers, and other gimmicks are offered as props. Political meetings are festive occasions complete with confetti and euphoria: supporters see film clips and dance to rock music or cheek to cheek.

Posters, too, have been transformed by the appeal of advertising. Aggressive, solemn, heavily symbolic posters have been replaced by posters featuring smiling political personalities, ties flapping in the breeze, figures exhibiting all the innocence of children. Advertisers have carried the day: political expression has to be "with it." Entertainment and creative communication are indispensable; the new posters and slogans, emotional and psychological in tone, appeal to feeling ("La force tranquille," "Vivement demain," "N'ayons pas peur de la liberté"). Telling the truth is not enough now. The truth must be told without boring anyone; it must be told with imagination, elegance, and humor. Humorous complicity and pastiches are coming to the fore; President Carter hired a gag writer to make his speeches more appealing. The spirit of "fun" continues to spread, in light-hearted political campaign literature published on posters or in newspapers in the form of comic strips ("Help! The Right is coming back!" "What big teeth you have, Grandma Right!" "The Great Disillusion: an exclusive twelve-month run"). The fashion process has restructured political communication: no one who is not seductive and casual makes the grade. Democratic competition takes the course of flirtatious games, passing through the artificial paradise of entertainment, looks, and media personalities.

Political seduction has unleashed a cross fire of more or less indignant condemnations. The refrain is familiar: hypnotized by star-leaders, mesmerized by the names of personalized images, artifices, and pretenses, the citizenry has been transformed into a community of passive and irresponsible spectators. Politics functioning as spectacle masks fundamental problems, offers charming personalities in place of programs, numbs the capacity for reasoning and judgment in favor of emotional reactions and irrational feelings of attraction and antipathy. With media politics, citizens are infantilized; they no longer participate in public life; they are alienated, manipulated by gimmickry and images; democracy is "denatured" and "perverted."[11] Show-business politics does not stop at anesthetizing citizens through entertainment; it transforms the very content of political life. Because the widest possible electorate must be targeted, political speakers have a tendency to gloss over the most controversial aspects of their programs, to look for a painless platform that will satisfy more or less everyone. Discourse on the right and left alike becomes more and more homogeneous, in a process of uniformization and neutralization that is "perhaps sapping the vitality of politics, or even doing it in altogether."[12] Under the spell of the show-business approach, communication renders collective debate anemic; it is fraught with consequences for the health of democracy.

If we measure the effects of spectacle-politics on democratic elections, we may conclude that not all those criticisms are unfounded. Indeed, it is no longer possible to maintain intact the well-known thesis that the influence of the media is weak, that it is less important than interpersonal communication, that only opinion leaders are really exposed to the action of the media. Since this theory was formulated in the 1940s, the importance of leaders, of the family, and of ideologues has declined considerably. In all the democratic nations we note a destabilization of voters' behavior: citizens identify less and less faithfully with a particular party, and voters' behavior tends increasingly to resemble that of an inconstant, pragmatic consumer. While we have known for a long time that the media have trouble influencing citizens with firm convictions, that the media tend to reinforce opinions rather than challenge them, we also know that the media play a non-negligible role with respect to the category of undecided voters, individuals who are not particularly motivated by political life. It is in this range of potential voters that the seduction process has full sway. Some surveys have shown that during one election campaign the intentions of undecided voters were significantly modified; a shift was noted among uncommitted voters, precisely the ones who determine the final outcome, electoral victory or defeat.[13] In a society in which the role of the mobile electorate has a good chance of growing, the role of political marketing is likely to take on increased importance. Far from being a peripheral manifestation, political seduction now has a significant and problematic impact on the trends of political life.

Why do so many analyses look at issues from just one side? Paradoxically, the denunciation of the fashion form in the political arena is limited to its most immediate, most superficial aspects. Its critics do not see that seduction also helps maintain democratic institutions, helps them take root in a lasting way. By adopting a spectacular form, political discourse becomes less boring, less "foreign"; people who have not cared much for politics may come to take some interest, if not in politics per se then perhaps in a tug-of-war between two leading figures, or the spectacle of the "man thrown to the lions." Major electoral debates and other live television performances by political figures are widely followed by the public, even if these events are perceived as belonging to the world of play and distraction. On such occasions the public is clearly in a situation of receiving and taking in information; public familiarity with the various political positions is thereby increased, however unevenly. Contrary to what opponents of the spectacle-state maintain, no sharp line of demarcation between information and entertainment can be drawn; the fashion form, far from being antithetical to an opening to politics, makes politics possible for a growing segment of the population. Seduction makes the debate that involves the collective whole less off-putting; at the very least it allows citizens to listen, to be better informed about the parties' various programs and lines of argument. It is more the instrument of a democratic mass political life than a new opium of the people.

Moreover, it is not true that the seduction process tends to neutralize content, to homogenize political discourse. The program of the French Left in 1981 was very different from that of its adversaries. Today, the political spectacle has not prevented the theses of the far-right National Front from being defended on the public stage. Hard-line neolibertarian programs have been deployed in countries like the United States in which the star system in politics is the most highly developed: the talents of the "great communicator" Ronald Reagan did not keep him from being the symbol of a different politics. If seduction tends to unify political communication in the direction of cordiality, simplicity, and personalization, it leaves intact the fundamental divisive issues, and maintains very broad possibilities for referential divergence.

Does this process entail a perversion of democracy, or a historical realization of one of the paths inscribed in its most fundamental dynamics? By acknowledging the collective will as the source of political sovereignty, democracy leads to the secularization of power; it turns the political agency into a purely human institution detached from any divine transcendence, from any sacred character. As a corollary, the state gives up the symbols of its own preeminent authority that it has unfailingly displayed in older systems. The state, having become an expression of society, has to resemble society more and more; it has to give up the signs, rituals, and mechanisms of its archaic dissimilarity. In this sense, the contemporary political spectacle only prolongs the process of political desacralization begun at the end of the eighteenth century. By showing off their hobbies, by appearing in turtleneck shirts and on television talk shows, the representatives of power take a supplementary step toward the secular path of dissolving the otherness of the state. Power has come down from its pedestal; the powerful are made of flesh and blood like other human beings, and their tastes and everyday interests are similar. What is involved is not a "cultural desecularization" that would reintroduce the underlying irrational and emotional components of traditional power,[14] but, on the contrary, a paroxysm of the democratic process of political secularization.

A spectacle-state? So be it. Nevertheless, the analogy between the contemporary political scene and the star system has its limits. Whereas the star system sets up "sacred monsters," the political spectacle brings the leading figures down off their pedestals; it brings power closer to individual citizens. The star system produces dreams; the political spectacle produces disenchantment. The more media politics is developed, the more the political element spills over into the consumable, into mass indifference, the floating mobility of opinions. The more seduction there is, the less Manicheanism, the fewer great political passions: one listens attentively or distractedly to political broadcasts, but the masses are not carried away. On the contrary, fervent militancy is discouraged; citizens are less and less inclined to invest emotionally in political causes, which are not "worth it" in their eyes. This is where the great democratic efficiency of the new communicational register comes in. Incompatible with aggressive hysteria, with the appeal to violence and hatred, "fashion" politics favors the self-discipline of speeches, the pacification of political conflicts (no matter how ferocious some negative advertising may have become), the respect for democratic institutions. Humor, variety shows, and the play of advertising all undermine the crusading, orthodox spirit; they discredit authoritarianism, excommunications, the exaltation of the values of war and revolution. In political conflicts, campaign slogans have to adopt a moderate tone; television adversaries have to be relaxed and smiling, have to acknowledge each other and talk to each other. Seduction is an instrument of civil peace that reinforces the democratic order. The spectacular only appears to lead to the dominion of the passionate or the emotional register; in fact, it works to reduce passion and to deidealize the political space, to expurgate its tendencies toward holy war. Is it lamentable, then, that hard-line propaganda has been replaced by one-man shows and creative advertising? Should we despair because politics no longer sends out calls for militant mobilization, no longer generates mass effusions? On the contrary, we might see the new situation as creating unparalleled conditions for the stability of democratic institutions and the legal alternation of power. By substituting seduction for the discourse of war, the new communication only reinforces public hostility to violence; it supports the predominant inclination of contemporary societies toward fair play, calmness, and tolerance. Certain manifestations are unquestionably worrisome, for example the political spot ads that occasionally drag down the level of political debate and that may also throw democratic competition out of balance because of their excessively high costs; in that respect, regulations are highly desirable. Yet considered as a whole, the frivolous process is not a threat to the democratic order; rather, it grounds the democratic order on a footing that is more serene, more open, broader but also smoother.

The explanation for the growth of seduction in politics only appears to be a simple one. It is shortsighted to view this phenomenon as merely a result of the television boom, an outgrowth of polls and advertising, as if the decor of the current political scene could be deduced directly from the new media technologies. But while the development of television in particular has undeniably played a crucial role, television is not responsible for everything. Political marketing corresponds in fact to the installation of the democratic societies in the era of fashion consumption: the values inherent in this order—hedonism, leisure, play, personality, psychology, cordiality, simplicity, humor—are the driving forces behind the restructuring of political performances. Politics based on advertising is more than a media effect; it has come into its own along with the new codes of democratic individualist sociability. Less distance, more evidence of cordiality and relaxation: how can we fail to see that these transformations are inseparable from cultural referents inherent in the frivolous age? The political class and the media have simply conformed to the new aspirations of the public at large. Consummate fashion has made human relationships less rigid in form; it has given impetus to tastes for the direct, the natural, the distracting. The intimacy that reflects the emergence of psychological values in the domain of human relations must also be related to the historic terminus of fashion, inasmuch as it has deepened social atomization while fostering subjective aims, the taste for self-knowledge and contact. This cultural upheaval has provided the background against which spectacle-democracy could be perceived.

CHAPTER VI

Culture, Media Style

Hits in Stock

MASS CULTURE is even more representative of the fashion process than is fashion itself. All of mass-media culture has become a powerful machine controlled by the laws of accelerated renewal, ephemeral success, seduction, and marginal differences. A culture industry organized according to the sovereign principle of novelty is coupled with a situation of exceptionally unstable consumption, where inconstancy and unpredictability in taste run rampant. In the 1950s, a full-length feature film ran, on the average, for about five years; now, the average is one year. The average life cycle of a hit song varies from three to six months. Best-sellers with a life span of more than a year are rare, and many bookstores no longer carry books published more than six months earlier. Certain television series have had remarkable longevity, to be sure: *Gunsmoke* lasted twenty years and *Dallas* ran almost as long. But these are exceptional cases in comparison to the quantity of new series introduced each year in the United States, very few of which manage to survive past the first thirteen episodes. New means of distributing audiovisual products have increased the life span of cultural products, too; films in particular can now be screened at will, independently of their first run and their availability in theaters. But what is true for movies is not true for music or books: every month, one recording drives out another, one book supplants another. Obsolescence reigns supreme.

At the heart of cultural consumption lies mass infatuation. In the span of just a few months, sales of a hit song can reach several hundred thousand copies, or even a million or more; dozens of platinum disks (a million copies) have joined golden ones (five hundred thousand). In 1984, twenty million Michael Jackson albums and ten million Prince albums were sold worldwide. For a few weeks, everybody is crazy about the same recording; radio stations play it ten times a day. The same thing happens in cinema, where seats sold for a successful new hit are counted in the millions. In Japan, in fewer than ten weeks, *E.T.* drew ten million spectators; in Buenos Aires, one spectator out of four saw that film. Fashion is translated in an exemplary manner by the scope of such infatuations, the mass success

evident in hit parades, charts, and best-sellers. Cultural infatuations have
a peculiar character: they upset nothing; they violate no taboo. For some
critics, fads are a subtle form of transgression; they offer the pleasure of
sidestepping norms and conventions. In this view, every new craze presents itself as "daring," and seeks to violate some social or aesthetic
taboo.[1] While some fads are indeed freighted with a certain subversive
charge (the miniskirt, for example, or early rock music, or avant-garde
fashion), the subversive element cannot be seen as an essential feature.
Where would we locate the transgression in the wave of enthusiasm focused at one point on a Michael Jackson recording, a moment later on
Madonna or Sade? Hits are original precisely because they generate crazes
that in most instances do not challenge any institution, any value, any
style. Hits do not express the pleasure of disturbing; they offer a pure
manifestation of the tranquil passion for small differences without disorder, without risk: the ecstasy of "change within continuity." They arouse
instant emotion linked to recognizable novelty, not to subversion.

   The culture industries are characterized by their highly random aspect.
Promotional techniques notwithstanding, no one can predict what will appear at the top of the hit parades. In France each year only about 20 record
titles sell more than 500,000 copies. The charts include only 7 percent of
the total production: of 24,000 numbers recorded over a three-year period,
only 320 singles made it to the hit parades.[2] In the United States, an estimated 70 percent of the musical titles produced each year run a deficit; the
losses are compensated by the huge profits realized by a small number of
others.[3] The movie industry is not exempt from randomness either: the
number of seats sold for films released in Paris varies from fewer than ten
thousand to two million. The same thing happens in book publishing: the
data are hard to verify, but it is estimated that a majority of novels published in France sell between three hundred and four hundred copies. This
uncertainty, which is part and parcel of the cultural marketplace, has the
effect of stimulating continual renewal. The multiplication of titles is a
way of insuring against risk, of increasing the chances of getting a hit or a
best-seller that will compensate for the losses incurred with the bulk of the
production. Thus a French record producer earns 50 percent of his profits
from just 3 percent of his records.[4] Even if the big recording studios or
publishing houses do not live exclusively on "big hits" (there are the back-
lists, the classics, and so on), they all look for hits by taking on new titles,
authors, and creators. All the culture industries are orchestrated by the
logic of fashion, by the goal of immediate success, by the race for novelty
and diversity. There were nine thousand recordings a year in France in
1970, twelve thousand in 1978. Even though record sales were dropping,
the total number of registered recordings still increased slightly between
1978 and 1981. And even though production in the major American film

studios went down sharply—from 500 to 138 full-length films a year—between 1950 and 1976, their production is once again on the rise: the overall number of films produced went from 175 in 1982 to 318 in 1984, 515 in 1986. Then there is the enormous output of television series, miniseries, and specials that add up to thousands of hours of programming. There always has to be something new. In an effort to limit the risk of launching new programs and in the hope of winning the ratings wars, trial balloons proliferate; a great many pilots are produced; test episodes are sent out "experimentally" to U.S. television screens before the decision to produce an entire series is made. In 1981, 23 completed programs were preceded by 85 pilots; for the 1983–84 season, 31 pilots were offered by NBC alone.[5] The culture industries are fashion industries through and through; accelerated renewal and diversification count among their strategic vectors.

To protect themselves against the uncertainty inherent in the demand for their products, the culture industries keep on raising their promotional and advertising budgets. In this area, book publishing is still lagging behind, at least in France. In the United States, however, the cost of promoting a book like Judith Krantz's *Princess Daisy*, which sold more than six million copies, can come to more than $200,000. In other areas, too, advertising costs are skyrocketing. It can cost as much to introduce a new record as to produce it, if not more, and the trend can only intensify with the development of MTV. Today in France it costs between 250,000 and 450,000 francs to produce a record, but the cost of a video clip to promote it can range from 100,000 to 400,000 francs. *Thriller* cost $500,000.[6] The average budget for an American-made movie is now estimated at $10 million (before postproduction costs); advertising expenses alone amount to $6 million. *Star Trek* cost $45 million to make, $9 million to promote. *Midnight Express* cost $3.2 million to make, while its advertising expenses came to $8.4 million. Furthermore, it may be argued that production expenses already include costs related to advertising in the form of fees paid to the stars; the inflation of marketing budgets parallels the spiral in stars' compensation. A paradoxical development: at the very moment when the great stars are fading, the fees they can command climb out of sight. Sean Connery, who earned $17,000 in 1962 for playing James Bond in *Doctor No*, later made $2 million for *Cuba*. Marlon Brando got $3.5 million for ten days of shooting in *Superman*; in the late 1970s, Steve McQueen was asking $5 million per film. More than any other industries, the culture industries are dependent on the fashion form, on advertising and the various vectors of seduction and promotion. The very escalation of budgets has a seductive effect: that a film or a video clip is the most expensive ever produced becomes a selling point, a factor in the product's success. The new so-called multimedia strategies not only make it possible to spread the very high risks inherent in the cultural marketplace over various subsidi-

aries, but they also make it possible to promote products that are multimedia by vocation. Thus the multimedia conglomerates are organized in
such a way that the growth of one activity benefits others: a successful film
leads to a television program; a book gives rise to a movie or a TV series;
movies are inspired by comic strips. "The characters of Warner comics
have turned up in countless films, starting with the three Superman movies, which in turn have led to new Superman products, including an Atari
game, dolls made by Knickerbocker Toys, and the franchising of the 'Superman' logo by Warner's Licensing Corporation of America."[7] Multimedia promotional operations are proliferating: a film, a record, a book,
and a toy, all in the same family, are introduced simultaneously, and each
benefits from the success of the others. The book that came out after the
showing of *Holocaust* in the United States sold more than one and a half
million copies, and the record from the movie *Saturday Night Fever* sold
thirty million copies.[8] Each product adds to the notoriety of the others and
gives them additional impetus, reinvigorating the current fad. Manufacturers no longer have to wait until a character becomes as famous as
Mickey Mouse to bring out derivative products: the release of a film or
cartoon is immediately accompanied by the sale of licensed toys and clothing. The *Dr. Slump* cartoon gave rise to eight thousand different derivative
products in a six-month period; toys, dolls, and publications drawn from
the *Marco Polo* series brought the R.A.I., the Italian state television organization, more than 1.4 billion lire;[9] in France, toys produced under licensing agreements in 1985 represented 11 percent of the profits of the entire
sector. With multimedia operations, a certain "rationalization" of fashion
is at work: not because fashions are to be thoroughly directed and controlled from this point on—that would be an absurd contention—but because each production functions as advertising for another; everything is
"recuperated" synergistically in order to enhance and accelerate the
phenomenon of success.

Culture Clip

The requirement of renewal that characterizes the culture industries is
completely different from the "tradition of novelty" that characterizes
modern art. Instead of obeying the avant-garde imperative of radical novelty, cultural products are shaped according to already tested formulas. As
Edgar Morin aptly put it, industrial culture synthesizes the original and
the standardized, the individual and the stereotype.[10] At bottom, this culture conforms to the fashion system in being an adventure without risk, a
variation on the style of an epoch, a logic of small differences. The product
always offers a certain individuality, but this distinctiveness is always

contained within a standard framework. Instead of avant-garde subversion, we find novelty within clichés, a blend of canonical forms and some unprecedented element. Certain works undeniably succeed in innovating, in departing from the beaten path, but the general rule is one of minimal variation within the known order: a hundred Westerns develop the same good guy/bad guy scenario, a hundred cops-and-robbers dramas stage the same type of confrontation in urban settings—each time with small differences that determine the success or failure of the product. *Dynasty* offers a different version of *Dallas*; each episode of a police series or a family saga exploits a recognizable style, an unchanged and repetitive formula that defines the image of the series. As with clothing or advertising, novelty is law, so long as it does not overtly disturb the public, so long as it does not upset the audience's habits and expectations, so long as it can be read and understood immediately by more or less everyone. Complexity is to be avoided; readily identifiable plots and characters must be offered; interpretation has to be provided. Today, television series go to great lengths to ensure maximum, effortless comprehension: the dialogues are elementary; feelings are expressed and insistently repeated through facial mimicry and background music. Mass culture is a culture of consumption, wholly constructed in view of immediate pleasure and mental recreation. Its seductiveness stems in part from its simplicity.

By cutting down on multiple meanings, by targeting the broadest possible public, by introducing "instant" products to the marketplace, the culture industries have brought into the sphere of spectacle the primacy of the temporal axis characteristic of fashion, namely, the present. Like fashion, mass culture is completely present-oriented, indeed triply so. First of all, because its explicit goal lies more than anything in immediate individual leisure. It is a matter of entertaining, not of educating, uplifting the mind, or inculcating higher values. Even though ideological contents clearly do turn up, they are subordinate to the goal of entertaining. Next, because mass culture retranslates all attitudes and discourses into the code of modernity. For industrial culture, the historical present is the measure of all things. It does not hesitate to adapt freely, to introduce anachronisms, to transplant the past into the present, to recycle the old in modern terms. Finally, because mass culture is a culture without traces, without a future, without a significant subjective extension, it is designed to exist in the living present. Like dreams and jokes, mass culture for the most part resonates in the here and now; its dominant temporality is the very same one that governs fashion.

The gulf that separates us from earlier times is obvious. During a major part of our history as human beings, higher-order works of the mind were constituted under the aesthetic authority of the ancients; they were produced in order to glorify heavenly or earthly sovereigns, the hereafter, or the realm of the powerful; they were primarily oriented toward the past or the future. It is true that, since the Renaissance at least, works of art have given rise to fashion fads. In courts and salons, different themes and styles could come and go; particular authors and artists could enjoy enormous success. Nevertheless, by virtue of their temporal orientation, the works in question were quite foreign to the fashion system and its inexhaustible thirst for renewal. The respect for rules from the past, the requirement that a work have a profound meaning, the search for sublime beauty, the desire to create a masterpiece were all factors that militated against, or at least limited, the headlong progress of change and the rate at which works became outdated. When art had the task of praising the sacred and the secular hierarchy, the temporal axis of artworks was the future much more than the ephemeral present. Artists had to bear witness to the eternal glory of God or to the greatness of a reign or a noble lineage; they had to offer up grandiose hymns, immortal signs of magnificence intended for posterity. Faithful to the lessons of the past and oriented toward the future, preindustrial culture was structurally immune to the production of fashion and the cult of the present. The subjective order of motivation worked in the same way: until recently, writers and artists created with an eye to eternity, immortality, nonephemeral fame. Whatever success they might win or seek, creators aspired to produce works that would outlast the unstable approval of their contemporaries. Petrarch maintained that true glory began only after death; much closer to our day, Mallarmé, Valéry, and Proust scorned the contemporary scene and found it natural to remain unknown most of their lives. Fashion, in such a context, is extrinsic to the creation of works of art; it may accompany the process, but it does not constitute its organizing principle. Industrial culture, on the contrary, is squarely installed in the realm of the perishable. It exhausts itself in a frenetic quest for instant success. Its ultimate criterion is the sales curve or the size of the audience. This does not preclude the creation of "immortal" works, but the overall trend points elsewhere—toward integral obsolescence, toward the vertigo of the present with no regard for tomorrow.

From this point on, the primacy of the present appears even in the rhythmic architecture of cultural products dominated increasingly by the ecstasy of speed and immediacy. The frenetic rhythm of advertising is winning out everywhere. Television production—in the United States in particular—is orchestrated around the sovereign principle of speed. Dead time, slow bits, are to be avoided at all costs. On the electronic screen, something must always be happening: a maximum of visual effects, a harassing of eye and ear, endless events, not much substance. A culture of narrative is being replaced, as it were, by a culture of movement; a lyric or melodic culture is being superseded by a cinematic culture constructed around shock and the deluge of images, the search for immediate sensation, the emotion of the syncopated cadence. Rock culture, advertising culture: since the 1950s, rock has been displacing the sweet nothings of the crooners. Now American programs and serials are waging a merciless war on slowness:[11] in police dramas (*Starsky and Hutch, Miami Vice*), in the personal and professional dramas of family sagas, everything happens at high speed, as if media time were nothing but a succession of competing instants. Music video—MTV—is only an extreme embodiment of this express culture. It is no longer a question of evoking an unreal universe or of illustrating a musical text; it is a matter of displaying an overstimulated parade of images, of changing in order to change faster and faster, less and less predictably, with increasingly arbitrary and extravagant combinations. We are now dealing with IPM rates (ideas per minute) and seduction-by-the-second. In video clips, each image is valid only for the present; all that counts is its capacity to stimulate and to surprise. Clips consist in nothing but disparate and precipitous accumulations of sensory impacts producing fashionable surrealistic effects in Technicolor. The video clip represents the ultimate expression of creativity in advertising and its cult of surfaces. The fashion form has conquered media imagery and media time; the rhythmic *force de frappe* is putting an end to the universe of depth and daydreaming. Only pure stimulation remains, without memory: reception in the fashion mode.

So why do critics continue to argue that mass programming serves the ideological function of "national and worldwide consensus,"[12] when such programming only puts images into temporary circulation and transports them nowhere? After the age of contemplative adoration, we have entered the era of the video trip. Viewers do not absorb the program's contents but rather unload their own; they explode in an excess of images, intoxicated by an overcharged sequence of images; no extrinsic purpose is served, only the pleasure of instant change, as in a mental stock-car race. Even soap operas, which are built around psychological continuities and clearly identified characters, are not taken seriously. There is no residue; everything is stirred together in perpetual combinations and recombinations. Verisimilitude is no longer a major concern; characters may change faces (as in *Dallas* or *Dynasty*), but the drama pursues its course. The narrative progresses at a very rapid pace; highly contrasted sequences and situations are presented in rapid succession with no transitions.[13] The point is to ward off boredom, to move quickly along to something else: identification with characters is blocked, ideological inculcation is neutralized, pulverized by the very speed of the video presentation. The rhythmic mode of televised products has short-circuited the alienation of spectators in favor of noninvolvement and amused detachment.

Everywhere, frenzied rushing is the rule: this is as true of pornography as of soap operas. Porno films also banish slowness in favor of "live" libidinal transmissions; nothing counts but the immediate plays of combinations, the speeded-up permutations of sex. It has been noted that pornography eliminates all ritual, all depth, all meaning; we might add that it is inseparable from a specific temporality: fast sex, instant sex. Unlike striptease, porno films and peep shows offer few mediations: they function in the mode of "everything, all at once." The overexposure of organs is accompanied by sustained haste, as in a sort of racing-car rally. The excitement induced by a zoom lens and the excitement of using a stopwatch are of the same nature. Pornography is an erotics of immediacy, of operational action and repetitive renewal; there is an endless stream of new positions and new partners in view of the unbridled mechanics of organs and pleasures. In this sense, pornographic films are sex clips, just as MTV clips are music-video porn. Each instant has to be filled with a new image, a spectacular libidinal spot. The fashion form and its discontinuous temporality have taken over even media sex.

Stars and Idols

Another reason mass culture is immersed in fashion is that it gravitates toward stars and idols, prodigiously successful and attractive figures who inspire infatuation and adulation in the extreme. Since the early decades of this century, the movies have continuously fabricated stars. Featured prominently on advertising posters, stars are important drawing cards to whom the faltering movie industry owed its reinvigoration in the 1950s. With stars, the fashion form shines in all its glory; seduction is at the height of its magic.

The stars' luxurious and frivolous life-style has often been described: sumptuous villas, gala evenings, elegant receptions, fleeting love affairs, a life devoted to pleasure, eccentricities in dress. The stars' role in fashion phenomena has also been stressed: they managed very early on to dethrone the preeminent women of the world where appearance was concerned, and they succeeded in gaining recognition as fashion leaders. Garbo started the trend to medium-length hair, along with the wearing of berets and tweeds; the vogue of the "platinum blond" came from Jean Harlow; Joan Crawford seduced the public with her elongated lips; Marlene Dietrich was all the rage with her plucked eyebrows. Clark Gable succeeded in making men's undershirts unfashionable after *It Happened One Night*. People imitated the behavior of certain stars on a massive scale: the way they made up their eyes and lips, their posture and facial expressions; in the 1930s there were even contests to find Dietrich and Garbo look-alikes. Later, Brigitte Bardot's ponytail or "bird's nest" hairstyles, James Dean's casual look and that of Marlon Brando, were widely imitated models. Today, young teenagers try to look like Michael Jackson. Stars are not only foyers of fashion, they are even more figures of fashion in themselves as *beings-for-seduction*, modern quintessences of seduction. Stars are characterized by the unique charm of their appearance, and the star system can be defined as the enchanted fabrication of images of seduction. As fashion products, stars have to please; beauty, even if it is neither absolutely necessary nor sufficient, is one of their principal attributes. Their beauty requires staging, artifice, aesthetic refabrication: the most sophisticated techniques—makeup, photographs with studied viewing angles, cosmetics, plastic surgery, massages—are used to create their incomparable image, their bewitching seductiveness. Like fashion, stars are artificial constructions, and if fashion is the aestheticization of clothing, the star system is the aestheticization of actors—not only their faces but their entire individuality.

More than beauty, personality is the star's ruling imperative. Stars shine and conquer the public essentially by the type of man or woman they succeed in conveying on the screen: Garbo incarnated the inaccessible and haughty woman, Marilyn Monroe the innocent, sensual, and vulnerable woman; Catherine Deneuve projects a glacial sensuality. Clark Gable exemplified the virile, complicitous, and impudent man; Clint Eastwood is identified with cynical, efficient, hard men. "Show me an actress who isn't a personality and I'll show you an actress who isn't a star,"[14] Katharine Hepburn used to say. The star is the image of a personality constructed on the basis of a physique and made-to-order roles, an archetype of stable or little-changing individuality that the public encounters over and over in all his or her films. The star system manufactures superpersonality, that is, the brand name of the divas of the silver screen.

Given this construction according to a principle of permanent identity, we might take the star to be at the opposite pole from fashion and its ineradicable versatility. To suppose this, however, would be to forget that the star system is based on the same values as fashion, on the sacralization of individuality and appearances. Just as fashion is the apparent personalization of ordinary human beings, so the star is the personalization of the actor; just as fashion is the sophisticated staging of the human body, so the star is the media staging of a personality. The "type" personified by a star is her identifying mark, just like a couturier's style; the cinematographic personality proceeds from a surface artificiality that is of the same essence as fashion. The same effect of personalization and individual originality is targeted in each case; both stars and fashion are constituted by the same work of spectacular staging. The star is a fantasy of personality just as fashion is a fantasy of appearance; together they exist only by virtue of the double law of seduction and the personalization of looks. Just as the couturier creates a design from start to finish, the star system redefines, in-

vents, and elaborates the profile and features of the stars. At work is the
same demiurgic-democratic power, the same ambition to recreate every
thing, to reshape everything with no preestablished models, for the greater
glory of the image, of artifice and radiant personality.

Stars may be media symbols of personality, but they are by no means
foreign to the system of small differences characteristic of fashion. That
phenomenon became manifest in the 1950s when a whole series of female
stars appeared, embodying variations on the theme of the child-woman:
Marilyn the innocent, Brigitte Bardot the sexy little animal, Baker the doll,
Audrey Hepburn the mischievous young woman. Something similar happened to male stars who embodied the theme of the tormented and rebel-
lious young hero; Marlon Brando and James Dean were the prototypes,
followed by Paul Newman, Anthony Perkins, Montgomery Clift, and
Dustin Hoffman. The cinematographic consecration of personality is accomplished according to the fashion process, according to a logic paralleling that of the combinatorial production of marginal differences.

Invented by the film industry, the star system quickly invaded the universe of song and the music hall. Singers with charm had crowds swooning
at their feet just like the movie stars; they attracted the same excitement,
the same curiosity, the same adoration. Tino Rossi, Bing Crosby, Frank
Sinatra, L. Mariano each received thousands of letters from their unswerving fans. The explosion of rock music combined with the LP revolution
and the pickup mike transformed the landscape of idols to some extent.
The proliferation of successful singers and groups triggered a significant
increase in the rate at which stars rise and fall. Although a few great rock
stars seem to have resisted the test of time, most of them have entered the
age of mobility and obsolescence. By producing more and more mini-idols
who are quickly eclipsed, show business has democratized the star scene,
as it were. It has removed stars from the realm of the immortals: there are
fewer pinnacles and divine altitudes, there is less immutable adulation.
Most idols have come down from Mount Olympus; in a way, they have
been conquered by progress toward equality of conditions. And while the
idols are being annexed by the capriciousness of fashion, their looks are
simultaneously taking on heightened importance. The phenomenon was
not created overnight; for a long time, popular singers sought to fix their
image visually by exhibiting some originality in stage dress: Maurice
Chevalier's straw hat, Trenet's rumpled hair, Piaf's little black dress. But
the spectacular dimension remained limited; the image did not institute a
real break with the everyday. What is more, the image was stable, more or
less ritualized for each artist. With singers wearing suits and ties or in
shirtsleeves, the visual world of the music hall signaled respectability and
sobriety. Under the convergent impetus of rock and advertising, the image
on stage now implies, on the contrary, a debauchery of originality and

endless renewal (Boy George, Prince, Sigue Sigue Sputnik): in place of the
discreet distinctive sign, we have the unmistakable mutant. Visual presentation is no longer simply a decorative element; it is constitutive of the
positioning, identity, and originality of groups, and its importance will
undoubtedly continue to keep pace with that of video clips. The more
groups and singers there are, the more a total advertising logic is required;
the more marginal difference there is, the more the logic of effect, spectacular impact, and fashion innovation is imposed.

While show business is cultivating hypertheatricality, movie stars are
gradually losing their glamour, their power to fascinate. The democratization of the stars' image prolongs a process begun half a century ago. Starting in the 1930s, star figures underwent major transformations that
brought them closer to the standards of reality and everyday life. The
unreal and inaccessible beauty of silent-film stars was replaced by the
more human, less royal beauty of stars who were not so much marble-
statue types.[15] The ethereal vamp gave way to a more tantalizing flesh-
and-blood woman; idealized heroes gave way to stars whose good looks
were less canonical but more interesting, more personalized. Stars closer
to the spectator's reality came into their own with the "sex appeal" of the
1950s (Bardot, Monroe), which desublimated the image of woman by
means of a "natural" eroticism. Under the subterranean impulse of the
work of equality, the stars left their remote, sacred universe behind. Their
private lives are now on display in magazines; their erotic attributes appear on screen and in photos; one sees them smiling and relaxed in the
most down-to-earth situations, with families, in town, on vacation. This
trend toward desacralization, which is in essence democratic, did not just
suddenly pop up out of nowhere. To be sure, cinema invented more-realis-
tic and less-distant stars, but they were always endowed with exceptional
beauty and seductive power. Clothing, photos, ideal measurements, an
ample bustline: the golden age of the star system did not abandon the
splendor of excess and the fantasy of the ideal all at once. Instead, it orchestrated a compromise formation: magical figures ostentatiously de-
taching themselves from the commonplace with whom the public could
nevertheless identify. At present, everything suggests that the process by
which the stars are being "humanized," their dissimilarities diminished,
has reached the end of its road. We are in the era of stars whose physique
is "nothing special"; they are no longer seductive because they are extraordinary, but because they are like us. "People don't look like him, he looks
like them"—this remark by one of Jean-Jacques Goldman's fans can ap-
propriately be addressed to these new "normal-looking" stars who lack
any obvious distinguishing features, such as Miou-Miou, Isabelle Huppert,
Marlène Jobert, Marie-Christine Barrault. Stars once were models; they
have become reflections. We are in the ultimate phase of the democratic

descent from Mount Olympus, the end of a process brought about by the code of communicational proximity, casualness, contact, pop psychology: people want "nice" stars. The psychological values in which we are immersed have caught the stars in the act of everyday ordinariness.

The universe of spectacles keeps rejoining real life, keeps getting involved in the world. While the stars keep their new aesthetic profiles on display, they also participate in large numbers in benefits for causes such as *Band Aid* or the *Restaurants du Coeur*. This phenomenon not only expresses the collective exhaustion of ideologies, it also reflects the irrepressible democratization of stardom. The idols are no longer content to be associated superficially with the great causes of history and the great choices in democratic elections; they now collect money, create associations for mutual support and for charity; they commit themselves to causes benefiting the most disadvantaged members of society. The demigods have taken up pilgrims' staffs; they have returned to the world, sensitive to the misfortunes of the wretched of the earth.

The more the stars are trivialized, the more media they penetrate. Multistars go along with multimedia. Once again, the phenomenon has its antecedents: stars have used their music-hall success for a long time to break into the film world (Bob Hope, Frank Sinatra, Bing Crosby, Yves Montand). Still rather exceptional until recently, the multistar pattern is in the process of becoming a rule; it is impossible to count the show-business idols who have propelled themselves into film (Johnny Hallyday, A. Souchon, Madonna, Tina Turner, Grace Jones). Screen stars become variety singers (Isabelle Adjani, Jane Birkin), singers take up writing (R. Zaraï, Jean-Luc Lahaye), while television stars become novelists and essayists (Patrick Poivre d'Arvor, François de Closets). The creatures of seduction seek to shed the yoke of image; they too aspire to profundity. Stars are no longer entirely superficial beings; like everyone else, they want to express themselves (autobiographies are legion), to bear witness, to deliver messages. Success opens the door to diversification. It calls for the all-out use of the star's name, the best possible advertising device. Fame in one area induces a probability of success elsewhere: one cannot produce a full-fledged vogue effect, but one can use stars to increase the audience and establish the best possible conditions for success.

The enigma of the stars has less to do with their seductive power than with the delirious cult devoted to them. Here is the most troubling question: how can we account for the emotional transports of fans, in a modern society with scientific and technological inclinations? Earlier, Edgar Morin took this phenomenon as an expression of the durability of religious and magical feelings at the heart of the rationalist world.[16] Stars have a share in divinity; they are demigods with their faithful followers who love unrequitedly and quarrel over the stars' intimate possessions, who go into delirium in their presence. The ritual does not amount to a totemic meal in the strict sense, but is more or less equivalent: an indigestion of confidences, interviews, indiscretions having to do with the god. Archaic magic has not been eliminated; it arises anew in the fetishistic adoration of stars. A religion of stars? But if so, why does this adulation find its privileged soil in youth? Why does it disappear so quickly with age? The ephemeral nature of that passion forces us to relate it not to a religious manifestation but to a fashionable passion, a temporary crush. The idolatry of the stars is not of the same essence as religious idolatry; it is only one of the extreme forms of modern infatuation. Unlike religious adoration, which is inseparable from a symbolic organization, from a transcendent meaning or content, the adoration of stars has the peculiarity of being an attachment to a pure image; it is the ecstasy of appearance. What moves fans is neither a human quality nor a message of salvation; it is the charm of a sublimated and aestheticized image. The cult of stars is a cult of personality, not a cult of the sacred; it is aesthetic, not archaic; an intimate revery, not a transcendent mysticism.

The continuity between love of gods and love of stars is merely formal and artificial, an abstract analogy masking the disparity of two forms of logic that have nothing in common. The *homo religiosus* basically stems from a symbolic institution that separates the earthly here and now from an originary elsewhere; it implies a social order that strictly determines the contents of belief, collective rituals, and required prescriptions. There is nothing of the sort with the idolatry directed at stars: that is not a social institution at all, but an expression of disparate personalities replete with subjective demands, fantasies, and delirium, aberrant, uncontrollable, unpredictable behavior. Behind the collective hysteria, there is the erratic movement of individualities; beyond imitation of the idol, there lie the incomparable aspirations and daydreams of individuals, as revealed in particular by fan letters. Far from being an archaic form of behavior, the cult of stars is a typically modern individualist phenomenon, based on the movement of individuals toward a free state: there is no dogma, no instituted body of beliefs, no obligatory ritual beyond the unleashing of fantastic amorous passions on the part of individual subjects.

Only one aspect of the phenomenon is visible when we refer to an acute form of alienation and dependency. The adulation of stars may actually lead to new behaviors: the young win a share of autonomy, however minimal, while shedding certain cultural influences, imitating new attitudes, extricating themselves from the influence of their original milieu. Unswervingly committed to their idols, fans reveal by that very token their personal tastes, their subjective preferences; they affirm their own individuality with respect to their familial and social environment. The cult of stars is at once a manifestation of the heteronomy of beings and, paradoxically, a springboard for the individual autonomy of youth. Having an idol is a way for young people to attest, ambiguously, to their own individuality, a way of gaining access to a form of subjective and group identity. If the phenomenon is manifested among the young, it is because at that age aesthetic tastes and preferences are the principal means of asserting one's personality. The cult of stars, at least during the golden age of film, was chiefly a female phenomenon: in the 1940s, about 80 percent of the fans were women. The reason for this is undoubtedly the same, for in a "phallocratic" society girls have far fewer means than boys to assert their independence. For generations of young women, devotion to stars has been a way of creating their own continent, opening up their personal horizons, and gaining access to new models of behavior.

Everything suggests that this difference between the sexes is in the process of being dissolved by women's liberation and the liberalization of mores. At present, the cult of stars is characterized less by the fans' gender than by the increasingly early age at which such cults develop: in recent years, ten-year-olds have succumbed to Michael Jackson fever. This is not so astonishing, really, in a society in which family authority is diminishing and in which education is based on the code of dialogue and communication. In such a social environment, the desire for independence appears earlier and earlier, more and more insistently. By displaying tastes and preferences that prevail among young adults, children and young teenagers set the dynamics of individual autonomy into motion, start the process of subjective separation, the conquest of their own criteria—even though the criteria are still those of the peer group.

Star worship is not a mass narcotic; it cannot be explained on the basis of the "wretchedness of need" or the dreary anonymous life of modern high-rises.[17] If it could, why would it not spread among adults? To the extent that the phenomenon is inseparable from the quest for identity and individual autonomy, it can only appear in a democratic universe in which the inegalitarian hierarchical order has been dissolved and the social fabric shredded by individualism. In a world in which places and roles have always been predetermined according to a preestablished order, there are no stars. The inequality between fan and star is not the same as the inequality that links the faithful to God. It is the inequality linked to the democratic revolution, where all human beings, detached and free, can recognize one another; where one wants to know everything about the daily private life of others; where one can express love without impediment or restraint, over and beyond differences of age, social standing, or celebrity. It is because there are no longer any regulated forms of collective belonging among human beings that amorous passion can take on unbridled intensity. It is because there is no longer any substantive inequality among individuals that we have the possibility of a form of adoration in which the being most admired is at the same time a confidant, an older sibling, a spiritual advisor, a sought-after lover; where mythic prestige does not exclude the desire to know the details of private life or rule out the spontaneity and proximity of contact. Amorous passion detached from any imperative social code can be invested in the most remote figures. There are no rules; the variable impulses of each individual are in the driver's seat. Underlying the "stellar liturgy," there is more than the magic of the star system, more than the anthropological need for dreams and imaginary identifications; there is also the dynamic of democratic equality that has liberated love from all ritual frameworks.

The Media Explode on the Screen

The ability of the various manifestations of media culture to offer a universe of exoticism, leisure, dreams, and oblivion probably accounts for its prodigious success. Thus it is not very risky to insist, as numerous empirical studies have done, that the need to *escape* is the principal need underlying cultural consumption. For sociologists like Lazarfeld or Merton, and even more so for philosophers like Marcuse or Debord, the culture of escapism has become the new opium of the people: its task is to make them forget the wretchedness and monotony of daily life. The industrial imagination, recreational and mind-dulling, offers its response to a generalized alienation. By increasing the degree to which work is fragmented and society is atomized, bureaucratic technological logic generates passivity, reduces professional competence, fosters boredom and irresponsibility, creates solitude and chronic frustration on the part of individuals. This is fertile terrain for mass-media culture, which has the power to make people forget reality; it allows them to glimpse an unlimited field of projections and identifications. We consume as spectacle what real life denies us: sex, because we are frustrated; adventure, because we have no excitement in our daily lives. This problem of alienation and compensation has been explored to the saturation point in a good deal of sociological and philosophical literature. Because it encourages passivity, dulls the faculties of initiative and creation, and discourages militant activity, mass culture simply broadens the sphere of subjective dispossession. It acts as an instrument for integrating individuals into the bureaucratic and capitalist system.

If mass culture is unquestionably destined, by and large, to satisfy people's need for escape, what long-term effects does it have? Those who analyze media culture as a means of distraction act as if everything is over and done with when the dream is fulfilled, as if the phenomenon leaves no trace, as if it does not modify the behavior and attributes of its public. This is obviously not the case. Above and beyond the evident psychological satisfactions it provides, mass culture has had a decisive historical function. It has reoriented individual and group attitudes, and has spread new standards of living. The attraction of mass culture cannot be understood unless we take into account the new ideological referents, the new existential models that it has successfully diffused at all social levels. On this point, Edgar Morin's analyses are entirely accurate. Beginning in the 1920s and 1930s, mass culture has been an active agent in the process by which rigorist values have been withering away with increasing rapidity. Mass culture has broken down forms of behavior inherited from the past while proposing new ideals and life-styles based on personal accomplishment, entertainment, consumption, and love. By way of stars and eroticism, sports and women's magazines, games and variety shows, mass culture has exalted the life of leisure, individual happiness, and well-being; it has promoted a new ethics for living based on play and consumption.[18] The central themes of mass culture have provided powerful support in the elaboration of a new figure of the modern individual, absorbed in his or her personal achievement and well-being. By offering, in multiple guises, models of self-realization and myths focusing on private life, mass culture has been a crucial vector in contemporary individualization, paralleling and even anticipating the revolution of needs.

But how is this individualism to be understood? It is remarkable that as soon as the real issue here was engaged, the critical thinkers most receptive to mass culture should have gone straight back to the problematics of negativity, alienation, and the consolation of consciousness. In their view, mass culture works only to produce pseudo-individuality; it renders "part of the life of its consumers fictitious. It turns spectators into phantoms, projecting their minds into a plurality of imagistic or imaginary universes, conveying their souls into the swarm of countless doubles that live for them vicariously. . . . Mass culture nourishes life on the one hand, depletes it on the other."[19] Its work is "hypnotic." It sacralizes the individual only in fiction; it magnifies happiness even as it makes concrete existence seem less real; it invites people to "live vicariously through the imagination." The result is a "sleepwalking" individualism, dispossessed of itself by enchanted figures from the realm of the imaginary. Individualist norms are presented as delusory; they merely extend the consolations offered by the opium of the people in another form. At the same time, such thinkers have obscured the real work of mass culture, work related to the democratic enterprise over the long haul; they have ignored the paradoxical but real contribution of mass culture to the rise of subjective autonomy. From the standpoint of the mythology of happiness, love, and leisure, fashion culture has permitted a generalization of the desire for self-assertion and individual independence. The hero seen as self-made man, the love stories presented in magazines and movies, the emancipated models provided by stars have made new reference points available to individuals, inciting them to live increasingly for themselves, to break away from traditionalist standards, to control their own lives. Mass culture as a whole functions the way the star system does: it provides an extraordinary way for human beings to detach themselves from their cultural and familial roots, to promote an ego that is more fully in charge of itself. By offering imaginary escapes, frivolous culture has played a part in the conquest of modern personal autonomy: less is imposed on the individual by the group, more models for self-identification and personal orientation are offered. Media culture has not simply disseminated the values of the petit bourgeois universe; it has also been a vector in the democratic individualist revolution. This point needs to be highlighted: the superficial cannot be reduced to its manifest effects. Artifice has its own historical reality; consummate fashion liberates people from confining and homogeneous social norms more than it subjects them to its own euphoric order.

However, a new phase is already on the horizon. The impact of industrial culture is no longer what it was; the model that began to form in the 1930s is no longer valid. During that entire golden age, mass culture brilliantly conquered a society that was quite extensively attached to traditionalist principles, to puritanical and conformist norms. The very fact of that disjunction has allowed mass culture to play a major role in the modernist adaptation and restructuring of behavior. The gap has now been closed, by and large; having massively assimilated the norms that had earlier been sublimated in films, society is no longer under the yoke of a different culture. Since the 1960s, mass culture has been engaged more in reproducing the dominant values than in proposing new ones. Mass culture once anticipated the spirit of the age; it was ahead of its time and the prevailing mores. Now it merely follows or accompanies them; it no longer offers poles of identification within a context of rift. The life-styles exhibited by media culture are precisely the ones that prevail in everyday life: marital conflicts, family dramas, drug abuse, problems of aging, issues of violence and personal security; the figures of the industrial imagination no longer offer anything absolutely new. At most, they magnify what we see around us every day. Fiction of course remains, with its hyperspectacular and unexpected universes, but in spite of its distance from the commonplace, the themes and myths it conveys tend more to echo society as it is than to anticipate where it is headed. Instead of initiating the audience to a new life-style, mass culture merely reinforces the individualist quest that is present at all levels of the social body. We can take *Dallas* as an example: in a sense, its universe has nothing whatever in common with our ordinary one (big business, jet sets, luxury), yet at every point we are reminded of concerns and problems we all have to deal with (couples separating, the drama of divorce, the desire for self-fulfillment). Culture still has some influence over aesthetic tastes, in music for example, but it has little influence over individual values, attitudes, or behavior. Increasingly, it is rediscovering its essence as fashion, as a superficial culture without consequences. If mass culture continues to accelerate the process of individualization, it does so less through its own thematics than through the cocktail of choices and diversity it offers: there can always be more musical styles, groups, films, series, so that this phenomenon can only generate more minimal differentiations, more possibilities for asserting more or less personalized preferences. For the most part, however, the process by which individuals develop their own subjectivity is carried out in other arenas.

"Information" is what has taken up the slack. The most important cultural and psychological effects of the era are now produced by information, broadly defined. Generally speaking, information has replaced works of fiction in the forward march of individualist democratic socialization. Newsmagazines, debates, and polls have more repercussions on consciousness than any box-office success. The French television programs *Psy Show* or *Ambitions* provide opportunities for more subjective redeployment than all the hours spent contemplating products of the industrial imagination. To be sure, information conveyed through print and radio has been broadening people's horizons for a long time. However, with the development of television, the scope of the phenomenon is of a new order of magnitude. By continually transmitting a vast diversity of information about life in society, from politics to sexuality, from dieting to sports, from economy to psychology, from medicine to technology, from theater to rock groups, the media have become powerful instruments for forming and integrating individuals. The explosion of contemporary individualism cannot be separated from the media explosion. With the proliferation of news sources and the knowledge they provide about other ways of thinking and behaving, individuals are inevitably led to "position themselves" with respect to what they are seeing. They review received opinions more or less rapidly; they make comparisons between where they are and elsewhere, between themselves and others, between the past and the future. Special reports, televised debates, and the daily news all familiarize us with different viewpoints and perspectives on a whole range of issues; they contribute toward the individualization of opinion, to the diversification of models and values, to the disruption of the shared traditional frames of reference; they help individuals become less dependent on an identical, unitary culture. Like a built-in zoom lens, information in democracies liberates minds from the limits of their own particular worlds; it functions as a machine for setting consciousness in motion, for multiplying the opportunities to make comparisons—and ever since Rousseau we have understood the primordial role comparison plays in the development of individual reason.

Information certainly has its "digest" aspect and its "distraction" aspect; be that as it may, there is no justification for continuing to assert that, owing to media-supplied information, "rational-critical debate [has] a tendency to be replaced by consumption," that "the consumption of mass culture leaves no lasting trace; it affords a kind of experience which is not cumulative but regressive."[20] The elitist intellectualist reflex is manifest here: something that amuses cannot possibly educate; something that distracts can only work against rational communication; something that seduces the masses has to give rise to irrational views; something that is easy and programmed can produce only passive assent. Such contentions are based on a profound misunderstanding. The universe of media information leads on a massive scale to the disruption of received ideas; it leads to reading, and to the development of the critical use of reason. It is a machine that adds complexity to the coordinates of thought, that stimulates a demand for reasoned argument, even if it does so within a simple, direct, and relatively unsystematic framework. The prevailing view of the media needs fundamental revision. Media consumption is not about to bury reason; the spectacular does not abolish the formation of critical opinions; news "shows" are pursuing the itinerary of the Enlightenment.

Information collaborates with the rise of individualism in still another way. We hear a lot of talk about the "global village," the media-induced contraction of the planet; at the same time, we need to note that the media are powerful instruments for overinvestment of the ego. They keep us informed about the multiple threats that surround us; they tell us about cancer, alcoholism, sexually transmitted diseases, and others; they are sounding boards for the various dangers that lurk on our highways and beaches and in contacts with other humans; they point out the precautions we need to take to stay slim and safe. This whole flood of information has centripetal effects: it leads individuals to pay more attention to themselves, to manage their bodies, appearance, and health "rationally"; people heed the disturbing, occasionally catastrophic tone of some media programming and are led to be more careful. The better informed people are, the more they take charge of their own lives, and the more the self is the object of concern, solicitude, and preventive measures. Even when the media make an effort not to dramatize issues, they generate worry and a diffuse anxiety that leads to narcissistic preoccupations. While they are distilling worry on the one hand, the media are in the process of removing culpability from many types of behavior on the other (drug use, rape, impotence, alcoholism, and so forth). Everything can be shown or talked about, but without value judgments; such information is presented as facts to be registered and understood, not to be condemned. The media display virtually everything and judge almost nothing. They help orchestrate the new profile of anxious but tolerant narcissistic individualism with open morality and a weak or inconsistent superego.

In various realms the media have succeeded in replacing churches, schools, families, political parties, and labor unions as agencies of socialization and the transmission of knowledge. More and more, it is through the media that we learn what is going on in the world; it is from the media that we get the new data that enable us to adapt to our changing environment. The socialization of human beings through tradition, religion, and morality is giving up more and more ground to the impact of media news and images. We have definitively left behind what Nietzsche called "the morality of mores": the cruel and tyrannical domestication of humans by humans that has been practiced from time immemorial, along with disciplinary instruction, has been replaced by a type of socialization that is entirely unprecedented; it is "soft," plural, noncoercive, and it functions in terms of choice, current events, the pleasure of images.

Information transmitted through the media has the peculiar ability to individualize consciousnesses and disseminate the social body through its countless contents, while at the same time it is working to homogenize the social body, as it were, by the very form of media language. Under its influence in particular, ponderous ideological systems continue to lose their authority; information is a determining agent in the process that turns people away from the great systems of meaning that have paralleled the contemporary evolution of democratic societies. Information in democratic societies is subtended by a logic of the factual, the contemporary, the new; it gradually reduces the impact of doctrinaire ambitions, and forges a consciousness that is more and more alienated from "religious" interpretations of the world, from prophetic and dogmatic discourses. And this applies not only to the fragmented, discontinuous, immediate daily news, but also to the daily broadcasts in which experts intervene, scientists and other specialists who explain the latest developments on the issues simply and directly to the public. The media function by way of the discreet charm of documentary and scientific objectivity. They undermine global interpretations of phenomena, preferring to register facts and syntheses that are largely "positivist." Whereas the great ideologies tended to free themselves from immediate reality, which they assumed to be misleading, and applied "the irresistible power of logic," implacable procedures of deduction, definitive explanations following from absolute premises,[21] information for its part glorifies change and emphasizes the empirical and "scientific" elements. It offers fewer glosses, but more images; fewer speculative syntheses, but more facts; less meaning, but more technical details. Hypercoherent arguments are replaced by events, value judgments by factual data, doctrines by news flashes, ideologues by experts, the radiant future by the fascinating present, by scoops and ephemeral current events. By putting novelties and the positivity of knowledge before the public, the media discredit the systematizing spirit; they propagate a mass allergy to totalizing visions of the world, to the exorbitant pretensions of hyperlogical dialectical reasoning. They favor the emergence of a *hyperrealist* spirit, enamored of facts, of what is "direct" or "live," of polls and novelties. Individual orientation through values has by no means disappeared; it is blended with the realist's appetite for information and with an openness to the voice of the other; and it has softened as faith in secular religions has eroded. If information is an accelerating agent for the dissemination of individualism, it is successful only inasmuch as it simultaneously diffuses the shared values of dialogue, pragmatism, and objectivity, by promoting a *homo telespectator* with realistic, relativistic, and open-minded tendencies.

If we grant that the media individualize human beings through the diversity of their contents but that they recreate a certain cultural unity by the way their messages are presented, we may be able to clarify the current debate on the social effects of "fragmented television." The terms of this debate are very familiar.[22] Sometimes the threat to the cultural unity of nations posed by the proliferation of communication networks is emphasized; in this view, the increase in the number of channels and programs can only further divide the collective body and be an obstacle to social integration. Sometimes, on the contrary, it is argued that the more audiovisual choices there are, the more social standardization there will be. This is a tired old debate: hyperdisaggregation versus hyperhomogenization. In reality, the media explosion will not have a profound impact on the process set in motion by the rise in mass communications; the phenomenon will develop the spiral of individualization and the spiral of cultural homogenization simultaneously. On the one hand, additional programs and channels can only disseminate individual tastes and accentuate the passion for personal autonomy. On the other hand, the multiplication of programs will obviously not go forward along radically contradictory paths. The same principles of communication will be invoked in each case: seduce the public, present current "hot" topics, aim for effect rather than academic demonstration. Whatever the range of choices may be, the same major problematic themes will be dealt with, and the same essential information will be imparted; successful programs will capture a broader audience. The media will keep on promoting a culture of current events, efficiency, communicational exchange, and objectivity. Fragmented telecommunications will boost the growing trend toward the autonomy of the individual along with the trend toward its hyperrealist acculturation. The social bond is not in danger of being torn apart; at most, it will become more supple, allowing for Brownian movements of individualities against a background of spot culture and ideologies whose passion is spent. Let us avoid science-fiction scenarios: the new individualism of the media is not a harbinger of social disintegration. Rather, the inverse is true: the more free choice and individualization there is, the greater the capacity for social integration becomes, and the more opportunities there are for individuals to recognize themselves in their society, to find in the media something corresponding to their own expectations and desires.

By discrediting ideological metasystems, by launching an event-centered culture, the media also contribute to developing a new relation of individuals to knowledge. Through the press and television, individuals have more and more information, in the superficial "digest" mode, about what is happening in the world. Entire segments of what we know come from the media: not only the latest scientific and technological knowledge, but also information concerning practical aspects of everyday life. Our choices are directed less and less by traditional knowledge and more and more by elements captured here and there in the media. How to eat properly, how to stay young and healthy, how to bring up children, what books to read—to all such questions, articles and popularizing texts bring not definitive answers but terms, data, and information appropriate to the discussion. What results is an essentially fragile mass knowledge, less and less assimilated in depth. The media have the effect of destabilizing the content and organization of knowledge: closed and limited knowledge of the traditional universe has been replaced by a mass culture that is much more extensive but also looser and more superficial. The media determine a type of individual culture characterized by turbulence, explosiveness, systematic blurring. Lacking access to fixed knowledge, overexposed to countless shifting messages, individuals are much more receptive to novelties from outside; they are tossed about according to the information they receive. Thus our relation to knowledge is increasingly elastic. We know many things, but almost nothing we know is solid, organized, or assimilated. Each person's culture resembles a mobile patchwork, a splintered construction over which our mastery is weak: "mosaic or rhapsodic culture," as Jean Cazeneuve calls it. While people keep their distance from monolithic ideologies, they are more receptive to information about the present and to novelties; people have been converted to a fuzzy skepticism with a realistic tinge. Information dissolves the strength of convictions and makes individuals permeable, ready to give up their own opinions and systems of reference without much of a struggle. The neonarcissistic individual—labile, uncommitted, a member of the chewing-gum culture—is a child of the media. With their weak and changeable opinions, their focus on reality and novelty, the media, together with consumerism, allow democratic societies to move to a more rapid and more supple pace of social experimentation. The media cannot be equated with a rationalization of social control, but with an increased superficiality and mobility of knowledge. They are vectors of a higher power of individual and collective transformation.

There should be little need, then, to underscore all that distinguishes the analysis I propose here from McLuhan's hypermaterialist analyses. It is obvious that the real message is not the medium. It is time to restore the contents conveyed by the media to their rightful place in the cultural and psychological transformations of our time. Thus television, as a "cold medium," has only a small role to play in the anthropological upheavals of the contemporary world. The explosion of news and information and their reorganization under the law of fashion have been the chief agents of the individualist leap forward. It is curious to read, in McLuhan's writings, that television stimulates "participation in depth," intense involvement of the self, whereas in fact, quite to the contrary, it makes the masses indifferent; it drains energy from the political scene and draws individuals away from the public sphere. We watch television from the outside; we listen distractedly; we skim over the pictures; we jump from channel to channel. Our relation to television is anything but intense involvement. The increased demand for personal motivation and expression that we see now concerns only the private self, not the increasingly corporatist, pragmatic, disillusioned public person. Everything leads us to voice serious reservations about the so-called power of the video image, as a "low-definition" image, to be the source of new habits of perception and experience. To say that a technologically poor picture compels the viewer at each instant to "'close' the spaces in the mesh by a convulsive sensuous participation that is profoundly kinetic and tactile"[23] is only an artifice of analysis, an act of argumentative gymnastics that gets us nowhere; it conceals the multiple and complex mainsprings of the future of democratic individualism. It is true that attitudes have become more relaxed and that tastes for intimacy and self-expression have developed, but these attitudes and tastes do not have to be linked to low-intensity video images; again, they have to be seen as related to the galaxy of democratic values (autonomy, hedonism, psychologism) driven by mass culture and more generally by the system of consummate fashion.

Information Plays and Wins

The crucial role of information in the process of socialization and individualization cannot be separated from its spectacular and superficial register. Committed to being factual and objective, media information is by no means exempt from the work of fashion. It is reshaped in large part by the imperatives of display and seduction. It aims to inform, but through plea-

sure, renewal, and distraction; all programming with a cultural or voca-
tional bent has to adopt the perspective of leisure. Mass communication
seeks mercilessly to weed out pedagogical approaches, dry and tedious
instruction. Reports have to be brief; commentary must be clear, simple,
and interspersed with fragmented interviews, slices of life, or anecdotal
elements; at all events the pictures have to distract, hold attention, and
shock the audience. The basic object is to hook the widest possible public
with the technology of rapid rhythms, flash sequences, and simplicity.
There is no need for memory, references, or continuity; everything must be
understood at once, and everything must change very quickly. The world
of animation and seduction is paramount: famous entertainers (Yves
Montand) and business stars (Bernard Tapie) are asked to present programs on the economic crisis or on setting up businesses. The same goal of
entertaining accounts for the proliferation of talk shows. To be sure, the
exoticism of imagery is lacking, but the thrill of live broadcasting compen-
sates: the cinema of personalities, the unexpected reactions, the jockeying
of minds and positions. Sometimes the exchange is courteous and mild-
mannered (*Les Dossiers de l'écran, L'Avenir du futur, Apostrophes*). On
other occasions it is less so: thus *Droit de réponse* merely pushed the democratic espousal of information and spectacular animation to its limits by
allowing the disordered, sympathetic, and confused confrontation of ideas
and milieus to play itself out. In any event, it is the "show" aspect that
determines the media quality of programs and that shapes the information
presented.

Media communication is orchestrated under the law of seduction and
entertainment. It is implacably restructured by the fashion process because it is governed by the law of polls, the race for audience ratings. In a
pluralist communicational universe subject to the resources of advertising,
the fashion form organizes the production and distribution of programs;
the fashion form governs their shape, nature, and timing. Once the media
bow to polls, the seduction process reigns supreme; it can claim even "scientific" and democratic value. The republic of ratings simply underlines
the sovereignty of fashion in the media, that is, the law of immediate success with the viewing public. The audiovisual explosion will not put a stop
to this process: the more competing channels and specialized media there
are, the more pitiless the principle of seduction, as measured by the ratings, will become. New charms will have to be aimed at the same limited
segments; new presentations and new formulas for keeping the public's
attention will have to be imagined. More than ever before, what seduces is
minimal difference.

Televised newscasts have fallen into step. The phenomenon is not a
recent one, but it is intensifying. To be convinced of this, it suffices to
observe the changes that have occurred in the tone and presentation of

televised news bulletins. We have moved from the news format dominated by an official and pedagogical tone that characterized the early days of the medium to less-distant, less-solemn, more-natural newscasting. Earlier journalists spoke in restrained, professorial voices, and the atmosphere was tense; now the tone is casual, and the ambience is cool. Television news has probably held on to some basic elements of gravity and seriousness; its brief flashes, free of rhetoric, have nothing in common with the carefree fantasy of fashion. Yet the imperative to seduce is obvious in the announcers, who are young, pleasant, attractive, and charming; their voices are reassuring. The law of glamour reigns: it is measured by the yardstick of numbers of viewers. For a long time, television has been nurturing great newscasters, stars such as R. Dimbedy in Great Britain or Walter Cronkite in the United States. The phenomenon merely multiplies as new avenues are exploited; all the channels are on the lookout for journalists with an attractive image. Newscasting is dominated by journalistic stars who can have a measurable influence on the ratings. Information is sold to millions of viewers via the announcer's personality, aura, or looks. We are in the age of the anchorperson; these stars have kept their high standing in the popularity polls even as the great film stars are fading away. Information manufactures and demands stars; it is as if the accomplished style of television newscasts had to have some human brilliance as a counterpart, a surfeit of individuality. It is the same with newscasts as with objects or advertising: the fashion form, the imperative of personalization and seduction, are at work everywhere.

For a long time it has been obvious that news programs and theater have the same mainsprings: the dramatization of facts, the search for sensational effects, the artificial creation of stars. All news tends to be caught up in the frenzy of the scoop, in the desire to deliver something new and unexpected according to a logic analogous to that of fashion. But television news grows out of the fashion form even more directly. More than any other news medium, television functions essentially by turning information into images—an invasion of images that are sometimes unfamiliar; they are often banal, devoid of special interest, merely illustrative. Images accompany commentaries and reported facts almost systematically: a half-hour television newscast presents more than twenty minutes' worth of pictures. Television news oscillates between the anecdote and the thriller; it is inseparable from visual pleasure, direct representation, and hyperrealist stimulation. All information comes via the kaleidoscope of images. Video tracks, visual effects, decorative elements (scenography, colors, titles, credits) are all-important: visual theater has colonized television news.

In the print media, the seduction process is reflected less by a profusion of images than by subtleties of page formatting, the tone of the writing, and the increasingly frequent use of humor in articles, headlines, and lead paragraphs. No newspaper is exempt from this any longer: the logic of information and the logic of play have been reconciled everywhere. Just as eighteenth-century fashion toyed with major and minor historical phenomena, using ribbons and hairstyles to poke fun at financial debacles or at popular uprisings, in the same way today's news continues to use a casual, fanciful style to present the events of the day, no matter how tragic. When it took over the media, the humoristic code shifted the register of information into the casual, playful logic of fashion. It is true that television newscasts do not have the same mocking, sometimes disrespectful tone: the need to use clear, synthetic discourse in a limited time span militates against the use of wordplay and innuendo. The announcer's humor can appear only incidentally, and discreetly. Television news seduces with high-toned chic: it combines seriousness of discourse with the increasingly frequent play of the new images made possible by electronic technologies and computers. In television news programs, we find multiple signs of sophisticated representation and visualization, scenographic gadgetry intended to produce effects and animation, to concoct a trademark image and a "look" for the channel. The new ways of treating images mean that mockups of television newscasts can be constructed; "screen-pages" can be designed with computer graphic techniques, electronic inserts, titles, illustrations, logos, and banners; images can be shifted on the screen, made smaller or larger at will, juxtaposed for duplex effects (the "embedded" man). Television news relies more and more on stylistic research (credits with special effects and modernistic rhetoric, abstract electronic imagery) and gives rise to a decorative display consisting of flashes, ephemeral embedded images, variations and recompositions of images that echo the modern spectacular and accelerated character of current events.[24] As the airwaves and their synthetic images are "dressed up," the fashion process of seduction is getting its second wind: news has made it into the fashionable era of electronic gadgetry.

The charges brought against media news are couched in familiar terms. Media news is avid for the sensational; it focuses on secondary or insignificant details; it puts incommensurable cultural phenomena on the same footing; it is the product of a "staging" that forestalls the critical use of reason and prevents any apprehension of the phenomenon as a whole. While it may be true that the spectacular is consubstantial with news, we nevertheless tend to forget too quickly that seduction also focuses attention, captivates the audience, increases the desire to see, to read and be informed. The effects induced are the same as those of political marketing: because of lively, entertaining programming, the most varied questions concerning scientific and technological progress, the worlds of art and literature, sexuality, and drugs are made accessible to everyone. By bringing specialists together, by producing magazine programs with the rhythm of variety shows, television puts blocks of knowledge at the disposal of the masses. What was once esoteric becomes familiar; what might have resembled an evening course becomes appealing and holds millions of viewers spellbound. The unreality of what Boorstin called the "pseudo-event" is much more than a device for manipulating or alienating the spectator; we have to speak of a partial reappropriation of a universe, a broadening of the horizon of knowledge for the greatest number of people, although within a somewhat ragged framework. What is at stake is not "subjection to power"[25] or degradation of the cultural use of reason, but a democratization of access to culture, an expanded possibility of forming freer opinions. However positive it may be, the phenomenon has obvious limits: if the sum of knowledge increases, the same is not true of the power to synthesize knowledge or to put the data received into perspective. By "blowing up" the present, news blurs the reference points for interpretation; it overexposes what is visible and anecdotal at the expense of what is invisible and fundamental; it obscures the larger picture in favor of a focus on events. This is at once the media's limitation and their power: they fragment knowledge and make it superficial. Nevertheless, on the scale of the history of democracies, they open up the public to the world, make it more critical and less conformist than before.

In the same way, the hasty judgment about the so-called decline of the public sphere in connection with the extension of the media ought to be revised. Theoreticians have competed to outdo one another with their critical denunciations: the media have instituted "communication without response" (Debord) and a "monopoly on speech";[26] they deprive the public of the possibility of speaking out and contradicting;[27] they are responsible for the disappearance of social contacts and relations of exchange. The ready-to-consume culture and the one-way architecture of the media short-circuit social communication and discussion among individuals. Casting human beings as passive, irresponsible consumers lacking in initiative, the media destroy human relations; they isolate people, reduce opportunities for people to get together, weaken the taste for exchange and conversation. People no longer speak to each other; instead, they consume messages. The media destroy sociability; they accelerate the decline of public man, all the more so in that the information they convey depends more and more on a positivist "performative" requirement that is "incompatible with communication." By valorizing the criterion of efficiency erected as a monopoly on truth, news that is predominantly objectivist blocks "the exchange of rational argument": it has "the effect of substituting exchanges of merchandise for what had been communicational interaction."[28] The era of mass communications entails the deterioration of human communication.

However, if we look somewhat more closely, we see that the media are also the occasion of countless discussions; they continue to furnish subjects of exchange among individuals. Numerous small relational circuits in the public itself are grafted onto media communication. Just as theatrical performances allow the exchange of points of view, television offers numerous subjects of conversation; documentary reports are discussed and evaluated in families and in society; is there anyone in France who has not talked about the *Psy Show* or *Dallas?* Televised series and films are topics for judgment and negotiation: "What are we going to watch tonight?" The media do not asphyxiate the sense of communication; they do not bring sociability to an end. They reproduce incidents of social exchange in a new way. They institute social exchange in a basically less ritualized and freer form. Individuals do not communicate less than ever: probably people have never communicated so much on so many issues with so many people. However, they communicate in a more fragmented, less formal, more discontinuous manner, in keeping with their taste for autonomy and speed.

The media do not create a space of communication comparable to that of the classic liberal public space as Habermas describes it when he evokes the salons, societies, and clubs in which people discuss, reason, and argue face-to-face. Even if his description of the public sphere is very idealistic, and even if this type of rational communication has only been realized historically to a very limited extent, we may accept the idea that the human communication incited by a media presentation does not look much like a coherent and systematic exchange of arguments. But this still does not justify speaking of the disintegration of the public sphere, if that term refers to the place where public opinion and criticism take shape. The media are wrongly viewed as mechanisms for manipulating the public in order to produce social consensus; the seduction of news and information is also an instrument of individual reason. It is important to understand that the development of individual reason comes about less and less through discussion among private individuals and more and more through consumption and the seductive paths of information. Even if there were a decline in social forms of discussion, it would not be legitimate to infer from this that the critical spirit had disappeared. Seduction does not abolish the practice of reason; it broadens and universalizes reason even as it modifies the exercise of reason. Indeed, the media have made it possible to generalize the sphere of the public debate: first, by allowing a constantly growing number of citizens to become more aware of the issues involved in political choices—allowing them to be better-informed judges of the political game;[29] second, by enlarging the space of questioning: from one perspective, television newscasts and documentaries, reports and discussions do no more than set off a dynamic of interrogation on all issues of public and private life. Prisons, homosexuality, nuclear power, euthanasia, bulimia, techniques of procreation—there are no issues left that have not been the object of news programs, analysis, and discussion. The public space has not ceased to be the place for critical discussion, no matter how much it has been penetrated by managerial concerns and by the system's standards for productivity. Experts and popularized presentations of scientific issues in no way preclude the possibility that basic rifts may develop over the way problems should be evaluated. Far from stifling public debate, the media nourish it and place it within the democratic space of endless questioning. Information is not colonized by the standards of utilitarian rationality. Through media debates, the various conflicts of values proper to the modern world arise, bringing standards of efficiency, equality, and freedom into conflict. The public is offered not only recipes, but also a multiplicity of approaches and viewpoints. The relative atrophy of social movements, the indifference to the political sphere, the frivolity of viewers do not point simply to the decline of the public sphere and a monopoly of the utilitarian ideology. Even as they succeed in producing a consensus, the media simultaneously pursue differences in perspective. Seduction integrates the public with contemporary society even as it develops criticism and civil polemics.

While the media broaden the space of critical interrogation, they also pacify its terms. There are occasional complaints about the muffled tones of television programs, about their aseptic worldliness. But those who make such complaints fail to appreciate the communicational effectiveness of such an apparatus. The media, recycled by the fashion process, educate the public about the ethos of the community. They diffuse in large doses the standard of peaceful conversation, a nonviolent model of sociability. Scenes of violence in movies and on television, it may be surmised, are in large measure counterbalanced by this staging of an endless dialogue and the exchange of arguments. The "simulation" of communication carried out by the media (questioning of the public, computerized polls, and so on), the debates, the pleasant tones of voice are essential: they produce the ideal of civility, and they disallow outrageous polemics and uncontrolled aggressivity. In this sense, the media have to be viewed as a major component in the consolidation of the democracies, which are henceforth committed to the code of verbal confrontation without bloodshed. The media socialize the public to accept the seductiveness of verbal exchanges and relational contact; they participate in the process of civilizing ideological and social conflict.

CHAPTER VII

Meaning Carries On

The Bearable Lightness of Meaning:

Fashion and Ideology

Like objects and mass culture, major discourses about meaning are caught up in the irrepressible logic of novelty, carried away by a turbulence that may not be absolutely identical to fashion in the narrow sense but is nevertheless analogous in principle. The world of consciousness, too, is now ordered by the ephemeral and the superficial: this is the new configuration of democratic societies. It would be patently absurd to claim that the frivolous process has completely taken over intellectual life and that ideological shifts are governed by a gratuitous logic of renewal. However, it can be argued that the fashion process succeeds in annexing even those spheres that are a priori most resistant to the play of fashion. We are not living through the end of ideologies; we are ushering in the era of ideologies recycled as fashion.

Never has change in cultural and ideological orientations proceeded so precipitously as it does in our societies; never has it been so dependent on fads. The speed with which frenzies of meaning have come and gone and proliferated over the last two or three decades is particularly striking. On the hit parade of ideas, coming one after another or overlapping, there has been the counterculture movement, antiauthoritarianism, third-worldism, libertarian pedagogy, antipsychiatry, sexual liberation, worker management, consumerism, and ecology. At the same time, in the more specifi cally intellectual sphere, France has embraced structuralism, semiology, psychoanalysis, Lacanianism, Althusserism, the philosophies of desire, and the "new philosophy." The ballet continued through the 1980s, with the spectacular turnaround of neolibertarianism: the "conservative revolution," the return of the sacred, the ecstasy of "roots," and the glorification of businesses. In the 1960s and 1970s, the hypercritical ideology of protest was a big hit, just like the miniskirt or the Beatles. Marx and Freud became superstars and gave rise to floods of ravished exegetes, mimetic discourses, imitators, and readers. And what is left today, in France? In a few short years, the most hallowed references have fallen into oblivion.

"May '68 is history!" What was once indispensable has become old-fashioned. Not by virtue of a critical movement, but simply through disaffection: one wave ends, another is launched with the same epidemic force. Taken to extremes, this phenomenon leads people to change the way they think just as they change addresses, cars, or spouses. Systems of representation have become consumer objects; they function almost according to the throwaway logic of fads and tissues.

One misunderstanding needs to be avoided from the outset. To speak about the fashion process in ideas does not mean that everything floats in a state of absolute nondifferentiation, that collective opinions oscillate from pole to pole without fixed anchor points. Consummate fashion makes sense only in the democratic age where there is consensus and strong, widespread, lasting attachment to the founding values of the modern ideology: equality, freedom, and human rights. The accelerated obsolescence of systems of representation can develop only against the background of the overall stability of modern democracies. Here is the paradox of consummate fashion: whereas democratic society is more and more capricious in its relation to collectively intelligible discourses, at the same time it is more and more balanced, consistent, and firm in its ideological underpinnings. Parodying Nietzsche, one might say that *homo democraticus* is superficial by way of depth; the securing of the principles of individualist ideology is what allows meanings to enter into their merry dance.

No one would claim that fashion is intruding on intellectual life for the very first time. Since the seventeenth century at least, the cultural sphere has been stirred up, in worldly and intellectual circles, by countless "frenzies," and even political views have gone through many cycles of alternation and change. However, if we look closely at the various ideological shifts that repeatedly jolted the democracies through the middle of the twentieth century, we do not find the fashion process at work; the tenor and emotional investment of the ideological formations characteristic of that era preclude the intervention of the fashion form. Republic, nation, proletariat, race, socialism, secularism, revolution—these were all sacred terms for the political ideologies that embraced the mission of renewing the world. These ideologies crystallized as dogmas calling for personal devotion and sacrifice. Modern revolutionary discourses, systems for global interpretation of the universe claiming to offer total knowledge of present, past, and future, have reintroduced a certain form of religious faith through their eschatological doctrines, their "scientific" ambition to articulate and maintain truth and justice with certainty. As "secular religions," they have given rise to militancy and absolute passions, unswerving submission to the correct line, total personal commitment, the gift of believers' lives and subjective individualities. Calling for renunciation of self in favor of revolution, nation, and party, the glorious age of ideologies is completely opposed to fashion and its relativism. Whereas the heroic reign of ideology requires the abnegation of individuality, the reign of fashion rests on the requirement of immediate individual happiness. Whereas ideology generates orthodoxy and scholasticism, fashion is attended by small individual differences and fluctuating commitments. Ideology is Manichean: it separates good from bad, cleaves society down the middle, and exacerbates social conflicts; fashion pacifies and neutralizes antagonisms. Whatever reversals may have come about in the sphere of political and social thought during the last two centuries, fashion did not succeed until recently in imposing its ephemeral legislation, countered as it was by ideologies with theological pretensions.

We have left behind the age of secular prophecy. Within just a few decades, the discourse of radical social change has been largely swept away. It has lost all its legitimacy and all social moorings. No one believes any longer in the glorious fatherland of socialism; no one believes in the saving mission of the proletariat and the party; no one militates for the "Great Day" ahead. The historical importance of this debacle of the revolutionary imagination cannot be overstressed. No sooner did eschatological convictions and beliefs in an absolute truth of history begin to crumble than a new regime of "ideologies" came into being: that of fashion. The ruin of Promethean visions opens up an unprecedented relation to values, an essentially ephemeral, mobile, unstable ideological space. There are no more megasystems; they have given way to the fluctuation and mutability of trends. Where we used to have faith, we now have infatuation. After the era of intransigent theology comes the era of frivolous meaning: interpretations of the world have shed their former seriousness and taken up the casual intoxication of consumption and express service. And the importance of the ephemeral in the ideological realm is very likely to intensify: in recent years, we have already seen the most politically convinced people make a clean sweep of their views and change direction by 180 degrees. Yesterday's French Marxists are supporters of religion, and the "angry young men" have become apologists for capitalism. The heroes of cultural confrontation have been converted to the cult of the self, and devotees of worker management promote the market economy. We are prepared to adore unconditionally what we were only recently ready to burn. This destabilization does not involve the masses alone; it also affects the political class, as the conservative vogue in the early 1980s attested. It is not limited to the average person in the street; it extends to intellectuals as well, as one can see from the repeated gyrations of some of the French intellectual starlets. Mobility of conscience is not an exclusive privilege of our era. What is unique to our era, on the other hand, is the way in which inconstancy has become generalized, virtually systemic: today it is taking over as the dominant "ideological" mode of operation.

To be sure, people still believe in causes, but casually, without committing themselves "to the bitter end." No longer inclined to die in great numbers for their ideas, human beings in modern democratic societies are always prepared for change; consistency has become old hat. People live less and less according to systems of dominant ideas; like the rest, such systems have been swallowed up by frivolity. Higher goals do not disappear, but they no longer stand out. Of course they are capable of mobilizing the masses on occasion, but indirectly, and in unpredictable ways, like passing flare-ups that are quickly extinguished, replaced by the longer-lasting quest for personal happiness. The dominant trend produces adjustable and expendable plans. A preference for provisional arrangements is winning out over fidelity, superficial commitment over motivation based on belief. We are embarked on an interminable process of desacralization and desubstantialization of meaning that defines the reign of consummate fashion. This is how the gods die: not in a nihilist demoralization of the West and anguish over the loss of values, but in small jolts of meaning. Not in the morosity of Europe, but in the euphoria of fleeting ideas and actions. Not in passive disillusionment, but in hyperanimation and temporary highs. There is no point in weeping over the "death of God": God is getting a Technicolor, fast-forward funeral. Far from engendering a will to nothingness, the death of God carries the desire for the new and its excitement to extremes.

The new flexibility has to be resituated within the continuity of the dynamics of democracy. By positing the organization of society as dependent on humans and no longer on a sacred agency, the modern ideologies had been the instituting matrixes of our democratic universe, a universe called forth by the will of the collective body alone. But by setting up intransigent dogmas and establishing an ineluctable meaning for history, this process of secularization in a sense stopped in its tracks. It reintroduced in secular guise the old religious apparatus of human submission to an inaccessible higher principle. The age of fashion represents one more step forward toward the democratic elimination of the intangible and the hieratic. Nothing now requires self-sacrifice; discourses are open to flexible debate, to correction, to the nondisruptive revision of principles. The fashion form reflects the final stage of the democratization of minds and meanings.

Beyond fashion's mood shifts, paradoxically, democratic society is digging a homogeneous furrow, pursuing an identical trajectory. One of the limits of the cyclical theory of collective behavior has to do with the way this theory sees the abrupt changes of ideological coordinates as back-and-forth movements, pendulum swings between private and public life,[1] as if there is nothing but historical discontinuity, reversals that are always radically opposed to whatever came before. Now if we consider the oscillations that have taken place over the past three decades, we are obliged to note that, despite these reversals, a single historical dynamic turns out, paradoxically, to be at work. To be sure, on the surface the utopian wave of the 1960s is in total contrast to our disillusioned, pragmatist, corporatist moment; an era of public commitment is radically distinct from an era defined by its hyperindividualistic preoccupations, no matter what partial social conflicts may erupt here and there. However, can the counterculture or the events of May 1968 be seen as anything but waves of transpolitical individualist claims?[2] Can radical feminism be seen as anything but a movement allowing women to claim new freedoms? The ideology of protest brandished the banner of revolution, but one of its mainsprings was the individualist goal of living freely, unhampered by organizations or conventions. This ideology helped in its own way to highlight the forward march of democratic individualism and to topple a certain number of ponderous, repressive frameworks that had been resistant to personal autonomy. There is not an irreducible gap between that moment and the present one; they represent nothing but two different paths along a single trajectory, that of the conquest of individuality. Today, the emphasis on personal values and even the return of a certain moral conservatism are pursuing the same historical effort to conquer autonomy in other ways. As soon as the reference points of dogmatic progressivism are blurred and new antinomic references are promoted, community pressures become weaker and less homogeneous; what is correct becomes less clear; the gamut of individual choice broadens, and the possibility of variegating the values that orient our lives increases as well. Reason has its ruses: yesterday the ideology of the Left served the historical progress of individualism; today the values of order and business are playing the same role in their turn, almost in spite of themselves. Their manifest reversals notwithstanding, temporary ideologies do not disrupt the age-old continuity of the democracies; rather, they accelerate its progress.

The fashion regime of collective representations did not replace the era of Promethean ideologies all at once. There was a turning point, a critical moment that functioned as a compromise formation between the historical phase of the revolution and the phase of consummate fashion. The last manifestation of the revolutionary spirit turned out to be curiously combined, in the 1960s, with its counterpart, the fashion spirit. On the one hand, the 1960s and their aftermath reintroduced the imaginary realm of revolution, through student demonstrations, the counterculture, radical feminism, and alternative movements. We saw the unfolding of an ideological escalation summoning us to change our lives, to destroy the hierarchical and bureaucratic organization of capitalist society, to free ourselves from all forms of domination and authority. With the evocation of the police state and the bosses' state, the return to general strikes, the "Internationale" and the barricades, the revolutionary mythology succeeded in refurbishing its coat of arms. On the other hand, the confrontations of the 1960s for the most part broke off the essential links that had connected that mythology with the demiurgic projects of building a new world that were crystallized in the nineteenth century. May 1968 in this respect constitutes an unprecedented moment: without any definite goal or program, the movement was an insurrection without a future, a revolution in the present tense attesting simultaneously to the decline of eschatologies and to the protesters' inability to offer a clear view of the society to come. Without an explicit project, subtended by a spontaneous ideology, May 1968 was just a short-lived parenthesis, a frivolous revolution, an infatuation with Revolution rather than a fundamental mobilization. It offered the spectacle of revolution, a joyous affirmation of revolutionary signs, not revolutionary stakes and confrontations. Unlike the bloody revolutions that had focused on the deliberate construction of a different future, May 1968 was organized around the temporal axis of fashion—the present—in a "happening" that looked more like a big party than like the days that shook the world. The springtime of the students did not make serious proposals or build anything lasting. It criticized and palavered; it brought people together in the streets and universities; it upset certainties; it called for "the rebellion of life," for "everything, all at once," for the total fulfillment of individuals as opposed to organizations and bureaucracies. The idea was to explode instituted hierarchies in order to live unhampered in the here and now: May 1968 was subtended by a libertarian individualist, hedonist, and communicational ideology at the opposite pole from the self-abnegation of earlier revolutions. The collective and subjective present was the leading temporal pole of May 1968. This was the first *fashion revolution*: frivolity won out over tragedy, and history espoused play. May 1968 mobilized revolutionary passions more on the surface than in depth. In parodying revolution, May 1968 did less to reignite the age-old flames than to carry to its apotheosis, briefly, *the fashion of protest*.

The ideological climate of the times played a preponderant role in the rise of the protest phenomenon in France. Neither the students' objective situation nor the deterioration of their job prospects or future outlook can account for the youthful utopian rebellion. In May 1968, no one was really worrying about the future; the students gave very little thought to the value of their diplomas. Quite the contrary: they rejected the adaptation of university instruction to the needs of the capitalist economy. The employment crisis had not yet sunk in. The spirit of May 1968 did not result from a social inclination to worry; it resulted above all from ideological inclinations, intellectual fashions, among a particular age group: social criticism was "in," as were revolutionary attitudes, Marxism, and anticapitalism, at the very moment when the real revolutionary perspective embodied in the party and the working class were disappearing. The vogue for revolution evolved as a counterpart to the decomposition of the French Communist party and the integration of the working class to neocapitalism. This vogue managed to attract a lot of attention precisely because it was discredited among the masses and their protest organizations, because it was able to serve the young as a sign of affirmation, a spectacle of visible difference. The intellectual break was of course particularly evident in hyper-politicized leftist groups, but in fact radical ideas were more or less widespread in very broad layers of the student movement. Police efforts to suppress the student movement contributed to student espousal of the anticapitalist ideology that was more or less in favor, and led to the propagation of the protest phenomenon. While they do not account for everything, radical chic and hypercritical conformity among young people are crucial to an understanding of the breadth and contagiousness of the spirit of May 1968.

Other cultural factors also played major roles in developing the spirit of protest. No circumstantial or structural explanation (the war in Vietnam, a centralizing and dominating state, the archaic nature of the university, the Gaullist regime in France) can account for a phenomenon that touched young people (in a variety of ways, to be sure—there were the hippies, the counterculture, the psychedelic movement, the *provos*, May 1968, the alternative movements, feminism, gay liberation), but that affected all the advanced democratic societies. The uprisings of the 1960s can be related to the increase in school populations, the fact that students stayed in school longer, the fact that teenagers and postadolescents led lives without responsibility, separated from the real world of work. But each of these factors was important only within the broader framework in which the new fashion organization of society was overturning the values of everyday life. At the heart of the individualism of protest, there is the empire of fashion as the springboard of individualist demands, of the appeal for personal freedom and fulfillment. The hedonist age of fashion and the cult of personal development that it inspires were vectors of the upheaval of the 1960s and early 1970s, an upheaval that came about among young people because that group was less subject to the older forms of socialization, because it had assimilated the new standards for living one's life more rapidly, more directly, and more intensely than other groups. Hedonist individualism bumped headlong into archaic, authoritarian frameworks for socialization; it was this antagonism between a culture centered on the values of fashion and a managerial society, a culturally blocked society, that fed the trend toward protest. At the deepest level, what was at stake was a revolt aimed at harmonizing and unifying a culture with its own new basic principles. This was not a "crisis of civilization," but a collective effort to draw society away from the rigid cultural norms of the past and give birth to more a supple, more varied, more individualistic society that would conform to the requirements of consummate fashion.

Revolutionary discourse has lost its attraction today. Eschatological narratives have lost their shock value; we are firmly ensconced in the terminal reign of the fashion of meaning. The disaffection with ideological odysseys and its corollary, the advent of "light" meaning, result not so much from a collective awareness of the totalitarianism of the Communist revolution, the inferno of the Gulag, than from the changes that have occurred within the Western world as it has been won over by the process of consummate fashion. The ludic-aesthetic-hedonistic-psychologistic life-style celebrated by the media is what undermined the revolutionary utopia and discredited discourse on behalf of a classless society and a harmonious future. The consummate-fashion system fosters the cult of individual health and life in the here and now; it holds sacred the personal happiness of individuals and the pragmatism of attitudes; it destroys class solidarities and consciousness in favor of explicitly individualistic demands and preoccupations. The empire of seduction has been a euphoric gravedigger for the great ideologies. Taking into account neither the singular individual nor the requirement of freedom to live *hic et nunc*, those ideologies found themselves poles apart from contemporary individualist aspirations.

The fluidity of meaning inherent in our societies is matched by more or less pronounced concerns about the vitality of the democracies. Stripped of belief in great causes, indifferent to major projects of collective edification, are not democracies highly fragile, vulnerable to threats from without, haunted by the spirit of capitulation? Under the reign of fashion, militant fervor is quenched: might not this phenomenon, under some circumstances, foster the establishment of dictatorial regimes? What becomes of the spirit of freedom, courage in the face of danger, or the mobilization of energies in a society that lacks higher goals, that is obsessed with the quest for personal happiness? These questions cannot be ignored, but it is illegitimate to draw hasty conclusions about the degeneration of the democratic spirit, a spirit gone soft owing to the flabbiness of citizens' convictions. One may well wonder whether, today, people would be ready to die in large numbers for the institutions of the republic; but once the question has been raised, how can one reasonably go further? No one can give a serious answer to the sort of question that situates us in a catastrophic scenario with necessarily unprecedented features. Has the will to fight been snuffed out by the cult of the self? If we look at the profile of contemporary society, we find nothing that authorizes us to answer categorically in the affirmative. The rout of heroic ideologies does not lead to generalized cowardice, to the paralysis of the citizenry and the rejection of war. Military service does not arouse enthusiasm, but it does not generate any movement toward collective refusal; except for extreme pacifists, the principles of armed defense, a credible dissuasive force, and the reinforcement of military potential are challenged by no one. While the democratic states, with the support of their own populations, continue to arm themselves, pursuing their military-industrial course, civil society for its part manifests collective calm and remarkable firmness of opinion in view of the expansion of terrorism. The temptation to give in to terrorist blackmail is rejected by the majority, despite the threats that weigh on public tranquillity; judges willing to pronounce a severe verdict against the head of a terrorist organization despite the risks have been widely welcomed by society and the political class. *Homo democraticus* does not dream of heroic sacrifice and an impressive show of weapons, to be sure; still, he does not fall into the cowardice and unconsciousness of capitulation and the immediate present. Terrorist violence has to be answered with strength and the enforcement of laws; threats by foreign nations have to be answered with the reinforcement of military might. Without enthusiasm but with lucidity, contemporary individuals have adopted the old adage: "If you want peace, you must prepare for war."

The withering away of hard-line ideological choices is not the same thing as the advent of the spirit of surrender and collective lack of foresight; moreover, it reinforces the social legitimacy of democratic institutions. Apart from tiny terrorist groups with far-out views rejected by all political formations, the democracies no longer harbor within themselves any unconditional adversaries. This is an entirely new situation: revolutionary parties no longer have any impact whatever. In a more relativist world, lacking any ardent historical faith, respect for institutions wins out over subversion; political violence makes no new converts and becomes illegitimate in the eyes of the community; in Western Europe, appeals to bloodshed and physical violence are rejected by the social and political body. Critics endlessly find things to criticize in our societies, and in the end they take a certain satisfaction in doing so: for the first time since the advent of the democratic age, human beings have no more social utopias; they no longer dream of a different society. On the surface, the twists and turns of fashion destabilize the democracies; at a deeper level, they settle them down, make them more stable and more resistant to holy wars, less threatened from within, less vulnerable to the hysterical delirium of total mobilization.

What we are seeing, then, is not the decline of the democratic spirit but its advance. The gentle drift of meaning is accompanied, to be sure, by a process in which the political is made more spectacular and more trivial, in which militancy and labor-union memberships decline, in which the spirit of citizenship is inflected toward consumerism, in which the public is less involved in the election process and sometimes disaffected—so many revealing aspects of a crisis of *homo democraticus*, ideally conceived. Yet we can hardly fail to see at the same time that the dissolving of ideologies and the dream of consummate fashion go hand in hand with a more autonomous civil society, one that is more mobilized around what touches it to the quick: women's rights, the environment, education. On the one hand, there is less and less religious commitment to political causes; on the other, there are more "social conflicts" attesting that civil society is not so passive as some make it out to be, that it intervenes more directly and spontaneously in matters involving the lives of individuals and families. Less boxed in by ponderous dogmas, more mobile, more attached to the quality of life and individual freedoms, society is freer to intervene, more able to bring pressure to bear on the state, more apt to express its hopes outside the traditional political parties and labor unions. The loss of faith in ideologies that characterizes our era leads to more open conflicts, to a greater involvement on the part of citizens with their own immediate affairs, to a less arrogant wielding of power on the part of electoral majorities. Society makes itself increasingly heard, and public power has to learn to imagine solutions that are less technocratic and more flexible, less authoritarian and more diversified, in harmony with the contemporary open individualistic world.

The Thrill of the Comeback

But let us consider the great ideological shift that is taking place in France before our very eyes. In a few short years, the Marxist paradigm has given way to the libertarian paradigm; the opposition to capitalism has yielded to the consecration of free enterprise and the limitation of state power. After the great nay-saying, there is the ecstasy of profit. Yesterday, utopias were in the air; today, there is pragmatism and managerial realism. The rehabilitation of competitive individualist values is a corollary of the ideological promotion of economic competition. As ambition, effort, and money take on enhanced prestige, the end of the " '68 recess" is being proclaimed; educational institutions are being denounced as increasingly flabby and subject to pedagogical ideology. Merit, excellence, and individual competence are winning out; after the euphoria of the counterculture and relationships, the global pendulum has swung back to efficiency.

Nevertheless, the neolibertarian wave is clearly a long way from carrying the day without false notes. If private enterprise and decreased state intervention are unquestionably in favor, this in no way prevents the social body, even in the United States, from supporting systems of social protection, social policies established within the framework of the welfare state. Distaste for state interventionism in economic matters in no way under-

mines the collective attachment to social justice, to establishing protec-
tions against major risks, to state intervention in social matters and even
in university affairs, as recent student movements in France and Spain
have shown. Entrepreneurial dynamism may be celebrated, but large
numbers of people manifest their attachment to acquired benefits and a
salary scale based on seniority. The will to restore the authority of teachers
and of knowledge itself does not undermine the importance of the relational dimension and the need to take subjective motives into consideration in the pedagogical realm. Fashion has its extremes, but in its social
diffusion it smoothes over the most pronounced wrinkles; it reconstitutes
itself heterogeneously; it gives up all doctrinal character in order to
achieve, de facto, a certain "continuity in change," a more rapid transformation of the collective body that still will not disrupt the great equilibri-
ums of democratic societies.

The current neolibertarian trend is much more a fashion than a hard-
line ideological credo; the attraction of the new and the image of privacy
are more seductive than the libertarian political program. Like any fashion, this one will secrete its own antitheses. No doubt, after a while, we
shall see new enthusiasm for the state and even for the rationality of the
universal; we shall have new waves of protesters, hirsute or not, along with
romantic utopias at war with the world of money, hierarchy, and work. As
soon as the theological age of ideologies ended, we were consigned to a
chronic instability of values, to the ebb and flow of actions and reactions,
to the "eternal return" of fashion, which keeps on recycling the old forms
and values in modern guise. In the 1980s, France resonates to the sound of
high-tech modernism and a backward-looking mongrel competitiveness;
but for how long?

This moment can be described as one of the cycles of modern history
characterized by overinvolvement in private affairs, in contrast with an
earlier phase of attachment to the public sphere. A shift with respect to the
public/private axis has in fact occurred; a new privatizing cycle is under
way, after the various collective engagements of the 1960s and the early
1970s. The question is whether such a fluctuation can be understood, even
partially, as a disappointment resulting from participation in public actions.[3] Through its stress on the role of dissatisfaction and personal frustration, Albert Hirschman's analysis accounts for the abruptness of the
collective reversals we have witnessed, over and beyond the consideration
of contingent objective factors and "rational actors." At the same time,
this analysis makes clear how much changes in preference owe to the
inconstancy and frivolity of human motivations: in a sense, the logic of
fashion underlies this theory of ideological and social oscillations. But the
importance attributed to disappointment is highly overestimated; as it
happens, that particular disappointment has little explanatory value in

the cycle that concerns us. Today, those who have been disappointed by the revolutionary mobilization are not the only ones who put their hopes in the private sphere; in a general way, the entire social body does the same—the silent majority itself, which has been quite apathetic politically for decades. This apathy has nothing to do with the disappointment provoked by actions taken in the public interest; it has been a long time since the masses played an active role in the great eschatological struggles and clung to the hope of changing the world. The same people who vaguely condemned capitalism and its excesses without being politically committed themselves have come to the point of revising their judgments in favor of free enterprise. What we are seeing is not disappointment, but the invincible attraction of the new. The current shift has less to do with the experience of dissatisfaction than with the ruin of the great ironclad ideologies; it has less to do with frustration than with the frenzy of change and the passion for all that exalts free individuals. Without the seductive power of novelty, the new libertarian ideas would never have won such a large audience so rapidly. The cultural promotion of free enterprise came about not only by way of realism in relation to the economic crisis, but also through the spirit of fashion.

Although it is in part a fashion, the new entrepreneurial culture still produces fundamental and presumably lasting changes in individual and collective behavior. With the change in the social image of business, the latter becomes less a place of exploitation and class struggle than a place of creation of wealth that calls for more widespread participation. In the Europe of the 1980s, the figure of the profiteer boss is yielding on a broad scale to that of the creator and hero-star of business. Labor unions are starting to take this change of climate into account in their language and practices: worker management looks like a has-been; capitalism is no longer evil incarnate; strikes are becoming weapons whose use is sometimes problematic. At the same time, the taste for enterprise is spreading and winning new social legitimacy. The winners' turn has come—the photogenic bosses, the yuppies. Here is a crucial ideological updating for the free societies that, having shed their image as inveterate exploiters, find themselves endowed with strengthened legitimacy and a culture at least theoretically favorable to a more realistic participation on the part of wage earners and to a process of conflictual cooperation in businesses.

A shift in ideological coordinates of this nature cannot leave the subjective sphere itself unchanged; it is carried away by new goals and meanings. We are far removed from the culture of marginal dissidence. We are now worrying about the future; effort, courage, and risk have returned to center stage; emulation, professionalism, and excellence are extolled. Still, does this new cultural environment toll the death knell of the narcissistic profile of contemporary personalities? The spirit of competition and ambition have been rehabilitated, and there is a consensus about business: is this not a new configuration incompatible with the reign of the self-absorbed ego, preoccupied with its own intimate sensations and well-being? In one sense, a page is about to be turned. Laxity, permissiveness, and scattershot popular psychology have all had their day; an entire sector of "cool" culture is being overtaken by referents that are more "serious," more responsible, more productive. But psychologizing individualism has not succumbed; it has recycled itself by integrating the new thirst for business, software, media, and advertising. A new narcissistic generation is on the move, in the grip of a frenzy for computers, productivity, business, and the image-meter. Not only are the pop-psychology cult, the idolatry of the body and of personal autonomy more active than ever, but the original, historically unique interhuman relation instituted by the second individualist revolution is being perpetually recuperated. To be sure, we are undergoing a meritocratic reaction: to be sure, the taste for success, competition, and business is returning at full strength. But how is this moment to be interpreted? Not at all as a classic reinvestment in hierarchical values and the primacy of other-directed criteria, but much more fundamentally as the pursuit, through other means, of the properly narcissistic process of reduction—which does not mean abolition—of the subjective dependence on collective criteria of social respectability. At the heart of what constitutes contemporary individualism, there is a new structure of interpersonal relations in which the ego wins out over social recognition, in which the individual quest for happiness and self-expression displaces the age-old primacy of the judgment of others (as reflected in concern with honor, conspicuous consumption, social standing, and so on). Far from being abolished, this shifting of the social relation among human beings pursues its own dynamic. It is simplistic to suppose that we are simply witnessing a comeback of competitive ideology, of the frenzied quest for success and social status; the new spirit of the times is simply getting on with the task of emancipating individuals with respect to the collective reference points of social success and the approval of others.

Even the craze for media recognition that henceforth drives artists, journalists, writers, bosses, and everyone else must not be understood as signaling the primacy of an obsession with others, but much more as autopublicity, the narcissistic pleasure of appearing on the screen, of being seen by as many people as possible. Media exposure satisfies the desire to be loved and to please more than the desire to be respected and admired for one's works. Narcissus is more eager to seduce than to be respected; he wants to be talked about, wants people to care about him, wants to be fussed over. As Patrick Poivre d'Arvor has declared to a major daily newspaper: "I need to be loved." It is once again respectable to earn money and social success, but the psychological mainsprings of these activities have little to do with the desire to rise in the social hierarchy, to hoist oneself up above others, to be envied, to win respectability. Ambition itself is caught up in the vertigo of intimate subjectivity: business offers as much a way to establish an economically comfortable place for oneself as a means for realizing one's own potential and outdoing oneself, a way to have a challenging goal in life. The narcissistic structure of the ego dominates; it is a matter on the one hand of having enough money to enjoy the goods and services of modern life in private, and on the other hand of doing something by and for oneself, of experiencing the excitement of adventure and risk. Competition has taken on a new tonality: it no longer connotes the effort to "make it," but rather a narcissism more attentive to oneself and one's intimate resonances than to social posturing, rank, and prestige. There is no rift between the new entrepreneurial cult and the multiple passions of individuals for writing, music, or dance; self-expression, "creativity," "in-depth participation" of the self prevail everywhere. In an increasing number of cases, people in business, the liberal professions, and others change their professional activities, not because their "career profiles" are blocked, but because as individuals they are not fulfilling themselves as they would like. The neonarcissistic age implies the subordination of the forms of competition to desires for personal accomplishment. The other is less an obstacle or an enemy than a springboard to being oneself. True, individuals measure themselves against one another, assert themselves individually in comparison with others; still, this does not mean that a new cycle is simply replacing hedonistic individualism. It is the very same process of narcissistic privatization that is widening the frontiers; the ego is becoming more and more the master of interpersonal competition, as in certain sports (footraces, nontournament tennis) in which competition with others is above all a way of relaxing, staying in shape, challenging oneself, or setting a personal record.

The neolibertarian vogue warrants our attention. How could free enterprise, which French intellectuals have denounced for so long, have won their hearts in such a short time? How can we explain the cultural reversal in favor of profit and markets? How, in a nation like France, so inclined for so long to the protective centralism of public power, could a movement like the disengagement of the state have come about? We know that, in the French case, the socialist experience of the early 1980s contributed more than a little to this shift. In particular, it revealed the limits of state action in an economy involved in the international market; it exposed constraints on the economy and the reality of international economic links; it undermined leftist dreams by putting into action, after an initial start-up phase, a pragmatic style of business management. Beyond the political alternation of right and left, the context of economic crisis was crucial. Its first, quite concrete impact came through the continued growth of obligatory payroll deductions: what appeared to be a means of protection, a guarantee of freedom and well-being, began to look to some like an obstacle to autonomy and individual responsibility. The increase in taxes and social contributions ceased to be taken for granted; they gave rise to the feeling that we were forging nations of welfare clients, immature democracies. At an even deeper level, the economic crisis was a pedagogical instrument converting minds to reality, making utopian visions and miraculous solutions by the all-purpose state obsolete. Lingering unemployment, zero-growth rates, industrial weakness, loss of competitiveness, deficits in the balance of payments—the new economic configuration led belatedly to an awareness that the European nations were running out of steam, and needed to acquire the means to emerge from the crisis state. This new configuration is at the root of the cultural promotion of the entrepreneur, the emphasis on risk and individual merit as means of giving our societies a new lease on life and opening up opportunities for the future.

Whatever their importance, all these factors could come into play only because they were grafted onto the transformations of values and life-styles that belong to the age of consummate fashion. By hyperindividualizing human beings, by developing the taste for personal autonomy, by privileging the registering of facts, the reign of objects and information led to a valorization of everything that relates to freedom and individual responsibility. The neolibertarian vogue is in part an ideological adaptation to ways of life that center on the independent individual unit, an entity resistant to omniscient systems, to intrusive, homogeneous, directive frameworks. It is impossible to separate the consensus over profit and enterprise from the action that characterizes the generalized fashion system, a system that continues to promote individual autonomy, as we have seen, and to uproot dogmatic eschatological beliefs. In the era of protest, individualist claims had free rein to denounce the bureaucratic capitalist system and to espouse revolutionary radicalism; this era constituted an intermediate phase between a militant revolutionary age and an age of individualism absorbed first and foremost in private preoccupations. Consummate fashion has pursued its course: the narcissistic individualism that governs us, hostile to great prophecies and fond of hyperreality, has been fertile ground for the libertarian renaissance. The requirement of flexibility, the moves to denationalize and deregulate, echo the transformations of individuality itself: it has become flexible, pragmatic, and eager above all for personal autonomy.

Alongside this second libertarian wave, various conservative manifestations are unfolding, reflecting just as spectacular a reversal of values. The ideology of law and order has the wind in its sails at the moment: in France, public opinion is running in favor of the death penalty, and many states in the United States have already reenacted and implemented it. As

far as French prisons are concerned, there is less and less emphasis on
rehabilitation and social reinsertion; we are told that we have had enough
"soft" prisons and lax justice, that we have to punish with a firm hand,
that we have to reestablish mandatory sentences. In England, there are
threats to restore physical punishment. "Therapeutic injunctions" for
drug addicts and penalties for substance abuse have been advocated. Numerous associations such as Pro-Life or *Laissez-les-vivre* (Let them live)
are crusading for the abolition of legal abortion. In the United States, attacks on abortion clinics are increasing, and since 1977 it has not been
possible to pay for voluntary abortions with public funds. Leading political figures in France as well as in America have declared that legalized
abortion must be brought to an end. A new moral order is struggling to
take hold; the slogan "work, family, fatherland" is coming back. After the
frenzy of sexual liberation and women's liberation, we now hear praise for
chastity, for virginity, occasionally for the role of woman as housewife;
contraception is stigmatized, while AIDS appears as a sign of divine wrath,
and intolerant statements against homosexuality are heard more often in
some contexts. More troubling still, racist and xenophobic themes are pop-
ping up shamelessly in public places. In France, people express doubts
about the Holocaust; attacks on foreigners are increasing; parties of the
extreme right do well in elections with slogans like "France to the French;
foreigners out." The antiauthoritarian and emancipatory climate of the
1960s and 1970s is behind us; conservatism is front-page news.

Can all these disparate phenomena—which nevertheless signal an unmistakable ideological reversal—be taken as manifestations of generalized
fashion? Are we not witnessing an authentic conservative and moralistic
comeback after the exacerbated cultural liberalism of recent years? Is this
not the very sign of fashion's eternal return, the alternation of old and
new, the recycling of the past, the alternating cycle of neo and retro? The
analogy is misleading: at its core, what is sometimes called the "conservative revolution" is antithetical to the spirit and logic of fashion. While
consummate fashion functions according to a logic of hedonism, seduction, and novelty, neoconservatism rehabilitates moralism, repression,
and tradition. The process under way opposes the frivolous order to the
moral order. Whereas the fashion form treats the individual subjective
choice as god, conservative rigorism attempts to crush diversity and freedom of choice. Fashion is fed by the insatiable desire for novelty; neoconservatism is rooted in dogma. Fashion responds to the taste for change; the
new moral order is a response to the anxieties produced by physical, economic, and cultural insecurity. Fashion exalts the present; the Moral
Majority is nostalgic for a past order. Conservatives are carrying out a
rigorous offensive in the area of morality; they are directing it explicitly,
moreover, against hypermodernism and the laxity of the fashion spirit,

which they accuse of having destroyed the values of effort, family, religion, work, and patriotism. What we are witnessing, in France and in the United States, is a reaction against permissive morality, against the destruction of authority and the family, against racial mixing and national "suicide," against Western "decadence," which is blamed on the unbridled reign of total fashion.

The desire for security aside, the rise of the Moral Majority in the United States is primarily the effect of a religious fundamentalism that consummate fashion has not succeeded in eradicating. The Moral Majority is not so much a fashion effect as an intolerant religious remnant, not so much an essential feature of contemporary democracies as a manifestation characteristic of nations in which fundamentalist groups and churches proliferate. Such groups have been able to win back their audience owing precisely to the earlier emancipatory tidal wave, the disintegration of social identities, and the individual and collective anxiety that disintegration generates. This neoconservatism does not reflect the flexible reign of consummate fashion; it reintroduces the hyperorthodox religious spirit of another age, in that it does not recognize the free action and judgment of private persons. Fashion's empire has not yet reached the end of its course. It has unearthed a number of cleavages, and in a few short years it has unleashed an unparalleled set of individualist claims. In societies in which the puritan sentiment is deeply rooted, the fashion process has come into conflict with intransigent faith and convictions that it has not managed to shake. Still, we should not be too quick to invoke a religious absolute impervious to worldly concerns: we must take the times into account, and we must acknowledge that the cultural effects of the wider fashion are only a few decades old. Let us not invoke, either, the omnipotent power of fashion's reign: there is nothing to suggest that it will ever succeed in changing the world of our beliefs into a realm of the consumable and the changeable. It is reasonable to suppose only that, because of the irreversible dynamics of fashion, fundamentalism will be less and less widely shared, less and less dominant in the modern democracies. However, there are no guarantees that it will ever disappear.

Although it cannot be identified as a form of infatuation, the rigorist and authoritarian phase is not unrelated to consummate fashion. In search of novelty, the media have powerfully inflated the traditionalist comeback, as if public opinion had suddenly switched sides. We know that this is not the case. At issue is more a pseudo-event than a basic cultural reality; in this respect, the "return to values" effect is inseparable from the media and at the same time, paradoxically, from fashion—even as it sets itself up to challenge fashion. All the polls point in the same direction: the passion for autonomy and the desire for personal pleasure keep on growing. Family values may be invoked, but the divorce rate keeps on rising and the birthrate continues to drop. People are getting married later and later in life, and in smaller and smaller numbers. In France, one child in five is now born out of wedlock. The decline of permissive sexuality may be announced, but in high schools in Paris one of every two boys is sexually active, and one girl in three is no longer a virgin; the overwhelming majority of high school students think that contraception and free adolescent sexuality are legitimate. The public is hostile to abortion? In the United States, the majority is opposed to prohibiting it by law, and in France, 30 percent of the right-wing National Front party voters are in favor of maintaining the right to abortion. Religious fundamentalism is on the rise in Western democracies? To suppose so is to fail to note that the practices and beliefs of a majority of believers are increasingly free, eclectic, and individualized. It is to forget that the phenomenon is developed by means of televangelism, Christian video advertising, Christian theme parks with laser shows, pools where you can swim in the daytime and get baptized at night. The phenomenon has many superficial echoes in the media, but few on the broad social scale: is this not in itself one of the characteristic features of fashion? A society restructured by the fashion form by no means keeps rigorist values out of the spotlight—but we have to recognize that the phenomenon remains a spectacle. Its effects may be non-negligible, but they are skin-deep and confined to a minority.

Like neopuritanism, claims and demands for security cannot be considered fashion movements. Restoration of the death penalty, stricter justice, identity checks in public streets, restriction of the right of exile, nationality codes—none of these manifestations has anything to do with the ephemeral fluctuations of fashion. The polls are unanimous: the struggle against criminality and the desire for personal security head the list of public preoccupations. We have not seen the last of the demands for law and order; this is because, at the deepest level, what is at issue is not an ideology but an unavoidable component of an orderly individualist society restructured by the fashion form. In a hyperindividualist society in which socialization excludes physical violence and cruelty, in which diverse populations meet, in which communication takes the place of repression and in which public order is very broadly assured, fear is part and parcel of the pacific, unarmed individual. Anxiety about personal safety is not a passing fancy; in a way, it is an invariant of democratic life. Tocqueville had already stressed this point: if democratic man has a natural taste for freedom, he has a still more ardent passion for public order; he is always ready, in difficult circumstances, to give up his own rights to stifle the seeds of disorder: "The taste for public tranquillity then becomes a blind passion, and the citizens are liable to conceive a most inordinate devotion to order."[4] Even as it is being inscribed in the prolongation of this democratic trend, the present moment nevertheless manifests a singular characteristic: in

effect, citizens are demanding both more security in their everyday lives
and more individual freedom. They want increased public order with no
decrease in individual rights. Still, the desire for security does not have as
its counterpart a willingness to give up political and personal freedoms, as
Tocqueville feared it would. We are not witnessing the beginning of a
trend toward restricting individual rights and increasing state prerogatives; instead we are seeing the crystallization of a heightened demand for
public control and protection at the heart of a society profoundly attached
to individual and democratic freedoms.

Just as security measures do not stem from a constituted ideology, the
resurgence of xenophobia is not inscribed within the continuity of classic
racist ideology. Today, the very citizens whose attitudes toward dark-
skinned people are least welcoming no longer advocate the destruction of
the other; they no longer proclaim the unchallenged superiority of the
Aryan or the Westerner. However many racist crimes there may be in
Western Europe, and there are too many, the phenomenon remains circumscribed; we no longer see pogroms, massacres, or systematic rape. Racism no longer has the virulence it once had; it is much more contained,
less aggressive. Many people dislike foreigners; few approve of bloodshed.
They avoid making contact, but they do not commit aggressive acts. The
frivolous age does not eliminate racism, but it modifies some of its features. No one imagines a "final solution" any longer; no one supports the
proposition that populations of color are genetically inferior. Western Europe has left the thematics of racial purity behind; contemporary xenophobia develops on the terrain of the obsession with personal security and
the protection of personal interests. In France, racism is going the way of
other ideologies: it is less heavily freighted with meaning; it has become
less sure of itself, less dominant, "postideological," more an expression of
individual anxiety than of a Manichean world view. It is hardly necessary
to specify that racism has not shifted, for all that—to say the least—into
the casual world of fashion.

Do-It-Yourself Enlightenment

Although the new social regulation of meaning is not antithetical to the
stable operation of democratic institutions, it does pose one thorny problem concerning the democratic ideal of subjective autonomy in the realm
of opinion. Can we really speak of individual freedom where the life of the
mind resonates to the rhythm of changing moods in fashion? If ideas oscillate with every capricious shift in fads, if we regularly adopt the "in"
trends, what becomes of the democratic individualist goal par excellence:
personal sovereignty or self-determination in the order of thought? The

question is a crucial one, as Tocqueville recognized. Tocqueville's nuanced pessimism regarding the future of democracies is well known: as equality of conditions advances, the yoke of habit and collective prejudice weakens, benefiting independence of mind and individual reasoning. However, even as individuals are led to rely increasingly on their own understanding, a counterforce develops that leads them to trust public opinion. On the one hand, individuals strive increasingly to seek truth in themselves; on the other hand, they are increasingly inclined to follow the majority verdict unquestioningly. In democracies, the action of ordinary opinion on isolated individuals has a new and incomparable power: it exerts itself as fashion, not through coercion but through the invisible pressure of numbers. Taken to the extreme, democratic epochs may bring about "the absolute power of a majority" and may induce people to "give up thinking at all, thus extinguishing intellectual freedom."[5] We can hardly fail to share Tocqueville's concern today, given the media's impact, the cult of best-sellers, the esoteric gurus, the entertainment programs, the proliferation of one-minute stars and of intellectual and ideological fashions.

Yet however ambiguous the frivolous economy of meaning may be, it hardly seems justifiable to represent it as an enterprise tending to eradicate individual freedom or as a sign of an increasing subjugation of human minds. Actually, the acceleration and proliferation of fashionable conformities are fostering a partial but effective autonomy of minds; the epidemics of mimesis produce progress toward greater individualization of thought. People take pleasure today in denouncing the sheeplike mindlessness of our contemporaries, their absence of reflection, their unfortunate tendency to be inconsistent and to go off on tangents. Still, we can hardly argue that minds were freer when religions and traditions attempted to produce a seamless homogeneity of collective beliefs, when the great messianic ideologies imposed dogmatic doctrines with no room for individual critical examination. It is easy to see what has been lost: today, convictions are less assured, there is less personal resistance to the seduction of the new and of majority opinion. It is harder to pinpoint what has been gained in the same process: people are more prepared to raise questions in the absence of preconceived answers, and they are more comfortable calling themselves into question as well. Under the reign of total fashion, the mind is less firmly made up than before, but more receptive to criticism; it is less stable but more tolerant; less sure of itself but more open to difference, more receptive to evidence and to the arguments of others. To identify consummate fashion with an unparalleled process of standardization and depersonalization is to take a superficial view; in reality, consummate fashion is the driving force behind a more insistent questioning, a multiplication of subjective viewpoints, a decrease in the similarity of small personal visions. The great ideological certainties are giving way before an explosion of individual microdifferences, subjective singularities that may not be very original, creative, or reflective but that are more numerous and more flexible than before. In the hollow space left by the collapse of catechisms and orthodoxies, fashion opens the way to the proliferation of subjective opinions. Nothing would be farther off the mark than to represent fashion with the features of an intellectual unanimity. Let us look at the current infatuation with libertarianism and a reduced role for the state: far from being reflected in a homogeneous discourse, it is accompanied by a whole range of variants and adaptations, from neo-libertarians to social democrats by way of neoconservatives and various others. Virtually all intellectual groupings, in varying degrees, share the infatuation of the moment, but none of them uses it in precisely the same way. A few years earlier, the same thing happened with revolutionary Marxist thought, which gave rise to a torrent of interpretations and combinations: spontaneism, self-management, Maoism, Freudo-Marxism, marginal utopia, structuralist Marxism, theoretical antihumanism, and so on. Fashion is a do-it-yourself enterprise in which individuals concoct for themselves a more or less made-to-order intellectual universe consisting of assorted borrowings and reactions to one thing and another. Our societies are committed to the flowering of small and large differences of opinion; individual consciousnesses, far from being homogenized by fashion, are being carried away in a process of broadened differentiation, of à la carte intellectual tinkering.

Progress is a term that is somewhat out of fashion today. However, we must not hesitate to reactivate the notion, even if by doing so we engage in head-on confrontation with thinking shaped by the posterity of Marx and Nietzsche. Yes, there is progress in freedom of thought, even despite the mimicry and conformity of fashion. Yes, the forward movement of enlightenment is continuing; people "as a whole," as Kant would say, continue to emerge from their status as "minors." In advanced democracies, ideological fanaticism is becoming extinct; traditions are coming undone; a passion for information is moving to the foreground. Individuals are increasingly capable of examining issues freely; they are less influenced by collective discourse, better able to use their own intellectual resources, to "think for themselves"—which obviously does not mean they are impervious to all influence. To be sure, fashion restores a form of external determination in the intellectual realm; it signifies one particular version of the influence of the other. But the authority is nondirective; it is accompanied by a greater desire for argumentation and a greater capacity for individual questioning. Consummate fashion is not an obstacle to the autonomy of human consciousness; it is the condition for a mass movement toward enlightenment. The notion of thinking without the help of others, apart from a nourishing intellectual and ideological climate, is in any case meaningless. "Somewhere and somehow authority is always bound to play a part in intellectual and moral life. The part may vary, but some part there must be. The independence of the individual may be greater or less but can never be limitless."[6] If, in a world of creative geniuses, the mimetic reign of fashion may damage personal autonomy, it nevertheless allows personal autonomy to come into play at the level of the majority of human beings.

Something always leads us to resist the idea that fashion might be considered an instrument of freedom. Beyond the apparent uniformity it achieves, does fashion not lead to discouraging thoughtful individual efforts in the search for truth and justice, operating as it does through seduction and relying on mimetic facility? Is not being master of one's own thoughts necessarily the result of individual effort, an act of courage and explicit construction? In one sense it is impossible to get around this point of view; however, it applies better to the work of intellectual discovery than to the constitution of people's more general thoughts. If we restrict ourselves to a voluntarist definition of intellectual autonomy, only a few professionals in the realm of concepts can claim to have access to freedom of mind; the masses are condemned, and properly so, to idolatry and spectacle, to the consumption of idea-images, on the assumption that they are incapable of reaching maturity, or of using their minds freely and creatively. It seems to me that such an elitist dichotomy fails to take into account the much more complex process that is under way in modern societies. The conquest of individual freedom may be carried out at a more empirical level, through the multiplicity of influences and their confrontations, through the play of diverse comparisons. The progress of self-determination in history is not accomplished via the royal road of individual speculative effort, but via a set of cultural and social phenomena that are in apparent contradiction with the Enlightenment. "Have the courage to use your own intelligence. That is the motto of the Enlightenment." The era of consummate fashion is one that allows very large numbers of people to think for themselves; this is because the timeless order of tradition has exploded and terrorist systems of meaning have lost their hold on human minds. People are subject to a great variety of influences, but no single one of them is strictly determining any longer; no single one does away with the capacity to reconsider. The critical spirit is expanding in and through the mimicry of fashion, in and through the fluctuations of "opinion": such is the greatest paradox of the dynamics of enlightenment. Autonomy is inseparable from the mechanisms of heteronomy.

Still, we ought to be wary of self-satisfaction: the impulsive reactions of the public, the phenomenon of sects, the various esoteric and parapsychological beliefs that often monopolize the news are here to remind us that enlightenment does not go forward without its contrary. The individualization of consciousness also leads to apathy and an intellectual vacuum, to "instant" thinking and mental hotchpotch, to the most irrational commitments and new forms of superstition, to "anything and everything." But no matter how real and spectacular they may be, these phenomena must not be allowed to obscure the underlying force that is modifying the relation of individuals to truth and meaning. People may devote little time to the work of thinking, but they speak more often in their own names. They may produce few deliberate meditations, but human beings have moved closer to adulthood and maturity. The irrationality of fashion contributes to the fashioning of individual reason; fashion has its reasons that reason does not know.

CHAPTER VIII

The Progressive Shifting
of the Social

THE REIGN of generalized fashion brings into sharp focus the enigma of togetherness that characterizes the democratic age. What we must try to understand is how a society based on the fashion form can get people to coexist. How can such a society institute a social bond when it is constantly broadening the sphere of subjective autonomy, increasing individual difference, emptying social regulatory principles of their transcendent substance, dissolving the unity of life-styles and opinions? By thoroughly restructuring both the production and the circulation of objects and culture under the influence of seduction, ephemera, and marginal differentiation, consummate fashion has overturned the economy of interpersonal relations. It has generalized a new type of encounter and relation among social units. Consummate fashion marks the mature stage of the democratic social state.

As a corollary to this unprecedented form of social cohesion, fashion has developed a new relation to duration, a new orientation of social time. The time frame that has always governed fashion—the present—is being increasingly generalized. Fashion society has definitively liquidated the power of the past as embodied in the universe of tradition. It has also inflected the investment in the future that characterized the eschatological age of ideologies. We are living in a time of short-term programs, perpetually changing standards, and exhortations to live for the moment. The present has taken over as the principal axis of social duration.

The Apotheosis of the Social Present

Now that fashion has ceased to refer exclusively to the domain of ephemera and has come to designate an overall logic and social temporality, it is useful and even necessary to take another look at the work that went furthest to clarify the problem, that of Gabriel de Tarde. Tarde was the first to succeed in carrying the theory of fashion beyond frivolous appearances, the first to give the subject of fashion conceptual dignity by acknowledging its specific social logic and social temporality. He was the first to see fashion as a general form of sociality, and the first to define entire epochs and civilizations through the principle of fashion itself.

For Tarde, fashion is essentially a form of human relationship, a social relationship characterized by the imitation of one's contemporaries and the love of foreign novelties. Society exists only by virtue of a common stock of ideas and desires. The resemblance among human beings is what institutes the social bond, to such an extent that Tarde can assert that "society is imitation."[1] Fashion and custom are the two great forms of imitation; they allow the assimilation of individuals to society. When the influence of one's forebears yields to the suggestions of innovators, ages of custom give way to ages of fashion. Whereas in ages of custom one obeys rules handed down from generation to generation, in ages of fashion one imitates novelties from elsewhere, as well as people from one's immediate surroundings.[2] Fashion is a social logic independent of its content. All behavior and institutions are susceptible to being carried away by the fashion spirit, by fascination with what is new. Two rigorously correlative principles characterize fashion in Tarde's eyes: on the one hand, interpersonal relations, governed by the imitation of contemporary models; on the other hand, a legitimate new temporality, the *social present*, which is accurately illustrated by the motto of fashion eras, "everything new is beautiful." In eras when fashion dominates, the traditional past is no longer the object of devotion. The current moment galvanizes people's awareness. Novelties have prestige: change and the present are venerated. By contrasting the periods in which fashion reigns to periods ruled by custom, Tarde powerfully emphasizes that fashion is much more than a frivolous institution. Fashion entails a specific temporality and a specific sociality.

Despite this major theoretical advance, Tarde did not succeed in grasping the link that makes fashion consubstantial with modern societies. In his search for universal laws of imitation and their irreversible progress, Tarde did not recognize fashion as an exclusive invention of the modern West; he saw it rather as an inevitable and cyclical form of social imitation. In this view, fashion is an invariant principle in humanity's vast historical trajectory; it appears as a transitory and revolutionary phase between two ages of custom. Social life is universally and necessarily punctuated by traditionalist phases in which the imitation of ancient and autochthonous models arises, and by fashion phases marked by waves of imitation of foreign novelties, waves that disrupt the customary equilibrium. "Imitation, which was at first custom-imitation and then fashion-imitation, turns back again to custom. . . . This general formula . . . sums up the whole development of every civilization."[3] Furthermore, this formula applies more to the various stages of social life taken one by one—

language, religion, morality, needs, government—than to the collective whole, for only in rare historical moments does fashion imitation conquer all spheres of social activity simultaneously (as it did in Greece in the fifth century B.C., in Florence in the fifteenth century, in Paris in the sixteenth century, and in Europe as a whole in the eighteenth and nineteenth centuries).[4] Trapped in a transhistoric concept of fashion, Tarde proceeded to extend the concept too broadly. He glossed over the historical discontinuity that it brings about; he applied it to types of civilizations in which social mechanisms tend to forestall its emergence. However, this did not prevent him from observing with lucidity the exceptional scope of fashion contagions in modern democratic societies. "The eighteenth century inaugurated the reign of fashion on a large scale. . . . we are unquestionably passing through a period of fashion-imitation, one which is preeminently remarkable for its breadth and permanency."[5]

No matter how powerful the waves of fashion may be, in Tarde's view, the prestige of forebears still continues to take precedence over that of novelty: it is a matter of social persistence. Even in the modern societies that are most susceptible to passing fads, the role of the traditional element is always preponderant; the prestige of ancestors is superior to that of innovators. "Imitation, then, that is engaged in the currents of fashion is but a very feeble stream compared with the great torrent of custom. And this must necessarily be so."[6] No social cohesion is possible without a community of beliefs, without similarities of hearts and minds. To keep the chain of generations unbroken, to keep children from being strangers to their parents, the respect for the old beliefs has to be maintained. Imitation of the same models from the past allows the generations to continue to resemble one another and to form a single society. The preeminence of tradition is a societal constant, a categorical imperative of the social bond, and this is the case no matter what fashion upheavals and crises may come into play.

At the time Tarde was writing, at the end of the nineteenth century, this analysis was probably justified. Fashion had not yet reached its fullest extension; it allowed large areas of collective life to subsist under the yoke of tradition and the authority of the past. However, the analysis cannot be reintroduced unchanged at a time when so much—economy, culture, meaning, everyday life—is governed by the ephemeral and by seduction. With consummate fashion, a critical mutation in the axis of social temporality has come about, a reversal in the distribution of strengths between fashion and custom. For the first time, the fashion spirit is winning out over tradition virtually everywhere; novelty is coming out ahead of inheritance. As fashion comes to encompass broader and broader spheres of collective life, the reign of tradition is eclipsed. It no longer represents anything but "a very feeble torrent" compared to the "great river" of fash-

ion. This is something new in history: our societies now function outside
the power of the past to regulate and integrate; the axis of the present has
become the socially prevalent temporality. Everywhere we look, the phenomena of fads and the logic of inconstancy are developing; everywhere,
the new is manifestly appreciated and valued. The standards that socialize
us and guide our behavior are fluctuating standards, continually realized
in new forms. The empire of fashion designates this immense inversion of
social temporality that consecrates the preeminence of the present with
respect to the past; it marks the advent of a social space buttressed by the
present—which is precisely the time frame of fashion. If fashion rules us,
it is because the past is no longer the norm that governs every detail of our
actions, tastes, and beliefs. The ancient decrees are largely discredited as
guides to behavior; the examples we follow come increasingly from around
us in a precarious environment. In every realm—education, knowledge,
hygiene, consumption, sports, human relations, leisure—we find our models here and now; they are not behind us. The ancestral legacy no longer
structures behavior and opinions, by and large. The imitation of forebears
has yielded to the imitation of moderns; the spirit of custom has given way
to the spirit of novelty. Fashion is in charge, because the love of novelty
has become general, regular, limitless; "curiosity has become a fatal, irresistible passion," as Baudelaire remarked. In most areas, individuals are
engaged in a passionate quest for novelty; veneration of the immutable
past has been replaced by the follies and fads of fashion. More than ever
before, we are governed by the motto "everything new is beautiful."

Fashion is our law because our entire culture holds the new sacred and
consecrates the dignity of the present—not only in technology, art, and
knowledge but in our very way of life, which has been reordered according
to hedonistic values. Characterized by the legitimizing of well-being and
material enjoyment, by free and guilt-free sexuality, by invitations to live
life more fully, to satisfy one's desires, to "get the most out of life," hedonistic culture orients human beings toward the existential present. It exacerbates fads and the search for individual salvation in the new, presenting
novelties as stimulations and sensations apt to produce a rich and accomplished life. The reign of the past has not been abolished, but it has been
neutralized, now that it is subject to the unchallenged requirement of individual, personal satisfaction.

This preponderance of the social present is only the culminating point
of the age-old secular transformation of the relation to time that has
caused modern societies to mutate as they shift toward the futurist age.
Centuries ago our societies began to put in motion an immense "shifting of
time" that detaches us from fidelity to the past and orients us more and
more toward the future. Accompanying the development of capitalism,
science, and the modern nation, an unprecedented temporal logic has been

established: the legitimacy of the foundational past characteristic of traditionalist societies has yielded to the legitimacy of the organization of the future.[7] There is no doubt, indeed, that administration of and responsibility for the future by various political and economic agencies is the basis for modern societies. There is no doubt, either, that the administrative democratic state, relieved of all transcendent references, is most profoundly legitimized by its ability to prepare an open future and to orchestrate collective change. Yet this orientation and this futurist legitimization shed no light on the nature of the social temporality that characterizes democratic societies in the age of consummate fashion. If public and economic powers are oriented toward management of the future, and if reference to the future has become constitutive of the operations of the state and of capitalism, interpersonal space for its part turns out to be increasingly dependent on the dictates of the present. On the one hand, there is the futurist organization of change; on the other, the love of novelties, fads, and trends, ever-wider fluctuations in the imitation of contemporaries, the precariousness of collective standards. The modern era can certainly be defined in terms of investment in and legitimization of the future, provided we add that, in a parallel development, a certain type of social regulation guarantees the preeminence and the legitimacy of the present. This is all the more perceptible since, in recent years, society's orientation toward the future has lost the detailed and definitive character that the great messianic ideologies used to confer on it.[8] Our vision of the future is no longer clear and distinct. The future appears blurry and open; by the same token, the idea of a pure, hard-line, political program preparing it is losing credibility. What we require now is flexibility, the ability to navigate by sight, to correct our positions rapidly in a world without predetermined dynamics. We find the same primacy of the present in the economic sphere, where the great dream of industrial policies is over. The rapidity of technological change implies mobility in decision making from now on, along with increasingly rapid adaptation to the sovereign marketplace, an aptitude for flexibility and experimentation under risky conditions. The management of the future has entered the orbit of the short term, a permanent state of urgency. The supremacy of the present is not in contradiction to the orientation toward the future; it only achieves that orientation, accentuates the tendency of our societies to shed the heavy burden of inheritance and to constitute themselves as virtually "experimental" systems. The reign of the present reflects the collapse of the demiurgic ideologies, the accelerated invention of tomorrow, the capacity of our societies to criticize themselves, to navigate without a preestablished model, to hasten the work of democratic autoproduction.

The supremacy of fashion signifies less the annihilation of tradition than the loss of its constraining collective power. A good number of customs have persisted: marriage, holidays, gift giving, cooking, religion, manners; however, they no longer succeed in imposing compulsory rules of social conduct. Standards inherited from the past persist without group coercion, but they are now subject to the influence of autonomous subjectivities. People continue to celebrate Christmas, but on ski slopes or southern beaches, or in front of a television set. Young women still wear white at their weddings, but by their own free choice: it is a matter of aesthetic pleasure, a form of play. Religious beliefs and practices are tenacious, but they tend to function à la carte. Italian specialties and French cuisine can be eaten kosher; Judaism itself has entered the supermarket era and leaves room for tinkering with its rites, prayers, and religious symbols—among Reform congregations in the United States, women lead prayers, wear emblems once reserved for men, and can become rabbis. Even if certain traditional forms are perpetuated, adaptation and innovation disrupt age-old continuities everywhere. Traditions are recycled in the register of openness, institutional and individual creativity. The spirit of collective tradition is dead. The present governs our relation to the past. We keep only that part of the past that is convenient for us, only what is not in flagrant contradiction to modern values, personal taste, and conscience. No collective rule has value in itself any longer if it is not expressly recognized by the will of an individual. Under these conditions, customs are dissolving in a process of personalization. They have the charm of days gone by, a past restored less through respect for ancestors than through a spirit of play and a desire for individualist affiliation with a given group. Paradoxically, traditions have become instruments for individualist assertion: collective norms are no longer imposed on me, it is I who deliberately adhere to them, through my personal will to identify with one set or another, through my individualist taste for displaying a difference, through my desire for privileged communication with a more or less limited social group.

In cultural and artistic matters, our relation to the past is unquestionably more complex. Indeed, the "classic" works are not discredited anywhere, quite the contrary: they are admired and appreciated to the highest degree. Opera and classical music have a broad public of faithful admirers. Major art exhibits (of the works of Raphael, Turner, or Manet, for instance) that have been organized in Paris in recent years have consistently attracted hundreds of thousands of visitors. To say that our society functions in the present does not mean that the past is devalued; it means that the past is no longer a model to reproduce and respect. The past is admired, but it no longer rules. The great works of the past have enormous prestige, but we produce "hits" designed not to last, works with built-in obsolescence.

This phenomenon does not involve mass culture alone. With artistic modernism and the avant-gardes, works have explicitly ceased to manifest any connection with the past; all ties with tradition have been severed as art has been opened up to the enterprise of radical rupture and permanent renewal. Avant-garde art has reacted against public taste and aesthetic standards in the name of a limitless creativity and the ultimate value of innovation. At war with academism, "good taste," and repetition, the avant-gardes have produced hermetic, dissonant, dislocated, scandalous works that are at the opposite pole from the logic of fashion and its submission to the spirit of the times. If the modernist process was initially modeled on revolutionary escalation, the fashion form has nevertheless succeeded, in a second phase, in absorbing the revolutionary form itself into its register: a structurally hybrid artistic field has been orchestrated, consisting simultaneously of revolt against custom and systematically capricious reversals. On the one side we find the spirit of subversion, on the other the inconstancy of back-and-forth movement, the ostentatious aim of producing what has never been seen before. The development of the avant-gardes has coincided more and more with the preponderance of the fashion form. Art has seen the search for originality and novelty run rampant no matter what the cost; deconstructionist chic, the sophisticated vogue for minimal art and conceptual art, the proliferation of "non-art" gimmicks (happenings, actions and performances, body art, landscape art, and so on) are based more on excess, paradox, gratuitousness, play, or outrageousness than on revolutionary radicalism. The artistic scene has shifted into an age of accelerated obsolescence: artists and avant-garde groups proliferate, only to be immediately used up, forgotten, replaced by other trends that are still more "in." The artistic sphere has become the theater of a frivolous revolution that no longer disturbs anyone: there is a great deal of theoretical posturing, but there are few actual ruptures. Instead of the profound upheavals that took place in the early part of this century, we find a multiplicity of micronovelties and marginal variations; instead of the conquests of the great historical avant-gardes, we find repetitious modernist academism and the immobility of pseudo-differences. Even while continuing to resort to the alibi of subversion, the tranquil comfort of fashion has won out over revolutionary discontinuity. Art is structured more and more by the ephemeral imperatives of the present, by the need to create an event, by the inconstancy of the vogues orchestrated by merchants and relayed by the media. The gap between creation in fashion and creation in art grows smaller and smaller. While artists no longer succeed in creating scandals, fashion shows seek to be more and more creative; there are now as many innovations and surprises in fashion as in the fine arts. The democratic age has succeeded in dissolving the hierarchical division of the arts by subjecting them equally to the order of fashion. Exaggerated originality, show, and marketing are winning out everywhere.

The postmodern moment (or "trans-avant-garde," "free figuration," return to tradition, and so on) has not modified the ongoing process at all.

By valorizing the reprise of the past and the artistic tradition, contemporary art perfects its transformation into fashion. As soon as breaking with the past is no longer an absolute imperative, one can mix styles in works that are baroque, ironic, more accessible (as in the case of postmodern architectures). Modernist austerity is declining in favor of the frontierless mixing of old and new. Art becomes concerned with effect; it seeks the complicitous nod, the "second-degree" ludic combinations and recombinations. Everything can come back; all the forms of the imaginary museum can be exploited, can contribute to the increasingly rapid declassification of what is in the forefront. Art has joined the fashion cycle of ephemeral oscillation between neo and retro, variations in which nothing is at stake and nothing is condemned; art no longer excludes, it recycles. Revival has become a recipe: there are the neofauves, the neoexpressionists, and before long no doubt there will be the neoneoabstractionists. Having abandoned the code of modernist rupture, art has no more reference points at all, no more evaluative criteria. Everything is possible, including starting over "in the manner of so-and-so," if one toys with an out-of-phase imitation of the past. Art is now better able to adopt the frivolous rhythms of the eternal return of forms, the speeded-up and tension-free dance of stylistic renewal. Whatever the postmodernists may claim, the artistic new is not a devalued value, and it is certainly no longer the same "new" that the "classic" avant-gardes were targeting; it is much closer to the "new" that governs fashion.

Conflict and Social Bonds

As individuals attempt to resemble their contemporaries instead of their ancestors, they increasingly imitate models from outside family groups and the environment of origin. Multiple influences are coming into play, replacing the closed determinism of bodies, classes, and countries. Consummate fashion corresponds to "the free and unimpeded domain of imitation,"[9] the social state in which mimetic contagions accelerate and operate beyond the closed realms of class and nation. Classes, nations, and age groups may still determine specific behaviors; however, influences of this type are less and less exclusive and one-sided. With the decompartmentalization and opening of mimetic trends, the democratic revolution is pursuing its work: it eradicates watertight separations between classes and countries; it erodes the principle of aristocratic influence and the monopoly certain high-status groups have exercised in terms of influence. The closed, global imitation characteristic of traditional eras is replaced by individual and partial imitation. We imitate this but not that; we copy one thing from one person and something else from another. Our borrowings no longer have a fixed origin; they are taken from myriad sources. Far from adding up to a uniformity of behavior, practice, and taste, the empire of fashion is tantamount to the personalization of individuals. In eras of custom, few people are imitated, but they are imitated in everything. In our societies it is just the opposite. Here I can do no less than cite Tarde's text in full, in its unsurpassable accuracy: "What is contrary to personal preeminence is the imitation of a single man whom people copy in everything. But when, instead of patterning one's self after one person or after a few, we borrow from a hundred, a thousand, or ten thousand persons, each of whom is considered under a particular aspect, the elements of thought or action which we subsequently combine, the very nature and choice of these elementary copies, as well as their combination, expresses and accentuates our original personality."[10]

How could one really endorse the idea, then, "that a fully democratic social state is a state in which there are, as it were, no more individual influences?"[11] To be sure, the Tocquevillean analysis is on target when it notes the progressive retreat of the powerful and lasting influence of families and groups. But that retreat does not mean that individual influences decline or disappear. Democratic society lets loose waves of imitation, and multiplies them; individual influences are less profound, but they are lasting and diverse. It is true that the great intellectual leaders are waning, that the authority of the masters is being eclipsed, that the higher classes are no longer preeminent models, that the stars themselves are no longer the magnetic poles they once were. But at the same time microscopic influences are proliferating; examples in kit form are taken from hither and yon. The welfare state governed by fashion is characterized on the one hand by the eclipse of the great controlling authorities, and on the other by the dissemination of small influences that are sometimes determining and sometimes superficial. It is an era of precarious influences à la carte.

The end of tradition, the instability of standards of socialization, the hyperindividualization of human beings: consummate fashion, as the ultimate stage of the modern welfare state, simply raises with greater insistence the question of what holds contemporary societies together. How can a society made up of free and independent units, with no substantial bond of sociability, be recognized as a society? How can a society liberated from the traditional bonds of community constituted by autonomous, floating, increasingly self-directed individuals escape the process of disintegration? The question has all the more resonance given that the democratic universe, far from relying on similarity of opinions and unity of beliefs, continually opens up numerous foyers of dissension, new conflicts of ideas and values. The unity of reference points has vanished; our societies are inseparable from permanent antagonisms of meaning. To be sure, the democratic societies are not at the zero-degree point on the values scale; freedom and equality in particular constitute the basis for a common ideal. But as abstract principles that are open to fundamental contrary interpretations, the major referents of the democratic age only stimulate a limitless process of criticism, discord, and renewed questioning of the established order. Even if the epoch of great political divisions and excommunications contemporary with the religious era of ideologies has in fact yielded to a universal consensus about democratic institutions and the imperatives of a strictly managed economy, we are by no means in a unified phase. Basic cleavages, major differences, irreconcilable viewpoints are at the heart of our debates; the image of a society "where differences of view are only matters of nuance"[12] cannot be applied to us. We have buried the hatchet of war over the dictatorship of the proletariat and the revolution, but new antagonisms have arisen: the death penalty, immigration, prisons, abortion, drugs, euthanasia, nuclear power, artificial insemination, social protection, surrogate motherhood, all these are questions on which there is no hope of reaching any measure of unanimity. Our societies are condemned to the tug-of-war of conflicting viewpoints.

The era of consummate fashion means many things, but it does not mean uniformity of convictions and behavior. It has indeed homogenized tastes and life-styles in the process of pulverizing the last vestiges of local customs, and it has indeed diffused universal standards of well-being, leisure, human and sexual relations; however, at the same time it has inaugurated an unparalleled process involving the fragmentation of life-styles. Even if hedonism and psychologism are dominant values, life-styles continue to proliferate in countless groupings that sociologists of everyday life attempt to catalogue. Attitudes toward consumption, the family, vacations, the media, work, and leisure activities are less and less uniform; the universe of life-styles has been conquered by disparity. If in our societies we go on widening the differential gaps that separate us in our beliefs and life-styles, what can ensure the stability of the collective body?

In an insightful analysis, Marcel Gauchet has shown how democratic society, inherently fragmented at the level of opinion, has succeeded in keeping citizens together in and through their oppositions and divergences. There is no need to follow Tocqueville's example and posit a unity of beliefs based on societal permanence. It is conflict itself, conflict involving social meanings and interests, that works to produce a dimension of community belonging. Divisions and social antagonisms create a symbolic social bond; they solder people together, in that the opposing parties continue to define themselves in terms of a shared world, they assert themselves as members of one and the same society, and they have a common stake in the way that society is to be transformed. Conflict is a means for getting individuals to participate, a way of implicating them in the definition of a common universe; it is thus a factor of socialization, social inclusion, and social cohesion.[13] Still, does social conflict maintain its pronounced integrative role when political parties lose their credibility on a large scale, when deunionization accelerates, when collective struggles become more sporadic and the cult of private life prevails? Social division played an undeniable assimilative role during the great historical struggles that established the features of the modern democracies. But today? Conflicts over public issues no longer have the character of holy wars; they no longer bring visions of irreconcilable worlds into confrontation; most often they mobilize collective passions only intermittently. The integrative force of social conflict is on the wane; it is far from sufficient to account for the cohesiveness of contemporary societies.

At present, social unity is maintained less through frontal opposition between citizens than through the neutralization of conflicts; it is perpetuated less by way of antagonisms than by way of individualist pacification of the collective debate. We are held together as societies by our democratic mores; these are the cement of our durability. While ideological and political rifts remain numerous, not only do they not succeed in shattering the social body, but they give rise only rarely to bloody confrontations. We do not see eye to eye, but we do not get out our guns; we do not try to make the other disappear. The cohesiveness of any collective body is inseparable from the extraordinary taming of conflict, the pacifying of individual and collective behavior that stems from the development of individualist values—respect for life, respect for and indifference to the other—and from the privatization of existences produced by the reign of fashion.[14] Even mass unemployment and terrorist attacks have not succeeded in disrupting individual and collective behavior patterns, which are for the most part tolerant and peaceful. Western Europeans can coexist in a heterogeneity of viewpoints because contemporary mores are governed by a peaceful relativism, because everything that relates to physical violence is rejected at a visceral level. The political leadership may go on talking in terms of irreducible opposition on occasion, but civil society remains astonishingly calm, resistant to the warfare of political and ideological harassment. If fashion's reign hastens the splintering of the social element, it simultaneously reconstitutes an invaluable bond of sociability by fostering the rooting out of antagonisms, by advancing the age-old process by which the mores constitutive of modern times become gentler, by reinforcing the taste for civil peace and the respect for democratic rules. Social divisions are no longer explosive; they function like fashion, in a nondramatic mode of marginal differences. Even radically antithetical viewpoints no longer give rise to inhibiting exclusions; underlying ideological differences do not succeed in breaking the social bond. Social conflict is structured like fashion: the major oppositions coexist with great civility. It is as if only superficial divergences were at stake: the ultimate reign of fashion inscribes as marginal difference what is in reality a disjunction of

principles. We have to restore mores to their rightful place in the maintenance of democratic societies. The collective whole stays together only
through a process of socialization that develops calm, individualist, democratic passions—only through a massively tolerant life-style. Tocqueville's
lesson must be heeded: "If in the course of this book I have not succeeded
in making the reader feel the importance I attach to the practical experience of the Americans, to their habits, opinions, and, in a word, their
mores, in maintaining their laws, I have failed in the main object of my
work."[15]

If the apotheosis of fashion works to reinforce civil peace, it certainly
does not preclude the eruption of social conflicts. These are often limited
in scope (as in the case of strikes by specific categories of workers), but
they may also be quite broad-based, as in recent years in France with
movements against proposed changes in legislation affecting private
schools and public higher education. Contemporary individualism does
not rule out participation in collective struggles, but it changes the tenor of
those struggles. It is simplistic to reduce contemporary individualism to
egocentrism, narcissistic froth, the mere quest for personal enjoyment.
Narcissism is the dominant penchant of democracies; it is not their exclusive orientation. From time to time, social struggles do arise, but far from
being antithetical to the individualist dynamic, they reproduce its values
and its features. Even when individuals move out of their strictly private
universe and get involved in collective actions, individualist logic remains
preponderant. Generally speaking, private interests win out over general
considerations; individual autonomy prevails over doctrinal orthodoxy;
the desire for immediate improvement of living conditions prevails over
unconditional devotion; free participation prevails over conscription;
"I've-had-it-up-to-here" prevails over militancy. Hyperindividualist society does not mean the disappearance of social conflict and the simple
smothering of the res publica; it signifies the development of collective
actions in which individuals are no longer subordinated to a higher order
that dictates the tenor of their ideas and actions. Consummate individualism reverses the relation of individual submission to doctrines and mass
parties in favor of free social actions, largely unpredictable and spontaneous, triggered more by the initiative of the grass roots or of civil society
than by that of parties and unions. The requirement of personal autonomy
is rediscovered in collective actions, which now originate independently of
the great labor unions and political organizations. Collective movements
have not been reduced to nothing, but have become more and more depo-
liticized, deideologized, and deunionized; they are supported by individualist demands for improvement in buying power and working conditions,
but also by demands for individual freedoms in action and in civil society.
In Western Europe, the reign of the ego is not being established in a social

desert; it has colonized the sphere of collective action itself, a sphere less and less hemmed in by the classic apparatuses that had directed social struggles, more and more buttressed by the direct preoccupations of individuals: the defense of private interests, the demand for the freedom to live as one pleases *right now*, far removed from the great historical and utopian hopes of the ideological age. On the one hand, contemporary society entails ever-increasing personal desires for freedom and personal accomplishment; on the other hand, it entails social explosions provoked by individualist motivations and demands: buying power, job security, fringe benefits, individual freedoms. Social actions reproduce the individualist motivations of private life. The tendency to reversal that defines the new democratic age is at work everywhere: we see it in the preeminence of corporatist interests over great global projects, and in the primacy of personal autonomy over the discipline of the great militant organizations and over the ideological direction of consciences. The forms of collective mobilization do not run counter to individualism; they are its corollaries and its reflection, its other face: perhaps less obvious, less immediately readable, but just as revealing of the irrepressible rise of the reign of the individual.

In May 1968, in France, individualist passions were celebrated on city walls. "It is forbidden to forbid." Individualism sought to change the world, to change life. Today, it has settled down and become "responsible," limited to demands like "keep your hands off my university" and "never again." It has gotten rid of the utopian matrix and it rejects all political perspectives, all party affiliations, all overarching worldviews. Mobilizations have concrete, targeted, achievable objectives in the short run, and, whatever may be claimed in this regard, they are driven less by an abstract ideal of equality than by a demand for individual autonomy and by personal anxiety in face of the future. The scope of the wave of protests by French high school and university students in the early 1980s can be fully understood only if it is related to young people's anxiety about their future. Where will they be able to go to college? Will they be able to afford it? Will they make it through? What other choices do they have? The movement has been considerably idealized and inflated by those who speak of "children with a heart," of a "generation of solidarity": whatever degree of generosity the movement may entail, the complexity of motivations ought to make us more reserved in our judgments. In fact, the student movements of the 1980s brought no evidence of a struggle against competitive individualist society and its flagrant inequalities; quite to the contrary, it brought evidence of the individualist desire to be integrated into society as it is, with its hierarchies and its injustices—the desire not to wait outside the door, not to foreclose the possibility of earning recognized diplomas, of being better placed in the competitive job market, of making more of one's life. The "generation of solidarity" can come to terms quite readily with the prevailing indifference toward the have-nots, with the society of business and careers, with the quest for personal enjoyment.

It is true that solidarity movements of an explicitly moral cast appeared around the same time; in France, SOS Racisme, Band Aid, Restaurants du Coeur, Sport Aid, and antiapartheid movements are examples. All these manifestations appear to have nothing in common with the reign of fashion and the individualist quest for well-being. However, here again the opposition is not so radical as it seems at first. The generalization of the fashion process is what has made such movements possible: by making the great historico-social utopias obsolete and replacing them with individual values, the frivolous age at the same time led to a strengthened concern for human rights and increased sensitivity to the familiar, concrete human drama of famine. The more individuals are socialized in the direction of personal autonomy, the more compelling the imperative of human rights becomes. The more society progresses toward hedonistic individualism, the more human individuality appears as an ultimate value. The more the historical megadiscourses crumble, the more life and respect for persons are established as absolutes. The more violence regresses in social mores, the more sacred the individual becomes. People do not join movements on behalf of systems; they are moved by the ignominy of racism, by the hellish situation of human beings condemned to hunger and physical degradation. The paradox deserves to be highlighted: the new charity is swept along by the euphoric and individualistic waters of fashion. Contemporary individualism is inconceivable apart from democratic reference points; it is thinkable only in the framework of a society in which there is profound commitment to the values of freedom and equality, and in which the primordial value is precisely the individual. To the extent that the reign of fashion shatters the superstructures of historical meaning, the leading ideals of democracy appear in the front rank and become an essential driving force for any mass action.

Not only is contemporary solidarity a child of the mature reign of fashion, but it also reproduces some of fashion's basic characteristics, most notably hedonism. No activist movement today is unacquainted with spectacle, show business, a focus on the participants' pleasure. We have become allergic to platitudes as well as to sermonizing; we require parties, rock concerts, good-humored parades bristling with slogans whose tone reflects that of humorous advertising. The actors on today's social stage espouse the universe of images, spectacles, the media, the star system, fashion, and advertising. Two million badges saying "Touche pas à mon pote!" (Hands off my buddy!) were sold in France within the space of a few months; then that frenzy began to fade. "Moral" commitment is at the same time emotional, "tuned-in," funny, festive, sports-related, musical. It is impossible not to see the globally weightless and ephemeral character of these forms of participation: apart from a declining number of militants, how many people do anything beyond buying a button or a bumper sticker, attending a concert or running a race, buying a record? Commitment of body and soul has been replaced by participation in passing, à la carte. People spend as much time and money as they like, they mobilize when and as they wish, in keeping with the primary desire for individual autonomy. Our era is one of minimal commitment, echoing the minimal ideology of human rights and the sensitization to the ravages of poverty. The fashion spirit has managed to penetrate the heart of the democratic individual; it has infiltrated the sphere of solidarity and ethics. The fashion age does not lead to consummate egoism, but to sporadic, flexible, nondoctrinaire commitment that requires no sacrifice. Fashion's reign is not a cause for despair; it broadens the path of human rights and opens people's eyes to human misfortune. We have less doctrinaire rigidity but more humanitarian concern; we manifest less ethical self-denial but more respect for life; we are less faithful but, as a group, more spontaneous—all of which produces neither the best of worlds nor the worst.

We should not take heart too quickly, however. The age of accomplished fashion is inseparable from the increasing breakdown of the community and from the deficit in intersubjective communication. More or less everywhere, people are complaining that they are not understood, that they are not listened to, that they cannot express themselves. Anemic social relations, difficulty understanding one another, a feeling that people talk only about themselves and do not listen to one another, all these are characteristic features of the final age of fashion, of the formidable thrust of individualist existences and aspirations. The dissolving of social identities, the diversification of tastes, the sovereign requirement of being oneself are all factors contributing to a relational impasse, an unparalleled crisis in communication. "Formal," stereotyped, conventional exchange is less and less satisfying; we want free, sincere, personal communication, and at the same time we want renewal in our relationships. We suffer not only from the rhythm and the organization of modern life, we also suffer from our insatiable appetite for personal accomplishment and for communication; we suffer from the endless demands we each make on others. The more we insist on our right to a genuine, authentic, rich exchange, the more we are condemned to the feeling that our communication is superficial. The more people reveal of their intimate selves, the more they open themselves up to others, the more they feel that intersubjective communication is a fleeting phenomenon. The more we assert our desires for independence and personal self-realization, the more intersubjectivity is condemned to turbulence and noncommunication.

As it invades the sphere of being-for-others, fashion reveals the hidden dimension of its empire: the drama of intimacy is at the very heart of the delight in novelty. Fashion is neither angel nor devil; there is also a *tragic lightness* established as a social system, a tragic dimension that cannot be eliminated at the level of subjective units. The consummate reign of fashion pacifies social conflict, but it deepens subjective and intersubjective conflict; it allows more individual freedom, but it generates greater malaise in living. The lesson is a harsh one: the progress of enlightenment and the progress of happiness do not go hand in hand. The euphoria of fashion has its counterparts in dereliction, depression, and existential anguish. We encounter more stimulations of all sorts, but also more anxiety; we have more personal autonomy, but also more personal crises. Such is the greatness of fashion, which always refers us, as individuals, back to ourselves; such is the misery of fashion, which renders us increasingly problematic to ourselves and others.

Epilogue

P
UBLICATION of the English translation of *L'Empire de l'éphémère* provides an opportunity not only to review the two fundamental aims of the original work but also to assess its conclusions in light of the social and cultural changes that have taken place since the book came out in 1987.

My primary goal in *L'Empire de l'ephémère* was to offer a new interpretation of fashion in a broad historical perspective, breaking sharply with the hegemonic epistemological model inherited from the nineteenth century and regularly adopted by historians and sociologists ever since: namely, the paradigm of symbolic class struggle and competition, or—as it has come to be called in the wake of Pierre Bourdieu's work—the logic of distinction.

A theoretical updating was needed because the model of social distinction had proved unable to account either for the historical invention of fashion in the fourteenth century or for the major organizational, behavioral, and aesthetic mutations that orchestrated its historical development. I did not seek to deny the impact of competition for social rank on fashion; rather, I sought to demonstrate that such competition has less explanatory value than the modern individualist ethic that has been present exclusively in the West for more than six centuries.

This conceptual revision took place in a specific intellectual context that it may be useful to spell out here. Starting in the mid-1970s, certain French thinkers have tended to recast the issue of individualism as a nodal phenomenon constitutive of modern democratic societies. This point warrants some clarification. The problem of individualism unquestionably has a long intellectual history, traversed by the great names in sociology. But as it happened, until the 1970s, the idea of individualism was generally identified with the principle of economic and democratic freedom; it was not singled out for serious conceptual, historical, or sociological analysis. The concept of individualism made it possible to characterize liberal systems in opposition to totalitarian collectivities; it functioned more as a label than as a problematic concept.

Following lines suggested by Tocqueville, the works of Louis Dumont and Marcel Gauchet have been of critical importance.[1] These works have reopened the issue of individualism by making the rediscovery of the individual the key to understanding modernity and its metamorphoses. In this context, individualism ceases to be mistaken for petit bourgeois ethos; it can be understood as a crucial factor underlying the ideological, political, and anthropological originality of modern societies. For Dumont, individualism designates not only the ideology characteristic of democratic equality but also a specific social state accompanied by social mores and interpersonal relations that have no equivalent in the past. By the same token, what has been most obvious in modernity (the values of equality and individual freedom) becomes what is most fundamental: no longer reduced to a class-bound ideological mystification, the idea of the individual can be accepted as the creative principle of a social and political bond producing ways of life of exceptional historical originality. The effort to conceptualize the individual—and to give conceptual legitimacy and sociopolitical efficacy to the principle of autonomy that is coextensive with the individual—constitutes one of the most innovative and promising trends to appear on the French intellectual scene in opposition to the Marxist, Heideggerian, or Foucaldian tendencies that have dominated interpretations of modernity.

The adoption of Dumont's theoretical model opposing holism to individualism and the traditional-hierarchical era to the modern democratic era paved the way for a new interpretation of fashion that avoids recourse to the schema of distinction. What is fashion, indeed, if not a modern social logic instituting a new legitimate temporality—the social present—that breaks with the traditional order venerating continuity and fidelity to the past? To the extent that fashion presupposes the social dignifying of the new and by the same token the valorization of individuality, it cannot be detached from the individualist universe, even though it developed over a period of four centuries in aristocratic societies, and that it has been accompanied by class-based phenomenon of mimicry and conformity. Fashion as it began to function in the nineteenth century has to be understood as one of the characteristic figures of "democratic revolution." This is still the case today: what we observe in contemporary fashion only emphasizes its democratic and individual aspect.

The second goal I was pursuing in *L'Empire de l'éphémère* focused much more directly on the present: I was seeking to show the new role and new meaning of fashion in contemporary democracies now that fashion has become a general principle restructuring entire facets of society. Hence the notion of "consummate fashion," which is simply an ideal type in Max Weber's sense. While this schema is by no means able to account for the full complexity of our societies, at least it allows us to grasp one of their most original and most paradoxical dimensions. A great number of phenomena indeed lie outside the scope of the fashion form or even run counter to it. But rather than speak in terms of contradictions, I am inclined to point to the paradoxes of our era as so many figures of the reign of generalized fashion.

Paradox 1. We speak of the expansion of fashion at the very moment when dress—the characteristic emblem of fashion—is continuing to lose its prestige and when spending on clothes is declining. Between 1970 and 1992, the percentage of the household budget allocated to dress and clothing in France went from 9.6 percent to 6.2 percent; it is expected to stabilize at around 5 percent in the year 2000.[2] At a time when more and more women have professional ambitions and activities, and when sportswear is becoming more and more prevalent, interest in fashion persists, yet clothes are losing their ability to elicit social admiration. For the most part, dress has ceased to be a vector of social affirmation and recognition, with the notable exception of certain categories of young people who seek to put their personal or collective identity on display. This does not mean that the logic of appearances has been abandoned; it is rather as though the center of gravity of that logic had been displaced. For the steady decline of clothing is paralleled by an increase in commercial activity linked to a growing preoccupation with the body. After the theatricality of clothing, we have the narcissistic cult of the body: it has its fashions, its aesthetic, dietetic, and athletic models. After the primacy of the social image of the individual we have the primacy of the bodily image—the very emblem of postmodern individualism. From this point on, seduction is incarnated less in attention-getting clothing than in the imperative of youthfulness, beauty, thinness, and vigorous good health.

The market sectors that focus on the body tend to become fashion industries themselves, caught up in the process of marginal differentiation and product renewal. For example, proliferating fitness centers sell an increasing variety of "products." In 1991, in France, four million people were enrolled in centers offering a wide array of activities, from body building to eutonics and cardio-funk. Gymnastics is no longer a uniform practice; it has evolved into hybrid forms such as stretching, toning, harmonics, and aerobics; endless new fashions, new "personalized" variations keep appearing on the market. In mountain and water sports, too, a whole palette of new activities has emerged: monoski, snow surfing, rafting, hydrospeed. In the United States, the consumption of goods and services devoted to the body has gone up significantly: home exercise equipment was one of the fastest-growing sectors in the consumer economy in the 1980s, along with microcomputers and low-calorie foods.[3] Participation in sports is growing everywhere. Individuals show increasing concern with maintaining their bodies in the best possible condition. The need to demonstrate one's physical worth, to develop one's muscles, to lose weight, has taken over as an individualist mass ideal. The cult of looks is no longer aimed at a display of rank; it is experienced as a way to stay young, to feel good, to maximize self-confidence. In the era of consummate fashion, the aesthetics of the body has become a matter of psychology and performance.

The beauty market has undergone a similar evolution. In 1980, 50 new perfumes were introduced worldwide; ten years later, the number had gone up to 114. L'Oréal, ranked number one in the world, has no fewer than 32,000 separate products. In 1992, some 300 new cosmetic products were introduced into the French market. Despite the economic slump, in 1992 in France profits in the cosmetic sector as a whole amounted to 50.7 billion francs, up 8.3 percent from 1991. And the world market, where the overall profits amount to 330 billion francs, appears likely to continue to grow by 4 to 5 percent per year. According to a recent study, Europeans are apt to spend around 44 billion francs on beauty products in 1995, and the Japanese now consume twice as many cosmetic products per capita as Europeans do.[4] Breast creams, anti-aging creams, moisturizing lotions, and restructuring creams proliferate, while at the same time liposuction, plastic surgery, and other cosmetic operations are on the rise. By the late 1980s, one American woman out of sixty had had breast implants, and plastic surgeons perform roughly 1.5 million operations a year.[5]

Then there is the new obsession with food, heralded by an unprecedented wave of diets and weight-loss programs. In 1992, 25 percent of all French men and 40 percent of French women wanted to lose weight. Seventy-one percent of the women and 46 percent of the men claimed that they wanted to lose weight primarily for aesthetic reasons. One and a half million French citizens have lost weight thanks to the Weight Watchers program. In the United States, 85 million people are on permanent low-calorie diets; in 1988, weight-loss programs earned $5.5 billion on the American market, and treatments in specialized diet clinics brought in $10 billion.[6] And "light" products now account for 10 percent of the food products sold in the major European countries, while new food products sold in Japan ("functional foods") claim to have multiple health benefits (toning, relaxation, anticancer, and so on) along with cosmetic benefits (they will make skin more "youthful," complexions more beautiful). In less than five years, such products have already conquered 5 percent of the Japanese food market; their annual profits may climb to 40 billion francs in 1995.[7]

Thus the theater of appearances has a new configuration. On the one hand, we are witnessing the end of diktats in the realm of dress. By virtue of the overwhelming diversification of "legitimate" styles, fashions in dress have ceased to be compelling or unanimous; no single line now succeeds in imposing itself on women. Women are more inclined to wear what they like, what becomes them, rather than choose fashion for fashion's sake. As evidence, we need only look at the latest effort to market long skirts. These were introduced in 1992–93 but adopted only eclectically; the style was never accepted as an exclusive canon of elegance. The directive mimesis characteristic of fashion has given way to an optional mimesis, the ultimate stage of frivolous individualism.[8] On the other hand, if the

despotism of dress is a thing of the past, there is a price: social norms
defining what constitutes attractive and healthy bodies are increasingly
powerful. The exhaustion of insistent signs of social respectability is coupled with an anxiety-producing cult of the body characterized by the desire to avoid looking old, to avoid cellulite and wrinkles, a desire manifested in the endless task of vigilance, prevention, and self-improvement.
This task is undertaken by both sexes, but it is much more systematically
internalized and practiced by women. Despite some major shifts, the
postmodern work of appearances remains inegalitarian, a primarily feminine territory.

Paradox 2. The fashion process continues to expand during a period
when many seemingly incompatible phenomena are emerging. Poverty on
a large scale is increasingly juxtaposed with abundance; consumers are
spending less and saving more; novelties are losing their appeal to the
imagination; impulse buying and status consumption are on the wane;
individuals spend less and less time in stores (four hours per month in 1991
as compared to twelve hours per month ten years ago, in the United
States); consumer demand is oriented less toward display than toward
quality, simplicity of use and care, practicality and environmental sound-
ness; members of the upper classes want to buy more cheaply and resist
the inflationary tendencies of luxury items.[9] At the same time, ostensibly
less seductive new commercial strategies are being developed: superdis-
count stores without displays and with a limited choice of items, generic
products, ecological products, a decrease in spending on traditional advertising in favor of nonmedia ("below the line") communication. Nevertheless, it is absurd to speak, as some critics do, of "the end of consumer
society." Whether it moves with or against the tide, the organization of the
world in fashion terms goes on and on. More than ever, companies are
obliged to innovate with increasing rapidity; economic competition requires advertising and the diversification of product lines. What is happening in Japan only illustrates more dramatically than elsewhere the
generalization of the fashion logic: in 1991, more than two hundred new
Walkman models and more than sixty new (or repackaged) beers were
introduced into the Japanese market; every month Seiko proposes sixty
new styles of watches, on the average; more than three hundred new non-
alcoholic drinks are introduced every year.[10] Europe and the United States
are not exempt from this law of market segmentation, marginal diversification, and accelerated obsolescence. In 1970, cars were initially produced in four different versions as opposed to twenty in 1990; in 1980,
twenty-seven hundred new mass-market consumer products were introduced into the American market as opposed to nine thousand at the end of
the decade; five thousand new products show up every year in European
supermarkets. The era of flamboyant advertising is no doubt declining

somewhat, but this is because it is being overtaken by other mechanisms of the fashion form, diversification and personalization applied to the vectors of communication itself (direct marketing, promotion, public relations, lobbying, sponsorship, and so on). Far from being exhausted, consumer-fashion society is pursuing its inexorable rise, although with somewhat less glitter, less faith in progress, less enthusiasm for novelty. What marketing specialists now call "cocooning" or "burrowing" only points to this new phase of fashion in which consumption is less euphoric and more ecological, more inward-looking than other-directed. The fashion system is not collapsing; it is becoming trivialized as it evolves into an increasingly privatized and cynical system of self-service consumption.

Paradox 3. To the extent that our needs are programmed by the specialized agencies of the consummate-fashion system, each of us becomes increasingly the agent of our own existence, the free operator of our own private life. The more the world is "bureaucratized," the more individuals are "autonomized"; among other pieces of evidence for this, we may look at the rising divorce rate and the increase in nonmarital relationships, the liberalization of sexual conduct, birth control, the decline in orthodox religious beliefs and practices, and the increased number of women in the work force. Eight French women out of ten now say that they would rather work than stay home; for the same number, a woman's life cannot be considered a success without a career. To be sure, advertising can still exploit the register of the housewife or the sexy woman; to be sure, there are still major inequalities between men and women in terms of salaries, power, unemployment, and household chores. However, the society of ephemera has allowed women's desire for autonomy and self-realization to break through, especially through salaried work. On the surface, the culture of consumption casts women in a childlike and inferior role; in reality, it works toward their ongoing emancipation. Stereotypical judgments of fashion society and the culture of consumption have to be reexamined.[11] Contemporary Western culture is continually denounced as a "soft" dictatorship, an enterprise of generalized domination and massification, whereas it also generates greater independence on the part of consumer-actors, more concern for self and for meaning, less obsession with social status. Far from being equivalent to totalitarianism, fashion distances us from totalitarianism; it opens up the space of existential choice through the multitude of standards and models it proposes. With generalized fashion, individual autonomy has become an important social phenomenon; it has shifted into the second phase of the historical trajectory inaugurated in the seventeenth and eighteenth centuries.[12]

Paradox 4. The more powerful the logic of fashion becomes, the more powerfully ecological demands are expressed. The paradox is manifest: the logic of fashion celebrates the present, artificiality, and novelty, while the ecological movement focuses on the future, on nature, on conservation. The former is playful while the latter is fearful. But there need not be an unbridgeable gap between ecological sensitivity and the empire of fashion; fashion plays a more subtle game. Unquestionably, the future of the planet and its safekeeping are going to be the focus of collective preoccupation from now on. But except for the advocates of "deep ecology," what drives "green" consciousness in particular is the individualist concern for the quality of life and health, the desire to live better in the present. Mass ecological passion is the expression of the postmodern age of fashion. It lacks an alternative thrust; it does not aspire to "change life"; it reflects the exhaustion of the great conquering historical projects: it is now a matter only of protecting and preserving the environment in view of a better-balanced existence. There is no radical opposition between environmentalist ecology ("shallow ecology") and the individualist logic of consumption, for the aim of the former is only to improve management in order to improve consumption. Ecological sensitivity is governed by an ecology of consumption and a specific form of hedonism, with its faddish ecological purchasing, organic products, health-food diets, gentle therapies, and green tourism. All these sectors are already giving rise to fashions, labels, specialized shops, and focused marketing. Ecoconsumption and ecobusiness represent a new stage of fashion, one in which the seduction of marketing annexes the "respect for nature" niche. There is no exit here from the global fashion system; the new is simply propelled in the name of saving the earth and preserving one's health. What is "real," lasting, the "green" antifashion, functions as the new vector of consummate fashion.

Paradox 5. The more the democracies commit themselves to the race for the new, the more they are fascinated with the past, and the more interest they show in rehabilitating, conserving, and valorizing what is old. The fashion era is at the same time the era of national patrimonies and cultural anniversaries. A new museum is opened, somewhere in Europe, every single day. In France, more than one thousand cultural and historical commemorations have taken place over the last six years. The United States and Europe alike are witnessing an extraordinary memorial proliferation, a growing collective taste for the past, as illustrated in particular by the hordes of tourists who visit monuments, museums, and old cities. The field of patrimony and commemoration has become infinite: practically everything is subject to preservation, even things that are very modest or not at all remote (artifacts from the 1950s and 1960s); every date is an occasion to celebrate some great name or event (an artist's birth or death, a 50th, 100th, 150th, 200th, or 500th anniversary).[13]

Still, let us not be misled: this commemorative bulimia is only in apparent contradiction to the fervor for the present that characterizes fashion.

On the one hand, the postmodern cult of the past is evidenced through souvenir industries, media solicitations, high-decibel laser spectacles, ad agencies, and tourist bureaus. The frenzy to commemorate is coupled with economic and touristic exploitation, with marketing investment oriented toward national or local promotion, along with efforts to sell the *image* of cities or regions. The sacralization of the patrimony is at one and the same time a "cultural enterprise" and a tourist industry, a stratum to be exploited. Stuffy ceremonies and official homages have been supplanted by television shows, folkloric reenactments, theatrical and musical performances: the fashion process has succeeded in phagocytosing our relation to our inheritance. On the other hand, commemorative inflation merely confirms the decline of any structuring influence of the past on our behavior and the correlated increase in the power of models of the present. The postmodern commemorative bulimia does not in any way signify faithfulness to the past, or any hold of the past over what we are today; rather, it signifies a loss of the constraining collective power of the past. The past is no longer a canon to be reproduced or faithfully imitated, but merely a realm to visit and to admire aesthetically. We are all the more prepared to celebrate the past in that it no longer serves as an example for us;[14] the old has shifted into the order of ephemeral animation of our lives, the order of mass cultural consumption.

Paradox 6. Even as our daily lives are orchestrated by the law of inconstancy, seduction, and images, ethical questions are resurfacing with a new intensity: bioethics, humanitarian acts, ecology, the morality of business and the media, debates about sexual harassment, abortion, politically correct language, antidrug and antitobacco measures. We are witnessing a vigorous return of ethical themes in the social discourse of the democracies. Even so, here too we must not forget that the comeback of ethics is not completely exempt from the influence of fashion; we have only to look at charity shows, those syntheses of ethics and diversion, of good intentions and rock stars, of generosity and decibels. "All I did," declared Bob Geldof, organizer of Band Aid, "was make famine fashionable"—in other words, he broadcast a painless, optional, emotional, and circumstantial ethics, an ethics adapted to the new individualist culture and stripped of regular, maximalist, sacrificial commandments. As for humanitarian interventions, it must be obvious by now that, however necessary they may be, they function as instruments of political communication intended to burnish the image of power in the public eye. The same logic governs, in part, the vogue for business ethics, one of whose central goals is to improve companies' performance ("ethics pays") through the management and marketing of values:[15] ethical codes, sponsorship, participation, institutional communication of an ethical nature. In our fashion societies, ethics has been instrumentalized; it has become a means of communication for internal and external use, a tool for managing brand names and human beings.

One may have reservations about this development; it is easy to emphasize its manipulative and demoralizing effects. Nevertheless, it offers proof that the consummate age of fashion is capable of giving priority once again to ethical standards. The frivolous universe of objects and the media does not lead inexorably to cynicism and the collapse of all values. If our societies have a strong penchant for an individualism with no holds barred, they also have a penchant for indignation; thus, they demand limits to the spiraling rise in subjective rights. At the same time, they manifest concern for future generations and for others in general, as the persistence and expansion of volunteerism attests. Alongside irresponsible individualism ("every man for himself"), a responsible individualism is being reconstituted; it includes a commitment to mutual aid and a respect for moral values. Yet alongside the ethical demand for realistic, liberal, and pragmatic solutions achieved through dialogue, a moralistic, even fundamentalist spirit is also being reconstituted (the "pro-life" movement, the antipornographers, the antivivisectionists, the antismoking lobby, the opponents to liberalization of drugs). The universe of frivolity has simply broadened the ethics "wars."[16]

Paradox 7. In this book, I have defended the idea that consummate fashion is a factor contributing to the consolidation of the liberal democracies. Yet what is happening before our eyes in Western Europe? Racist and xenophobic discourse is resurfacing in the public arena; extreme rightist parties are staking out places for themselves in the political landscape; immigrant hostels are burned in Germany and Jewish cemeteries are desecrated in France. Must our positive assessment of the ultimate reign of fashion thus be revised?

One thing at least needs to be made clear. If it is manifestly—and regrettably—the case that the frivolous democracies do not prevent racism and xenophobia, at least we must note that up to now they have succeeded in confining bloody violence to small numbers of young people who lack a legitimate and credible ideological program, and who are not supported by governing political parties, public opinion, or the press. Here is where the present situation differs from the one that prevailed between the two world wars. For the first time since the end of the eighteenth century, the democracies have no project but democracy itself; there is no longer any party whose declared goal is the destruction of democracy and the use of political violence. The new democratic citizenship undeniably tends to be passive, apathetic, and abstentionist; still, that has not stood in the way of huge street demonstrations in Germany, Austria, and Italy against the rise of racism. Major German corporations have organized advertising campaigns against xenophobia. These reactions on the part of civil society have nothing in common with those of the previous era, an era that was nevertheless subtended by an intransigent culture of civic and moral duty. The extreme right is not going to disappear anytime soon, but everything indicates that, at least in France, it has gotten all the votes it is going to get, that it will remain a marginal protest formation incapable of subverting democratic institutions. It is not the fashion system that makes liberal regimes fragile, it is rather the gaps in that system, when individuals find themselves excluded from its order, when they see their future threatened, when career choices are closed off, when poverty and underconsumption are on the rise. The age of the superficial does not protect us against all xenophobia and all racism, but it is in reality what protects us best against totalitarian temptations, civil wars, and political violence.

The real danger facing us is not the return of fascism, it is the dualization of democracies, the gap between rich and poor, between exclusive neighborhoods and ghettos, between the work force and the unemployed, between well-integrated citizens and marginal figures, between high-quality education and a deteriorating school system, between hospitals on the cutting edge and a disastrous system of health insurance.[17] The age of fashion has obviously not succeeded in conjuring away the social chasms within democracies; it has not stemmed the rise of poverty, underemployment, social exclusion, or delinquency. But let us not be too quick to blame all society's ills on the fashion universe. All developed societies today confront the same challenges (worldwide competition, declining employment, marginalization of certain social groups, drug addiction), but they do not all react in the same way, they do not all enact identical policies in the realms of social welfare, education, health, industry, or urban life. Fashion is a social form independent of societies' policies, choices, and intentions. The problems of the future will obviously not be settled by fashion logic; however, nothing lasting will be accomplished without that logic, either. Let us not fool ourselves: no exit from the system of the ephemeral and of seduction is thinkable or even desirable. We have to regulate that system through the voluntary action of individuals and governments. Fashion entails neither fatality nor pure determinism: fashion has to be restructured and finalized in terms of our values. Whatever constraints may be imposed by the "system," people do have a margin of liberty and creative autonomy with regard to the future. Consummate fashion does not signify "the end of history"[18] but the constantly renewed *invention* of democracy and the marketplace; it signifies the responsibility of citizens facing the construction of a future whose keys no individual now holds. The unreasonableness of fashion calls for, and paves the way for, an extra measure of enlightened reason.

Total fashion generates a host of antithetical effects. At one point, it increases the capacity of individuals to reject dogmas; at another, it supports the return of esoteric beliefs, the multiplication of sects, the unexamined life. At one point, it allows more universalist openings, more outpourings of imitation and hybridization; at another, it is accompanied by new ethnocentric fashions, by cultural separatism, by closed cults based on self-identification.[19] In one place, tolerance and heterodoxy are in the forefront; in another, new ideologically "correct" codes are arising that challenge freedom of expression and teaching, that define what one has the right to say and not to say, that seek to punish any and all discriminatory verbal behavior. The democracies of the fashion era are for the most part undoing the old catechisms and dogmatisms, but at the same time they are reinstituting new minority modes of meaning, new mimetic contagions that function like thought police.

This litany of paradoxes could go on and on. In one place, consummate fashion erodes the value of work in favor of leisure, private life, the sovereignty of money; in another, it encourages individuals to find self-realization in business and professional life. For some, it leads to self-destruction via drug addiction; for others, it entails holding the aesthetic and hygienic body sacred. In one place, corruption, illegal transactions, and fiscal fraud are on the rise; in another, the populace votes in favor of moralizing measures. Everywhere, the individualism of fashion society progresses by taking on two radically opposing facets: more self-control, more mobility, more integration for the majority; more marginalization, more delinquency, more irresponsible lawlessness for the rest. Here is the challenge of the twenty-first century. While the frivolous democracies have defeated the totalitarian regimes, they now have to win the battle for democratic progress, for the quality of life, for individual and collective responsibility, in an ongoing struggle at the very heart of our societies.

Notes

INTRODUCTION

1. Gilles Lipovetsky, *L'Ere du vide* (Paris: Gallimard, 1983).

PART ONE
THE ENCHANTMENT OF APPEARANCES

1. Gabriel de Tarde, *The Laws of Imitation* (1890), trans. Elsie Clews Parsons (Gloucester, Mass.: Peter Smith, 1962).

2. For example in Georg Simmel, where fashion is grafted onto psychological tendencies viewed as universal and in contradiction with imitation and individual differentiation; see "Fashion" (1904), in *On Individuality and Social Forms: Selected Writings*, ed. Donald N. Levine (Chicago: University of Chicago Press, 1971), pp. 294–323. See also René König, *A la Mode: On the Social Psychology of Fashion* (1971), trans. F. Bradley (New York: Seabury Press, 1973).

CHAPTER I
FASHION AND THE WEST

1. Fernand Braudel, *Civilization and Capitalism, 15th–18th Century* (1967–79), trans. and revised by Siân Reynolds (New York: Harper and Row, 1981–84), 1:312.

2. Tarde, *Laws of Imitation*, p. 247.

3. François Boucher, *20,000 Years of Fashion: The History of Costume and Personal Adornment*, expanded ed. (New York: Harry N. Abrams, 1967), pp. 191–98. See also Paul Post, "La Naissance du costume masculin moderne au XIVe siècle," in *Actes du 1er Congrès international d'histoire du costume* (Venice, 1952), pp. 28–41.

4. Edmond de Goncourt, *The Woman of the Eighteenth Century: Her Life from Birth to Death, Her Love, and Her Philosophy in the Worlds of Salon, Shop and Street* (1862), trans. Jacques Le Clercq and Ralph Roeder (New York: Minton, Balch, 1927), p. 234.

5. Boucher, *20,000 Years of Fashion*; Yvonne Deslandres, *Le Costume, image de l'homme* (Paris: Albin Michel, 1976); Henny Harald Hansen, *Costume Cavalcade: 689 Examples of Historic Costume in Colour* (1954), trans. Mrs. Lenner, 2d ed. (London: Methuen, 1972). On late-medieval dress, see Michèle Beaulieu and Jeanne Baylé, *Le Costume en Bourgogne, de Philippe le Hardi à la mort de Charles le Téméraire (1364-1477)* (Paris: Presses Universitaires de France, 1956).

6. Philippe Braunstein, "Toward Intimacy: The Fourteenth and Fifteenth Centuries," in *A History of Private Life* (1985), ed. Philippe Ariès and Georges Duby, trans. Arthur Goldhammer (Cambridge: Harvard University Press, Belknap Press, 1988), 2:580–81.

7. Françoise Piponnier, *Costume et vie sociale: La Cour d'Anjou, XIVe–XVe siècles* (Paris: Mouton, 1970), p. 9.

8. Michel de Montaigne, *The Complete Essays of Montaigne* (1595), trans. Donald M. Frame (Stanford: Stanford University Press, 1958), part 1, chap. 49, p. 216.

9. See the remarkable study by Louise Godard de Donville, *Signification de la mode sous Louis XIII* (Aix-en-Provence: Edisud, 1976), pp. 121–51.

10. Edward Sapir, "Fashion" (1931), in *Selected Writings of Edward Sapir in Language, Culture, and Personality*, ed. David G. Mandelbaum (Berkeley and Los Angeles: University of California Press, 1949), p. 376.

11. König, *A la Mode.*

12. Tarde, *Laws of Imitation*, p. 247.

13. Ibid.

14. On the influence of combat equipment on the appearance of the short male costume in the fourteenth century, see Post, "La Naissance," p. 34.

15. Bernard Grillet, *Les Femmes et les fards dans l'Antiquité grecque* (Paris: Centre National de la Recherche Scientifique, 1975).

16. Norbert Elias, *The Court Society* (1969), trans. Edmund Jephcott (New York: Pantheon Books, 1983), pp. 104–6.

17. Godard de Donville, *Signification de la mode*, pp. 208–12.

18. Ibid., pp. 170–84.

19. Edmond Goblot makes this point clearly in *La Barrière et le niveau* (Paris: Presses Universitaires de France, 1967), p. 47.

20. Fitelieu, *La Contre-Mode* (1642), cited along with other important texts by Godard de Donville, *Signification de la mode*, p. 28.

21. Piponnier, *Costume et vie sociale*, p. 245.

22. See for example John Carl Flügel, *The Psychology of Clothes* (1930; reprint, London: Hogarth Press, 1950), pp. 138–39; see also Goblot, *La Barrière et le niveau*, p. 49.

23. This thesis is at the heart of Pierre Bourdieu's work, particularly *Distinction: A Social Critique of the Judgement of Taste* (1979), trans. Richard Nice (Cambridge, Harvard University Press, 1984); see also König, *A la Mode*, pp. 106–10.

24. Thorstein Veblen, *The Theory of the Leisure Class* (1899; reprint, New York: Penguin, 1979), p. 173.

25. Ibid.

26. Ibid., p. 176.

27. Ibid., pp. 174–76.

28. See Paul Veyne, *Le Pain et le cirque: Sociologie historique d'un pluralisme politique* (Paris: Seuil, 1976).

29. Veblen, *Theory of the Leisure Class*, p. 178.

30. Max Weber, *Economy and Society: An Outline of Interpretive Sociology* (1925), trans. Ephraim Fischoff et al. (New York: Bedminster Press, 1968), 3:1106.

31. Danielle Régnier-Bohler, "Imagining the Self: Exploring Literature," in *A*

History of Private Life (1985), ed. Philippe Ariès and Georges Duby, trans. Arthur Goldhammer (Cambridge: Harvard University Press, Belknap Press, 1988), 2:379.

32. Philippe Ariès, *L'Homme devant la mort* (Paris: Seuil, 1977), pp. 99–288.

33. Thus in the fifteenth century King René could offer Louis XI and members of his household the gift of modest, unglamorous clothing, precisely because of the social value already attached to novelty; see Piponnier, *Costume et vie sociale*, pp. 210–12.

34. Georges Duby, *The Age of Cathedrals: Art and Society, 980–1420*, trans. Eleanor Levieux and Barbara Thompson (Chicago: University of Chicago Press, 1981).

35. Alberto Tenenti, *Sens de la mort et amour de la vie: Renaissance en Italie et en France* (1977), trans. Simone Matarasso-Gervais (Paris: L'Harmattan, Serge Fleury, 1983).

36. Lucien Febvre, *The Problem of Unbelief in the Sixteenth Century: The Religion of Rabelais*, trans. Beatrice Gottlieb (Cambridge: Harvard University Press, 1982).

37. René Nelli, *L'Erotique des troubadours* (Paris: Union Générale d'Editions, 1974), 1:204; and Henri-Irénée Marrou, *Les Troubadours* (Paris: Seuil, 1971).

38. Post, "La Naissance," p. 39.

39. Ibid.

40. This point has been particularly emphasized by Marcel Gauchet in *Le Désenchantement du monde* (Paris: Gallimard, 1985), pp. 97–98. In a much more limited realm, Erich Auerbach showed earlier the way in which the integration of all human events in the high style of Western literature, as well as the realist-serious representation of what is individual, daily, and social, was Christian in origin; see *Mimesis: The Representation of Reality in Western Literature* (1946), trans. Willard Trask, 2d ed. (Garden City, N.Y.: Doubleday Anchor Books, 1957).

41. Gauchet, *Le Désenchantement du monde*, pp. 108–30.

CHAPTER II

A CENTURY OF FASHION

1. Alexis de Tocqueville, *Democracy in America*, ed. J. P. Mayer and Max Lerner, trans. George Lawrence (New York: Harper and Row, 1966), vol. 1, intro., p. 12.

2. Germaine Deschamps, "La Crise dans les industries du vêtement et de la mode à Paris pendant la période de 1930 à 1937," Ph.D. diss., Paris, 1937.

3. Philippe Simon, "Monographie d'une industrie de luxe: La haute couture," Ph.D diss., Paris, 1931, p. 102.

4. Jean-Charles Worth, "A propos de la mode," *La Revue de Paris* (15 May 1930): 295–311.

5. Cited in Edmonde Charles-Roux, *Le Temps Chanel* (Paris: Chêne-Grasset, 1979), p. 211.

6. A good deal of information about this phenomenon is provided by Bruno du Roselle in *La Mode* (Paris: Imprimerie nationale, 1980); see also Marylène Delbourg-Delphis, *Le Chic et le look* (Paris: Hachette, 1981).

7. Cited in Meredith Etherington-Smith, *Patou* (New York: St. Martin's/Marek, 1983), p. 55.

8. The 1960s, characterized by rapid and abrupt variations, especially in skirt lengths (mini, maxi), represent the last phase of that "directed" mass unanimism.

9. Cited in Charles-Roux, *Le Temps Chanel*, p. 327.

10. James Laver, *Costume and Fashion: A Concise History*, revised ed. (London: Thames and Hudson, 1982), p. 232.

11. Cecil Beaton, *The Glass of Fashion* (London: Weidenfeld and Nicolson, 1954).

12. Cited in Catherine Lebas and Annie Jacques, *La Coiffure en France du Moyen Age à nos jours* (Paris: Delmas International, 1979), p. 162.

13. Goncourt, *Woman of the Eighteenth Century*, pp. 226–27.

14. Cited in Anny Latour, *Kings of Fashion* (1956), trans. Mervyn Savill (London: Weidenfeld and Nicolson, 1958), p. 7.

15. Goncourt, *Woman of the Eighteenth Century*, p. 226.

16. Deslandres, *Le Costume*, p. 134.

17. Charles Baudelaire, *The Painter of Modern Life and Other Essays* (1863), trans. Jonathan Mayne (London: Phaidon, 1965), pp. 32, 31.

18. Goncourt, *Woman of the Eighteenth Century*, pp. 226–27, 229.

19. Latour, *Kings of Fashion*, p. 14.

20. Tocqueville, *Democracy in America*, vol. 2, book 3, chap. 19, p. 603.

21. John C. Prevost, *Le Dandysme en France, 1817–1839* (Paris: Minard, 1957), pp. 134–62.

22. Paul Bénichou, *Le Sacre de l'écrivain* (Paris: José Corti, 1973).

23. Jean Starobinski, *Portrait de l'artiste en saltimbanque* (Geneva: Skira, 1970).

24. Paul Poiret, *King of Fashion: The Autobiography of Paul Poiret* (1930), trans. Stephen Haden Guest (Philadelphia: J. B. Lippincott, 1931), pp. 295–96.

25. Ibid., p. 148.

26. Claude Lefort, *L'Invention démocratique* (Paris: Fayard, 1981).

27. Poiret, *King of Fashion*, p. 148.

28. Ibid., p. 301.

29. Roland Barthes, *The Fashion System* (1967), trans. Matthew Ward and Richard Howard (New York: Hill and Wang, 1983), pp. 254–55.

30. Poiret, *King of Fashion*, p. 299.

31. Marc Bohan in Claude Cézan, *La Mode, phénomène humain* (Toulouse: Privat, 1967), p. 137.

32. Simon, "Monographie," p. 90.

33. Latour, *Kings of Fashion*, p. 189.

34. Marcel Gauchet and Gladys Swain, *La Pratique de l'esprit humain* (Paris: Gallimard, 1980), pp. 163–66.

35. For a fuller treatment of this issue, see Simon, "Monographie," pp. 25–31.

36. Gaston Worth, *La Couture et la confection des vêtements de femme* (Paris: Imprimerie Chaix, 1895), p. 20.

37. See Bourdieu, *Distinction*; Pierre Bourdieu and Yvette Delsaut, "Le Couturier et sa griffe: Contribution à une théorie de la magie," *Actes de la recherche en sciences sociales* 1 (January 1975): 7–36; see also Philippe Perrot, *Les Dessus et les*

dessous de la bourgeoisie: Une histoire du vêtement au XIXe siècle (Paris: Fayard, 1981).

38. For example, see Perrot, *Les Dessus et les dessous*, p. 325.

39. G. Worth, *La Couture*, chap. 2.

40. See the end of part 2, chap. 2 herein.

41. Poiret, *King of Fashion*, p. 290.

42. Ibid., pp. 76–77.

43. Ibid., p. 77.

44. Ibid., p. 148.

45. Ibid., pp. 292, 294.

CHAPTER III
OPEN FASHION

1. In 1982, direct profits from domestic sales and exports (excluding perfume) came to 1.4 billion francs, and indirect profits (that is, profits from brand-name licensing agreements and subsidiaries throughout the world) were 9.3 billion. In 1985, these figures had risen to 2.4 billion and 17.3 billion respectively.

2. Françoise Vincent-Ricard, *Raison et passion: La mode, 1940–1990* (Paris: Textile/Art/Langage, 1983), p. 83.

3. Ibid., pp. 85–87.

4. Roselle, *La Mode*, pp. 264–66.

5. Cited in Cézan, *La Mode*, p. 129.

6. Saint-Laurent, cited in ibid., p. 130.

7. Cited in ibid., p. 126.

8. Made-to-order clothes represented 10 percent of clothing expenses per person in 1953 and 1 percent in 1984.

9. The vast array of differentiated products is subtended by an industry that is itself very fragmented; this fragmentation permits rapid adaptation to changes in fashion. In 1984, there were slightly more than a thousand enterprises in France employing more than ten salaried workers, and nearly 84 percent of these enterprises employed fewer than fifty people.

10. As a comparison, in the mid 1950s, the twenty-eight Dior workshops produced twelve thousand items per year, for three thousand women customers.

11. Bourdieu and Delsaut, "Le Couturier et sa griffe," p. 33.

12. Ibid.

13. Yves Saint-Laurent, cited in Cézan, *La Mode*, p. 130.

14. Ibid., p. 130.

15. Caroline Roy, "Les soins personnels," in *Données sociales* (Paris: I N.S.E.E., 1984), pp. 400–401.

16. Cited in Vincent-Ricard, *Raison et passion*, p. 171.

17. Delbourg-Delphis, *Le Chic et le look*.

18. Paul Yonnet, *Jeux, modes et masses: La Société française et le moderne, 1945–1985* (Paris: Gallimard, 1985), p. 355.

19. Jean Baudrillard, *L'Echange symbolique et la mort* (Paris: Gallimard, 1976), pp. 131–40.

20. Between 1958 and 1968, the overall profits of the French perfume industry grew, in constant francs, by a factor of 2.5. Expenditures on perfume products, per year and per person, came to 284 francs in 1970, 365 francs in 1978, and 465 francs in 1985, again in constant francs.

21. In a survey carried out by SOFRES, a French polling firm, in 1983, 63 percent of the women interviewed thought that the multiplication of products related to beauty and hygiene gave them more freedom because they could change their looks according to their immediate circumstances and desires. Thirty-four percent thought that the phenomenon gave them less freedom, because they felt obliged to follow a fashion.

22. Marcel Gauchet, "Tocqueville, l'Amérique et nous," *Libre* 7 (1980): 43–120.

23. Tocqueville, *Democracy in America*, vol. 2, book 3, chap. 26, p. 637n.

24. See Nicolas Herpin, "L'Habillement: Une dépense sur le déclin," *Economie et statistique*, I.N.S.E.E. 192 (1986): 68–69.

25. Nicolas Herpin, "L'habillement, la classe sociale et la mode," *Economie et statistique*, I.N.S.E.E. 188 (1986): 35–54.

26. Herpin, "L'Habillement: Une dépense sur le déclin," pp. 70–72.

PART TWO
CONSUMMATE FASHION

1. Alexandre Kojève, *Introduction to the Reading of Hegel* (1947), trans. James H. Nichols, Jr. (New York: Basic Books, 1969), pp. 159–62.

CHAPTER IV
THE SEDUCTION OF THINGS

1. Cited in Vance Packard, *The Waste Makers* (New York: David McKay, 1960), p. 71.

2. Abraham Moles, *Psychologie du Kitsch* (Paris: Denoël, 1971), p. 199.

3. Jean Baudrillard, *La Société de consommation: Ses mythes, ses structures* (Paris: S.G.P.P., 1970), pp. 171–72.

4. Paul Yonnet, "La société automobile," *Le Débat* 31 (1984): 136–37; reprinted as "Automobile. La société de mobilité," in *Jeux, modes et masses*, pp. 243–93.

5. The expression is borrowed from David Riesman, *The Lonely Crowd: A Study of the Changing American Character* (1950; reprint, Garden City, N.Y.: Doubleday Anchor Books 1953), p. 64.

6. Baudrillard, *Le Système des objets* (Paris: Denoël, 1968), p. 163.

7. Ibid., pp. 172–76.

8. Packard, *Waste Makers*, pp. 102–17.

9. Jean-Paul Ceron and Jean Baillon, *La Société de l'éphémère* (Grenoble: Presses Universitaires de Grenoble, 1979).

10. Packard, *Waste Makers*, pp. 118–27.

11. Henri Van Lier, "Culture et industrie: Le Design," *Critique* 246 (November 1967): 935–52.

12. Ibid., pp. 948–50.

13. Victor Papanek, *Design for the Real World: Human Ecology and Social Change* (New York: Pantheon, 1971), p. 6.

14. Jean Baudrillard, "Le Crépuscule des signes," *Traverses* 2, Le Design (1975): 30–31.

15. Raymond Guidot, "Et que l'objet fonctionne," *Traverses* 4, Fonctionnalismes en dérive (1976): 144–45.

16. Jean Baudrillard, *Pour une critique de l'économie politique du signe* (Paris: Gallimard, 1972).

17. Ibid., p. 34.

18. Ibid., p. 40.

19. Ibid., p. 39.

20. Paul Dumouchel and Jean-Pierre Dupuy, *L'Enfer des choses: René Girard et la logique de l'économie* (Paris: Seuil, 1979).

21. Herbert Marcuse, *One Dimensional Man: Studies in the Ideology of Advanced Industrial Society* (Boston: Beacon Press, 1964), pp. x, xv.

22. Bourdieu, *Distinction*, pp. 230–32.

23. Ibid., p. 233.

24. Today the speed of microwave ovens is a factor in the purchasing decisions of seven consumers out of ten.

25. Tarde, *Laws of Imitation*, p. 246.

CHAPTER V
ADVERTISING ON THE OFFENSIVE

1. Daniel Boorstin, *The Image: A Guide to Pseudo-Events in America* (1962), (New York: Atheneum, 25th anniv. ed., 1987), pp. 211–12.

2. Jean-Marie Dru, *Le Saut créatif* (Paris: Jean-Claude Larrès, 1984), pp. 187–97.

3. Jacques Séguéla, *Hollywood lave plus blanc* (Paris: Flammarion, 1982).

4. See Boorstin, *Image*, pp. 211 and 224–25; see also Baudrillard, *Le Système des objets*, pp. 196–203.

5. John Kenneth Galbraith, *The New Industrial State* (Boston: Houghton Mifflin, 1967), pp. 206–29.

6. This idea is found in Marcuse, *One Dimensional Man* (for example, pp. xv–xvi, 1–3), and also in Guy Debord, *Society of the Spectacle* (Detroit: Black and Red, 1970). On the subject of "motivation research" in advertising, Vance Packard evoked the nightmarish Orwellian world in *The Hidden Persuaders* (New York: David McKay, 1957), pp. 7, 232.

7. Calling the bluff of journalistic criticism, Cornélius Castoriadis writes: "The advertising imposture is, in the long run, no less dangerous than the totalitarian imposture. . . . The commercial-advertising domination does not differ much, from this viewpoint, from the totalitarian domination," in *Domaines de l'homme, les carrefours du labyrinthe II* (Paris: Seuil, 1986), pp. 29, 33.

8. Gauchet and Swain, *La Pratique de l'esprit humain*, pp. 106–8.

9. Hannah Arendt, *The Origins of Totalitarianism* (New York: Harcourt Brace Jovanovich, 1973), p. 458.

10. Doris-Louise Haineault and Jean-Yves Roy, *Unconscious for Sale: Advertising, Psychoanalysis, and the Public* (1984), trans. Kimball Lockhart and Barbara Kerslake, Theory and History of Literature 86 (Minneapolis: University of Minnesota Press, 1993), pp. 184–85.

11. Roger-Gérard Schwartzenberg, *L'Etat spectacle: Essai sur et contre le star system en politique* (Paris: Librairie générale française, 1978).

12. Roland Cayrol, *La Nouvelle Communication politique* (Paris: Larousse, 1986), pp. 10, 155–56.

13. Ibid., pp. 178–80.

14. Schwartzenberg, *L'Etat spectacle*, pp. 353–54.

CHAPTER VI
CULTURE, MEDIA STYLE

1. Olivier Burgelin, "L'Engouement," *Traverses* 3, La Mode (1976): 30–34.

2. Antoine Hennion, *Les Professionnels du disque* (Paris: A.-M. Métailié, 1981), p. 173.

3. Patrice Flichy, *Les Industries de l'imaginaire* (Grenoble: Presses Universitaires de Grenoble, 1980), p. 41.

4. Ibid., pp. 41–42.

5. Armand Mattelart, Xavier Delcourt, and Michèle Mattelart, *La Culture contre la démocratie? L'audiovisuel à l'heure transnationale* (Paris: La Découverte, 1983), p. 176.

6. José Ferré, "Transnational et transtechnologique," *Autrement* 58, Showbiz (1984): 78.

7. Cited by Bernard Guillou, "La Diversification des entreprises de communication: Approches stratégiques et organisationnelles," *Réseaux* 14 (1985): 21.

8. Flichy, *Les Industries de l'imaginaire*, p. 196.

9. Mattelart, Delcourt, and Mattelart, *La Culture contre la démocratie?* p. 179.

10. Edgar Morin, *L'Esprit du temps* (Paris: Grasset, 1962), 1:32–37.

11. Mattelart, Delcourt, and Mattelart, *La Culture contre la démocratie?* p. 180.

12. Ibid., pp. 183–85.

13. Jean Bianchi, "Dallas, les feuilletons et la télévision populaire," *Réseaux* 12 (1985): 22.

14. Cited in Ken Wlaschin, *The Illustrated Encyclopedia of the World's Great Movie Stars and Their Films* (London: Salamander Books, 1979), p. 6.

15. Edgar Morin, *Les Stars* (Paris: Seuil, 1957), pp. 21–35.

16. Ibid., pp. 8, 94–97.

17. Ibid., p. 91.

18. Morin, *L'Esprit du temps*.

19. Ibid., p. 238.

20. Jürgen Habermas, *The Structural Transformation of the Public Sphere: An Inquiry into a Category of Bourgeois Society* (1965), trans. Thomas Burger (Cambridge: MIT Press, 1989), pp. 161, 166.

21. Arendt, *Origins of Totalitarianism*, pp. 468–79.

22. Jean-Louis Missika and Dominique Wolton, *La Folle du logis: La Télévision dans les sociétés démocratiques* (Paris: Gallimard, 1983), pp. 265–73.

23. Marshall McLuhan, *Understanding Media: The Extensions of Man* (New York: McGraw Hill, 1964), p. 314.

24. Pierre Moeglin, "Une scénographie en quête de modernité: De nouveaux traitements de l'image au journal télévisé," in *Le JT: Mise en scène de l'actualité à la télévision* (Paris: I.N.A., La Documentation française, 1986), pp. 33–69.

25. Louis Quéré, *Des miroirs équivoques: Aux origines de la communication moderne* (Paris: Aubier, 1982), pp. 153–75.

26. Baudrillard, *Pour une critique de l'économie politique du signe*, pp. 208–12.

27. Habermas, *Structural Transformation*, pp. 170–71.

28. Quéré, *Des miroirs équivoques*, pp. 141, 146.

29. Missika and Wolton, *La Folle du logis*, pp. 307–8.

CHAPTER VII
MEANING CARRIES ON

1. Albert Hirschman, *Shifting Involvements: Private Interest and Public Action* (Princeton: Princeton University Press, 1982).

2. See Gilles Lipovetsky, "Changer la vie, ou l'irruption de l'individualisme transpolitique," *Pouvoirs* 39 (1986): 91–100.

3. Hirschman, *Shifting Involvements*.

4. Tocqueville, *Democracy in America*, vol. 2, book 4, chap. 4, p. 653; see also vol. 2, book 2, chap. 14, pp. 512–13, and vol. 2, book 4, chap. 3, p. 647.

5. Ibid., vol. 2, book 1, chap. 2, pp. 400–401.

6. Ibid., p. 399.

CHAPTER VIII
THE PROGRESSIVE SHIFTING OF THE SOCIAL

1. Tarde, *Laws of Imitation*, p. 87.

2. Ibid., pp. 244–48.

3. Ibid., pp. 253–54.

4. Ibid., pp. 254, 338.

5. Ibid., pp. 293, 357.

6. Ibid., p. 244.

7. Krzysztof Pomian, "La Crise de l'avenir," *Le Débat* 7 (1980): 5–17; see also Gauchet, *Le Désenchantement du monde*, pp. 253–60.

8. Gauchet, *Le Désenchantement du monde*, p. 262.

9. Tarde, *Laws of Imitation*, p. 369.

10. Ibid., preface to the 2d French ed., p. xxiv.

11. Pierre Manent, *Tocqueville et la nature de la démocratie* (Paris: Julliard, 1982), pp. 26–27.

12. Tocqueville, *Democracy in America*, vol. 1, book 2, chap. 4, p. 179.

13. Gauchet, "Tocqueville, l'Amérique et nous," pp. 116–17.

14. For a more detailed discussion of this point, see Lipovetsky, *L'Ere du vide*, chap. 6.

15. Tocqueville, *Democracy in America*, vol. 1, book 2, chap. 9, p. 284.

EPILOGUE

1. Louis Dumont, *From Mandeville to Marx: The Genesis and Triumph of Economic Ideology* (Chicago: University of Chicago Press, 1977); Dumont, *Essays on Individualism: Modern Ideology in Anthropological Perspective* (Chicago: University of Chicago Press, 1986); Gauchet, "Tocqueville, l'Amérique et nous"; Gauchet, "De l'avènement de l'individu à la découverte de la société," *Annales: Economies, Sociétés, Civilisations* 3 (May–June 1979): 451–63; Gauchet, "Changement de paradigme en sciences sociales?" *Le Débat* 50 (1988): 165–70; Gauchet and Swain, *La Pratique de l'esprit humain*.

2. Dominique Darmon and Philippe L'Hardy, "Consommation: Santé et loisirs au premier plan," *Economie et statistique*, I.N.S.E.E. 190 (1986): 68.

3. "1980's Shoppers Charged into a Brave New World of Goods," *Los Angeles Times*, 31 December 1989, cited by Jean-Jacques Courtine in "Les Stakhanovistes du narcissisme: Body-building et puritanisme ostentatoire dans la culture américaine du corps," *Communications* 56 (1993): 246.

4. Luc Dettier, "Un Marché bien dans sa peau," *Challenges* (March 1993): 60–64.

5. See Susan Faludi, *Backlash: The Undeclared War against American Women* (New York: Crown, 1991), p. 218.

6. Ibid., pp. 500–501, n. 10.

7. Eric Labouze, "Vers des aliments high tech?" *Science et Vie* 182 (March 1993): 24–30.

8. This logic applies principally to leisure wear and evening dress. It does not hold up for working clothes, where relatively strict codes manifestly continue to organize women's and men's appearance alike.

9. Thus in the United States, which is, with 32 percent of the world market, the top-ranking country in consumption of luxury products, the index of luxury-item prices in 1991 went up less than the consumer price index for the first time since 1984 (*Le Monde*, 26 May 1992). Luxury items will not disappear, but they will become less and less ostentatious; they will be consumed increasingly behind closed doors, in a continuation of an essentially democratic movement inaugurated in the nineteenth century.

10. Dominique Turpin, "Le Marketing est aussi japonais," *Revue française de gestion* 91 (November-December 1992): 64–71.

11. In the United States, several works have also sought to produce a less systematically negative interpretation of consumption: see William R. Leach, "Transformations in a Culture of Consumption: Women and Department Stores, 1890–1925," *Journal of American History* 71 (September 1984): 319–42; Michael Schudson, *Advertising: The Uneasy Persuasion* (New York: Basic Books, 1984); Schudson, "Delectable Materialism: Were the Critics of Consumer Culture Wrong All Along?" *American Prospect* (Spring 1991): 26–35; Daniel Miller, *Material Culture and Mass Consumption* (New York: Basil Blackwell, 1987).

12. Concerning this "second industrial revolution," see Lipovetsky, *L'Ere du vide*.

13. Françoise Chouay, *L'Allégorie du patrimoine* (Paris: Seuil, 1992); Jean-Michel Leniaud, *L'Utopie française: Essai sur le patrimoine* (Paris: Mengès, 1992);

Pierre Nora, "L'Ere de la commémoration," in *Lieux de mémoire*, vol. 3, *Les France: De l'archive à l'emblème* (Paris: Gallimard, 1992); William Johnston, *Celebrations: The Cult of Anniversaries in Europe and the United States Today* (New Brunswick, N.J.: Transaction Publishers, 1991).

14. Johnston, *Celebrations*, pp. 6 and 161.

15. Robert C. Solomon and Kristine R. Hanson, *It's Good Business* (New York: Atheneum, 1985); *Ethics in American Business: A Special Report* (New York: Touche Ross, 1988); James O'Toole, *Vanguard Management: Redesigning the Corporate Future* (Garden City, N.Y.: Doubleday, 1985).

16. Gilles Lipovetsky, *Le Crépuscule du devoir: L'Ethique indolore des nouveaux temps démocratiques* (Paris: Gallimard, 1992).

17. See, among other texts, Philippe Delmas, *Le Maître des horloges* (Paris: Odile Jacob, 1991), and Michel Albert, *Capitalisme contre capitalisme* (Paris: Seuil, 1991).

18. Francis Fukuyama, *The End of History and the Last Man* (New York: Free Press, 1992).

19. Arthur M. Schlesinger, *The Disuniting of America: Reflections on a Multicultural Society* (Knoxville, Tenn.: Whittle Communications, 1991).

Works Cited

Albert, Michel. *Capitalisme contre capitalisme*. Paris: Seuil, 1991.

Arendt, Hannah. *The Origins of Totalitarianism*. New York: Harcourt Brace Jovanovich, 1973.

Ariès, Philippe. *L'Homme devant la mort*. Paris: Seuil, 1977.

Auerbach, Erich. *Mimesis: The Representation of Reality in Western Literature* (1946). Translated by Willard Trask. 2d ed. Garden City, N.Y.: Doubleday Anchor Books, 1957.

Barthes, Roland. *The Fashion System* (1967). Translated by Matthew Ward and Richard Howard. New York: Hill and Wang, 1983.

Baudelaire, Charles. *The Painter of Modern Life and Other Essays* (1863). Translated by Jonathan Mayne. London: Phaidon, 1965.

Baudrillard, Jean. "Le Crépuscule des signes." *Traverses* 2, Le Design (1975): 27–40.

———. *L'Échange symbolique et la mort*. Paris: Gallimard, 1976.

———. *Pour une critique de l'économie politique du signe*. Paris: Gallimard, 1972.

———. *La Société de consommation: ses mythes, ses structures*. Paris: S.G.P.P., 1970.

———. *Le Système des objets*. Paris: Denoël, 1968.

Beaton, Cecil. *The Glass of Fashion*. London: Weidenfeld and Nicolson, 1954.

Beaulieu, Michèle, and Jeanne Baylé. *Le Costume en Bourgogne, de Philippe le Hardi à la mort de Charles le Téméraire (1364–1477)*. Paris: Presses Universitaires de France, 1956.

Bénichou, Paul. *Le Sacre de l'écrivain*. Paris: José Corti, 1973.

Bianchi, Jean. "Dallas, les feuilletons et la télévision populaire." *Réseaux* 12 (1985): 19–28.

Boorstin, Daniel. *The Image: A Guide to Pseudo-Events in America* (1962). New York: Atheneum, 25th anniv. ed., 1987. Originally titled *The Image: or, What Happened to the American Dream*.

Boucher, François. *20,000 Years of Fashion: The History of Costume and Personal Adornment*. Expanded ed. New York: Harry N. Abrams, 1967.

Bourdieu, Pierre. *Distinction: A Social Critique of the Judgement of Taste* (1979). Translated by Richard Nice. Cambridge: Harvard University Press, 1984.

Bourdieu, Pierre, and Yvette Delsaut. "Le Couturier et sa griffe: Contribution à une théorie de la magie." *Actes de la recherche en sciences sociales* 1 (January 1975): 7–36.

Braudel, Fernand. *Civilization and Capitalism, 15th–18th Century* (1967–79). 3 vols. Translated and revised by Siân Reynolds. New York: Harper and Row, 1981–84.

Braunstein, Philippe. "Toward Intimacy: The Fourteenth and Fifteenth Centuries." In *A History of Private Life* (1985), edited by Philippe Ariès and Georges

Duby, translated by Arthur Goldhammer, 2:535–630. Cambridge: Harvard University Press, Belknap Press, 1988.

Burgelin, Olivier. "L'Engouement." *Traverses* 3, La Mode (1976): 26–43.

Castoriadis, Cornélius. *Domaines de l'homme, les carrefours du labyrinthe II.* Paris: Seuil, 1986.

Cayrol, Roland. *La Nouvelle Communication politique.* Paris: Larousse, 1986.

Cazeneuve, Jean. *L'Homme téléspectateur.* Paris: Denoël, 1974.

Ceron, Jean-Paul, and Jean Baillon. *La Société de l'éphémère.* Grenoble: Presses Universitaires de Grenoble, 1979.

Cézan, Claude. *La Mode, phénomène humain.* Toulouse: Privat, 1967.

Charles-Roux, Edmonde. *Le Temps Chanel.* Paris: Chêne-Grasset, 1979.

Chouay, Françoise. *L'Allégorie du patrimoine.* Paris: Seuil, 1992.

Courtine, Jean-Jacques. "Les Stakhanovistes du narcisissme: Body-building et puritanisme ostentatoire dans la culture américaine du corps." *Communications* 56 (1993): 225–51.

Darmon, Dominique, and Philippe L'Hardy. "Consommation: Santé et loisirs au premier plan." *Economie et statistique*, I.N.S.E.E. 190 (1986): 55–69.

Debord, Guy. *Society of the Spectacle.* Detroit: Black and Red, 1970.

Delbourg-Delphis, Marylène. *Le Chic et le look.* Paris: Hachette, 1981.

Delmas, Philippe. *Le Maître des horloges.* Paris: Odile Jacob, 1991.

Deschamps, Germaine. "La Crise dans les industries du vêtement et de la mode à Paris pendant la période de 1930 à 1937." Ph.D. diss., Paris, 1937.

Deslandres, Yvonne. *Le Costume, image de l'homme.* Paris: Albin Michel, 1976.

Dettier, Luc. "Un Marché bien dans sa peau." *Challenges* (March 1993): 60–64.

Dru, Jean-Marie. *Le Saut créatif.* Paris: Jean-Claude Larrès, 1984.

Duby, Georges. *The Age of Cathedrals: Art and Society, 980–1420.* Translated by Eleanor Levieux and Barbara Thompson. Chicago: University of Chicago Press, 1981.

Dumont, Louis. *Essays on Individualism: Modern Ideology in Anthropological Perspective.* Chicago: University of Chicago Press, 1986.

———. *From Mandeville to Marx: The Genesis and Triumph of Economic Ideology.* Chicago: University of Chicago Press, 1977.

Dumouchel, Paul, and Jean-Pierre Dupuy. *L'Enfer des choses: René Girard et la logique de l'économie.* Paris: Seuil, 1979.

Elias, Norbert. *The Court Society* (1969). Translated by Edmund Jephcott. New York: Pantheon Books, 1983.

Etherington-Smith, Meredith. *Patou.* New York: St. Martin's/Marek, 1983.

Ethics in American Business: A Special Report. New York: Touche Ross, 1988.

Faludi, Susan. *Backlash: The Undeclared War against American Women.* New York: Crown, 1991.

Febvre, Lucien. *The Problem of Unbelief in the Sixteenth Century: The Religion of Rabelais.* Translated by Beatrice Gottlieb. Cambridge: Harvard University Press, 1982.

Ferré, José. "Transnational et transtechnologique." *Autrement* 58, Show-biz (1984): 75–82.

Flichy, Patrice. *Les Industries de l'imaginaire.* Grenoble: Presses Universitaires de Grenoble, 1980.

Flügel, John Carl. *The Psychology of Clothes*. 1930. Reprint. London: Hogarth Press, 1950.

Fukuyama, Francis. *The End of History and the Last Man*. New York: Free Press, 1992.

Galbraith, John Kenneth. *The New Industrial State*. Boston: Houghton Mifflin, 1967.

Gauchet, Marcel. "Changement de paradigme en sciences sociales?" *Le Débat* 50 (1988): 165–70.

———. "De l'avènement de l'individu à la découverte de la société." *Annales: Economies, Sociétés, Civilisations* 3 (May–June 1979): 451–63.

———. *Le Désenchantement du monde*. Paris: Gallimard, 1985.

———. "Tocqueville, l'Amérique et nous." *Libre* 7 (1980): 43–120.

Gauchet, Marcel, and Gladys Swain. *La Pratique de l'esprit humain*. Paris: Gallimard, 1980.

Goblot, Edmond. *La Barrière et le niveau*. Paris: Presses Universitaires de France, 1967.

Godard de Donville, Louise. *Signification de la mode sous Louis XIII*. Aix-en-Provence: Edisud, 1976.

Goncourt, Edmond de. *The Woman of the Eighteenth Century: Her Life from Birth to Death, Her Love, and Her Philosophy in the Worlds of Salon, Shop, and Street* (1862). Translated by Jacques Le Clercq and Ralph Roeder. New York: Minton, Balch, 1927.

Grillet, Bernard. *Les Femmes et les fards dans l'Antiquité grecque*. Paris: Centre National de la Recherche Scientifique, 1975.

Guidot, Raymond. "Et que l'objet fonctionne." *Traverses* 4, Fonctionnalismes en dérive (1976): 135–45.

Guillou, Bernard. "La Diversification des entreprises de communication: Approches stratégiques et organisationnelles." *Réseaux* 14 (1985): 9–32.

Habermas, Jürgen. *The Structural Transformation of the Public Sphere: An Inquiry into a Category of Bourgeois Society* (1965). Translated by Thomas Burger. Cambridge: MIT Press, 1989.

Haineault, Doris-Louise, and Jean-Yves Roy. *Unconscious for Sale: Advertising, Psychoanalysis, and the Public* (1984). Translated by Kimball Lockhart and Barbara Kerslake. Theory and History of Literature 86. Minneapolis: University of Minnesota Press, 1993.

Hansen, Henny Harald. *Costume Cavalcade: 689 Examples of Historic Costume in Colour* (1954). Translated by Mrs. Lenner. 2d ed. London: Methuen, 1972.

Hennion, Antoine. *Les Professionnels du disque*. Paris: A.-M. Métailié, 1981.

Herpin, Nicolas. "L'Habillement, la classe sociale et la mode." *Economie et statistique*, I.N.S.E.E. 188 (1986): 35–54.

———. "L'Habillement: Une dépense sur le déclin." *Economie et statistique*, I.N.S.E.E. 192 (1986): 65–74.

Hirschman, Albert. *Shifting Involvements: Private Interest and Public Action*. Princeton: Princeton University Press, 1982.

Horkheimer, Max, and Theodor W. Adorno. *Dialectic of Enlightenment* (1944). Translated by John Cumming. New York: Herder and Herder, 1972.

Johnston, William. *Celebrations: The Cult of Anniversaries in Europe and the United States Today*. New Brunswick, N.J.: Transaction Publishers, 1991.

Kojève, Alexandre. *Introduction to the Reading of Hegel* (1947). Translated by James H. Nichols, Jr. New York: Basic Books, 1969.

König, René. *A la Mode: On the Social Psychology of Fashion* (1971). Translated by F. Bradley. New York: Seabury Press, 1973.

Labouze, Eric. "Vers des aliments high tech?" *Science et Vie* 182 (March 1993): 24–30.

Latour, Anny. *Kings of Fashion* (1956). Translated by Mervyn Savill. London: Weidenfeld and Nicolson, 1958.

Laver, James. *Costume and Fashion: A Concise History*. Revised ed. London: Thames and Hudson, 1982.

Leach, William R. "Transformations in a Culture of Consumption: Women and Department Stores, 1890–1925." *Journal of American History* 71 (September 1984): 319–42.

Lebas, Catherine, and Annie Jacques. *La Coiffure en France du Moyen Age à nos jours*. Paris: Delmas International, 1979.

Lefort, Claude. *L'Invention démocratique*. Paris: Fayard, 1981.

Leniaud, Jean-Michel. *L'Utopie française: Essai sur le patrimoine*. Paris: Mengès, 1992.

Lipovetsky, Gilles. "Changer la vie, ou l'irruption de l'individualisme transpolitique." *Pouvoirs* 39 (1986): 91–100.

———. *Le Crépuscule du devoir: L'Ethique indolore des nouveaux temps démocratiques*. Paris: Gallimard, 1992.

———. *L'Ere du vide*. Paris: Gallimard, 1983.

McLuhan, Marshall. *Understanding Media: The Extensions of Man*. New York: McGraw Hill, 1964.

Mâle, Emile. *Art and Artists of the Middle Ages* (1982). Translated by Sylvia Stallings Lowe. Redding Ridge, Conn.: Black Swan Books, 1986.

Manent, Pierre. *Tocqueville et la nature de la démocratie*. Paris: Julliard, 1982.

Marcuse, Herbert. *One Dimensional Man: Studies in the Ideology of Advanced Industrial Society*. Boston: Beacon Press, 1964.

Marrou, Henri-Irénée. *Les Troubadours*. Paris: Seuil, 1971.

Mattelart, Armand, Xavier Delcourt, and Michèle Mattelart. *La Culture contre la démocratie? L'audiovisuel à l'heure transnationale*. Paris: La Decouverte, 1983.

Miller, Daniel. *Material Culture and Mass Consumption*. New York: Basil Blackwell, 1987.

Missika, Jean-Louis, and Dominique Wolton. *La Folle du logis: La Télévision dans les sociétés démocratiques*. Paris: Gallimard, 1983.

Moeglin, Pierre. "Une scénographie en quête de modernité: De nouveaux traitements de l'image au journal télévisé." In *Le JT: Mise en scène de l'actualité à la télévision*, pp. 33–69. Paris: I.N.A., La Documentation française, 1986.

Moles, Abraham. *Psychologie du Kitsch*. Paris: Denoël, 1971.

Montaigne, Michel de. *The Complete Essays of Montaigne* (1595). Translated by Donald M. Frame. Stanford: Stanford University Press, 1958.

Morin, Edgar. *L'Esprit du temps*. 2 vols. Paris: Grasset, 1962.

———. *Les Stars*. Paris: Seuil, 1957.

Nelli, René. *L'Erotique des troubadours*. 2 vols. Paris: Union Générale d'Editions, 1974.

Nora, Pierre. "L'Ere de la commémoration." In *Lieux de mémoire*, vol. 3, *Les France: De l'archive à l'emblème*. Paris: Gallimard, 1992.

O'Toole, James. *Vanguard Management: Redesigning the Corporate Future*. Garden City, N.Y.: Doubleday, 1985.

Packard, Vance. *The Hidden Persuaders*. New York: David McKay, 1957.

———. *The Waste Makers*. New York: David McKay, 1960.

Papanek, Victor. *Design for the Real World: Human Ecology and Social Change*. New York: Pantheon, 1971.

Perrot, Philippe. *Les Dessus et les dessous de la bourgeoisie: Une histoire du vêtement au XIXe siècle*. Paris: Fayard, 1981.

Piponnier, Françoise. *Costume et vie sociale: La Cour d'Anjou, XIVe–XVe siècles*. Paris: Mouton, 1970.

Poiret, Paul. *King of Fashion: The Autobiography of Paul Poiret* (1930). Translated by Stephen Haden Guest. Philadelphia: J. B. Lippincott, 1931.

Pomian, Krzysztof. "La Crise de l'avenir." *Le Débat* 7 (1980): 5–17.

Post, Paul. "La Naissance du costume masculin moderne au XIVe siècle." In *Actes du Ier Congrès international d'histoire du costume*. Venice, 1952.

Prevost, John C. *Le Dandysme en France, 1817–1839*. Paris: Minard, 1957.

Quéré, Louis. *Des miroirs équivoques: Aux origines de la communication moderne*. Paris: Aubier, 1982.

Régnier-Bohler, Danielle. "Imagining the Self: Exploring Literature." In *A History of Private Life* (1985), edited by Philippe Ariès and Georges Duby, translated by Arthur Goldhammer, 2:311–93. Cambridge: Harvard University Press, Belknap Press, 1988.

Riesman, David. *The Lonely Crowd: A Study of the Changing American Character*. 1950. Reprint. Garden City, N.Y.: Doubleday Anchor Books, 1953.

Roselle, Bruno du. *La Mode*. Paris: Imprimerie nationale, 1980.

Roy, Caroline. "Les soins personnels." In *Données sociales*, pp. 400–401. Paris: I.N.S.E.E., 1984.

Sapir, Edward. "Fashion" (1931). In *Selected Writings of Edward Sapir in Language, Culture, and Personality*, edited by David G. Mandelbaum, pp. 373–81. Berkeley and Los Angeles: University of California Press, 1949.

Schlesinger, Arthur M. *The Disuniting of America: Reflections on a Multicultural Society*. Knoxville, Tenn.: Whittle Communications, 1991.

Schudson, Michael. *Advertising: The Uneasy Persuasion*. New York: Basic Books, 1984.

———. "Delectable Materialism: Were the Critics of Consumer Culture Wrong All Along?" *American Prospect* (Spring 1991): 26–35.

Schwartzenberg, Roger-Gérard. *L'Etat spectacle: Essai sur et contre le star system en politique*. Paris: Librairie générale française, 1978.

Séguéla, Jacques. *Hollywood lave plus blanc*. Paris: Flammarion, 1982.

Simmel, Georg. "Fashion" (1904). In *On Individuality and Social Forms: Selected Writings*, edited by Donald N. Levine, pp. 294–323. Chicago: University of Chicago Press, 1971.

Simon, Philippe. "Monographie d'une industrie de luxe: La haute couture." Ph.D. diss., Paris, 1931.

Solomon, Robert C., and Kristine R. Hanson. *It's Good Business*. New York: Atheneum, 1985.

Starobinski, Jean. *Portrait de l'artiste en saltimbanque*. Geneva: Skira, 1970.

Tarde, Gabriel de. *The Laws of Imitation* (1890). Translated by Elsie Clews Parsons. Gloucester, Mass.: Peter Smith, 1962.

Tenenti, Alberto. *Sens de la mort et amour de la vie: Renaissance en Italie et en France* (1977). Translated by Simone Matarasso-Gervais. Paris: L'Harmattan, Serge Fleury, 1983.

Tocqueville, Alexis de. *Democracy in America*. Edited by J. P. Mayer and Max Lerner, translated by George Lawrence. 2 vols. in 1. New York: Harper and Row, 1966.

Turpin, Dominique. "Le Marketing est aussi japonais." *Revue française de gestion* 91 (November–December 1992): 64–71.

Van Lier, Henri. "Culture et industrie: Le Design." *Critique* 246 (November 1967): 935–52.

Veblen, Thorstein. *The Theory of the Leisure Class*. 1899. Reprint. New York: Penguin, 1979.

Veyne, Paul. *Le Pain et le cirque: Sociologie historique d'un pluralisme politique*. Paris: Seuil, 1976.

Vincent-Ricard, Françoise. *Raison et passion: La mode, 1940–1990*. Paris: Textile/Art/Langage, 1983.

Weber, Max. *Economy and Society: An Outline of Interpretive Sociology* (1925). Translated by Ephraim Fischoff et al. 3 vols. New York: Bedminster Press, 1968.

Wlaschin, Ken. *The Illustrated Encyclopedia of the World's Great Movie Stars and Their Films*. London: Salamander Books, 1979.

Worth, Gaston. *La Couture et la confection des vêtements de femme*. Paris: Imprimerie Chaix, 1895.

Worth, Jean-Charles. "A propos de la mode." *La Revue de Paris* (15 May 1930): 295–311.

Yonnet, Paul. *Jeux, modes et masses: La Société française et le moderne, 1945–1985*. Paris: Gallimard, 1985.